D0207640

THOUGHT AND KNOWLEDGE
An Introduction to Critical Thinking

THOUGHT AND KNOWLEDGE

An Introduction to Critical Thinking

DIANE F. HALPERN
California State University, San Bernardino

LEA

1984 LAWRENCE ERLBAUM ASSOCIATES, PUBLISHERS
Hillsdale, New Jersey London

BF
455
.H255
1984

Copyright © 1984 by Lawrence Erlbaum Associates, Inc.
All rights reserved. No part of this book may be reproduced in any form, by photostat, microform, retrieval system, or any other means, without the prior written permission of the publisher.

Lawrence Erlbaum Associates, Inc., Publishers
365 Broadway
Hillsdale, New Jersey 07642

Library of Congress Cataloging in Publication Data

Halpern, Diane F.
Thought and knowledge.

Includes bibliographies and indexes.
1. Thought and thinking. 2. Knowledge, Theory of.
I. Title.
BF455.H255 1984 153 84-7988
ISBN 0-89859-381-6
ISBN 0-89859-514-2 (pbk.)

Printed in the United States of America
10 9 8 7 6 5 4

Contents

Preface **ix**

1. THINKING: AN INTRODUCTION **1**

The Need for Critical Thinking Skills *1*
Thinking About Thinking *6*
Metacognition *15*
About This Book *20*
Chapter Summary *22*
Suggested Readings *23*

2. THE RELATIONSHIP BETWEEN THOUGHT AND LANGUAGE **25**

Thought and Language *25*
Comprehension *30*
Persuasion and Propaganda *36*
Distinguishing Fact from Opinion *43*
Chapter Summary *45*
Suggested Readings *48*

3. DEVELOPMENT OF REASONING SKILLS **51**

Logical and Psychological *53*
Syllogistic Reasoning *56*
Linear Ordering *71*
If, Then Statements *74*
Reasoning in Everyday Contexts *82*
Chapter Summary *86*
Suggested Readings *91*

4. THINKING AS HYPOTHESIS TESTING **93**

Understanding Hypothesis Testing *94*
Determining Cause *102*
Self-Fulfilling Prophecies *111*
Thinking as an Intuitive Scientist *112*
Chapter Summary *113*
Suggested Readings *116*

5. UNDERSTANDING PROBABILITIES (LIKELIHOOD AND UNCERTAINTY) **119**

Probabilistic Nature of the World *120*
Using Probability *123*
Expected Values *132*
Subjective Probability *135*
Statistical Abuse *148*
An Application of Probability Models *153*
Chapter Summary *154*
Suggested Reading *158*

6. DEVELOPMENT OF PROBLEM SOLVING SKILLS **159**

Anatomy of a Problem *161*
Stages in Problem Solving *163*
Insight *164*
Well-Defined and Ill-Defined Problems *165*
Problem Solving Strategies *166*
Problem Solving Problems *199*
Chapter Summary *202*
Suggested Readings *207*

7. DECISION MAKING **209**

Making Sound Decisions *210*
Decision Making Among Trained Professionals *212*
Pitfalls and Pratfalls in Decision Making *213*
Uncertainty and Risks *223*
Elimination by Aspects *225*
Multidimensional Comparisons *225*
Preparing a Worksheet *228*
Postdecision Commitment and Evaluation *236*
Chapter Summary *238*
Suggested Readings *241*

8. MEMORY **243**

Acquisition of Knowledge *243*
Learning and Memory *244*
Human Information Processing *245*
Marijuana *261*
Emotions and Memory *263*
Metamemory *267*
Mnemonics *268*
Chapter Summary *275*
Suggested Readings *278*

9. INTELLIGENCE **281**

The Nature of Intelligence *282*
The Intelligence Quotient (IQ) *285*
Is There Bias in Intelligence Testing? *290*
Learning to be Intelligent *298*
Piagetian Model of Intelligence *300*
Chapter Summary *307*
Suggested Readings *312*

10. CREATIVE THINKING **315**

Creativity *316*
Measuring Creativity *322*
Encouraging Creativity *325*
Strategies for Creative Thinking *327*
Chapter Summary *338*
Suggested Readings *341*

11. APPLICATIONS OF CRITICAL THINKING SKILLS **343**

Thinking is a Unitary Concept *343*
Consumerism and Advertising Claims *344*
Utilizing Research *345*
Legal Testimony *346*
Medical Decisions *347*
Politics *349*
Games of Chance *352*
Food Labels *353*
Personal Decision Making and Life Planning *354*

Glossary **357**
References **373**
Author Index **385**
Subject Index **391**

Preface

During the last century, psychologists have sought to understand how we think and know about the world around us. As they have gathered information to answer these questions, many have wondered if we could use our knowledge about the way that the mind works to help people improve how they think. It seems clear that we can. The purpose of this book is to apply the research and theories of cognitive psychology to the development of critical thinking skills. It's sort of a user's guide to an immensely complex and highly efficient information processor—the human mind. Because it was written from the perspective of a cognitive psychologist, it can also serve as an introduction to the general area of cognitive psychology.

Traditionally, instruction in how to think has been a neglected component in American education. Students were more often taught what to think than how to think. Education has primarily been concerned with presenting students with the "facts" on a wide variety of topics—the "knowing that"—while offering little on how to utilize this information or how to discover facts on their own—the "knowing how." Domerque (cited in Parnes, Noller, & Biondi, 1977, p. 52) summarized this situation well when he said, "Some people study all their life, and at their death they have learned everything except to think."

I recently had a conversation with a senior partner of a large law firm, during which he lamented the current state of recent law school graduates. He complained that although they could recite the relevant laws, they didn't know how to think. Complaints like this one have been raised by many people in almost every discipline. Consider, for example, the A+ student who could recite in order each of the major Chinese dynasties, yet had no idea what a dynasty was. More importantly, it never occurred to him to ask about the meaning of this term, as he had never made it a habit to be mindful of his thoughts or to monitor his own thought processes for understanding. Perhaps vignettes like these that demonstrate the need for critical thinking instruction shouldn't be surprising, since students are rarely given explicit instruction on how to improve their thinking. Modern educators have recognized that this gap exists and have begun instituting courses with the primary objective of teaching students how to improve their thinking. Most students, teachers, and administrators will agree that this is an idea whose time is long overdue.

It is my hope that you, the reader, will take something very valuable away with you after reading this book. You should be able to think more clearly about any topic, recognize muddy thinking, whether your own or someone else's, monitor what you know and, more importantly, what you don't know, and improve your memory, problem solving, decision making, reasoning, and creative thinking skills. These are lofty objectives, yet ones that can be achieved with a little hard work. Current and relevant examples of each thinking skill have been utilized throughout the book. Many of them may be immediately applicable in your own life. I hope that you'll find this book to be informative, worthwhile, and fun.

ACKNOWLEDGMENTS

Many people have assisted in the preparation of this book. Mr. Jack Burton, Vice President, Lawrence Erlbaum Associates, Inc., has guided me through the publication process with tact and wisdom. In the process, he has become an admired and respected friend. Dr. George Mandler at the University of California, San Diego has read and reread the manuscript, offering expert advice and practical good sense. His wise counsel has been very much appreciated. My dear "aunt," Dr. Katharine D. Newman, now retired from the English Department at West Chester State College, has not only commented on the manuscript, offering helpful suggestions and corrections, but has also served as a life-long role model. She has influenced greatly the course of my life. Dr. Susan Nummedal at California State University, Long Beach, has afforded me the benefit of her expertise with helpful suggestions on the manuscript and has given me support and encouragement with this project. It is deeply appreciated. Dr. Dorothy Piontkowski at San Francisco State University provided several useful insights, especially on Chapter II, The Relationship Between Thought and Language. I would also like to thank an "anonymous philosopher" for comments on the Reasoning Chapter. Ms. Sandi Guideman, production editor, deserves special thanks for all of her help in "pulling the book together" and contributing to its format.

The people most responsible for this text are my husband, Sheldon, and my children, Evan and Joan. Sheldon has read and commented on the entire manuscript, suffered through low points in the writing, encouraged me throughout this project and in almost every endeavor in my life. Evan and Joan have helped in numerous ways, but mostly by just being there and taking pride in my accomplishments. Thanks to all of you.

Diane F. Halpern

To
Sheldon, my husband, and
Evan and Joan, my children—
for their support, encouragement, and love.

1 Thinking: An Introduction

Contents

The Need for Critical Thinking Skills 1
Directed and Nondirected Thought 3
Learning How to Think: Can It Be Done? 3
Changing How People Think 4
Improving Thinking Skills 6
Thinking About Thinking 6
Thinking as a Biological Process 6
Thinking as Imagery and Silent Speech 7
Thinking as Human Information Processing 11
Metacognition 15
Being Mindful 16
Individual Differences 19
About This Book 20

Many people would sooner die than think. In fact they do.
—Bertrand Russell

"Think about it!" How many times have you heard this phrase or said it yourself? Look around you. Watch someone who is solving a calculus problem, or someone who is "debugging" a computer program, or someone who is trying to decide if nuclear energy poses a genuine health hazard. Watch a child absorbed in a fairy tale or an adult constructing a skyscraper or deciding how much sugar to use in a cake recipe. What are they doing that makes their faces appear so serious, so quizzical—so much like Rodin's famous statue, "The Thinker," which appears on the cover of this book? They are all "lost in thought," yet lost seems like a strange word to describe the process of thinking—maybe "found in thought" would be a more appropriate phrase.

THE NEED FOR CRITICAL THINKING SKILLS

Although the ability to think critically has always been important, it is imperative for the citizens of the 20th and 21st century. For the first time in the history of the human race, we have the ability to destroy all life on earth. The decisions that we make as individuals and as a society regarding defense, the economy, conserva-

GRIN AND BEAR IT by Lichty & Wagner

"Fifty cents for my thoughts?"

tion of natural resources, and the development of nuclear weapons will affect future generations of all people around the world. We are also called upon to make decisions on a wide range of important local topics. For example, in a recent election voters had to decide if they favored or opposed an increase in property taxes, the construction of a canal that would divert water from one part of the state to another, and a rent control ordinance in addition to deciding which candidate they preferred for diverse political offices including governor, state treasurer, county commissioner, and trustee of the local library system. Consumers need to decide if the nitrates in their hot dogs are carcinogens, if the public school system is providing an adequate education, and whether prepaid health plans are preferable to plans with a deductible. Because every citizen is required to make countless important decisions, it seems obvious that, as a society, we should be concerned with the way these decisions are made.

Despite what may seem to many to be an obvious need in higher education, it is only in recent years that educators have been concerned with designing educational programs to improve thinking and decision making. It's difficult to imagine any area where the ability to think clearly is not needed. Yet, few of us have ever received explicit instructions on how to improve the way we think. Traditionally, our schools have required students to learn, remember, make decisions, analyze arguments, and solve problems without ever teaching them how. There has been a tacit assumption that adult students already know "how to think." Recent research has shown, however, this assumption is not warranted. Psychologists have found that only 25% of first year college students possessed the skills needed for logical thought (McKinnon & Renner, 1971).

Directed and Nondirected Thought

The term **critical thinking** is used to describe thinking that is purposeful and goal directed. Critical thinking is also called **directed thinking.** Whenever we solve a problem, make an inference, or arrive at a decision, we are engaging in critical thinking. Daydreams, night dreams, and other sorts of thinking that are not engaged in for a specific purpose are not subsumed under the critical thinking category. Neither is the type of thinking that underlies our daily routinized habits such as getting up in the morning, brushing our teeth, or driving to school and work. These are examples of the kind of thinking called **nondirected thinking.**

The focus of this book is on the development and improvement of those skills that characterize clear, precise, purposeful thinking. It is a practical book, based primarily on applications of cognitive psychology to reasoning, problem solving, creativity, intelligence, language, and decision making.

Although psychology has been concerned with the way people think for much of its 100+ years of existence as an academic discipline, cognitive psychology, the branch of psychology that is concerned with thought and knowledge, has virtually dominated the field of psychology over the last 15 years. Psychologists have been concerned with learning about the skills and strategies used in problem solving, reasoning, and decision making and the way these abilities relate to intelligence. All of this interest in human thinking processes has given birth to a new area of psychology that has come to be known as **cognitive process instruction.** Its goal is to utilize the knowledge we have accumulated about human thought processes and mechanisms in ways that can help people improve how they think. For example, by examining correct and incorrect responses in a variety of situations, psychologists have found that most people's spontaneous and intuitive approaches to problems are frequently wrong. Furthermore, they can often predict when an incorrect response will be made either because of the nature of the problem or because of biases that a problem solver may bring to the problem. This knowledge is already being put to use to solve a host of applied problems that range from providing military personnel with map reading skills to designing "user-friendly" (easy to use) computer programs.

Learning How to Think: Can It Be Done?

The answer to this question is a somewhat qualified, "No." Every one of us knows how to think. It's something we've done, most often without thinking much about it, from birth. It comes as naturally as breathing. On a more positive and relevant note, although it may not be possible to teach someone how to think, it is possible to *improve* the way someone thinks.

It may seem that if I'm concerned with improving the way people think, then I should be able to offer a good definition for the term "thinking." Although this is a reasonable expectation, unfortunately there are no satisfactory definitions of thinking. The lack of a definition isn't because people haven't tried to formulate one; it's just that words seem to fail us in our attempt to capture the meaning of this term. Consider the definition and question offered by Bourne, Ekstrand and Dominowski (1971, p. 5): "Thinking is a complex, multifaceted process. It is essentially internal (and possibly nonbehavioral), involving symbolic representations of events and objects not immediately present, but is initiated by some external event (stimulus). Its function is to generate and to control overt behavior. This expression seems straightforward enough, a reasonable working hypothesis. But is it?"

This definition, like any definition, is arbitrary. Most people would agree that thinking is complex and that it guides our behavior. In addition, for most people, thinking is dynamic; it's something we do, an action in itself. Thinking involves "going beyond the information given" (Bruner, 1957). We take new information, combine it with information stored in memory and end up with something more than and different from what we started with. It's also private, in that no one else can know about our thoughts unless we choose to communicate them. Furthermore, thinking is so private that no one has conscious awareness of her or his own thinking processes. As Mandler (1975) reminds us, we usually have no knowledge of how we think; we only know the products of our thoughts. The lack of a good definition of thinking shouldn't prevent us from finding ways to improve it. After all, as Munson (1976, p. 3) astutely observed, "The truth is that not a whole heck of a lot about a complicated subject can be learned from a definition of it."

Changing How People Think

The whole idea of influencing the way people think may seem scary. It suggests terms like "mind control" and "propaganda," or perhaps even a "Big Brother," like the one in Orwell's chilling novel *1984,* who knew what you were thinking. When Orwell wrote his book (in 1949), he was writing about the horrors of a society 35 years into the future. Interestingly, the publication date of this text is 1984, and the topic, "thinking," is very much on the minds of educators and students, but for reasons opposite from those raised by Orwell. Learning the skills of clear thinking can help everyone to recognize propaganda and thus not fall prey to it, to analyze unstated assumptions in arguments, to realize when there is deliberate deception, to consider the credibility of an information source, and to think a problem or a decision through in the best way possible.

Let's consider some examples of the need to think critically in a variety of contexts. A good place to start is with commercials. Sponsors pay substantial sums for the opportunity to persuade customers to purchase their products. Most of their advertising campaigns are rated as successful if more of the product is sold after the advertisements are run (on television, radio, billboards, newspapers, etc.), and the additional sales more than cover the cost of the advertisement. One of my favorite examples is a cigarette advertisement. As most of you know, every cigarette advertisement must carry the message, "Warning: The U.S. Surgeon General has determined that cigarette smoking is dangerous to your health." It would seem that this message would conjure up visions of hacking coughs, stained teeth, and lung cancer, and thus reduce the effectiveness of any cigarette advertisement. To counter the surgeon general's warning, many cigarette advertisements show smokers in natural outdoor surroundings (with crystal lakes, clear blue skies, and tall, green, pine trees). One cigarette advertisement reads, "Come to where the clean is." Have you ever stopped to consider the association of cigarette smoking and the beauty of an outdoor scene? Does cigarette smoking seem healthier when it is associated with beautiful people in beautiful settings? We don't know how many people have been influenced by this advertisement. It is reasonable to assume, however, that since the advertisement has been used so frequently, it is persuading people to smoke the brand of cigarettes being advertised.

Another example of the need for critical thinking comes from a conversation I once had with a cab driver. Our conversation got around to the way laundry products are advertised. He told me that he never paid any attention to advertisements and that they had no affect on his decision about which product to buy. He went on to say that he always buys the blue liquid detergent that is good at getting out "ring around the collar." Do you see the inconsistency in his statements? While he believed that he was not allowing the advertising claims to influence him, in fact, they were directly determining his buying habits. I doubt if many people worried about "ring around the collar," "waxy-yellow build-up on their kitchen floor," "fresh smelling carpets," or "soft elbows" before commercials told us that we were remiss and socially undesirable unless we attended to these details. The unstated assumption in these commercials is that the "problems" they raise (e.g., dark lines on the inside neck portion of shirts, or floors that aren't as clear as new ones) are important ones that can be remedied if you purchase their products. The cab driver, for example, accepted the problem as a valid concern and then purchased the advertised product *without* any conscious awareness of the ways his thoughts and behaviors had been influenced.

In a recent political campaign, one candidate told voters he was opposed to waste, fraud, pollution, crime, and overpaid bureaucrats. This speech was followed with cheering and applause. What's wrong with his speech? He never really said anything. I've never heard any candidate claim to be *for* waste, fraud, pollution, crime, or overpaid bureaucrats. Voters should have asked him to be more explicit about his goals, *how* he would accomplish them and where the money would come from to finance his plans.

As you read the chapters in this book, you should become aware of the need to think critically in a variety of contexts. The results should be well worth the effort you put into learning the material.

Improving Thinking Skills

Evidence has been accumulating to support the idea that people can learn to think more effectively. One of the pioneers in this area is Moshe Rubinstein, who has developed a long-running course at UCLA designed to teach students the skills of critical thinking and problem solving. An educator at a midwestern university who has adopted Rubinstein's program reported that 82.4% of the students who have taken his course scored higher on a test of intelligence than they did before the course began (Rubinstein, 1980). Other evidence that thinking skills can be improved with instruction specifically designed for this purpose is presented by Fox, Marsh, and Crandall (1983). They found that college students who had been taught general problem solving skills showed significant gains on a test of abstract thinking ability while a control group of college students who had not received the problem solving training showed no such gains.

In a recent attempt to improve thinking skills, Schoenfeld and Herrmann (1982) taught college freshmen and sophomores either general techniques of problem solving or "structural programming" which involved "an orderly way to solve nonmathematical problems using the computer." Students who received the general strategy instruction approached mathematical problems in ways that were similar to the approaches used by professors of mathematics. The general strategy approach demonstrated substantial improvement in problem solving scores, while those in the computer course showed little improvement over the scores obtained before taking the course. There are numerous other examples (for example, see Cyert, 1980; Lochhead & Clement, 1979) that all point to the same conclusion: Better thinking can be learned with appropriate instruction.

THINKING ABOUT THINKING

Thinking as a Biological Process

Researchers from many fields have spent their lifetimes trying to understand what people do when they think. Biologists and neuropsychologists have attempted to answer this question by examining patterns of **brain waves** that can be recorded with electrodes that have been attached to a person's skull. A graph of wavy lines (brain waves) called an **electroencephalograph,** or brain wave recording, shows the place on the skull where brain activity is greatest at the time of the recording. (The graph gives no clue about what the subject is thinking.)

Brain researchers are interested in understanding how the brain and other parts of the nervous system work. Every time you have a thought, feel an emotion, or receive information through your senses, your nervous system is involved. If you could examine your own brain, you would no doubt be surprised to find that it looks like a giant mushy walnut with the consistency of a soft-boiled egg. There is nothing in its appearance to even suggest that it is the foundation of human thought. Brain researchers study the brain in their attempt to unravel the mystery of the human mind. They have found that different areas of the brain become more active with different kinds of tasks suggesting that different portions of the brain are specialized for certain functions.

The human brain is divided into two halves or **hemispheres.** Recent research has shown that for most people each hemisphere may be dominant or superior with respect to certain functions. It seems that for most right-handed people and many left-handed people, the left hemisphere (left half of the brain) is dominant for language, mathematics, and other logical sequential functions, whereas the right hemisphere (right half of the brain) is dominant with respect to spatial skills, music, art, and dance. The rest of the population either uses both hemispheres about equally for all of these tasks, or, in a minority of people, the specialization of the right and left hemispheres is reversed. Although brain researchers discovered fascinating links between the biology (and anatomy) of the brain and intellectual skills, there is still much to learn. As a discipline, brain research is still in its infancy and thus, at present, has little to contribute to the development of our ability to think critically. Because we are certainly not able to control or direct neural processes, the biological approach has little to suggest about how to improve the way we think. Current science fiction notions about brain transplants, pills to make us smarter, or miracle foods that prolong life still remain in the realm of late-night movies and Saturday afternoon matinees.

Current biological suggestions for better thinking are much more mundane. From a biological perspective, clear thinking will be facilitated if individuals take care of their health by making certain that they get adequate nutrition and sleep, and by avoiding mind-altering drugs, (e.g., alcohol, marijuana, cocaine, etc.). You may have heard that some people think better or more creatively when they are under the influence of drugs. This is *not* true. There is no evidence that being drugged has ever improved the quality or clarity of anyone's thoughts, and there is *much* evidence that drugs are detrimental to the ability to think.

Thinking as Imagery and Silent Speech

Thinking is the talking of the soul with itself.
—Author Unknown
Found in a Fortune Cookie

THE FAMILY CIRCUS® **By Bil Keane**

"Thinking is when the picture is in your head with the sound turned off."

Psychologists at the beginning of the century believed that thinking was comprised of mental images. Later in the century, other psychologists hypothesized that thinking was simply a form of "silent speech," much like talking to yourself without vocalization. In order to test these hypotheses, psychologists would ask subjects to describe what they did when responding to certain questions. Let's try some examples. As you answer each question posed below, try to be aware of what you did when you "thought about it."

1. How many windows are in your living room?
2. What does your mother look like?
3. What letter comes after N in the alphabet?
4. Name a word that rhymes with "shoe."
5. How much is 2 + 3?
6. Can you define "critical thinking?"

As you answered these questions, were you aware of the use of images and/or words? Most people find that when they are asked to describe some concrete object, like the number of windows in their living room or their mother, they are aware of picture-like images. In fact, it seems almost impossible to answer these questions without generating an internal representation or utilizing **imagery** in some way. Can you describe your mother or anyone else without creating an image? Questions like 3 or 4, which involve the order of letters in the alphabet and the sounds of words, usually require an individual to recite silently the items. (Did you sing l-m-n-o-p to yourself in order to answer Question 3?) When answering questions like 5 and 6, people are often unable to say how they arrived at an answer. (By the way, if you couldn't answer 6, go back and reread the beginning sections in this chapter.) Most people feel that the answers just seemed to "pop into their heads" without any conscious awareness of the "medium" or "stuff" of thought.

Currently, research psychologists are debating whether the "true" medium of thought involves imagery, or sentence-like propositions, or both. For most people, the question is moot, as almost everyone reports that, at least under some circumstances, they are aware of both mental images and "silent speech" during sentence structure. Most of the time, however, we have little or no conscious awareness of what happens when we think.

Sometimes, thinking can be improved if we "work at" generating an image or using speech-like thought. Albert Einstein often credited his ability to solve difficult problems to his extensive use of imagery. The most famous use of imagery was recorded by the chemist Kekulé. He knew that if he could understand the structure of a benzene molecule he would have hit upon one of the most important discoveries in organic chemistry. Kekulé knew that most chemical molecules are long strands of atoms, and that the structure of a benzene molecule had to be different. In order to solve this problem, Kekulé practiced generating visual images that might help him to find the right one. His hard work was rewarded when the historic answer came to him this way:

> Again the atoms were gamboling before my eyes. . . . My mental eye . . . could now distinguish larger structures . . . all twining and twisting in a snakelike motion. But look! What was that! One of the snakes had seized hold of its own tail, and the form whirled mockingly before my eyes. As if by a sudden flash of lightning I awoke (Kekulé, quoted in Koestler, 1964).

The image of a snake biting its own tail led Kekulé to the discovery that the benzene molecule was structured as a closed ring and not like strands of the other molecules. Thus, he was able to use visual imagery to direct his thoughts about a complex topic.

Words also serve to direct and stimulate thought. Although it may be obvious that thoughts are usually communicated with language, it is also true that language helps to generate thoughts. The generative role of language can be seen in an experiment by Glucksberg and Weisberg (1966). There is a classic problem in the psychology literature that was originally devised by Duncker (1945). In this problem, subjects are required to attach a candle to a wall so that it could be lit. They are given a candle, a box of matches, and some thumb tacks. Stop now and think how you would go about solving this problem if you were given only these materials (see Fig. 1.1). Don't go on until you've thought about it.

FIG. 1.1. Using only the materials shown in this figure, how would you attach the candle to the wall so that it can be burned?

The best solution is to dump the matches from their box, tack the box to the wall and set the candle in the box. Most subjects have difficulty with this task because they fail to think of the box as part of the solution—they see it as a "box of matches." Glucksberg and Weisberg had people solve this problem under one of two conditions. The items were either labeled ("box," "tacks," "candle," and "matches") or they were not labeled. Subjects in the labeled condition solved the problem in about 1 minute, while those in the unlabeled condition took an average of 9 minutes. The labels directed their attention to the relevant items and changed how the subjects solved this problem.

Let's consider a somewhat different example of the way language directs thought. There is a popular riddle that goes something like this:

> A young boy and his father went for a Sunday drive. A drunken driver swerved in front of their car, killing the father on impact. The young boy was rushed to the nearest hospital where the chief of neurosurgery was summoned to perform an operation. Upon seeing the boy, the chief of neurosurgery cried out, "I can't operate on him, he's my son!" How is this possible?

When I've posed this riddle to students, some of their answers included: "The chief of neurosurgery is the boy's step father"; "The real father didn't die"; and "It's impossible." Have you guessed the answer? The answer is that the chief of neurosurgery is the boy's mother. The reason for the difficulty is that in our society, terms like chief of neurosurgery lead us to consider only males. The words we use determine the kinds of thoughts we think. (This concept is developed more fully in chapter 2.)

Have you ever listened to two professionals in the same field discussing their work? Most professionals have highly developed specialized terms to communicate their thoughts. Often, these specialized terms also serve to guide the way the professionals think:

> How did the surgeon acquire his knowledge of the structure of the human body? . . . It has taken hundreds of dissections to build up the detailed and accurate picture of the structure of the human body that enables the surgeon to know where to cut. A highly specialized sublanguage has evolved for the sole purpose of describing this structure. The surgeon had to learn this jargon of anatomy before the anatomical facts could be effectively transmitted to him. Thus, underlying the "effective action" of the surgeon is an "effective language." Learning this anatomical language was a prerequisite to the transmission of the factual information that is needed here for effective action. (Bross, 1973, p. 217)

Thus, as the author points out, technical jargons not only facilitate communication among professionals, they are an inherent part of the development of ideas in a specialized discipline.

The use of jargon can serve as an efficient shorthand for communication among professionals. Specialized terms, however, can also serve as a barrier that keeps lay persons from understanding. Have you ever gone to a physician and found you were unable to communicate with him because you didn't understand the technical terms he used? A physician with a clear understanding of the problem should be able to communicate the nature of your problem in plain English. Beware of anyone who scatters terms indiscriminately or uses them as labels for simple phenomena.

A friend of mine once went to an allergy specialist who, after extensive tests, announced that my friend had "chronic rhinitis." Although she found this diagnosis alarming, with further questioning, she learned this means "runny nose,"—a diagnosis she could have made by herself.

Thinking as Human Information Processing

A currently popular approach to understanding human thought utilizes computers to model the ways humans think. One approach that psychologists and others concerned with computer models of thought (engineers, linguists, medical personnel) have taken is to program a computer so that the processes and strategies it uses in solving a problem are similar to those used by humans. Thus, programs were written that would *simulate* or imitate human thought. This approach is called **computer simulation.** One problem with this approach is that we need to have very good ideas about the ways humans think in order to tell a computer to do it the same way.

One way of finding out how people think is to ask them to say out loud everything that they consciously thought about as they solved a problem. Thus, experimenters would collect **think aloud protocols,** which are verbatim records of what the subject says he is doing while working on a problem. We have already tried something like this earlier in the chapter, using very simple questions. Let's try it with a more complex problem. As you try to work through this problem, say out loud every thought you have while working on the problem. It's important that you try to say all of your thoughts out loud. Your false starts, mistakes, repetitions, etc. are all valuable in understanding *how* you think.

Your friend has invited you to a birthday party. She has a square cake that she wants to share equally among the seven guests and herself. Using only *three* cuts with a knife, how would you cut the cake into eight equal slices? *Stop now,* and recite out loud how you would go about solving this problem. If you have a tape recorder available, tape your think aloud protocol so that you can analyze the thought processes you reveal in the protocol when you're finished. If you don't have a tape recorder, find a friend who is willing to take detailed notes of what you're saying. This gives you the added advantage of having someone with you to discuss your thinking process.

Most people find that they try several combinations of three slices before they hit upon the correct answer or give up. (The correct answer involves slicing the cake into quarters with two cuts, then placing the cake on its edge and slicing through the cake.) After collecting data from many subjects, a computer can be *programmed* (given a set of instructions in a computer language) to "think" about similar problems the way people do. If the simulation is successful, then the computer would also make the same mistakes that people do. Now that you've gotten the idea of think aloud protocols, try it again with the next problem. "Given Jug A, which contains 9 quarts; Jug B, 42 quarts; and Jug C, 6 quarts, measure out exactly 21 quarts" (Hayes, 1982, p. 65). Stop now, and verbalize aloud how you go about solving this problem. Be sure to say everything that you're thinking, even if it doesn't seem relevant. As before, you'll find the process more interesting if you can tape your responses so that you can review them later. Don't go on until you've tried to solve this problem.

Compare your protocol with the one presented here. Did you try the same problem-solving strategy used by the 37 year old lawyer who answered this way?

> OK, I want to, uh, see what is the highest number that will go into 21, of those 3 numbers. A, B, and C . . . 42 is too high, uh, 9 will go into 21 twice . . . and leaves a remainder of, uh, 3 . . . that doesn't work, uh . . . I, uh, will then take 6; 6 will go into 21, 3 times . . . that's no good; it leaves a remainder of 3 . . . If I make it twice, that's 12; that will leave a remainder of 9 quarts and I can use A. That's 9 quarts, so I've got two of the C's the 6 quarts and one of the A's that's 9 quarts.

Psychologists use think aloud protocols to understand how people think. In **protocol analysis,** the protocol is broken down into segments so that each segment can be analyzed separately. Sometimes psychologists have theories about the processes involved and try to confirm or disconfirm them with the protocol. Other times, the purpose of the analysis is exploratory. Specific theories about the processes involved are presented in chapter 3.

Think aloud protocols have proven to be useful in both understanding thought processes and improving them. Thomas Good, an authority on research in mathematics education, has found that mathematics students learn best when the teachers actively work with them and model out loud the problem-solving process. It seems that when teachers think out loud they provide "a structure and a way of thinking about the information . . . so [students] can better understand relationships" (Cordes, 1983, p. 7). One way to improve thinking is to analyze the think aloud protocols of experts and then model your own thought processes after them. This modeling technique has been found to be a useful aid in developing the thinking processes of novices.

Artificial Intelligence

The term **Artificial Intelligence** (AI) is sometimes used to refer to the way computers solve problems when there has been no attempt to simulate or mimic human behavior. In AI, the programmed instructions to the computer may be very different from the way humans solve the same problem.

Have you ever played chess with a computer? Many computer programs are designed to simulate the moves that humans make. Other chess programs take advantage of the vast "memory" of the computer and have it evaluate the consequences of several different possible moves. Several chess programs can consider between 5,000 and 50,000 possible combinations of moves (Berliner, 1977). Several years ago, it was predicted that world chess championships would all be won by computers. This has not happened. Our best human chess players can still beat the computers with regularity—a fact that makes most of us humans very happy.

Computer simulation and AI are more than toys. They can be used to guide military and economic decisions and to provide tentative answers to questions like, "What would happen if . . . ?" They also can infer information that is not specifically stated. For example, suppose that I told you that Jerome wanted to make an omelette. He noticed that he was out of butter and went to the market to buy some. Given only this information, answer the following question: Did Jerome have eggs in his house? Undoubtedly, you said, "Yes," since he only went to buy butter, he must have eggs. You can't make an omelette without eggs; and if he had been out of eggs, he would have also bought them at the store. Sophisticated computer programs can also make this inference. They can infer the truth about information not given (e.g., he must have eggs in the house) in much the same way that we humans do.

Computers have also been used to "talk" to people, much as some psychotherapists do. There is a type of psychotherpy called Rogerian therapy (named for Carl Rogers, its creator) in which the therapist rephrases the client's message. A famous computer program (Weizenbaum, 1966) does exactly the same thing. Here is an example of a "conversation" between a Rogerian computer therapist named Eliza and a human client. The conservation took place via typed message on a computer keyboard.

Patient: Men are all alike.
Eliza: In what way?
Patient: They're always bugging us about something or other.
Eliza: Can you think of a specific example?
Patient: Well, my boyfriend made me come here.
Eliza: Your boyfriend made you come here.
Patient: He says I'm depressed much of the time.
Eliza: I am sorry to hear you are depressed.
Patient: It's true. I am unhappy.
Eliza: Do you think coming here will help you not to be unhappy?
Patient: I need some help, that much seems certain.
Eliza: What would it mean to you if you got some help?
Patient: Perhaps I could learn to get along with my mother.
Eliza: Tell me more about your family.

Does this seem like an ordinary session between a patient and a psychotherapist? The therapist, Eliza, is a computer. If you examine her contributions to the conversation, you'll realize that she really doesn't add much. Eliza is programmed to respond to certain key phrases (e.g., "I feel . . .") by paraphrasing the words that come after them or by adding noncommital "filler" phrases.

Can Computers Think?

The answer to the question of whether or not computers can think is tied to the way we choose to define thinking. If thinking is defined as a human activity that is dependent upon the neural structure of the brain, then, by definition, computers would not qualify. Suppose we don't rule out a priori the notion that computers can think. How would you go about answering this question? The late A. M. Turing (1950) suggested a test for deciding if a computer can think. Appropriately, it's called **Turing's Test.** Suppose that you are sitting alone in a room with a typewriter keyboard. You can type in any question you want and the typed message will go to two different rooms. In one of these rooms there is a person; in the other there is a computer. Each will send their answer back to you, again via typewriter keyboard. You can ask any question that you want except, "Are you a computer or a human?" According to Turing's Test, if you can't tell from the messages you receive which is the person and which is the computer, then it has been demonstrated that computers can think. What do *you* think about Turing's Test?

Most people find that they are unwilling to conclude that a computer can think just because they couldn't distinguish the computer's answer from a human's answer. After all, is mimicking thought the same as thinking? Suppose I designed a robot that would come to your front door every day and take your dog for a walk. The end result would be the same as if a person had walked the dog, but would you be willing to conclude that the robot had exercised its muscles?

Just because the end product is the same, it doesn't follow that the process was the same.

On the other hand, consider the following line of reasoning. The most famous mathematical treatise of the 20th century, *Principia Mathematica,* was written in 1925 by Whitehead and Russell. All of us would agree that these outstanding mathematicians were exceptional thinkers. More recently, the information that was known prior to Whitehead and Russell's mathematical discoveries was fed into a computer that rapidly proceeded to derive most of the same theorems that these famous mathematicians had derived. When this intellectual feat was accomplished by humans, it was hailed as extraordinary thinking. Are we then also obliged to label the same feat in the same way when it is done by a computer?

Of course, computers and humans differ in many basic ways. Their underlying hardware—neural patterns for humans, electronic circuits for computers—are different. And, of course, humans reproduce themselves, while computers rely on humans for their production. It could be argued that computers don't really think since they rely on programs to tell them what to do; however, a similar argument could be made for humans since they rely upon their experiences, genetic programs, and input from other humans to tell them what to do. In any case, premonitions of a world ruled by computers like Hal in the movie *2001* still remain in the realm of science fiction.

METACOGNITION

Ultimately, it is not we who define thinking, it is thinking that defines us.

—quote from Carey, Foltz & Allan
Newsweek, February 7, 1983.

Metacognition refers to what we know about what we know, or, in more formal language, our knowledge about knowledge. It seems that most people have little awareness of the nature or even the existence of the thinking processes that underlie their judgments, beliefs, inferences, and conclusions about complex issues (Nisbett & Wilson, 1977).

There are many experimental examples of how little we know about the variables that influence our thinking. I'll demonstrate this point with one of my favorites. Researchers (Wilson & Nisbett, 1978) asked consumers in a large bargain store to select which of four pairs of nylon pantyhose they preferred. The stockings were hung on a rack above the researcher's table. The consumers examined the weave, the heel, and the toe. Very few had difficulty making a choice. The stocking in the left-most position was preferred by 12% of the consumers; the one to its right by 17%; the next one to the right by 31%; and the right-most stocking by 40%. This indicates that there were clear preferences among the shoppers. This is especially interesting in light of the fact that the four stockings were identical. Position alone accounted for the consumer preferences, yet none of the consumers indicated that position influenced his or her decision. People are simply not aware of the variables that affect how they think.

Being Mindful

In order to develop basic thinking skills, it is necessary to direct your attention to the processes and products of your own thoughts. You need to become consciously aware of the way you think and to develop the habit of examining the end products of your thought processes—the solution you've arrived at, the decision you've made, the inference that you believe to be true, or the judgment you've formulated. In short, you need to become mindful or aware of how and what you think.

Consider what happens when a student in mathematics or the sciences learns to rely on formulas that she does not understand. She may be able to substitute numbers for the algebraic symbols, then work through the appropriate arithmetic and arrive at the correct answer without ever understanding the principles involved or the meaning or importance of the answer.

Students in the sciences and in mathematics are taught a technical jargon. Too often, they believe that scattering these terms in a discussion is evidence that they understand the concepts, when in fact their understanding of the phenomena involved is shallow and consists mainly of the ability to label events. Students are required to memorize formulas with little understanding of when and how to apply them. Wickelgren (1974, p. ix) addressed this problem when he wrote:

> In the mathematics and science courses I took in college, I was enormously irritated by the hundreds of hours that I wasted staring at problems without any good idea about what approach to try next in attempting to solve them. I thought at the time that there was no educational value in those 'blank' minutes, and I see no value in them today.

Griffiths (1976, p. 81) raises an interesting question when he asks: "Physics teaching: Does it hinder intellectual development?" Griffiths answers this question by noting that the way physics is currently taught with vocabulary drills and reliance on formulas, prevents students from learning how to reason or think critically about the issues. In studying how students think about physics problems, Griffiths (1976) found that; "In many instances, when a conflict was apparent between the predicted results and the experimental evidence, a technical term was imposed to explain the discrepancy." Here is one of his student's responses to a classic problem involving an inclined plane, "You have to calculate it. You must set all forces to zero, then sum all the forces acting on the body equal to zero, then solve it for what it really means" (p. 84). You don't need to know anything about physics to realize that this student is in trouble. He has acquired a meaningless vocabulary and has not acquired the ability to think in a cogent way. More troublesome than the student's lack of knowledge in this case is the fact that he doesn't know that he doesn't know. He has not developed the ability to monitor his knowledge and recognize the difference between scattering terms and understanding concepts. He has no awareness or self-monitoring process for his own knowledge.

Consider the following example: Working alone, Stacy can mow her front lawn in 2 hours, while it takes her sister Carole 4 hours. How long will it take them to mow the lawn if they work together? Many students routinely apply the well-known formula for finding an average. They add 2 + 4 and divide by 2, concluding that it will take them an average of 3 hours if they work together. Few students stop to realize that this is an unreasonable answer, since it implies that it will take them longer if they work together than it would if Stacy were working alone! Why are students misled into thinking that this is a correct answer? I believe that they have been overly trained to rely on rote applications of formulas. They have not learned to stop and think about the kind of answer they should expect (e.g., a number less than 2); nor have they learned the skills of working through a problem. They have never learned the importance of being mindful. (In case you've been working on this problem and want to check your answer, the correct answer is 1 hour and 20 minutes.)

Several years ago, **programmed learning** was hailed as psychology's greatest contribution to education. In a programmed learning approach, students proceed through a set of materials in "small steps" with much repetition deliberately built into the learning materials. The emphasis on a "small-step" approach (introducing only a small amount of new material at any one time) sometimes means that the reader will lose sight of main ideas or the way concepts interrelate. Although it's true that some use of repetition will facilitate learning, heavy doses invariably lead to boredom. In most programmed learning texts, students are required to respond to questions with a single word or two-word phrase. There is no room for elaboration or reflection about the materials. Students are not encouraged to relate the concepts or to think beyond the material presented.

Students want to be creative in the way they approach problems, and they want the skills needed to function successfully in novel situations. The repetitious, stereotyped responding that is required in programmed learning packages is the antithesis of these skills (Schwartz, 1982). Unfortunately, programmed learning approaches are making an educational revival. Several new programmed learning packages are being designed for use with computers. Computer-assisted instruction is only as good or as bad as the computer program that is being used. Educational programmers need to understand that the ability to think critically about an issue can never be learned from rote (unthinking) responding.

The results of a 1982 national test of mathematics, which was conducted at federal expense by the National Assessment of Educational Progress, showed that students have improved in mathematical performance relative to their 1978 counterparts. However, a closer analysis of the results by Stephen Willoughby, a New York University mathematics professor, is less encouraging. He has concluded, "We've succeeded in teaching only those things that can be handled better by a machine" (Savage, 1983, p. 1). He found that gains in rote computations were being offset by losses in "questions that required thinking, estimation, or analysis." Much of the blame for these disheartening results has been placed on the routine use of calculators and computer software packages that don't require any real thinking. Computers and calculators are not inherently bad. They can be used in creative ways that foster intellectual development, and they can perform many of life's tedious tasks. The problems arise when they serve as a substitute for thinking instead of a tool for thinking. Early in this century, psychologists demonstrated that rodents could be taught to press a lever in response to an environmental cue. Let's be careful not to consider the same behavior in humans as indicative of the higher level processing we want to promote.

Another way that thinking may be discouraged in educational settings is in the kinds of examinations that are used to assess learning. Too often, learning is measured solely with fill-in-the-blank, true-false, and multiple-choice questions that are concerned only with recitations of previously presented material. It is possible for students to be able to place the correct word in the correct blank while not understanding very much about the topic.

One of contemporary psychology's best known spokespersons is B. F. Skinner. It was Skinner's work on the relationship between reinforcement and learning that led to the development and widespread use of programmed learning materials. In 1968, Skinner stated:

> It has been said that an education is what survives when a man has forgotten all he has been taught. Certainly few students could pass their final examinations even a year or two after leaving school or college. What has been learned of permanent value must therefore not be the facts and principles covered by examinations but certain other kinds of behavior often ascribed to special abilities. Far from neglecting these kinds of behaviors, careful programming reveals the need to teach them as explicit educational objectives (pp. 89–90).

I believe that in this passage, Skinner is arguing for specific instruction on how to think instead of the usual instruction in what others have thought. Like many other people, I believe that this is an idea whose time is long overdue.

Perhaps one of the most poignant examples of the way that education has not fostered thinking skills is presented by Carpenter (1981). She presented college students with a novel problem devised by the Swiss psychologist, Jean Piaget. (See the Intelligence Chapter for additional Piagetian tasks.) Students were given a small container of water, a large, heavy wooden block, and a small, light wooden block. Their task was to determine if either or both blocks would float and to explain their results. They found that the large, heavy block floated while the small, light one did not. When faced with the task of explaining the results, the college students assumed that they ought to know the answer and tried to remember formulas and terms. The college students who had taken several science courses brought in the terms "center of gravity," "specific gravity," and "surface tension." They were unwilling to test the situation or to explore the materials that were provided. In general, they were unable to generate testable hypotheses. This may be symptomatic of the discomfort many college students feel with science and mathematics courses. (The correct answer concerns the relationship between weight and area.)

The college students' approach to the problem can be sharply contrasted to the one used by 6th grade children when they were presented with the same task. The 6th graders manipulated the materials and revised their hypotheses as they tested the relevant variables of size and weight. Unburdened with technical jargon or the expectancy that this problem could be solved best with a formula, the 6th graders were more likely to generate testable hypotheses and to manipulate the materials in order to solve the problem than their college counterparts!

Individual Differences

When you offer someone a penny for his thoughts, you usually don't expect to get a bargain.
—Beardsley (1950, p. x)

Certainly we are all different in many ways, including the ways in which we think. An early study (Bloom & Broder, 1950) examined individual difference in the thinking processes of college students. Although this study is an old one, many of their conclusions remain valid today.

College students were tested on a series of reasoning problems. They were required to think out loud so that their thinking processes could be monitored. Here is a sample item (assume that these statements are true):

Any action that impedes the war effort of the United States should be made illegal.

All strikes impede the war effort of the United States.

Conclusions: (pick one)

A. All strikes should be made illegal.
B. Some restrictions should be placed on the right to strike, but it would be unwise to make them all illegal.
C. Some strikes should be made illegal.
D. Unjustifiable strikes should be made illegal.
E. None of the foregoing conclusions follows.

Don't worry if you're having difficulty answering this question. Reasoning problems like this one are discussed in detail in the chapter on the Development of Reasoning Skills. (The correct answer is A.)

Bloom & Broder compared the kinds of answers given by poor thinkers to those who answered correctly and found several important differences. The students who performed poorly utilized "one-shot" thinking instead of the extended sequential thinking processes of the good thinkers. The poor thinkers were willing to allow gaps in their knowledge to exist. There were basic differences in the attitude of the good and poor thinkers. The poor thinkers rushed through the instructions or skipped them altogether. They were passive rather than active in their approach to the problems. When the problems were difficult, they utilized only a few clues to answer the questions or guessed at an answer. They failed to break down complex problems into their constituent parts.

The researchers developed a remedial course to improve these students' performance. Students were given experts' think-aloud protocols for model solutions. They were taught how the correct answer was obtained, not merely the correct answer. The researchers reported significant success with this program.

There will always be difference in how people think and, as the French would say, *Viva la difference!* But differences among good thinkers are more desirable than differences among poor ones.

ABOUT THIS BOOK

Some people study all their life and at their death they have learned everything except to think.
—Domerque (quoted in Parnes, Noller, & Biondi, 1977, p. 52)

There are no quick and easy crash programs that will make you a competent thinker overnight. There is, however, substantial evidence that with hard work, determination, and the right learning experiences, most people can improve the way they think. It's certainly an objective worth working toward. This is a skill oriented text with frequent examples of each "thinking skill" for the reader to follow. Occasionally, relevant research and theories are presented to provide the reader with a background in the psychology of thinking. Because this is an introductory text, it does not attempt to provide exhaustive coverage of all possible topics. I hope that this book will spark an interest in the reader, leading you to explore the topics in greater depth. The suggested readings at the end of each chapter can serve as guideposts for finding out more about the most fascinating of all human activities: the thinking process.

Many of the major concepts that are presented appear in several places throughout this book because basic thinking skills are broadly applicable in a variety of situations. This should also serve as an aid in learning them, since research in learning and memory has shown that when information is learned in a variety of contexts, it is easier to remember and utilize.

Each chapter has been written to "stand alone" so that the chapters can be read in any order. Use the outline at the beginning of each chapter to establish a framework for the material. Paying attention to headings and subheadings will help you to organize hierarchically the information.

It is important to work through each sample problem to gain experience with each of the skills presented. Reread difficult sections and *paraphrase* (restate in your own words) each section. Chapter summaries are provided to serve as a recall cue and aid for the information in each chapter. Review the key terms and concepts and be sure that you can answer the end-of-the-chapter questions. Each chapter, except this one, ends with problems so that you can apply the skills presented in that chapter. In addition, a glossary of terms is provided at the back of the book.

Think up your own problems that are like the ones presented in this book, and be sure to keep alert for ways to apply these skills in your life. Read billboards and textbooks critically. Think about your school problems. Examine letters to newspaper editors with care. In short, develop the attitude of a critical thinker. I can't imagine any endeavor more exciting or worthwhile!

One of the goals of this text is to increase the reader's awareness of her or his own thinking process. In order to achieve this goal, the reader will have to work through numerous participatory exercises. As you read through this book, you'll become aware of the ways language influences thought, learn some strategies for approaching and solving problems, develop the skills needed to reason clearly and make sound decisions, understand how hypotheses are tested and how to use probabilities, learn what to do to help you remember, understand the concept and measurement of intelligence, enhance your ability to think creatively, and apply this knowledge to a wide range of situations.

It has been said that the head remembers what it does. Markle (1977) has claimed that the first axiom of learning is, "It is not what is presented to the student but what the student is led to do that results in learning" (p. 13). I doubt that very much has ever been learned in a passive manner. So, get involved with the material, work the exercises, discuss them with others, raise questions and enjoy yourself. Thinking is not a spectator sport! Nutritionists warn that you are what you eat. I believe *instead* that you are what you think.

CHAPTER SUMMARY

1. It is imperative that citizens of the 20th and 21st century think critically, yet recent tests have shown that only 25% of first year college students have the skills needed for logical thought.

2. There is considerable empirical evidence that cognitive skills can be learned in specific courses designed to teach them.

3. While it is possible to view thinking as a biological process, this perspective will not be helpful in devising ways to improve thinking.

4. People report that thinking sometimes seems to rely on visual imagery and sentence-like propositions.

5. Think aloud protocols are used to understand and improve human thought. In computer simulation, they are used to write computer programs that mimic human thought.

6. Metacognition refers to people's knowledge of their own thought processes. We usually have little conscious awareness of how we think. Self-monitoring your own thought processes is one way to improve how you think.

7. Some traditional educational experiences have actually hindered intellectual development. These negative experiences include rote applications of rules or formulas, excessive reliance on technical jargons that are not well understood, and most programmed learning techniques that do not allow students to elaborate or reflect about the materials. Critical thinkers are *mindful* of the processes and products of their thoughts.

8. Researchers have found many differences between good and poor thinkers. The poor thinkers had a poorer attitude toward the reasoning problems that they were asked to solve. They were more likely to skip the instructions, work hastily, and guess at the answer. With remedial instruction, they showed considerable improvement.

9. Remember, you are what (and how) you think! Have fun with this book.

Terms to Know

You should be able to define the following terms and concepts. If you find that you're having difficulty with any term, be sure to reread the section where it is discussed.

Critical Thinking
Directed Thinking
Nondirected Thinking
Cognitive Process Instruction
Programmed Learning
Brain Waves
Electroencephalograph
Hemisphere (Brain)
Imagery
Human Information Processing
Computer Simulation

Think Aloud Protocols
Protocol Analysis
Artificial Intelligence
Turing's Test
Metacognition

Be sure that you can answer the following questions:

1. How is thinking defined in this chapter? Can you come up with a better definition for this term?

2. Why was the author critical of the political candidate who opposed waste, fraud, pollution, crime, and overpaid bureaucrats? Shouldn't we be concerned with these issues?

3. Cite some examples of the ways certain instructional programs can be detrimental to the development of thinking skills.

4. How do biologists study thinking?

5. Explain the idea that thinking is done with images and/or verbal statements. Give an example of each.

6. In what important ways are humans and computers similar? What are the important differences?

7. How can the analysis of think aloud protocols help psychologists understand how people think?

8. What points were raised in this chapter when trying to decide if computers think?

9. What are some differences in the way good and poor thinkers solve reasoning problems?

10. Explain the notion that critical thinkers are "mindful."

SUGGESTED READINGS

There are many fine books that can serve as an introduction to critical thinking and the psychology of thinking. If you're interested in the use of visual imagery to improve how you think, you'll enjoy Arheim's (1971) *Visual Thinking* and McKim's (1980) *Thinking Visually: A Strategy Manual for Problem Solving.*

One of the older classic "thinking books" is Flesch's (1951) *The Art of Clear Thinking*. Every chapter in this clever book begins with quotable quotes from the famous and not so famous. Another classic in the field is *New Think: The Use of Lateral Thinking in the Generation of New Ideas* by de Bono (1968). A historical overview is presented by Johnson (1972) in *A Systematic Introduction to the Psychology of Thinking.*

If you're interested in the way education has responded to psychology's views of thinking, you'll find the collection of papers in *Problem Solving and Education: Issues in Teaching and Research,* edited by Tuma and Reif (1980) and *Cognitive Process Instruction: Research on Teaching Thinking Skills,* edited by Lochhead and Clement (1979) to be informative.

A large and somewhat rambling book that reflects on the nature of thought is *The Act of Creation* by Koestler (1964). My personal favorite for a nonscientific introduction to thinking is *The Mind's Best Work* by Perkins (1981). It's an interesting book filled with strange illustrations and thoughtful questions. It is good food for thought.

A review article that presents some of the most recent psychological perspectives in this area is aptly titled "Thinking" by Erickson and Jones (1978). An old classic with a contemporary flavor is Bartlett's (1958) book *Thinking: An Experimental and Social Study*. If you are interested in the earlier work in the area of thinking, a good source for this is *The Psychology of Thinking* by Bourne, Ekstrand, and Dominowski (1971).

2 The Relationship Between Thought and Language

Contents

Thought and Language 25
Psycholinguistics 26
Underlying Representation 26
Language: Tool or Master of Thought? 27
Comprehension 30
Rules for Clear Communication 31
Implication and Inference 31
Barriers to Comprehension 34
Persuasion and Propaganda 36
Persuading With Language 36
Defending Against Persuasive Techniques 42
Distinguishing Fact From Opinion 43

There is an old story about three umpires that goes something like this:

> Three umpires were unwinding at a local pub after a very tough day. All three had endured abusive shouts like, "Kill the Umpire" and had numerous offers for new pairs of eyeglasses. After a few mugs of brew, they began discussing how they decide to call balls and strikes. The first umpire, Jim, explained that it was really quite simple. "I simply call them as I see them." Donnie, the second umpire, disagreed when he said, "I see them as I call them."
>
> Neil, the third umpire emphatically shook his head in disagreement with the other two. "You're both wrong," he said, slurring his words somewhat. "They don't even exist until I call them."

Neil had a good point. Whether a ball whizzing past home plate is a ball or a strike depends on what the umpire labels it. The words he uses both interpret and define reality.

THOUGHT AND LANGUAGE

How do you express your thoughts in words and sentences? How influenced are you by your particular language? You will have difficulty answering these questions because you use both so automatically and because you have no conscious awareness of the way your thoughts give rise to the words you use to express them. In fact, if you try to monitor your speaking process, you'll find yourself stuttering and interfering with the fluid speech that you normally create so easily. It's as though our speech emerges automatically and preformed. Conscious attention directed at the process tends to interfere with it.

Psycholinguistics

Communication is primarily an exercise in thinking.
—Pitt and Leavenworth (1968, p. vii)

Psycholinguistics is the field of psychology that is concerned with how we acquire and use language. Language is a complex cognitive activity that all normal humans perform with skill and apparent ease. As speakers, we select the words we want to use and produce them in a grammatically correct form. As listeners, we use the information in another's utterance in order to share the expressed thoughts. What do we know about the way speakers and listeners share thoughts through the medium of language?

Underlying Representation and Surface Structure

Language appears to be simply the clothing of naked thought.
—Miller (1972, p. 43)

The sequence of sounds that we produce must correspond to our intended meaning if we are to communicate successfully. Psychologists who are concerned with the way people use and understand language divide language into two components or structures. The **underlying representation** of language refers to the meaning component of language—it's the thought you want to convey. **Surface structure** refers to the sounds of the verbal expression that you use. The problem in producing language is deriving surface structure from underlying representation, while the problem in comprehending language is getting from the surface structure back to the speaker's (or writer's) underlying representation.

When language is ambiguous, the surface structure can have more than one meaning or underlying representation. Some examples of ambiguous sentences are:

Visiting professors can be boring. (This can be interpreted to mean either that it is boring to visit the homes of professors or that it is boring when professors visit campus.)

They are kissing fish. (This can be interpreted to mean either that they are a variety of fish called "kissing fish," or that they are a variety of fish who kiss, or that at least two people have their mouths in the fish bowl and are engaging in the somewhat kinky behavior of kissing fish.)

He cooks carrots and peas in the same pot. (I won't explain the two possible interpretations).

Each of these sentences is ambiguous because there is a single surface structure (the sound of the sentence) and at least two possible underlying representations or interpretations. Clear communications will be unambiguous. With only a little effort, an ambiguous statement can be made clear so that it corresponds to only one underlying representation. For example, the first sentence can be made unambiguous with simple changes:

It is boring to visit professors.

or

Visiting professors are boring.

Language: Tool or Master of Thought?

Learn a new language and get a new soul.
—Czech proverb.

We use language not only to convey our thoughts, but also to mold and shape them. Language and thought are inextricably related concepts that exert mutual influences on each other. Some psychologists believe that language, at least in part, determines thought. The hypothesis that the language we use affects how we think is called the **Sapir–Whorf hypothesis of linguistic relativity,** or more informally, the *Sapir–Whorf hypothesis* (Sapir, 1960; Whorf, 1956).

"How do I know what I mean until I see what I say?" (Miller, 1972, p. 43). In a humorous way this question examines the relationship between thought and language. Although it seems clear to most people that our thoughts influence the language that we use, it is sometimes more difficult to understand the reciprocal nature of the relationship. Anthropologists and psychologists have studied whether people who speak different languages also think somewhat differently. Perhaps you have had the experience of translating a passage from one language to another and had difficulty conveying exactly the same meaning. Jokes are a good example of this. Ethnic jokes that are told in their native language frequently lose their humor when they are told in translation. Could this indicate that ways of thinking, as reflected in language, differ across cultures?

Some chilling implications of the Sapir–Whorf hypothesis appeared in George Orwell's classic book, *1984*. In *1984*, he wrote about a repressive society that was able to control the thoughts of its citizenry by redefining some words and removing others from the language. By gaining control of the language, this futuristic society dictated which thoughts were possible and which were not.

The Orwellian example is an extreme interpretation of the Sapir–Whorf hypothesis that language absolutely determines thought. According to this view, if a term does not exist within a language, speakers do not have the corresponding thought. Do you believe that if the word "love" didn't exist in our language, then people wouldn't be able to feel this emotion? Most people would disagree with the strong form of the Sapir–Whorf hypothesis. Cross-cultural research that has examined the way different languages influence thought has not supported the strong version of the Sapir–Whorf hypothesis (Berlin & Kay, 1969; Rosch, 1977). A weaker version of the Sapir–Whorf hypothesis is that language influences, but does not determine thinking. As an example of this, consider the following terms carefully and decide if each evokes a somewhat different thought: senior citizen; old man; golden-ager. Did each term connote a different thought? Did you think about a different type of person with each word? Most people agree that they did. (See Fig. 2.1.)

As an example of the weak version of the Sapir–Whorf hypothesis consider the heated debate between those for and against abortion. The faction opposed to

Senior Citizen Old Man Golden Ager

FIG. 2.1. The words we use influence how we think. Compare the different thoughts that are evoked by the terms "senior citizen," "old man," and "golden ager."

abortion realized that it is better to be for something than against something and therefore decided to call their stance "pro-life." On the other side, those who favored abortion certainly didn't want to be called "anti-life" and decided to label their stance "pro-choice." They hoped that people would think differently about a position that is "pro-choice" than they would about one that is "anti-life." Of course, the position hasn't changed—only its label or name has changed, but presumably the way the position is labeled influences how people think about it.

When you want to influence how people think, choose your words carefully. You also need to be aware of the ways others attempt to manipulate your own thoughts by the labels they use. It's fairly easy to find examples of this around election time. During a recent election, a group called "Citizens for Sane Laws" opposed a proposition, while another group called "Citizens for Better Government" favored it. The political advertisements continued to broadcast these group names and the message to vote "No on 10" or "Yes on 10" depending on who financed the advertisement. Very little meaningful information was ever given on the merits or problems of the proposition. Be wary of attempts to influence your thinking though the use of positive and negative labels, especially on the important issues that concern social and political policies.

Advertisers and merchants like to price their wares in uneven amounts, like $19.99 and $24.95. Have you ever wondered why they don't simplify matters and price garments to the nearest dollar so that $19.99 would be labeled $20.00 and $24.95 would become $25.00? They believe that consumers will think that $19.99 is considerably less than $20.00. Of course, the one cent difference is negligible, but it does seem to change how people think about the price.

Consider the following problem:

> Imagine that the U.S. is preparing for the outbreak of an unusual disease, which is expected to kill 600 people. Two alternative programs to combat the disease have been proposed. Assume that the exact scientific estimate of the consequences of the programs are as follows:
>
> If Program A is adopted, 200 people will be saved.
>
> If Program B is adopted, there is ⅓ probability that 600 people will be saved, and ⅔ probability that no people will be saved.
>
> Which of the two programs would you favor? (Tversky & Kahneman, 1981, p. 453)

Now, consider the same problem, and select between the following two programs:

> If Program C is adopted, 400 people will die.
>
> If Program D is adopted there is ⅓ probability that nobody will die, and ⅔ probability that 600 people will die.
>
> Which of these two programs would you favor?

When this problem was presented to college students, 72% of those given the first set of choices selected Program A, while 78% of those given the second set of choices selected Program D. Look closely at the choices. Program A and C are effectively identical—they differ only in that A is described in terms of the numbers of lives saved, while C is described in terms of the number who will die. Program B and D are also identical, differing only in the language used to describe the outcomes. The percentage of people who prefer each alternative differs significantly depending on the language used to describe each alternative. This is an important result, showing that human judgments and preferences can be readily manipulated by changes in the way questions are asked or framed.

Another example of the influence of language on thought comes from a study by Loftus (1975, p. 561). Forty people were asked questions about their headaches. A key question was posed in one of two ways:

"Do you get headaches frequently, and, if so, how often?"

or

"Do you get headaches occasionally, and, if so, how often?"

Can you anticipate the results of this study? The respondents who answered the first question reported an average of 2.2 headaches per week, while those who answered the second question reported an average of .7 headaches per week. It seems that if people are asked questions with the word "frequently," they will believe they have experienced more headaches than if they are asked the same question with the word "occasionally." Note that while this example does not seem to contain any deliberate attempts to mislead or direct respondents' answers, the changes in wording have accomplished exactly that end. Pay careful attention to the way that questions are posed. Always consider if slight changes in the language used would result in different responses.

COMPREHENSION

Language is the first medium of the rational mind.
—Ferguson (1981, p. 120)

The purpose of language is communication of ideas. The goal is to transfer the thoughts that reside in the mind of the speaker or writer to that of the listener or reader. Language is the vehicle or mode for the transfer of ideas. *Comprehension* occurs when the listener arrives at the intended meaning. Comprehension is the goal of communication and the reason for language. We've all heard the familiar complaint "Nobody understands me," representing an obvious failure in communication. Either the speaker didn't make herself or himself clear or the listener was insufficiently sensitive to the meaning in the message or somewhere along the transmission route, the message went astray, much like excessive static over telephone wires. The next section is concerned with the ways that meaningful information can be clearly transmitted and with some of the barriers to clear communication.

Rules for Clear Communication

In order to communicate effectively, you need to know a great many things: What is the purpose of the communication? What are your listener's characteristics? That is, what is your listener's age and social status? How much does the listener know or want to know about the topic? The answers to all of these questions shape the nature of communications. Without giving much thought to them, we implicitly change the way we speak or write, depending on how we answer these questions. Communication is governed by rules that we all obey, although you may never have consciously considered them.

Rule 1: Tell listeners what you believe they want to know.

Consider how you would answer a simple question like, "Where do you live?" If I met you in Europe and asked you this question, you would probably respond, "In the United States." If I asked you this question in New York, you would respond with the name of a state, "In Pennsylvania." If I asked you the same question on your college campus, you might respond, "In the dorms." If I asked you this question while we were in the dorms, you might respond, "In Wing D, Room 331." The same question could be asked each time, yet you would give a different answer that depended upon the context of the question and what you thought I wanted to know. The level of information you choose to convey depends on the purpose of the communication.

Rule 2: Don't tell listeners what they already know.

In the first chapter, I began by introducing the topic of thinking and the need for the development of critical thinking skills. You probably did not think that this was unusual. Suppose I started every chapter in this book the same way. You would not only think that this was unusual, you would also question my mental status.

When you present information to an audience, you balance the amount of new information that you present with the old or already known information. If you present too much new information at once, listeners will be lost and will not be able to extract the intended meaning; if you present too much old or known information, listeners will be bored. The relative proportion of old information to new information is known as the **given/new distinction** (H. Clark & Haviland, 1977).

The ratio of given or known information to new information is a determinant of the difficulty of a communication. If a passage (spoken or written) contains too much new material for a listener or reader, it will be difficult to comprehend. No one would take an advanced course in biochemistry without first obtaining the requisite background in biology and chemistry. The educational process, if successful, fosters the transformation of new information into the students' systems of known information.

Rule 3: Vary the style of your communication, depending upon the knowledge, age, and status of the listeners.

Suppose you are an expert computer programmer given the task of describing the operations of a computer center to a group of visitors. You would vary the way you convey the necessary information for each of the following: a group of politicians; a third grade class from an elementary school; your history professor; a close friend; or an expert programmer from another university.

Your communication would be more or less technical depending on what you believe your listener knows about the topic. You might tell the politicians about the high costs of maintaining a computer center; the third grade class might simply be told about the general use of computers; you might explain to your history professor how computers can be used in research; your close friend might be told that you feel you're being underpaid; and the visiting programmer might be told about the capacity of the computers.

Rule 4: Tell the truth.

When we communicate with each other, it is assumed that the information being conveyed is truthful. This is an imperative for meaningful communication. Of course, sometimes people lie. How do you process information when you believe that the speaker is lying? All components of the communication are scrutinized. In general, the communication process breaks down when the listener suspects that the speaker is violating this rule.

Rule 5: Use a simple straightforward style.

Mark Twain said this best when he said, "Eschew surplusage." Information is transmitted best when simple and precise language is used. Some people think that use of multisyllabic words and intricate sentence structures is a sign of intelligence. This is not true. It is a far more difficult task to express complex thoughts in simple language than to express simple thoughts in complex language. The transformation of our private thoughts into easily understood language is the benchmark of human cognition.

Rule 6: Utilize manner and context to clarify meaning.

Meaning depends not only on the words that we use, but also on the context and the manner we use to convey it. Have you ever tried to explain to someone why it is funny when Steve Martin says, "Wel-l-l excuse me?" The humor is not in the words themselves, but in the way he says them. We often rely on intonation, hesitations, and nonverbal behaviors to clarify intended meanings. Often these secondary clues will negate a verbal expression. Have you ever had the experience of having someone say, "I'll be happy to do that for you" in a manner that clearly showed that she was most unhappy?

Context is a critical aid for comprehension. "The food is on the table" can be an invitation to eat or a simple descriptive statement, depending on the context.

Context is also used to decide which of two possible meanings is the intended meaning for ambiguous sentences. The intended meaning of "They are kissing fish" is usually straightforward when spoken in context.

Our judgments or evaluations of events depend on context. Parducci (1968) asked subjects to decide how bad it is to "pocket the tip which the previous customers left for the waitress." Half the subjects were asked to judge this event along with the following mild infractions: stealing a loaf of bread from a store when you are starving; playing poker on Sunday; cheating at solitaire. The other half of the subjects were asked to judge the same event (pocketing the tip which the previous customers left for the waitress) along with the following infractions: spreading rumors that an acquaintance is a sexual pervert; putting your deformed child in the circus; murdering your mother without justification or provocation.

Taking a waitress' tip was judged to be a more serious offense when it was presented along with milder infractions than when it was presented among a list of serious infractions. The event (pocketing a tip) was exactly the same in each case, and the wording was identical. Changes in the context in which it was presented created changes in the way it was evaluated. Context is an important determinant of the meaning we assign to events.

Implication and Inference

Communication depends as much on information that is implied as it does on the words that are explicitly stated. Comprehension of meaningful material will always require the listener or reader to make inferences by going beyond the words uttered. Consider this very simple three-sentence story:

> Matt inherited a great deal of money.
> Bertha loves diamonds and furs.
> Bertha married Matt.

Although very little factual information was provided, it is a meaningful story. Readers infer that Bertha married Matt for his money and that she will use his money to buy diamonds and furs. Most communication requires the receiver to fill in gaps between given bits of information to understand intended meanings. In the first chapter of this book, one definition of thinking was "going beyond the information given." Understanding language by making inferences is a prime example of this definition of thinking.

When you produce speech, the intended meaning is implied or suggested by the words you use, the context in which it is embedded, and verbal and nonverbal expressions. It is often possible to say one thing while communicating something quite different. This technique is often used by advertisers who want to persuade you to buy their products, yet have legal restrictions on the kinds of statements they can make.

A recent television commercial for American Express Travelers Cheques goes something like this:

> "Oh, no, we've lost our travelers cheques! What will we do? (Couple wrings their respective hands at this point, obviously looking distressed.)
>
> The voice of a distinguished actor comes on, "What kind were they?"
>
> Distressed couple responds, "American Express."
>
> The distinguished actor calmly reassures them, "Good thing you have American Express Travelers Cheques. You can get a refund at their conveniently located office across the street."
>
> The now-smiling couple walk off the screen to the tune of "Don't leave home without them."

Other traveler check companies have complained about this advertisement because it *implies* that people who lose other brands of travelers checks may not get a refund. Notice that while this is never stated, it is a reasonable inference from the information offered.

Perhaps you're familiar with a popular advertisement for Listerine, a brand of mouthwash. A middle class mother bundles her children in warm clothing while discussing colds and flus. She earnestly states how much she dislikes "scratchy sore throats" and "runny noses." To keep her family healthy, she sees that they eat right, get plenty of rest and exercise, and "gargle with Listerine." Of course, she never says that Listerine will prevent or cure colds. This would be a false claim since there is no evidence that it does. Yet, this information is implied. Studies with fictitious commercials have shown that viewers do infer that mouthwash will protect against colds from advertisements like this one (Harris, 1977).

Moreoever, Harris (1977) found that people remember the implied meaning of a message, and not the actual statements that were made. If you have already read the chapter on the development of memory skills, this shouldn't be surprising to you. Meaningful information is more easily remembered than nonmeaningful information. People remember the meaning or gist of the message and not the actual words that were spoken. We rarely remember statements verbatim. Thus, our memory of events depends on the interpretations we give them when they occur.

Barriers to Comprehension

When I use a word," Humpty Dumpty said, in a rather scornful tone, "it means just what I choose it to mean—neither more or less.

The question is," said Alice, "whether you can make words mean so many different things.

The question is," said Humpty Dumpty, "which is to be master—that's all.
—Lewis Carroll (Through the Looking Glass)

Bureaucratese and Euphemism

A student once told me that while she really wanted to understand the material in her textbook, she found that the information went "in one eye and out the other." In other words, it "didn't stick" or seem to involve her brain at all. She was unable to understand or remember the material. We can all sympathize with her since we've all had this experience at one time or another. Comprehension failures often result from the language used to express an idea and not from the difficulty of the idea itself. Good teachers know how to communicate complex ideas so that they can be easily understood, while poor teachers could talk or write for days without conveying the ideas to their students.

Two language barriers to comprehension are bureaucratese and euphemism. **Bureaucratese** is the use of formal, stilted language that is often unfamiliar to people who lack special training. The same information can be expressed better with simpler terms. Bureaucratese is different from the use of precise technical terms that may be needed in specialized disciplines; in bureaucratese the style and language hinders our understanding instead of aiding it. The legal profession is often guilty of bureaucratese. I once read a legal document that began with the term "Witnesseth." Of course, I questioned what meaning was being conveyed with the use of this term, which is standard on many legal forms. The answer was, "very little." It could have been deleted altogether or replaced with "Notice" or "Read this document," both of which would have been more meaningful than the obscure, "Witnesseth."

Euphemism is the substitution of a desirable term for a less desirable or offensive one. The result is often a loss of communication. Euphemism is common in hospital and medical facilities where bodily functions need to be discussed. Hospital personnel may ask a patient if he has "voided his bladder." Many patients do not realize that this refers to urination. In fact, it has been shown that a majority of patients do not understand the language that is commonly used in their interactions with medical staff. Many do not understand words like "malignant," "benign," "terminal," and "generic." You can imagine a solemn physician telling a patient that she is "terminal," with the patient then inquiring when she'll get better. It is easy to see how use of euphemisms can lead to misunderstandings.

Euphemisms abound in advertisements of all sorts. Do "bathroom tissue" and "feminine hygiene products" seem more desirable and glamorous than toilet paper and sanitary pads? Euphemisms often obscure the intended meaning. Although polite speech is a necessary rule of society, euphemistic terms that are not commonly used interfere with the communication of ideas, and thus should be avoided.

Vagueness

Vagueness refers to a lack of precision in a communication. If your friend Valerie told you to bake a cake in a hot oven, you'd probably ask her how hot it should be. In this context, the word "hot" is too vague and needs to be specified further. Similarly, if you were told that your blind date for tonight is overweight, you'd want to know how much overweight. A communication is vague if it does not specify enough details for its intended purpose.

PERSUASION AND PROPAGANDA

Language! The blood of the soul, sir, into which our thoughts run and out of which they grow.
—Oliver Wendell Holmes

We use language not only to communicate ideas, but to persuade or convince others to "see things our way." Much of our communication is concerned with changing its recipient by getting him or her to act or think in a certain way. *The American Heritage Dictionary of the English Language* (Morris, 1969, p. 1048) defines **propaganda** as "material disseminated by the proselytizers of a doctrine." In other words, it is material that is written or spoken by people who want others to believe that what they are saying is true. This broad definition is applicable to a great variety of situations. Propaganda, like beauty, is in the eyes of the beholder. It does not require that the information be false or misleading; it merely has to be presented for the purpose of covert persuasion. Frequently, the information provided is charged with appeals to emotion rather than reason.

In 1983, the United States government required that a Canadian film that is opposed to nuclear energy carry a warning that it is propaganda. Civil rights and antinuclear groups vowed to fight this mandatory label all the way to the Supreme Court. These groups claimed that the information presented in the film is an accurate account of the dangers of nuclear radiation, and thus is educational. They maintained if this film is propaganda then so are films that teach children how to maintain good dental health and films like, "Oregon, A State of Many Beauties." The purpose of propaganda is to persuade people. An examination of common persuasive techniques should help you to recognize when they are being used.

Persuading With Language

Through clever and constant application of propaganda, people can be made to see paradise as hell, and also the other way round, to consider the most wretched sort of life as paradise.
—Adolf Hitler (from *Mein Kampf*)

Humans are very clever in using techniques that aim to influence others' thinking. We have already looked at how advertisers rely on inference to sell their products. Now, we turn to a more direct technique often referred to as propaganda. It is impossible to list every propaganda technique that has been employed to change how people think. The list would be too long to be useful, with only subtle differences among several of the techniques. Accordingly, only the most common and representative techniques are discussed. If you understand how propaganda works in general, you'll be better prepared to recognize and defend against it.

Mere Exposure Effect

Suppose that you walked into a voting booth on a primary election day and were faced with the following choice:

County Solicitor (Choose One)
Myron Jones
John Adams
Victor Light

Unfortunately, you have not kept up with local politics, and are unfamiliar with the record of any of these candidates. Which candidate would you vote for? Studies indicate that you probably chose John Adams.

In a recent election in New Hampshire, John Adams, an unemployed cab driver who did not campaign, won the Republican nomination for the State's First Congressional District. Why did John Adams, a man who spent no money on his campaign and who never gave a speech, win his party's nomination? Psychologists believe that when voters were confronted with three names they didn't recognize, they picked the one linked in history with a political figure. Hence, prior exposure creates a sense of familiarity, which in turn can enhance your liking for the stimulus, a phenomenon known as the **mere exposure effect.**

Political commercials often operate on this principle. They repeatedly hark, "Vote for Brandon Lee, He's The One!" Such commercials give absolutely no information about the candidate. They rely on the well-documented effect that familiarity will enhance liking. Based on this principle, repetition was commonly used in Nazi Germany and North Korean prison camps during World War II in an attempt to make their political ideologies more palatable to the prisoners.

What should you do if you face unknown candidates' names in a voting booth? If you can't vote intelligently for an office, skip that section and vote for the offices that you're familiar with. Intelligent voters ask themselves, "What do I know about these candidates?" and do not fall prey to a familiar sounding name.

Association Effect

One of the oldest principles in psychology is the notion that if two events occur close together in time and/or space the mind will form an *association* between them. Thereafter, when one occurs, the other is expected to occur. This principle has become widely used in the political arena, especially to create guilt by association. Suppose you read in a newspaper that a violent mass murderer endorsed a presidential candidate. This endorsement would be detrimental to the candidate, even if she did not desire it and did nothing to promote it.

An example of the propagandistic use of association came from a political group called "California Tax Reduction Movement." In their 1983 literature they stated: "This court, *dominated by Jerry Brown appointees,* and having radical views close to those of *Jane Fonda and Tom Hayden,* has twisted the words until we don't even recognize them!" You might be wondering what Jane Fonda and Tom Hayden are doing in a sentence about the California Supreme Court. They had no connection with the court. This literature was written with the belief that people who favor tax reductions will also be opposed to Jane Fonda and Tom Hayden. The Court is being made guilty by association with Jane Fonda and Tom Hayden. The actual association is somewhat convoluted. When Jerry Brown was governor of California, he appointed judges to the State Supreme Court. Jane Fonda and Tom Hayden were supporters of Jerry Brown. Although it is implied, it does not logically follow that the Supreme Court therefore has views similar to Jane Fonda and Tom Hayden. It may or may not have had such views. (Note also the use of the emotion laden word "radical.") Whenever you see examples of associations with no justifiable connection like this one, be wary of the rest of the message. It is likely to contain an appeal to your emotions rather than to your cognitions.

Just as one can have **guilt by association,** it is also possible to have **virtue by association.** In this instance, the names or label attached to the person are "good" ones. Perhaps this is why certain political offices tend to run in families. People expected the Kennedy brothers to be similar as politicians because of their obvious association with each other. This expectation is being passed onto their children, many of whom are now considering political careers. Would you vote for or against an unknown Kennedy simply because he or she is in the Kennedy family?

A wary recipient of messages that rely on association will ask about the nature of the association. If a leader is a member of the Ku Klux Klan, then associating the doctrine of the Klan with this indivdiual is reasonable. If, on the other hand, a friend of the candidate's mother is a member of the Klan, the association is ludicrous.

Arguments Against the Person

Arguments against the person is the formal term for name calling or, in its Latin form, *argumentatum ad hominem.* This form of persuasion or propaganda attacks the people who support a cause, and not the cause itself. As an example of this, the Nazis believed that the theory of relativity was wrong because its discoverer was a Jew named Albert Einstein. They never considered the evidence for or against the theory, just the religion of its originator. It is basically another form of the association effect. In this case, the association that is being made is between an idea and a person. The underlying principle is that if you don't like the person who supports an idea, then you should also oppose the idea itself because the idea and the person are associated. It's interesting to note that arguments against the person and the remaining techniques of persuasion and propaganda presented in this section have been studied primarily by philosophers. The switch between areas traditionally considered the domain of psychology and philosophy occurs in several places throughout this book. This switch is a natural one since both psychology and philosophy are concerned with critical thinking and have developed both separate and overlapping areas of expertise.

Suppose you were serving on a jury that had to decide which of two witnesses was telling the truth. Would you be swayed if one attorney told you to disregard one man's testimony because he had been divorced twice? Presumably not, because the man's marital status is irrelevant to the issue. Suppose you were told that one of the men had two previous convictions for lying to a jury. Would this argument against the person be relevant? I would think so. Consider the strength and relevancy of the argument and don't be misled by irrelevant attacks on the supporters or detractors of any position.

Appeals to Pity

An **appeal to pity** is easy to spot. "Support this position" or "buy that product" because it needs your help. A rental car agency has made it well known that they're #2 in their business, and therefore will try harder. They hope that consumers will root for the "underdog" and support the company that is #2. Does this conclusion logically follow from the fact that they're #2? No! You could also logically conclude that the #1 company will try harder to retain their lead.

Appeals to pity are often found in legal pleadings. A defendant's poor background or turbulent home life will often be brought up during a trial. These appeals to pity have nothing to do with the question of whether a defendant is guilty or innocent, although they may be persuasive appeals for leniency in sentencing if the defendant is found guilty.

Popularity and Testimonials

The **popularity** technique (also known as the "bandwagon") relies on the need for conformity for its persuasive power. It is persuasive because it explains that *everyone* supports a position or buys a certain product. It is expected that the message recipients will adopt the belief or buy the product in order to feel as if she or he belongs to the groups mentioned. Implicitly, the message is, "If everyone is doing it, it must be right."

A variation of the popularity technique is **testimonials.** Respected politicians or movie stars endorse a belief or product. It is believed that since people will want to be similar to the people they respect, they will choose to use the same deodorant or hair spray or support the same causes. The recipients of testimonials are expected to infer a conclusion from the information stated. (See the chapter on the Development of Reasoning Skills for a related discussion on forming conclusions from stated information.) It is expected that they will reason along these lines: Christie Brinkley is a gorgeous model. She uses the advertised beauty product. If I use this beauty product, I will look like Christie Brinkley. Of course, this conclusion does not follow from the first two sentences, but many people believe that it does or at least that it might.

Consider this classic television commercial:

She's lovely.
She's engaged.
She uses Ponds.

Of course, it is never stated that she became engaged because she uses Ponds. This is an implied conclusion. It is also implied that everyone who uses Ponds will get engaged.

Sometimes, however, the popularity technique and testimonials can be valid persuasive techniques. If, for example, all of the members of any unbiased expert panel established to study the effects of a drug decide that it is unsafe, I would consider this information relevant to the question of the drug's safety. Similarly, if a leading educator endorses a reading text, this might properly have an impact on your evaluation of the text. Both of these examples presume that the "experts" have no personal motives for their endorsements—i.e., they're not being paid for saying these things—and that their expertise is relevant to the position or product that they're supporting.

False Dichotomy

Don't give him two sides to a question to worry him. Give him one; better yet, give him none!
—Ray Bradbury (*Fahrenheit 451*)

There are very few political or social decisions that have simple answers or that can be solved with simple choices. Yet, simple slogans are the **prototype** or most common and representative form of persuasive techniques. **False dichotomy** is sometimes called *simplification* or the **Black or White Fallacy** since readers are asked to decide between two positions, without allowing other alternatives or "gray areas" that would combine aspects of both choices.

The following question appeared in a questionnaire that was sent by an Assemblyman to his constituents (Assemblyman Montjoy Needs Your Views, 1983):

"Would you prefer that government cut spending or increase taxes?

cut spending increase taxes

Does this question bother you? It should. The answers to our fiscal problems are not this simple. You should ask where and how the cuts would be made and how and how much taxes would be increased. Perhaps "cuts" could be combined with small or temporary increases in taxes. Can you guess which answer the Assemblyman prefers? Given this choice, I believe that most people will respond with "cut spending," yet an entirely different response would result from a question that was worded differently.

When you are faced with a false dichotomy or the simplification of a complex issue, don't ask yourself if the ideas are good or bad. Ask instead what is good about the ideas and what is bad about them. Consider other alternatives and combinations of ideas.

Appeals to Pride or Snobbery

Speech was given to man to disguise his thoughts.
—Talleyrand

An **appeal to pride or snobbery** usually involves praise or flattery. A blatant and humorous example can be found in an advertisement that was mailed to me at home. (Notice that it begins with my name, a sure attention-getting technique.)

Dear Dr. Halpern,

You may just be the solution.

Here is the problem: How do you find the right subscribers for an extraordinary magazine that is about to be published—BUT, a magazine that isn't for everyone? A magazine that is, in fact, for only a handful of bright, literate people, people who still in this world of instant communication love to sit down with a good book.

I'd love to believe that the publishers know me personally, and have written a magazine just for the kind of person I'd like to be. The truth is, this letter went to thousands of people whose names were bought as part of various mailing lists. Clearly, they are attempting to persuade me to purchase their magazine by appealing to my pride or snobbery.

Consider the following question which appeared as part of a "1982 Congressional Questionnaire" (Congressman Carlos J. Moorhead Reports, Summer, 1982):

> In an attempt to make federal social programs more responsive to citizens' needs, less wasteful and more efficient, the Administration has proposed a New Federalism where the programs and funds—in the form of block grants—are transferred to local government for management and administration. Do you think that you, your neighbors, and your local officials have the ability to handle this new responsibility?
>
> yes no

Do you think that this question is slanted toward a "yes" response? The appeal to pride or snobbery is less obvious in this question than in the first example, possibly making it even more potent. The question is really, "Are you and your friends smart enough to handle X?" It doesn't matter what X is; most people believe that they are smart. The congressman has also posed the wrong question. You may be able to "handle this new responsibility" without believing that block grants are a good idea. Responses to this question were subsequently used to support the idea of block grants. Be wary of persuasive communications that include flattery. While flattery is not in and of itself wrong, it may be used to obscure real issues.

Card Stacking or Suppressed Information

Card stacking or suppressed information operates as a persuasive technique by omitting information that supports the unfavored view. An automobile company recently compared the car they were advertising on television with a competitor. The advertisers stressed that their car got better mileage and cost less. What about the variables they omitted? Which car needed fewer repairs, had the more comfortable seating, or accelerated better? What about other makes of cars? Did a brand that was not mentioned exceed the advertised one on all of these dimensions? When considering persuasive information, be sure to consider what has *not* been stated along with the stated claims.

Defending Against Persuasive Techniques

The persuasive techniques listed earlier do not constitute a complete compendium of techniques designed to change attitudes and actions. A complete list may be impossible, given that there may be an endless number of ways to attempt to convince others that a position or product is good or bad. Once you are aware of some of the common persuasive techniques, you'll be surprised how frequently they're used. One of the best ways of dealing with these techniques was suggested in 1951 by Flesch in his chapter entitled "How Not to Be Bamboozled." He suggests that you ask two questions whenever you spot persuasion: "So what" and "Specify."

If you hear a movie star endorsing a product, ask "So What?" What does it matter if Dolly Parton uses So-Soft Hair Spray? If a toothpaste promises you "sex appeal," ask—"specify?" How will whiter teeth make you sexier? When a politician claims that there is too much "bureaucratic fat" in government," make him specify where it is and how it might be reduced. Consider the relevance of the technique to the issue. Pay careful attention to emotionally laden words. Are they being used as a smokescreen to conceal real issues? With a little care and careful thought, you can spot persuasive techniques and make your own rational issue-based appeals for policies and products you believe in.

Evaluate the Source

Whenever you are faced with a persuasive message, ask yourself, "Who says so?" Consider the credibility and motives of the information source. The most credible sources are experts in the field who have proven themselves to be honest and trustworthy and who have no personal stake in the outcome. Because this eliminates virtually everyone, we usually need to consider the *relative* credibility of our sources. Suppose that the president of General Motors tells you that the braking system on their new cars is absolutely safe. The president of General Motors has an obvious financial stake in making you believe that General Motors cars are the safest. He or she may be telling the truth, but you need to be more cautious about this information than you would need to be if Ralph Nader, a consumer advocate, had told it to you. Recent research has shown that people trust corporate presidents who endorse their company's products in advertisements. You may have noticed that Lee Iacocca, the President of Chrysler, has been shown in many commercials touting his company's cars. People tend to see him as a credible information source because of his responsible position. Keep in mind that he has a highly vested and biased interest in making you believe that his cars are best. It would be wrong to dismiss automatically all claims by people with stakes in the outcome, since the outcome they prefer may be the best one; however, it is prudent to consider the information source along with the information.

In our complex, technical society, we often need to rely on the opinions of knowledgeable experts who have analyzed systems that we can't understand. Most often, the knowledgeable experts disagree. Few of us are able to assess independently the safety of nuclear reactors. However, when you consider the pros and cons of complex issues, be sure to evaluate the source.

DISTINGUISHING FACT FROM OPINION

Facts have a verifiable truth value—e.g., Gravel-O's breakfast cereal has 100% of the recommended daily requirement of iron. **Opinion,** on the other hand, reflects how an individual or group has assessed a position or product—e.g., "Vote for Max Lake; he's the best man for the job!" Often, the distinction between fact and opinion is a fine one. If we say that Gravel-O's is a good cereal because it has 100% of the recommended daily requirement of iron, this is an opinion. While it is a fact that it contains iron, it is an opinion that iron makes it a good cereal. Although we (hopefully) base our opinions on a careful assessment of the facts, they are two distinct statements.

"Pure" facts that are untainted by opinion are often hard to come by. Take, for example, your daily newspaper. Although news reporters are obligated to provide readers with facts, their opinions certainly color what they report and how they report it. Compare the way two different newspapers cover the same story. One newspaper could make it the headline on page one, thus making it important news that will be read by many, whereas the other could place it on an inside section in smaller print; thus making sure that fewer people will read the story. Look at the words used to convey the same story. A quiet night in Poland during a period of martial law could be described as "Poland Enforces Martial Law" or as "All is Quiet in Poland." Both of these headlines could be factually correct, yet they clearly convey different ideas about current Polish life.

You may be thinking that at least one source of honest facts is your textbooks. While it is usually safe to assume that text authors do not set out deliberately to mislead students, the facts that they report are also subject to interpretation. Easily quantified and verifiable information such as the number of soldiers sent to a South American country or the size of the national deficit are probably correct or as close to correct as possible, presuming that there has been no deliberate attempt to lie. Other facts such as the sequence of events and their importance in causing a war, or strategies at political conventions, or poverty in America need to be interpreted by the text author who will decide how to describe them. The words she or he uses, the events included and omitted, and the amount of information given, all contribute to the "factual" information that is printed. Personal bias can, of course, influence the way the ideas are presented.

It has been said that there is never just one war fought. Each side has its own version, and rarely do they agree. Unfortunately, there is always fighting somewhere around the world so that you can verify this statement for yourself. It is not unusual for each side to claim that the other fired first, or for both sides to claim victory in a battle. Obviously, in the absence of verifiable truth there is no way to know which, if either, side is presenting the truth.

Even though it may sometimes be difficult to be certain of a fact, opinions are usually easier to spot. Advertisements make extensive use of opinions *dressed up* as fact. Consider the advertisements for headache remedies. Often they will show an attractive man in a white laboratory coat, obviously selected to portray a physician. He tells you that, "Bufferin works fast on headache pain." While this may seem like a fact, it is an opinion. "Fast" is a vague term, and therefore it is a matter of judgment. If the appropriate tests with a large number of people had shown that, on the average, Bufferin brings pain relief in 20 minutes, this information would be a fact. If you are in doubt as to whether information is fact or opinion, check for vague or evaluative terms (fast, better, lovelier, etc.), and ask yourself if the information is verifiable.

CHAPTER SUMMARY

1. Psycholinguistics is the branch of psychology that is concerned with understanding how people produce and comprehend language.

2. Psychologists view language as comprised of two components or levels: a meaning component (underlying representation) and a speech sound component (surface structure).

3. Language is ambiguous when a single surface structure has two or more possible underlying representations.

4. Language and thought exert mutual influences on each other with our thoughts determining the language we use and, in turn, the language we use reshaping our thoughts.

5. Six *rules* of communication were presented. Every time we attempt to communicate with others, we utilize these rules to determine what information we will convey and how to express the information.

6. Language comprehension requires that the listener make many inferences.

7. The use of obscure, euphemistic, and/or vague terms hinders the communication of ideas.

8. Frequently, people will come to like a stimulus with which they are familiar. This is known as the *mere exposure effect*. Other common persuasive techniques include forming positive or negative associations, attacking the people who support a cause, appealing to the reader's pity or pride, explaining that *everyone* agrees, simplifying complex issues, and stacking the evidence so that only favorable information is presented.

9. When considering information, be sure to evaluate its source.

10. Facts have a verifiable truth value while opinions contain evaluative terms like good, better, and faster. Opinions tend to be vague, while facts are usually quantified and specific.

Terms to Know:

You should be able to define or describe the following terms and concepts. If you find that you're having difficulty with any term, be sure to reread the section where it is discussed.

Psycholinguistics
Underlying Representation
Surface Structure
Sapir–Whorf Hypothesis of Linguistic Relativity
Given/New Distinction
Bureaucratese
Euphemism

Vagueness
Propaganda
Mere Exposure Effect
Virtue by Association
Guilt by Association
Arguments Against the Person
Appeals to Pity
Popularity Technique (or Bandwagon Technique)
Testimonials
False Dichotomy (or Simplification)
Prototype
Black or White Fallacy
Appeals to Pride or Snobbery
Card Stacking (or Suppressed Information)
Fact
Opinion

Be sure that you can answer the following questions:

1. Explain the relationship between underlying representation and surface structure. Why has the gap between them been called the "problem" of producing and comprehending language?

2. What is the Sapir–Whorf hypothesis of linguistic relativity?

3. Distinguish between the strong and weak forms of the Sapir–Whorf hypothesis. What do you think about the truth of each of these forms?

4. Two experimental studies were presented to demonstrate empirically how slight changes in wording can cause substantial differences in the way people think. Describe these studies.

5. What are the six *rules* for communication? How do we implicitly use them to shape our communications?

6. List and explain some of the barriers to comprehension.

7. Explain the following sentence which appears in this chapter: "Propaganda, like beauty, is in the eyes of the beholder."

8. How did psychologists explain the recent election of a relatively unknown political candidate?

9. List and describe the eight common persuasive techniques described in this chapter.

10. How can we distinguish between fact and opinion? Give three examples of each.

Exercises

Using your knowledge of common persuasive techniques and barriers to comprehension, explain how they are being used in each of the following:

1. Never trust politicians to protect your basic right to social security. Since they don't participate in social security, they'll never protect our rights.

2. "At last, four new residences designed to delineate a new level of luxury. Some visitors will find the opulence disturbing. Perhaps you will recognize a unique opportunity. From one-half miliion dollars . . ." (quote from an advertisement for condominiums, Los Angeles Times, 1983).

3. Of course, the new senator will be conservative. His father and mother are conservatives, and his brother-in-law is head of "Conservatives for Better America."

4. Every good American will support Josh Day for dog catcher.

5. "Your honor, the defendant came from a broken home."

6. California State University is the best school for you. It has a better computer major than Colorado State and is cheaper than Harvard.

7. Vote for Lincoln Lewis.
   Vote for Lincoln Lewis.
   Vote for Lincoln Lewis.
This message has been brought to you by The Committee for Better Government.

8. Eddie Murphy comes from a middle class background. He can never accurately portray the experiences of poor Americans.

9. Walter Cronkite buys his clothes at Snooty Brothers. He's a man who knows. Shouldn't you be shopping here too?

10. You'll get a better tasting cake with Happy Homemaker Cake Mix.

11. We can either send troops to the Middle East or we can pull out entirely. Which course of action do you prefer?

12. His petty bourgeois capitalist ideology will surely ruin the European Common Market.

Carefully consider the following statements. For each statement, decide if it is a fact or an opinion. If it is a fact, decide if it is an important or relevant one.

13. Bold has a new and improved formula to get clothes even whiter.

14. Speedo is a faster acting cold remedy.

15. Tang has more Vitamin C than plain orange juice.

16. Pearl Gray is the best candidate for the job!

17. Josh is the best pitcher on the team.

18. Josh hit more home runs than anyone else on the team.

19. Ray got 83% of the arithmetic problems correct.

20. Druggies hits a higher level of pain relief.

21. Three out of four dogs prefer the taste of Crunchies brand dog food.

22. Diamonds are a good investment.

23. Mr. T. uses Hair-So-Neat hair cream.

24. Interest rates have dropped three percentage points since March.

25. The national debt must be reduced.

26. As free Americans, we have the right to bear arms.

27. George Washington had wooden teeth.

28. Keep a record of the persuasive techniques that appear on billboards, radio and television. A particularly good source for this sort of material is the solicitations for political and charitable organizations that are mailed to your home. Letters to the editor in newspapers and political cartoons also rely on common persuasive techniques to "make their point."

SUGGESTED READINGS

The suggested readings for this chapter fall into two distinct categories—those concerned with psycholinguistics and those dealing with persuasion and propaganda. Although these two topics have a logical bond in that they both are concerned with the way language is used to convey and influence thoughts, psycholinguistic research is primarily conducted by experimental psychologists and propaganda research has remained in the domain of social psychologists.

An excellent and easy-to-read text in psycholinguistics is Clark and Clark's (1977) *Psychology and Language: An Introduction to Psycholinguistics* is highly recommended for anyone who wants to learn more about this area of psychology. Slobin's (1974) slim text, appropriately titled *Psycholinguistics,* is also a good starting place for an introduction to the field.

A somewhat rambling book that is difficult to classify is Brown's (1958) *Words and Things*. It's provocative reading on the wide range of topics that concern language. Pollio, Barlow, Fine, and Pollio (1977) have compiled an interesting series of papers on the psychology of language in their book with the intriguing title, *Psychology and The Poetics of Growth.*

Although much has been written over the past three decades about persuasion and propaganda, three classic texts that are still contemporary in their content are Flesch's (1951) *The Art of Clear Thinking* and an even older book by Thouless (1939) *Tests of Logical Reasoning: How to Think Straight.* Also recommended is Thouless' earlier book written in 1932, entitled *Straight and Crooked Thinking.* The last chapter in this gem of a book is called "Thirty-Four Dishonest Tricks." It is a list of persuasive techniques that are as current as the day it was written. Most importantly, he tells us how to defend against them.

An interesting book that describes the interpersonal aspects of communication is Adler, Rosenfeld, and Towne's (1980) *Interplay: The Process of Interpersonal Communication.* It is easy reading. Two texts that view the relationship between thought and language from the perspective of an English professor are *Word, Self, Reality: The Rhetoric of Imagination* by Miller (1972) and *Good Reason for Writing* by Barry (1983).

A colorful and well-illustrated source of information on persuasion and propaganda is Sparke, Taines, and Sidell's (1975) *Doublespeak: Language for Sale.* Billing itself as "a guide to propaganda for students of propaganda, for citizens generally who are objects of propaganda, and for propagandists'' (p. vii), is Lee's (1953) worthwhile book, *How to Understand Propaganda*. Kahane's (1980) text *Logic and Contemporary Rhetoric: The Use of Reason in Everyday Life* also contains numerous examples of political and advertising techniques designed to sell goods and politics to consumers. Hitchcock's (1983) *Critical Thinking: A Guide to Evaluating Information* lists and discusses a variety of persuasive techniques in a structured outline-like format. It's a clearly written text that could also serve as an introduction to the general area of argument analysis.

3 Development of Reasoning Skills

Contents

Logical and Psychological 52
Inductive and Deductive Reasoning 54
Syllogistic Reasoning 56
Ecological Validity 63
Common Errors in Syllogistic Reasoning 64
Linear Ordering 71
If, Then Statements 74
Content Effects 77
Probabilistic Reasoning 77
Negation 79
Confirmation Bias 80
Reasoning in Everyday Contexts 82
Computer Logic 83
Logic Flowcharts 83

Everyone agreed that it was a true tragedy. The front page headlines read, "Young Boy Killed by Police Officer." How did it happen? How could it be explained? It was late at night when the police officer, a white man with an unblemished record on the police force, was called to investigate a possible disappearance in an overcrowded, predominantly black neighborhood. The apartment manager let him in the outer door. The door to the only bedroom was tied shut with string. Nervously, he untied the string and called for any occupants to come out. No one responded. He kicked open the door. In the dark room, illuminated only by the flickering light of the television set, he saw a crouched figure pointing a gun at him. In a panic, the police officer shot at the shadowy figure, only to realize that it was a small boy with a toy pistol.

Everyone agreed that it was a tragic event, but that is the only thing that was agreed upon. Some concluded that it was a blatant racial incident because the officer was white and the child was black. Protestors picketed city hall, calling attention to the alleged racist nature of the killing. Some observers decided that the agitators must be Communists because it's good Communist propaganda to point

ALLEGHENY CAMPUS LIBRARY

out inequities and injustices in our political system. Others concluded that the child's mother was negligent and unloving because only an uncaring mother would leave a young child alone in an apartment with the door tied shut. The current political administration was blamed because it had not provided low cost day care that the child could have attended, and the mother's employer was blamed for not offering on-site day care.

The issue is emotional. Which of these conclusions follow from the facts? Why can't reasonable people agree?

LOGICAL AND PSYCHOLOGICAL

The trick, of course, is to reason well. It isn't easy and it isn't automatic.
—Kahane (1980, p. 3)

Reasoning is often taken to be the hallmark of the human species. Colloquially, reasoning tells us "what follows what." It allows us to reach conclusions about the nature of the world. When we reason, we use our knowledge about the truth of one or more statements to determine if another statement, the *conclusion,* is true. A **conclusion** is an inferential belief that is derived from other statements.

When we reason logically, we are following a set of rules that specify how we "ought to" derive conclusions. **Logic** is the branch of philosophy that explicitly states the rules for deriving valid (correct) conclusions. A conclusion is **valid** if it necessarily follows from the premise. Conclusions that are not in accord with the rules of logic are **illogical.** According to the rules of logic, we should *not* be concerned with the truth of the statements or whether the conclusion is factually correct or even probably correct. We should only consider whether a conclusion follows from given statements. Thus, according to logic, a conclusion can be valid even if the assumptions are false. Although we maintain that the ability for rational, logical thought is unique to humans, all too often we reach invalid or illogical conclusions. This fact has led Hunt (1982, p. 121) to award "A flunking grade in logic for the world's only logical animal."

The psychological approach, by contrast, is concerned with *how* people process information in reasoning tasks. As a psychologist, I have an (understandable) bias for the approach taken by psychologists. I believe that an understanding of how people do reason is essential for getting people to improve the way they reason.

The fact is that in our everyday thinking, the psychological processes quite often are not logical. In a classic paper on the relation between logic and thinking, Henle noted that while everyday thought does not generally follow the formal rules of logic, people use their own imperfect rules. If we were not logical, at least some of the time, we wouldn't be able to understand each other, "follow one another's thinking, reach common decisions, and work together" (Henle, 1962 p. 374). To demonstrate this point, stop now and work on one of the problems Henle posed to her subjects in one of her studies:

> A group of women were discussing their household problems. Mrs. Shivers broke the ice by saying: "I'm so glad we're talking about these problems. It's so important to talk about things that are in our minds. We spend so much of our time in the kitchen that, of course, household problems are in our minds. So it is important to talk about them." (Does it follow that it is important to talk about them? Give your reasoning.) p. 370.

Do not go on until you decide if it is valid to conclude that Mrs. Shivers is correct when she says that it is important to talk about household problems. Why did you answer as you did?

According to the rules of logic, it doesn't matter if Mrs. Shivers is correct when she says the women need to talk about things that are on their minds. Neither does it matter if she is correct when she says that household problems are on their minds. Regardless of the truth of these two statements, it still logically follows that it is important for them to talk about household problems.

When Henle posed this problem to graduate students, she found that some arrived at the wrong answer, whereas others arrived at the right answer for the wrong reasons. Consider the following answer given by one of her subjects: "No. It is not important to talk about things that are in our minds unless they worry us, which is not the case" (p. 370). Where did this subject go wrong? Instead of deciding if the conclusion followed logically from the earlier statements, she added her own opinions about what sorts of things it is important to talk about. Thus, while the answer is incorrect as evaluated by the standard rules of logic, it is correct by the subject's own rules. Consider this answer: "Yes. It could be very important for the individual doing the talking and possibly to some of those listening, because it is important for people to 'get a load off their chest,' but not for any other reason, unless in the process one or the other learns something new and of value" (p. 370). This time, the subject gave the correct answer, but for the wrong reasons. This subject, like the first one, added her own beliefs to the problem instead of deriving her conclusions solely on the basis of the information presented. Henle has termed this the **failure to accept the logical task.** It seems that in everyday use of reasoning, we don't determine if a conclusion is correct solely on the basis of the statements we're given—a procedure that is correct according to the rules of formal logic. Instead, we alter the statements we're given according to our beliefs and then decide if a conclusion follows from the altered statements. We function under a kind of "personal logic" in which we utilize our personal beliefs about the world to formulate conclusions about related issues. The reliance on "personal logic," while incorrect from the perspective of the rules of formal logic, is not necessarily bad. In fact, if we utilize our knowledge and beliefs about the truth of the premises, we can spot "holes" or "gaps" in advertising and political rhetoric. (A related discussion is presented in the chapter on The Relationship Between Thought and Language.)

Inductive and Deductive Reasoning

A distinction is often made between inductive and deductive reasoning. (See the Thinking as Hypothesis Testing chapter for a related discussion of this topic.) In **inductive reasoning** observations are collected that support or suggest a conclu-

© King Features Syndicate

sion. For example, if every person you have ever seen has only one head, you would use this evidence to support the conclusion (or hypothesis) that everyone in the world has only one head. Of course, you can't be absolutely certain of this fact. It's always possible that someone you've never met has two heads. If you met just one person with two heads, your conclusion must be wrong. Thus, with inductive reasoning you can never *prove* that your conclusion or hypothesis is correct, but you can disprove it.

When we reason inductively, we collect facts and use them to provide support or disconfirmation for conclusions or hypotheses. We either do this informally as in the course of everyday living, or formally as in experimental research. For this reason, hypothesis testing is sometimes described as the process of inductive reasoning.

In **deductive reasoning,** you would begin with statements known or believed to be true, like "everyone has only one head," and then conclude or infer that Karen, a woman you've never met, will have only one head.[1] This conclusion follows logically from the earlier statement. If we know that it is true that everyone has only one head, then it must also be true that any specific person will have only one head.

Although it is common to make a distinction between inductive and deductive reasoning, the distinction may not be particularly useful. In everyday contexts, we switch from inductive to deductive reasoning in the course of thinking. Our hypotheses and beliefs guide the observations we make, while our observations, in turn, modify our hypotheses and beliefs. In formal deductive logic, statements and rules are given, and their truth is irrelevant. The task for the individual is to derive conclusions that must follow from the statements, usually called *premises*. In the logic of everyday life, we rarely accept statements without considering their truth value. Instead, we evaluate them to determine their truthfulness and then decide which conclusions are valid or correct. Often, this process will involve a continuous interplay of inductive and deductive reasoning.

Consider the following argument (which may be familiar to you). The Equal Rights Amendment would require that women and men be treated equally under the law. Equal treatment would mean that women and men use the same public bathrooms. Does it logically follow that if you would be opposed to having women and men use the same public bathrooms, then you should vote against the Equal Rights Amendment? According to the laws of formal logic, "Yes." However, the initial statements are incorrect. The Equal Rights Amendment has nothing to do with unisex bathrooms, although its distractors have used this argument several times. It is necessary to assess the truthfulness of statements in real life contexts. In addition, we need to consider other truthful statements that may have been omitted. For example, you may vote for a political candidate who

[1]Note that this is a psychological definition in that it describes what people usually do. According to the standard rules of logic, the truth of a statement is irrelevant.

advocates some policies with which you don't agree if you believe that he will act correctly on other issues that you believe are important. People will often vote in favor of tax increases even though they really don't want to pay higher taxes. People often realize that if they want quality schools and other government services, tax increases are sometimes necessary. Thus, it might be perfectly reasonable to vote for a specific tax increase after weighing your priorities even though, as a general matter, you don't want to pay higher taxes.

A psychological approach to reasoning is emphasized in this chapter (as distinct from a philosophical one). Useful principles for everyday reasoning are presented, as are methods for deciding if a conclusion validly follows from given statements. Unfortunately, there are no simple guidelines for deciding if the statements you're asked to consider are true or whether there are other important considerations that bear upon the conclusion that you should make. Disagreements often arise over these issues. When we're dealing with real life, complex issues, it's often difficult to obtain agreement. Nine of the "best thinkers" of our time comprise the United States Supreme Court, yet a majority of their most difficult decisions are not unanimous. Attorneys for each side of the cases that are considered by the Supreme Court attempt to convince the justices that their own particular interpretation of the law is the correct one and that they have accurately presented the important facts. The justices must decide which conclusions follow logically from the true and important facts and from the relevant laws. If you have ever followed legal proceedings of any kind, you know that they are often exercises in reasoning. The crux of our legal system depends on the use of precedent (previous legal decisions) and the attempt to determine if a new set of facts is consistent with the precedent or different enough to require an alternate legal decision. Because we are likely to be all participants at some time in legal proceedings, either as attorneys, defendants, plaintiffs, jurors, or interested parties, an understanding of the basic reasoning principles involved will insure our intelligent participation.

SYLLOGISTIC REASONING

Nothing intelligible ever puzzles me. Logic puzzles me.
—Lewis Carroll (1887)

Syllogistic reasoning is a form of reasoning that involves deciding whether or not a conclusion can properly be inferred from two or more statements. One type of syllogistic reasoning is *categorical reasoning*. **Categorical reasoning** involves **quantifiers** or terms that tell us how many. Quantifiers are terms like "all," "some," "none," and "no." The quantifiers indicate how many items belong in specified categories. A famous example of syllogistic reasoning is attributed to Abraham Lincoln. It goes something like this, "You may fool all of the people some of the time; you can even fool some of the people all of the time, but you can't fool all of the people all of the time.''

A **syllogism** usually consists of two statements that are called **premises** and a *conclusion*. In categorical syllogisms quantifiers are used in the premises and conclusions. The task is to determine if the conclusion follows logically from the premises.

The premises and conclusion of a syllogism are classified according to **mood.** There are four different moods, or combinations of positive and negative statements with the terms ''all'' or ''some.'' The four moods are:

Mood	*Abstract Example*	*Concrete Example*
Universal Affirmative	All A are B.	All students are smart.
Particular Affirmative	Some A are B.	Some video games are fun.
Universal Negative	No A are B.	No smurfs are pink.
Particular Negative	Some A are not B.	Some democrats are not liberals.

As you can see from this list, a statement is universal if it contains the terms ''all'' or ''no''; it is particular if it contains the term ''some''; it is negative if it contains ''no'' or ''not''; and it is affirmative if it is not negative. Thus, it should be easy to classify the mood of any statement by searching out the key terms.

Several syllogisms are presented here. Each consists of two premises and a conclusion. Work through each syllogism and decide if the conclusion is true or false. If you decide that a conclusion is false, write down what a valid conclusion would be, given the premises. Don't go on until you have worked through these syllogisms.

1.	Premise #1	All A are B.	
	Premise #2	All B are C.	
	Conclusion	All A are C.	T or F
2.	Premise #1	Some A are B.	
	Premise #2	Some B are C.	
	Conclusion	Some A are C.	T or F
3.	Premise #1	All A are B.	
	Premise #2	Some B are C.	
	Conclusion	Some A are C.	T or F
4.	Premise #1	No A are B.	
	Premise #2	All B are C.	
	Conclusion	No A are C.	T or F
5.	Premise #1	No A are B.	
	Premise #2	No B are C.	
	Conclusion	No A are C.	T or F
6.	Premise #1	All zaks are creb.	
	Premise #2	All creb are bips.	
	Conclusion	All zaks are bips.	T or F

7.	Premise #1	Some flubs are gluck.	
	Premise #2	Some gluck are chez.	
	Conclusion	Some flubs are chez.	T or F
8.	Premise #1	All vox are thed.	
	Premise #2	Some thed are hef.	
	Conclusion	Some vox are hef.	T or F
9.	Premise #1	No crim are bub.	
	Premise #2	All bub are glot.	
	Conclusion	No crim are glot.	T or F
10.	Premise #1	No zevs are hip.	
	Premise #2	No hip are crep.	
	Conclusion	No zevs are crep.	T or F
11.	Premise #1	All boys are athletes.	
	Premise #2	All athletes are muscular.	
	Conclusion	All boys are muscular.	T or F
12.	Premise #1	Some lawyers are honest.	
	Premise #2	Some honest people eat oatmeal.	
	Conclusion	Some lawyers eat oatmeal.	T or F
13.	Premise #1	All judges are wise.	
	Premise #2	Some wise people are fat.	
	Conclusion	Some judges are fat.	T or F
14.	Premise #1	No teenagers are happy.	
	Premise #2	All happy people are rich.	
	Conclusion	No teenagers are rich.	T or F
15.	Premise #1	No professors are cool.	
	Premise #2	No cool people are punk.	
	Conclusion	No professors are punk.	T or F

According to the rules of logic, it should not matter if the syllogisms are presented in abstract terms of As and Bs, nonsense terms like zev and creb, or meaningful terms like lawyers and fat. The logical rules for deciding if a conclusion can be validly inferred from the premises remain the same. However, from a psychological perspective, there are important content differences. Did syllogisms #6 to #10 seem easier to you than #1 to #5? Did the last five syllogisms seem the easiest? Did you realize that the same five syllogisms were used in each set with only the content words changing?

Venn Diagrams

How did you go about deciding if the conclusions were valid? There is a relatively easy method of diagramming the relationships among the terms known as **Venn Diagrams,** named for a nineteenth-century English mathematician and logician who first introduced them. These are the same diagrams that you probably used in mathematics classes if you ever studied set theory. (A related method of diagramming relationships is known as *Euler Diagrams*. According to popular lore, this method was devised by Leonhard Euler, an 18th century Swiss mathematician, who was given the task of teaching the laws of syllogistic reasoning to a German princess. Because the princess was having difficulty understanding the task, Euler created a simple procedure that could be used to understand the relationships among the terms and to check on the validity of inferences.) In Venn Diagrams, circles are used to indicate category membership. Let's draw Venn Diagrams for Syllogisms #1, 6, and 11 since they are identical except for content.

Premise #1 states that "All A are B." Draw a circle indicating all things that are A.

A second circle will be drawn to indicate all things that are B. Since all A are B, the circle containing B must also contain A. Thus,

or

both represent the relationship. Using the language in Syllogisms #6 and #11, these figures become:

or

and

or

The left hand figure indicates that there are some B that are not A (some creb are not zaks or some athletes are not boys), while the right hand figure indicates that all B are A (all creb are zaks or all athletes are boys). There are important differences between these two figures. Although either figure could be correct given the information presented in the syllogism, they will lead to different conclusions. For example, if you only drew the left hand figure, you would conclude that "Some B are not A" while if you only drew the right hand figure, you would conclude that "All B are A." Given the information presented in the syllogism, you have no way of determining which of these conclusions is true. Both of these interpretations are possible given the first premise. We have no way of knowing which is correct. (It is interesting to note that according to the laws of formal logic only the left hand figure is correct. However, recent psychological research has shown that most people tend to consider only the interpretation depicted in the figure on the right (Erickson, 1974). The reasons for this bias are presented later in this chapter when common errors in syllogistic reasoning are discussed.) Consider the second premise, "All B are C." Thus, the circle containing B must be enclosed in the circle containing C. When we want to represent both premises, it is necessary to add a third circle to the diagrams, we get:

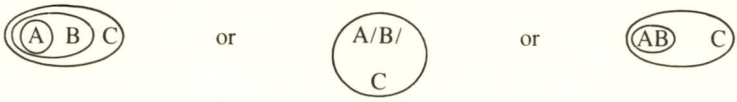

Using the terms in Syllogisms #6 and #11, they become:

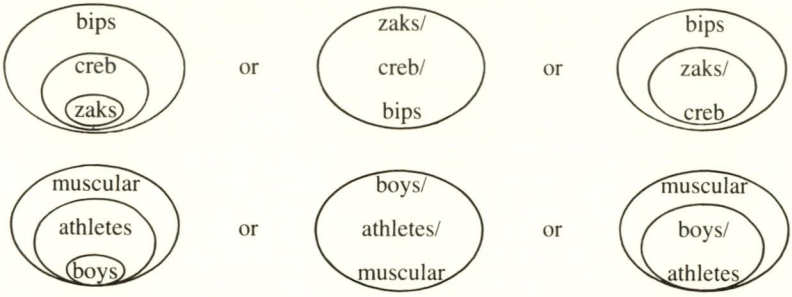

Now, look closely at the diagrams and decide if it is necessarily true that all A are C? The answer is "yes" since the entire circle containing A is inside C, or coterminus (has the same boundaries) with the circle containing C. Suppose that the conclusion had been "All C are A." Would this conclusion necessary be true? I hope that by examining the diagrams, you've decided that in this case, the answer is "no" since the circle containing C is not necessarily within A, or coterminus with A.

Let's try the same procedure with syllogisms #2, #7, and #12. The first premise is "Some A are B." In logic, "Some A are B" could mean exactly that, or it could also mean "All A are B." Thus, possible diagrams for this relationship include:

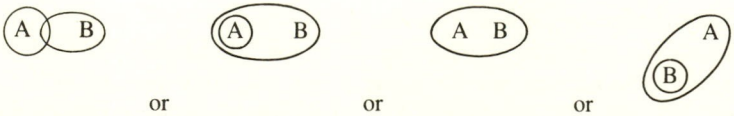

(There is some overlap between A and B.) (There are some B that are not A.) (A and B are the same.) (There are some A that are not B.)

Adding the second premise, "Some B are C," the above diagrams become:

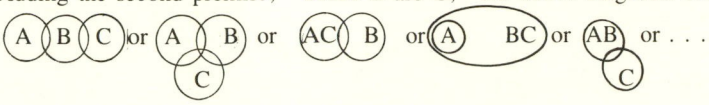

(There are many more possibilities.)

As you can see, if you have tried to diagram this syllogism, the number of combinations or possible circles to describe these relationships is quite large. Knowing that "some B are C" tells us nothing conclusive about the A and C relationship. Using the language of Syllogisms #7 and #12, we don't know if some flubs are chez or whether some lawyers eat oatmeal. Thus, the conclusions don't necessarily follow from these premises. They *may be* true, but given the information we've been given, we cannot make any valid conclusions. For reasons that are discussed later, errors on this type of syllogism are quite common. Can you guess why?

The first premise of Syllogisms #3, #8 and #13, "All A are B" is identical to the first premise in #1, #6, and #11. Let's add the second premise, "Some B are C" to the Venn diagrams.

All A are B.

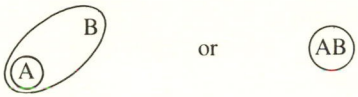

Some B are C.

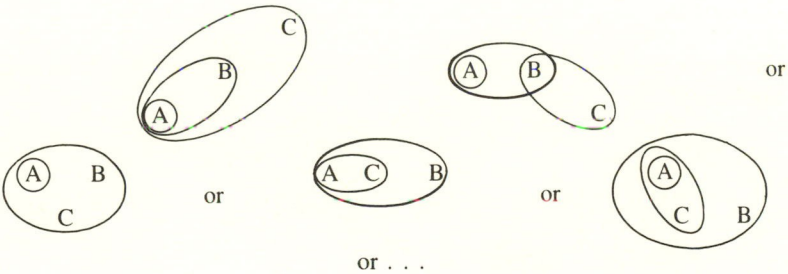

Again, there are a large number of possible diagrams that could describe this relationship. Does it necessarily follow that "Some A are C?" No, since the B that are C (or thed that are hef, as in Syllogism #8; or wise people who are fat, as in Syllogism #13) are not necessarily the B that are A (or the thed that are vox, or the wise pepole who are judges).

Stop now, and diagram the remaining two syllogisms. Don't go on until you have drawn the Venn diagrams for Syllogisms #4, #9, and #14; and #5, #10, and #15.

The diagrams you drew for Syllogisms #4, #9 and #14 should have looked like this:

No A are B

All B are C

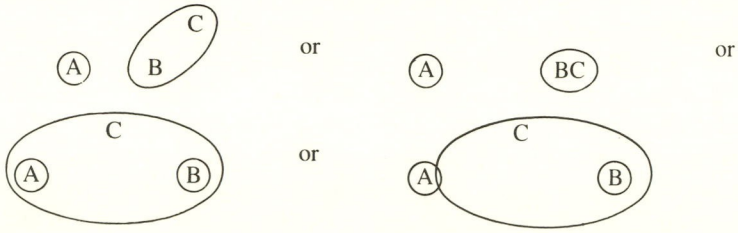

As you can see from the last two diagrams, it is not true that "No A are C." Look closely at Syllogisms #14. While no teenagers are happy, and all happy people are rich, it is possible to be an unhappy teenager who is rich. This syllogism is easier to solve when the terms are meaningful words than when it uses abstract letters (A, B) or nonsense words (crim, bub, glot), although the problems are logically identical.

How did you diagram the last set of syllogisms?

Did they look like this?

No A are B

No B are C

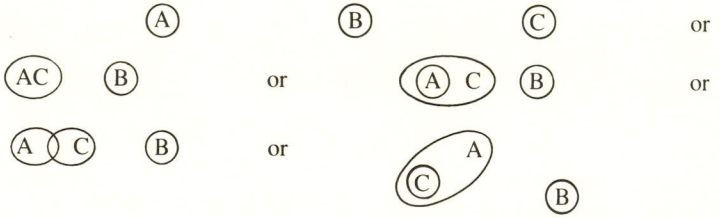

It is easy to see from these diagrams that the conclusion that "No A are C" is not necessarily valid.

If your diagrams didn't look like these or if you're still feeling unsure about how to drawn Venn Diagrams, reread this section and work through each problem again.

Johnson-Laird and Steedman (1978) have done much of the seminal work on understanding the way people solve syllogisms. They proposed a theory to explain their results. What do people do when faced with syllogisms like this one?

> No florists are bowlers.
> Some bowlers are athletic.

The psychologists' study indicated that people imagine a roomful of florists and bowlers, each wearing different hats to symbolize that "No florists are bowlers." Some of the bowlers are also wearing athletic clothing to symbolize that "Some bowlers are athletic." People then use these imagery-like depictions to derive conclusions. Although this may be an adequate description of the way untrained subjects solve syllogisms, it is a fallible system that will sometimes lead to invalid conclusions. Since none of the imaginary florists are wearing athletic clothing, people tend to falsely conclude that "No florists are athletic." If you use Venn diagrams and remember to diagram *all* of the possible relations, you'll find a substantial improvement in your reasoning skills.

Ecological Validity

Somewhere during the last section, you may have said to yourself, "Why bother!" It may seem that syllogisms are artificial stimuli created solely to make work for students and teachers. If you did have this thought, you were questioning the **ecological validity** of syllogisms. Ecological validity concerns the real world validity or applications of a concept outside of the laboratory or classroom. In other words, do people use syllogistic reasoning in real-world contexts?

Syllogistic reasoning and the other types of reasoning (linear ordering and if–then statements) that are discussed later in this chapter are sometimes considered as a subset of problem solving. Often, when solving a problem, we begin with statements that we believe or know to be true (the premises) and then decide which conclusions we can logically infer from them. (In the language of problem solving, the premises are called "givens" and the conclusions can take the form of either "operations" or "subgoals." See the chapter on the Development of Problem Solving Skills for a discussion of these terms.)

Syllogisms also appear implicitly in normal English prose. Of course, in natural context, the premises and conclusions aren't labeled, but the underlying structure is much the same. They are especially easy to spot in legal and political arguments and thus often appear on standardized tests for college, graduate, and law school admissions.

Here is an example of syllogistic reasoning that may seem more like the kind of syllogism you'd find in everyday contexts:

> There are some crimes that are so heinous that the perpetrator of the crime should be put to death. Police officers play a vital role in maintaining a civilized society and thus the shooting of a police officer is a heinous crime.

Can you conclude from these statements that people who shoot police officers should be put to death? Try to formulate these sentences into standard syllogism form (two premises and a conclusion). Use Venn diagrams to check on the validity of the conclusion. Stop now and work on this natural language syllogism.

Your syllogism should be similar to this:

Premise #1: All perpetrators of some heinous crimes should be killed.
Premise #2: Shooting a police officer is a heinous crime.
Conclusion: People who shoot police officers should be killed.

(Remember: When the term "some" is used in a syllogism it can also mean all.)

The Venn Diagrams should be:

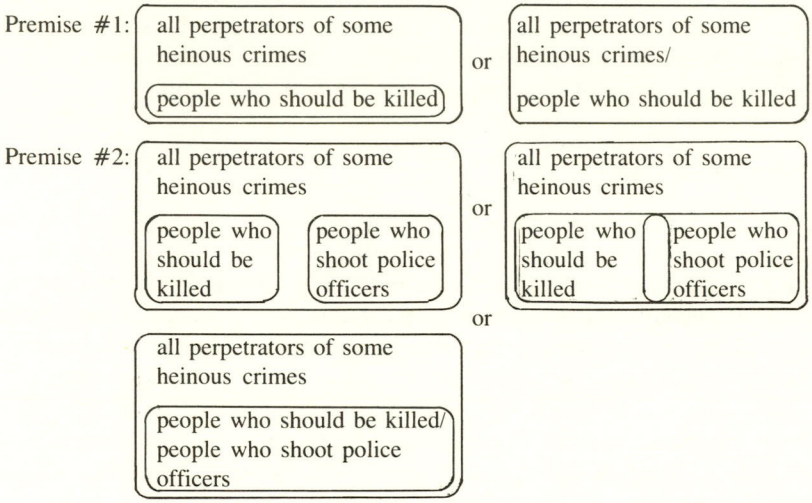

Conclusion: As can be seen from these diagrams, it does not necessarily follow that people who shoot police officers should be killed. Look at the first Venn diagram following Premise #2. While both "people who should be killed" and "people who shoot police officers" are categorized under "all perpetrators of some heinous crimes," they can be distinct categories. Pay careful attention to the way this short paragraph has been diagrammed. Be sure that you understand how these three different diagrams can be used to describe the reasoning in this paragraph and how the diagrams are used to determine the truth or validity of a conclusion.

Common Errors in Syllogistic Reasoning

At this point in the history of psychology, when it is claimed that machines can think, it seems strange to say that people cannot.
—Ceraso & Protivera (1971 p. 400)

© 1982, Sidney Harris, created for Discover.

Research has shown that some syllogisms are more difficult to solve than others. An analysis of the erroneous conclusions that people make has revealed that the errors fall into distinct types or categories. Categories of errors include illicit conversions, atmosphere effects, belief biases, and content effects. Each is discussed briefly.

Illicit Conversions

When most people read statements like, "All A are B," the representation they form in their mind is one in which it is also true that "All B are A," (Chapman & Chapman, 1959). As you should realize by now, these two premises are not equivalent. Transforming a premise into a nonequivalent form is a type of error known as an **illicit conversion.** Using Venn Diagrams to visualize illicit conversions, the premise "All A are B" is represented only by the diagram on the left, while the diagram on the right is not considered.

All A are B.

People tend to consider this A–B relationship.

People tend to ignore this A–B relationship.

It should be clear to you by now that either of these representations is correct, given that the mood of the premise is universal affirmative. (If you don't remember what these terms mean, you'll need to do some careful reviewing.) Many people interpret this statement to mean that A is the same as B, and thus illicitly convert or change the meaning. It is clear that people do not reason the way that logicians believe that they should. People systematically misinterpret the premises and/or fail to consider all possible interpretations.

Another common illicit conversion is the belief that "Some A are not B" also implies that "Some B are not A." The second statement is not equivalent to the first. What would Venn diagrams of "Some A are not B" look like? Either of these two diagrams is a possibly correct interpretation:

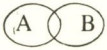

"Some A are not B" and
"Some B are not A"

or

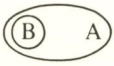

"Some A are not B" and
"All B are A."

The left hand diagram would support the conversion, while the one on the right would not. Again, this conversion most likely occurs when people fail to consider all possible meanings of syllogism premises. In a study by Ceraso and Protivera (1971), subjects were given modified syllogisms that would help them to consider all possible interpretations of the premises. For example, the traditional form of the premise, "All yellow blocks are striped" was modified so that it became, "Whenever I have a yellow block, it is striped, but there are some striped blocks which are not yellow" (p. 403). Subjects who were given the modified instructions made correct interpretations of the premises, and they did not make the illicit conversions. Stating the premise in its modified form helped them to improve their reasoning.

Atmosphere Effect

The **atmosphere effect** was an explanation of reasoning errors in syllogisms that was recognized for the first time in 1935 (Woodworth & Sells). The basic idea is that the logical terms "some," "all," "no," and "not" create an atmosphere or global impression that leads subjects to accept certain types of conclusions as true. In this way, the atmosphere effect is like a "set" in problem solving. Certain terms predispose people to accept certain conclusions that may or may not be correct. Begg and Denny (1969) have listed three components of the atmosphere effect, as exemplified in the following syllogisms:

1. No Smurfs live in Illinois.
   <u>All people who live in Illinois are new wave.</u>
   No Smurfs are new wave.
   True or False?
   The correct answer is False.
   Whenever one or more of the premises is negative, people tend to reach a conclusion that will be negative.

2. Some politicians are dishonest.
   Some dishonest people are rich.
   Some politicians are rich.
   True or False?
   The correct answer is False.
   Whenever one or more of the premises contains the word "some" (particular form), the most commonly accepted conclusion will contain the word "some."

3. All professors are intellectuals.
   All snobs are intellectuals.
   All professors are snobs.
   True or False?
   The correct answer is False.
   Whenever both premises contain the word "all" and are affirmative (universal affirmative), the most commonly accepted conclusion will contain "all" and be affirmative.

If you drew Venn diagrams to depict these syllogisms, you should have avoided falling prey to the atmosphere effect errors. The Venn diagrams for these three syllogisms are:

1. Premise #1
   No smurfs live in Illinois

   Premise #2
   All people who live in Illinois are new wave.

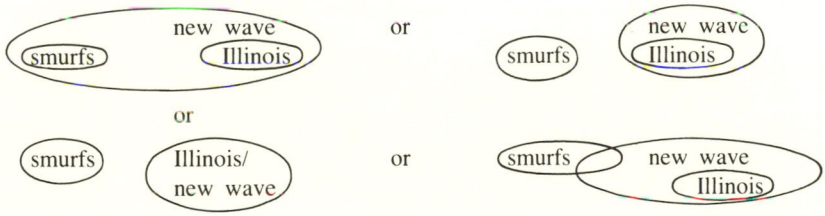

The first and fourth diagrams show that smurfs can be new wave, thus the conclusion that "No smurfs are new wave" is invalid.

2. Premise #1
   Some politicians are dishonest. (Remember that in logical reasoning "some" can also mean "all.")

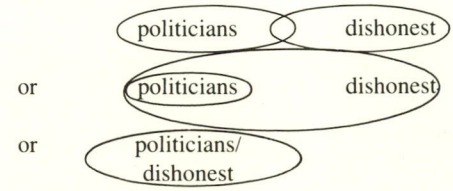

Premise #2
Some dishonest people are rich.

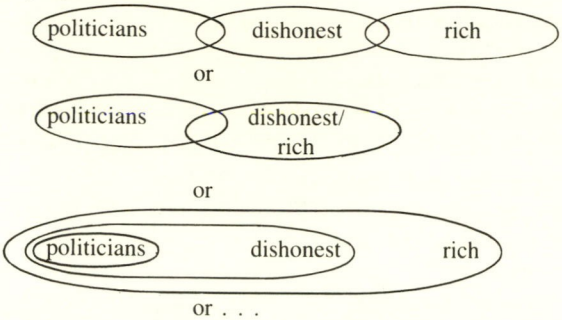

The first diagram after Premise #2 depicts a situation in which no politicians are rich. (The circles do not overlap.) Thus, it would be wrong to conclude that some politicians are rich.

3. Premise #1
All professors are intellectual.

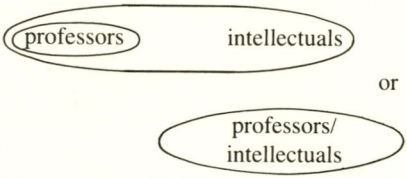

Premise #2
All snobs are intellectuals.

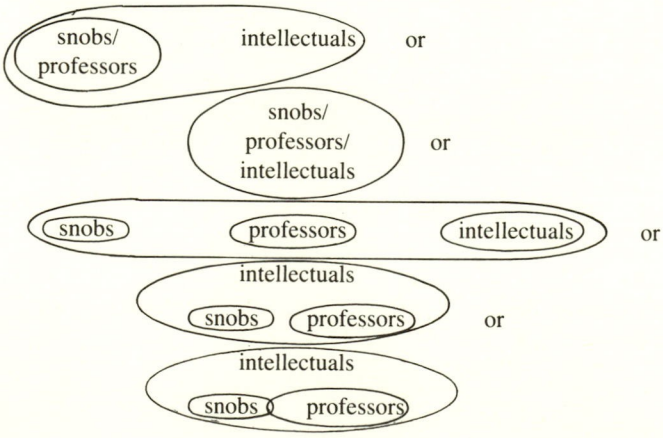

The last three diagrams show that some professors are not snobs. Thus, the conclusion that all professors are snobs is false.

Research on the kinds of illogical conclusions that people are willing to accept as true has shown that people who have never had formal training in logic often make the kinds of mistakes predicted by the atmosphere effect. J. R. Anderson (1980) has suggested that people rely on the atmosphere effect for understanding difficult syllogisms. They rely on a few key words (all, some, not, no) without working through the problem. Furthermore, Anderson argues that while the atmosphere effect will sometimes lead to erroneous conclusions, ". . . used by itself, the atmosphere heuristic leads to performance more than 80 percent correct. This is not bad for such a crude heuristic" (p. 321). (A *heuristic* is a "rule of thumb" or informal strategy for making decisions.)

Research has shown that it is easy to learn to avoid errors caused by the atmosphere effect. Simpson and Johnson (1966) explained the atmosphere effect to their students using an explanation similar to the one presented in this section, and after only a few minutes of training, their students substantially reduced the number of atmosphere effect errors that they made.

Belief Biases

Although the rules of logic dictate that content is irrelevant in the conclusions we formulate, the truth is that content does influence how we choose valid conclusions. It is possible to construct syllogisms so that the beliefs most people maintain conflict with logical conclusions. **Belief bias** occurs when an individual's beliefs interfere with her or his selection of the logical conclusion. Here are some examples from a study by Morgan and Morton that was published in 1944. Obviously, most Americans in 1944 had very strong beliefs about World War II, which clearly influenced their reasoning process. Syllogisms like the following one were devised to investigate the way beliefs affected how people reason.

> Usually, countries that are forced into war against their will make poor soldiers; since the Italian people were forced into this war against their will:
>
> 1. Italian people make poor soldiers.
> 2. Italian people may make poor soldiers.
> 3. Italian people do not make poor soldiers.
> 4. Italian people may not make poor soldiers.
> 5. None of the given conclusions seems to follow logically. (pp. 46–47)

Notice that this syllogism is presented in a natural prose format without specifically labeling the premises. The logical response is number 5 because there is no valid conclusion. The atmosphere effect would predict that most people would select number 2 since the first premise contains an implicit "some," as does conclusion number 2. This, in fact, is the most frequently selected answer. The interesting result from a belief bias perspective is the percentage of people who selected response number 1, the response that is consistent with what was presumed to be the belief of most American college students who served as subjects. When the syllogism was presented in the terms shown, 27% of the students selected response number 1; whereas, only 6% selected this response when the syllogism was presented in abstract terms using the letters X, Y, and Z. It seems clear that their beliefs influenced how they selected the correct conclusion.

Here is another example from Morgan and Morton's (1944) study:

> Some ruthless men deserve a violent death; since one of the most ruthless men was Heydrich, the Nazi hangman:
>
> 1. Heydrich, the Nazi hangman, deserved a violent death.
> 2. Heydrich, the Nazi hangman, may have deserved a violent death.
> 3. Heydrich, the Nazi hangman, did not deserve a violent death.
> 4. Heydrich, the Nazi hangman, may not have deserved a violent death.
> 5. None of the given conclusions seems to follow logically. (p. 48)

The logically correct answer is number 5. The authors presumed that response number 1 reflected the beliefs of American college students who served as subjects. When the same syllogism was presented, 38% selected response number 1 as compared to 1% when the syllogism was presented in abstract terms using the letters X, Y and Z.

It should come as no surprise to you that human reasoning becomes illogical when we are discussing emotional issues. This is true for people in every strata of society, even for Justices of the United States Supreme Court. When Justice William O. Douglas was new to the Supreme Court, Chief Justice Charles Evans Hughes gave him these words of advice, "You must remember one thing. At the constitutional level where we work, ninety percent of any decision is emotional. The rational part of us supplies the reasons for supporting our predilections" (quoted in Hunt, 1982, p. 129). Unfortunately, appellate legal proceedings are sometimes exercises in politics, with decisions changing as frequently as the political climate. Legal "reasoning" has sometimes served as a framework to persuade others that a conclusion is valid. If you understand how to formulate valid inferences, you'll be able to withstand and recognize its misuse by those who would use it to their advantage.

Content Effects

The content or topic of the syllogism influences how we think, even when the topic is not an emotional one. In everyday reasoning, we use what we know about a topic to determine if a conclusion is logical. We don't rely (and probably should not rely) on the information given in the premises. Consider these two syllogisms (Bucci, presented in Braine, 1978, p. 2):

> All football players are strong.
> *This man is strong.*
> Is this man a football player?

This is a simple syllogism. Most people will decide that they don't know.

All oak trees have acorns.
This tree has acorns.
It is an oak tree?

Most people will readily respond, "Yes" although this syllogism is identical in form to the one about football players. Braine (1978, p. 2) concludes that "In general, then, the common fallacies of syllogistic reasoning can be seen as due to the intrusion into formal reasoning of habits characteristic of practical reasoning and ordinary language comprehension." In other words, we use our knowledge about the world when we reason and do not merely decide what logically follows from the premises we've been given.

LINEAR ORDERING

Reasoning is simply a matter of getting your facts straight.
—B. F. Anderson (1980, p. 62)

Joel is stronger than Donald, but not as strong as Richard. Richard is stronger than Joel, but not as strong as Bill. Who is strongest and who is second strongest?

Although I'm sure that you've never met Joel, Donald, Richard, and Bill, I'm also sure you could answer this question. The premises or statements in this problem give information about the orderly relationship among the terms, hence it is called a **linear ordering** or **linear syllogism.** Like the syllogisms presented in the last section, the premises are used to derive valid conclusions; only this time we're concerned with orderly relationships instead of class inclusion and exclusion as denoted by terms like "all," "some," "no," and "not." How did you solve the problem about Joel, Donald, Richard and Bill? Most people work line-by-line, ordering the people as specified in each line:

"Joel is stronger than Donald, but not as strong as Richard" becomes

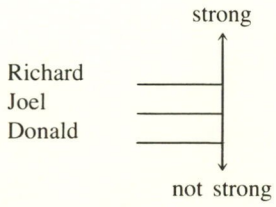

"Richard is stronger than Joel, but not as strong as Bill" becomes

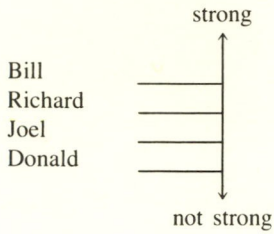

Thus, it is easy to "see" that Bill is strongest and Richard is second strongest.

Research with linear syllogisms has shown that people rely, at least in part, on spatial imagery or some sort of spatial representation to answer the question. Spatial imagery, however, is only part of the process.

According to a study by DeSoto, London and Handel (1965), Mickey Mantle and Willie Mays were both having a bad day at an exhibition baseball game which prompted a fan to shout, "I came to see which of you guys was better, Mantle or Mays. Instead I'm seeing which is worse" (p. 513). How did they know that they had been insulted? The term "better" conveys a sense that both are good, whereas the term "worse" conveys a sense that both are bad. According to the laws of logic, "Mantle is better than Mays" should be equivalent to "Mays is worse than Mantle," but they clearly are not. Comparisons like this one obey a logic of their own. The term **paralogic** has been coined to denote that while people are not strictly logical, they do utilize logic-like standards when interpreting these statements.

Work through the following pairs of linear syllogisms. Try to decide if one member of each pair is easier to solve than the other.

1. A. Julio is smarter than Diana.
   Diana is smarter than Ellen.
   Who is smartest? Julio, Diana, Ellen, or don't know.

   or

   B. JoAnne is taller than Susan.
   Rebeccah is taller than JoAnne.
   Who is shortest? JoAnne, Susan, Rebeccah, don't know.

2. A. Pat is not taller than Jim.
   Jim is shorter than Tiffany.
   Who is shortest? Pat, Jim, Tiffany, don't know.

   or

   B. Les is worse than Moshe.
   Harold is worse than Moshe.
   Who is worst? Les, Moshe, Harold, don't know.

3. A. Stuart doesn't run faster than Louis.
   Louis doesn't run slower than Dena.
   Who is slowest? Stuart, Lois, Dena, don't know.

   or

   B. Howard is darker than Ace.
   Ace is lighter than Kyla.
   Who is lightest? Howard, Ace, Kyla, don't know.

As you worked through these problems, did some seem more difficult to you than others?

You probably found problem 1A to be the easiest. Research has shown that when the second term in the first premise is the first term in the second premise (Diana in problem 1A), and when the comparison terms are congruent (smarter, smarter, smartest), the linear ordering is fairly easy to solve. Problem 1B does not follow this simple form. The comparisons are between JoAnne and Susan and Rebeccah and Susan. In addition, the comparison terms are not congruent (taller, taller, shortest). The correct answer is 1A for Julio. The correct answer for 1B is Rebeccah.

Problem 2A contains the negation term "not," which adds to the complexity of the problem. In addition, information is given in terms of both taller and shorter which makes this a difficult problem. The correct answer is Pat. Although problem 2B contains all congruent comparison terms (worse, worse, worst), some people find it tricky since we don't know if Les or Harold is worst. In addition, research has shown that it is more difficult to use terms like "worse" than it is to use terms like "better" because it denotes that all three are bad, while "better" is a more neutral term. (The correct answer is "don't know".) Problem 3A contains two negative terms as well as incongruent comparison terms (faster, slower, slowest). From the information given, we can't determine who is slowest. Problem 3B is somewhat easier since it doesn't contain negatives, but it does contain incongruent comparison terms (darker, lighter, lightest). The answer as to who is lightest can't be determined.

Hopefully, as you worked through these problems, you discovered some of the following psychological principles of linear orderings:

1. Orderings are easiest to solve when comparison terms are congruent.
2. Solutions will be facilitated if the second term in the first premise is the first term in the second premise.
3. Negations make the problem more difficult.
4. Comparisons between adjacent terms (e.g., Julio and Diana in problem 1A) are more difficult than comparisons between end terms (Julio and Ellen) (Potts, 1972).

5. When you are faced with a difficult syllogism, a good strategy for solving it is to draw a linear spatial array, like the one presented at the beginning of this section, so that the relationship among the terms can be visually inspected.

6. Comparison terms that limit the meaning of a sentence, like worse and dumber, are more difficult to process than more general and neutral terms like better and smarter. The adjectives that connote a bias (e.g., worse, dumber) are called **marked adjectives,** while the neutral adjectives are called **unmarked adjectives.**

These summary remarks can be used as an aid for clear communication of linear ordering information. If you want someone to understand a linear ordering, use congruent terms, make the second term in the first premise the first term in the second premise, and avoid negations and marked adjectives.

IF, THEN STATEMENTS

Reason, of course, is weak, when measured against its never-ending task. Weak, indeed, compared with the follies and passions of mankind, which, we must admit, almost entirely control our human destinies, in great things and small.
—Albert Einstein

"If, then" statements, like the other examples of reasoning presented in this chapter, utilize premises that are known or believed to be true to determine if a third premise validly follows. "If, then" statements are concerned with **contingency relationships**—some events are dependent or contingent upon the occurrence of others. *If* one of the premises is true, *then* a second premise must also be true. If, then statements are sometimes called **conditional logic** or **propositional logic.** Work through the four following if, then statements. Decide if the third premise is a valid conclusion.

1. If she is rich, she wears diamonds.
   She is rich.
   Therefore, she wears diamonds.
   True or False?
2. If she is rich, she wears diamonds.
   She isn't wearing diamonds.
   Therefore, she isn't rich.
   True or False?
3. If she is rich, she wears diamonds.
   She is wearing diamonds.

Therefore, she is rich.
True or False?

4. If she is rich, she wears diamonds.
She isn't rich.
Therefore, she isn't wearing diamonds.
True or False?

In each of these problems, the first premise begins with the word "if"; the "then" is not explicitly stated ("*then* she wears diamonds"). The first part of this premise (If she is rich) is called the **antecedent;** the second part (she wears diamonds) is called the **consequent.**

How did you answer problm 1? The conclusion is valid. The technical term for problem is *affirming the antecedent.* In this case, the second premise affirms or indicates the antecedent is true; therefore, its consequent is true.

Problem 2 also contains a valid conclusion. Because the second premise indicates that the consequent is not true, this sort of problem is technically called *denying the consequent.*

Many people are willing to conclude that problem 3 is also valid when, in fact, it is not. Although it must be assumed to be true that if she is rich, she wears diamonds, it is also possible that poor people wear diamonds. I have found that intelligent college students have difficulty with this problem. Because the second premise states that the consequent has occurred, this sort of problem is called *affirming the consequent.* It is fallacious to believe that because the consequent is true, the antecedent must also be true. "If," in these reasoning problems, doesn't mean "if and only if," which is how many people interpret it. Of course, she may be rich, it may even be more likely that she is rich, but we cannot conclude that she is rich just because she is wearing diamonds.

Problem 4 is also invalid, although it is tempting to conclude that if she isn't rich, she isn't wearing diamonds. Can you guess the technical term for this sort of problem? It's called *denying the antecedent* because premise 2 states that the antecedent is false.

A summary of these four kinds of reasoning, with examples of each, is shown in Table 3.1.

Several popular advertisements take advantage of people's tendencies to make invalid inferences from "if, then" statements. A highly successful yogurt commercial goes something like this:

> Some very old people from a remote section of the Soviet Union are shown. We're told that it is common for people in this remote region to live to be 110 years old. We're also told that they eat a great deal of yogurt. The conclusion that the advertisers want people to make is that eating yogurt will make you live 110 years.

Implicitly, we're being told that if we eat yogurt, then we'll live to be 110 years old. Of course, it's possible to live to be 110 without ever tasting yogurt,

TABLE 3.1
Four Kinds of Reasoning with If, Then Statements

	Antecedent	*Consequent*
Affirming	*Affirming the Antecedent* *Valid Reasoning* *Example:* If I am dieting, then I will lose weight. I am dieting. ——— Therefore, I will lose weight.	*Affirming the Consequent* *Invalid Reasoning* *Example:* If Harry went to the supermarket, then the refrigerator is full. The refrigerator is full. ——— Therefore, Harry went to the supermarket.
Denying	*Denying the Antecedent* *Invalid Reasoning* *Example:* If it is raining, then my hair is wet. It is not raining. ——— Therefore, my hair is not wet.	*Denying the Consequent* *Valid Reasoning* *Example:* If Judy and Bruce are in love, then they are planning to marry. They are not planning to marry. ——— Therefore, Judy and Bruce are not in love.

and we have no reason to believe that yogurt added years to their lives. These remote Russians engage in strenuous physical labor most of their lives and do not come into contact with many outsiders who carry potentially contagious diseases. Either of these facts, or countless others, including heredity, could account for their longevity. (It is also possible that the longevity claim is subject to question.) The advertisers are obviously hoping that the viewers will fall prey to the fallacy of affirming the consequent and say to themselves, "If I want to live to be 110 years old, I'd better eat yogurt."

The fallacy of affirming the consequent is similar to the syllogism error, illicit conversion, that was discussed earlier in this chapter. If you recall (if you don't, you'd better reread this section), illicit conversions occur when people think that "All A are B" also means that "All B are A." Illicit conversions, in "if, then" statements occur when people believe that "If A, then B" also means "If B, then A." In formal language, this error is called affirming the consequent, but you should be able to see that it is just another type of illicit conversion.

"If, then" statements, like syllogisms and linear orderings, appear implicitly in standard prose. Of course, we seldom find them neatly labeled "premise and conclusion." Yet, they are often the basis for many common arguments. The fallacies of denying the antecedent and affirming the consequent in everyday contexts are quite common.

There is currently an acrimonious debate over the issue of providing junior and senior high school students with contraceptive information. The pro side argues that if students are given this information, then they will act responsibly when engaging in intercourse. The con side argues that because teenagers should not engage in sexual activity (whether responsible or not), they therefore should not be given contraceptive information. This is an example of the fallacy of denying the antecedent. It does *not* follow that if they are not given contraceptive information, then they will not engage in sexual activity.

Content Effects

A point that has been made repeatedly throughout this chapter is that people do not reason according to the laws of formal logic. In everyday (practical) reasoning, we use information that is not stated in the premises in order to decide if the conclusion follows from the premises. One sort of knowledge we rely on is our knowledge about the content of the premises. The following two sentences demonstrate this point (Braine, 1978, p. 19):

If Hitler had had the atomic bomb in 1940, he would have won the war.
and
If Hitler had had one more plane in 1940, he would have won the war.

Many people would decide that the first sentence is probably true and the second sentence is false because they confuse truth with validity. When we interpret "if, then" statements in everyday contexts, we rely on our knowledge about the content to decide if a conclusion follows. According to the rules of logic, reasoning should be independent of content. We should all arrive at identical, logically correct conclusions no matter what the content is. Of course, humans are not perfect logic machines. We do and should determine if the premises are true before deciding if a conclusion follows.

Certain contents seem to require that we understand them in a way that is inconsistent with the laws of logic. Suppose you are told:

"If you mow the lawn, I'll give you five dollars" (Taplin & Staudenmeyer, 1973, p. 542). This statement invites the interpretation, "If you do not mow the law, I won't give you five dollars." In the everyday inference we make from language, this is a valid conclusion, although it is erroneous from the perspective of formal logic. In understanding statements of the "If p, then q" variety, the conclusions that we are willing to accept as valid depend very much on what p and q are.

Probabilistic Reasoning

The straight path of reason is narrow, the tempting byways are many and easier of access.
—Joseph Jastrow

In everyday reasoning, we don't view premises as "truths" that will necessarily require certain conclusions; instead we think of premises as statements that either support or fail to support certain conclusions. *Probabilistic* reasoning occurs when we use the information we have to decide that a conclusion is probably true or probably not true. The laws of logic are concerned only with conclusions that are necessarily true—conclusions that *must* follow from the premises. In everyday reasoning, we rely on notions of probability to assess the likelihood of a conclusion being true. Although probability is discussed in the chapter on Understanding Probability, it is also a reasoning skill.

Suppose you learn that people who have untreated diabetes are frequently thirsty, urinate often, and have a sudden weight loss. You notice that you have these symptoms. Does it necessarily follow that you have diabetes? No, of course not, but these symptoms do make a diagnosis of diabetes more likely. In everyday contexts, much of our reasoning is probabilistic, and thus does not obey the laws of formal logic.

Consider this example presented by Polya (1957, p. 186):

> If we are approaching land, we often see birds.
> *Now we see birds.*
> Therefore, it becomes more credible that we are approaching land.

In a shorthand format this becomes:

> If A, then B.
> *B is true*

Therefore, A is more probable than it was before we knew that B is true.

Much of our everyday reasoning is of this sort, and while A is not guaranteed with probabilistic reasoning, it does become more probable after we've told the second premise. Probabilistic reasoning is often a good strategy or "rule of thumb," especially since few things are known with absolute certainty in our probabilistic world. From the standpoint of formal logic, probabilistic reasoning is invalid. As long as you understand the nature of probabilities and the distinction between probabilistic and valid (must be true) reasoning, considering probabilities is a useful way of understanding and predicting events. When we reason in everyday contexts, we consider the *strength* and likelihood of the evidence that supports a conclusion and often decide if a conclusion is probable or improbable, not just merely valid or invalid.

Our beliefs in the premises of syllogisms are not usually all-or-none. For example, consider this syllogism:

> Premise 1: If a liberal candidate is elected to the school board, then the dress code will be abolished. Premise 2: Jane Fonda, a liberal candidate, will be elected to the school board.
>
> Conclusion: The dress code will be abolished.

Suppose that you believe that there is an 80% chance that the first premise is true and a 75% chance that the second premise is true. How would this affect your belief in the conclusion? It should seem clear that you would believe that while the abolition of a dress code is likely, it is not a certainty. The mathematical method for determining the actual probability of the conclusion occurring (in this case, abolishing the dress code), is given in the chapter on Understanding Probabilities.

As much of our reasoning is dependent on both the rules of logic and probability, McGuire (1981) has coined the term **probabilogical** to describe the joint effects of these disciplines on the way we think. Accordingly, we place greater faith in conclusions when we believe that the premises are highly probable than when we believe that the premises are unlikely.

Negation

The use of negatives ("no," "not") in a reasoning problem makes it much more difficult to solve (Wason, 1969). Consider these two sets of premises:

Either Chuck is handsome, or else he is famous.
Chuck is not famous.
What can you conclude?
Either Chuck is handsome, or else he is not famous.
Chuck is famous.
What can you conclude?

The conclusions to both of these sets of premises is the same—Chuck is handsome. Most people find the second set of premises to be much more difficult to comprehend. (I hope that the switch from "if, then" to "either, or" didn't confuse you. "Either, or" premises are also commonly used in reasoning. These premises can easily be recast in an "if, then" format, e.g., If Chuck is handsome, then he is not famous.)

In "if, then" statements, difficulties arise when the antecedent is negative. For example, (Evans, 1972, p. 32):

If the letter is not D, then the number is 7.
The number is not 7.
What, if anything, can you conclude?
If the letter is B, then the number is not 4.
The number is not 4.
What, if anything, can you conclude?

Most people incorrectly decide that no conclusion can be drawn from the first set of premises, whereas they readily believe that it is correct to conclude that "The number is 4" from the second set of premises. In the first set of premises, it is necessary to translate the statements into, "It is not D", an obviously difficult form for comprehension. The correct conclusion is, "The letter is D." I once heard a politician make a statement similar to this one. He said, "It is not true that I do not favor the legislation." It took me a few seconds to realize that he said that he favored the legislation. Recall that negation also makes linear orderings difficult to solve. In order to communicate clearly, avoid negations whenever possible.

Confirmation Bias

Confirmation bias, the predilection to seek and utilize information that supports or confirms your hypotheses or premises, is a topic that has received a great deal of attention in recent years. It appears in several places in this text because it is seen in so many contexts. (See the chapters on the Development of Decision Making Skills and Thinking as Hypothesis Testing for related discussions.)

Demonstrate this effect for yourself (Johnson-Laird & Wason, 1970):

> Four cards are lying face up on a table in front of you. Every card has a letter on one side and a number of the other. Your task is to decide if the following rule is true, "If a card has a vowel on one side, then it has an even number on the other side." Which card or cards do you need to turn over in order to find out whether the rule is true or false? You may turn over only the *minimum* number necessary to determine if this rule is true. Please stop now and examine the cards below to determine which ones you would want to turn over. Don't go on until you have decided which cards you would want to turn over.

A	D	4	7

Few people select the correct cards in this problem, which has become known as the **four-card selection task.** Most people respond "A only" or "A and 4". The correct answer is "A and 7." Can you figure out why? If A doesn't have an even number on the other side, the rule is false. Similarly, if 7 has a vowel on the other side, the rule is false. What about D and 4? D is a consonant. It doesn't matter if there is an even or odd number on the back since the rule says nothing about consonants. Since 4 is an even number, it doesn't matter if there is a vowel or a consonant on the back. The reason that this is such a difficult problem is that people interpret the rule to also mean "If a card does not have a vowel on one side, then it does not have an even number on the other side" or, without negatives, "If a card has a consonant on one side, then it has an odd number on the other side." These alternate interpretations are incorrect. Do you recognize the error as denying the antecedent? This is a robust (strong) effect. It is an extremely difficult task because of the crucial role of disconfirmation. People fail to appreciate the importance of a falsification strategy. This is exacerbated with the incorrect assumption that the converse of the rule is also true. The only correct way to solve this problem is to select only cards that can falsify the rule.

Part of the difficulty people have with this task may be related to the abstract nature of the problem. After all, there is very little we do in our everyday life that relates vowels and even numbers. Try out a more realistic and less abstract version of this task (adapted from Johnson-Laird, Legrenzi, & Legrenzi, 1972):

> In order to understand this task, you may need some background information (depending on your age). Several years ago, the United States Post Office had two different postage rates known as first class and second class mail. You could pay full postage which was 5¢ if you sealed your letter (first class), or you could pay a reduced, 3¢ rate, if you merely folded the flaps closed and didn't seal them (second class). (First class mail had priority for delivery over second class mail.)
>
> Suppose you are a postal employee watching letters as they move across a conveyor belt. The rule to be verified or disconfirmed is: "If a letter is sealed, then it has a 5¢ stamp on it." Four letters are shown in Fig. 3.1. Which ones would you have to turn over to decide if the rule is true?

Stop now and work on this problem. Don't go on until you've decided which letters (at a minimum) you would have to turn over to test this rule.

Did you notice that this is the same task that was posed earlier? The correct answer is the first (sealed) envelope and the last envelope (the one with the 3¢ stamp). This is an easier problem than the more abstract one because people find it easier to understand that a letter that is not sealed could also have a 5¢ stamp on it than it is to understand that if the letter is not a vowel it could also have an even number on the back.

Johnson-Laird and Wason (1977) found that when the problem is presented in this realistic manner, 22 out of 24 subjects selected the correct alternatives. In the abstract version, only 7 out of 24 subjects were able to solve the problem. Johnson-Laird and Wason concluded that our everyday experiences are relevant in determining how we reason. They believe that a bias to confirm our hypotheses rather than seek to disconfirm them may be indicative of a general pervasive cognitive bias.

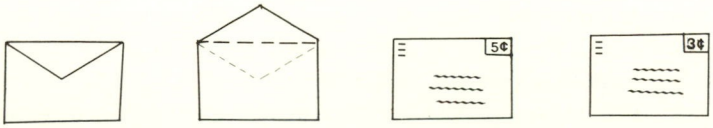

FIG. 3.1. Which of these letters would you have to turn over to decide if the following rule is true: "If a letter is sealed, then it has a 5¢ stamp on it." (Adapted from Johnson-Laird, Legrenzi, and Legrenzi, 1972.)

REASONING IN EVERYDAY CONTEXTS

Reasoning is the only ability that makes it possible for humans to rule the earth and ruin it.
—Scriven (1976, p. 2)

Syllogisms, linear orderings, and "if, then" statements are commonly found in everyday conversation. Of course, they are embedded in discourse and not labeled by premise or conclusion. They are sometimes used in ways that seem to be either deliberately misleading, or at least to capitalize on the common reasoning errors that most people make.

If you pay careful attention to bumper stickers, you'll probably be surprised to find that many are simple reasoning problems. Consider the bumper sticker I recently saw on a pick-up truck:

Off-road users
are not abusers.

The off-road users that this bumper sticker refers to are dirt bike riders who enjoy racing through open land (unpaved areas). Many people are concerned that this sport is destroying our natural resources by tearing up the vegetation. This bumper sticker is designed to present the opposing view. Notice how this is accomplished. The term "all" is implied in the first premise, when in fact "some" is true. You should recognize this as a syllogism with an implied conclusion that is invalid.

Another popular bumper sticker is:

If guns are outlawed,
only outlaws will have guns.

This is a standard "if, then" statement. The implied conclusion is "don't outlaw guns." What do you think about this statement? Some questions to ask yourself when evaluating claims of this sort are: (1) Are the premises true; (2) Does the implied conclusion logically follow; (3) Are there other relevant arguments (e.g., police would still have guns)?

Suppose someone responded to this bumper sticker by suggesting that if guns are outlawed approximately 80% of the crimes of violence and 90% of the petty crimes that are committed with a gun would probably be committed with a less dangerous weapon. How does an argument like this refute the "if, then" statement and its implied conclusion on the bumper sticker?

Consider a common argument that often appears in a slightly disguised form:

If minorities are not as bright as whites, then they will score lower on tests of intelligence.
<u>Minorities score lower on tests of intelligence.</u>
Obviously, a conclusion is implied.

The implied conclusion is that it therefore follows that minorities are not as bright as whites. I hope that you realize that this is an invalid conclusion. (See the Intelligence chapter for a discussion of this topic.) It is possible that minorities will score lower than whites on intelligence tests for a host of other reasons (e.g. test bias, culture differences, etc.). It does *not* necessarily follow that they are not as bright.

Linear orderings can also be used in misleading ways in everyday contexts. Suppose you find a political argument to be simply:

Communism is preferable to Socialism.
Communism is preferable to Capitalism.
An implied conclusion is that Socialism is preferable to Capitalism.

As you can easily see, this is an invalid conclusion. We have no (stated) basis for comparing Socialism and Capitalism.

Be alert for potentially misleading and erroneous examples of reasoning. Good sources of bad reasoning are the letters to the editor page of most newspapers, bumper stickers, commercials, and political rhetoric.

Computer Logic

One of the greatest sociological phenomena of this decade is the explosive growth of the computer industry. Computers are no longer the mysterious tools of physicists and mathematicians. Children as young as two and three are learning on them, and few people will go through high school or college without interacting, in some way, with a computer.

Instructions that are given to a computer are called programs. **Computer programs** contain explicit, logical, and sequential instructions. A brief introduction to the logic of computer programs may be helpful in the development of your own reasoning skills.

Logic Flowcharts

Before computer programs are written, the **programmer** (person who writes the program) needs to be clear about what he or she wants the computer to do and how to go about doing it. The sequence of operations that the computer uses in solving problems is usually written in a graphical form called a **flowchart.** Flowcharts allow the programmer "to plan the sequence of operations in a program before writing it" (McCracken, 1965, p. 23). Although the actual programs are not considered here since they vary with the computer language being used, a brief introduction to the logic of flowcharts provides readers with a useful strategy that can be used to solve reasoning problems.

Flowcharts utilize a variety of symbols for their notational system. A few of these symbols are:

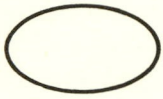

Ovals are used to indicate the beginning and end of a program.

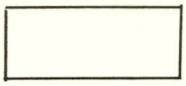

Rectangles indicate that a procedure (e.g., arithmetic) is to be executed.

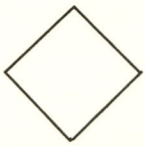

Diamonds indicate that a decision is to be made. These are used in "if, then" statements.

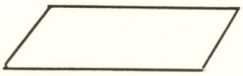

Parallelograms tell the computer to "read" or "write" something. (In computer jargon, this is called input and output.)

Giving instructions to a computer is like telling a small child what to do. You need to be very clear and very explicit. Every step must be spelled out, without skipping any steps.

A simple computer program might consist of adding two numbers together. If you want to tell the computer how to do this, you would have to *tell* it to start, read the numbers, add them, write out the answer, and then stop. If you skip any of these steps, the program won't run. Using the symbols just introduced, the flowchart for this program would be:

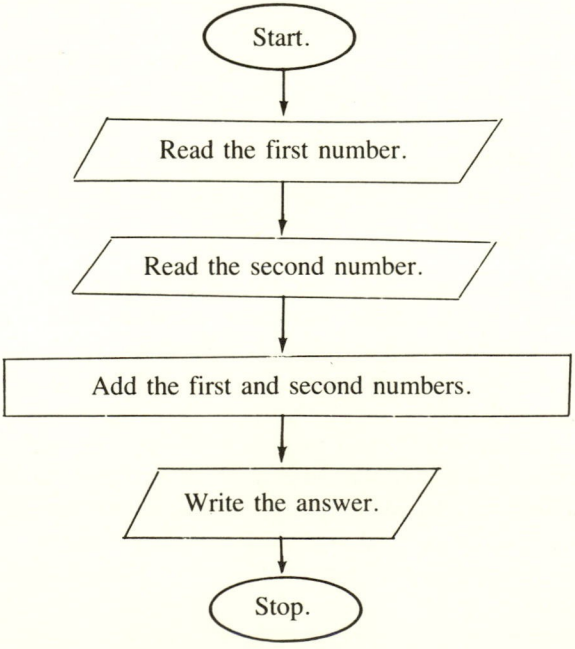

Notice that arrows are used to indicate the sequence in which the steps are to be executed. If you were really using this flowchart to write a computer program, you'd translate each step in the flowchart to a statement in a computer language (e.g., BASIC, FORTRAN, COBOL) that the computer can utilize. No matter which language you use, the logic of the flowcharts remains the same.

Suppose you want to tell the computer how to solve a linear ordering. This problem is in a slightly different form than the one presented earlier. Actual number values are given instead of terms like "taller than." The problem is conceptually the same as the linear orderings considered earlier. Only the format has changed. Arnold is 6′1″ tall. Bernard is 5′3″ tall. Clyde is 5′2″ tall. Who is tallest?

To solve this problem, we'll need to introduce the diamond shaped symbol into our flowcharts. When you encounter a diamond in a flowchart, a decision will have to be made about a simple question. If the answer is "yes," then one sequence of steps will follow, and if the answer is "no" then a different sequence of steps will follow. Pay careful attention to the following flowchart:

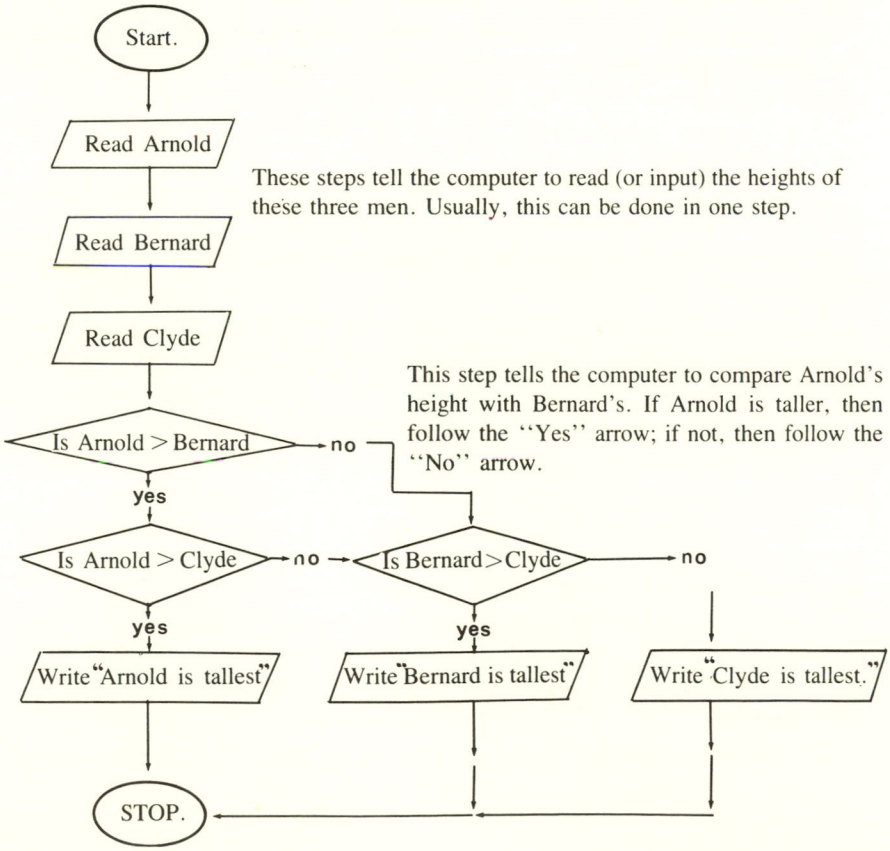

These steps tell the computer to read (or input) the heights of these three men. Usually, this can be done in one step.

This step tells the computer to compare Arnold's height with Bernard's. If Arnold is taller, then follow the "Yes" arrow; if not, then follow the "No" arrow.

Answer each question, and then follow the appropriate arrow to the stop symbol.

The decision diamonds are really "if, then" statements. If one term is larger, then you will follow one sequence of operations; if it is not, then you will follow a different sequence. As you can see, computer programming is a logical sequence of operations that is similar in many respects to the reasoning problems presented in this chapter.

CHAPTER SUMMARY

1. Reasoning is the use of premises or statements to derive valid conclusions.

2. People don't approach reasoning problems according to the laws of formal logic. Instead of determining if a conclusion logically follows from the premises as they are stated, people alter the premises according to their own beliefs and then decide if a conclusion follows from the altered statements.

3. In everyday contexts, people assess the truthfulness of premises and consider additional premises that may have been omitted.

4. Syllogisms indicate which terms belong in the categories that are specified. Statements in syllogisms can take one of four different moods: universal affirmative, particular affirmative, universal negative, and particular negative.

5. It is easier to solve syllogisms with meaningful terms than syllogisms that contain nonsense terms or letters.

6. Venn diagrams are used to understand relationships and check inferences in syllogisms. Circles are used to illustrate category memberships.

7. A common error in syllogisms is to interpret "All A are B" as also meaning that, "All B are A."

8. The atmosphere effect leads to erroneous conclusions because certain terms in syllogisms (e.g., all, some, no) predispose people to consider answers that contain similar terms.

9. Human reasoning is often biased by beliefs about emotional issues.

10. In everyday reasoning, we are usually concerned with whether a conclusion is probably true or probably not true and not just whether it is necessarily true.

11. In linear orderings, we use premises to establish conclusions about ordered relationships. A good strategy for solving linear orderings is to utilize a spatial representation with the items arranged in an ordered manner.

12. In "if, then" statements a conditional relationship is established. As in syllogisms and linear orderings, the premises that are given are used to determine valid conclusions.

13. "If" is frequently interpreted as "if and only if" in "if, then" statements. This is a common error.

14. Content is an important determinant of which conclusions we will decide are valid in "if, then" statements.

15. Confirmation bias is the predilection or tendency to seek and utilize information that supports or confirms the hypothesis or premise that is being considered. The "four-card selection task" is a demonstration of this robust bias.

16. Whenever you encounter attempts to persuade you with reasoning, keep in mind the following three questions: (1) Are the premises true? (2) Does the conclusion necessarily follow from the premises? (3) Are there other relevant arguments?

17. Instructions are given to computers in the form of programs. Flowcharts are diagrams of the sequence of operations that the computer will be told to use in working a problem.

Terms to Know:

You should be able to define or describe the following terms or concepts. If you find that you're having difficulty with any term, be sure to reread the section where it is discussed.

Reasoning
Conclusion
Logic
Illogical
Failure to Accept the Logical Task
Inductive Reasoning
Deductive Reasoning
Syllogistic Reasoning
Quantifiers
Categorical Reasoning
Syllogism
Premise
Mood
Universal Affirmative
Particular Affirmative
Universal Negative
Particular Negative
Venn Diagrams
Ecological Validity
Illicit Conversions
Atmosphere Effect
Belief Bias
Content Effects
Linear Ordering
Linear Syllogism
Paralogic
Marked Adjectives
Unmarked Adjectives
If, Then Statements
Contingency Relationships
Conditional Logic (also known as Propositional Logic)

Antecedent
Consequent
Probabilogical
Confirmation Bias
Four-Card Selection Task
Computer Programs
Flowcharts
Programmer

Be sure that you can answer the following questions:

1. Are the psychological processes that people use in formulating conclusions the same ones that are specified by the laws of formal logic? How do they differ? (This should provide a helpful hint for the first question.)

2. Why is the legal process described as an "exercise in reasoning?"

3. What is a syllogism?
   State the mood for each of the following premises:

   No drugs are good.
   Some dogs can't bark.
   All birds have feathers.
   Some junk food is good.

4. Explain what Venn diagrams are. Why are they used?

5. How does content affect the way we reason with syllogisms? How does this differ from the rules of logic?

6. List and describe five common errors in the way people interpret syllogisms. Can Venn diagrams be used to prevent these errors?

7. How are linear orderings similar to syllogisms? What are some factors that determine the ease with which we solve linear orderings?

8. What are the common errors that occur when people reason from "if, then" statements?

9. How do probability and logic interact to influence our belief in the validity of conclusions?

10. Confirmation bias is a ubiquitous effect. What is it? How is it demonstrated in the "four-card selection task?" Explain the correct answer to this problem.

11. How are computer flowcharts like reasoning problems?

Exercises

Try out the reasoning skills you've learned in this chapter.

I. Use Venn diagrams to select the valid conclusion in these syllogisms:
   A. Some baseball players are scholars.
      No blondes are baseball players.

Therefore:
1. All blondes are scholars.
2. Some blondes are scholars.
3. No blondes are scholars.
4. No definite conclusion.

B. All cats have nine lives.
All animals with nine lives are mammals.
Therefore:
1. All cats are mammals.
2. Some cats are mammals.
3. No cats are mammals.
4. No definite conclusion.

C. Some accountants are honest.
Some honest people are dancers.
Therefore:
1. All accountants are dancers.
2. Some accountants are dancers.
3. No accountants are dancers.
4. No definite conclusion.

D. No presidents are young.
All young people like LaVerne and Shirley.
Therefore:
1. No presidents like LaVerne and Shirley.
2. All presidents like LaVerne and Shirley.
3. No people who like LaVerne and Shirley are presidents.
4. No definite conclusion.

E. Some poor people do not own houses.
All homeowners have assets.
Therefore:
1. Some poor people have assets.
2. No poor people have assets.
3. Some people with assets are poor.
4. No definite conclusion.

II. Solve these linear orderings:

A. Carl is smarter than Abby.
Dan is smarter than Bruce.
Carl is smarter than Dan.
Who is smartest?
Who is dumbest?

B. The dog is to the left of the rooster.
The newt is to the right of the rooster.
The hyena is to the left of the giraffe.
The newt is to the left of the hyena.
Which animal is on the right?

III. Which of these conclusions is valid?

A. If gun control reduces violent crime, then people will vote for it.
People are voting against gun control.

Therefore:

1. Gun control reduces violent crimes.
2. Gun control does not reduce violent crime.
3. No definite conclusion.

B. If the Lakers were second, the 76*ers* came in first.
The Lakers were second.
Therefore:

1. The 76*ers* came in first.
2. The 76*ers* did not come in first.
3. No definite conclusion.

C. If Robin doesn't phone home, her parents worry.
Her parents are worried.
Therefore:

1. Robin didn't phone home.
2. Robin phoned home.
3. No definite conclusion.

D. If Edna doesn't practice, she won't play well.
She doesn't play well.
Therefore:

1. Edna doesn't practice.
2. Edna does practice.
3. No definite conclusion.

IV. "Mrs. Cooke had studied home economics in college. 'Youth is a time of rapid growth and great demands on energy,' she said. 'Many youngsters don't get enough vitamins in their daily diet. And since some vitamin deficiencies are dangerous to health, it follows that the health of many of our youngsters is being endangered by inadequate diet.' (Does it follow that the health of many youngsters is being endangered by inadequate diet? Give your reasoning)" (Henle, 1962, p. 371).

V. Consider the four cards below (adapted from Wason, 1969).

Every card has a triangle on one side and a circle on the other. Every card which has a black triangle on one side has a black circle on the other side. Your task is to indicate which of the cards you need to turn over in order to find out whether this rule is true.

VI. Present the four-card selection task to your family and friends. Explain the correct answer to them.

VII. Find examples of valid and invalid reasoning from the newspaper, television, billboards, and conversations. If the reasoning is invalid, explain what is wrong with it. Use Venn diagrams to check on the conclusions in syllogistic arguments.

SUGGESTED READINGS

The literature on reasoning dates back, at least, to Aristotle's time, and probably earlier. Currently, reasoning texts are written either by philosophers or psychologists, and each field has a different perspective on the area. The philosophical approach tends to be more proscriptive or concerned with what reasoning should be, while the psychological approach tends to be more descriptive or concerned with the way people actually reason. There is, however, considerable overlap between these two disciplines.

Some recommended texts that assume a philosophical viewpoint are Wright's (1982) *Better Reasoning*, Salmon's (1973) *Logic*, and Hitchcock's (1983) *Critical Thinking: A Guide to Evaluating Information*.

Recommended books in psychology are Revlin and Mayer's (1978) *Human Reasoning*, Wason and Johnson-Laird's (1972) *Psychology of Reasoning* and Evans' (1982) *The Psychology of Deductive Reasoning*. An old classic text in psychology with a good basic section on reasoning is Bruner, Goodnow and Austin's (1956) *A Study of Thinking*.

A useful and clever guide to logical pitfalls is Thouless' (1932) *Straight and Crooked Thinking*. The back section of the book contains a wealth of everyday examples of faulty logic. It may help you win at arguments.

If you're looking for additional reasoning problems to practice and sharpen your skills, you'll enjoy Summer's (1968) *New Puzzles in Logical Deduction* and Summers' later book (1972) *Test Your Logic: 50 Puzzles in Deductive Reasoning*. Some of the material presented in Summers' books is similar to the topics covered in the chapter on the Development of Problem Solving Skills. This shouldn't be surprising to you since early in the chapter, reasoning was described as one kind of problem solving. Two edited volumes with good collections of articles on this topic are Wason and Johnson-Laird (Eds.) (1968) *Thinking and Reasoning* and Johnson-Laird and Wason's (Eds.) (1977) *Thinking: Readings in Cognitive Science*.

Additional information on flowcharts can be easily found in almost any beginning computer language text. If the idea of reading these books terrifies you, you can start with one written for elementary school children, Lipson's (1982) *It's Basic: The ABC's of Computer Programming*. A more advanced, although still easy to read, text on the topic is Boillot, Gleason and Horn's (1979) *Essentials of Flowcharting*.

4 Thinking as Hypothesis Testing

Contents

Understanding Hypothesis Testing 94
Explanation, Prediction and Control 94
Inductive and Deductive Methods 95
Operational Definitions 97
Independent and Dependent Variables 98
Populations and Samples 99
Determining Cause 102
Isolation and Control of Variables 102
Prospective and Retrospective Research 104
Correlation and Cause 104
Measurement 108
Convergent Validity 109
Illusory Validity 110
Reliability 111
Self-fulfilling Prophecies 111
Thinking As An Intuitive Scientist 112

> The conversation was getting heated. "Look, I know what I'm talking about," Kay said to Chris in an angry tone. "Busing school children for the purpose of integration works. My daughter is now close friends with both white and black girls, and her grades have improved since busing was adopted in her district."
>
> "Oh, yeah," Chris answered. "Well, my son has become more prejudiced since they forced him to be bused across town, and his grades are barely passing."
>
> "Your son's grades were barely passing before he was bused," Kay responded, "And furthermore, my neighbor thinks that busing is good, too. You're just too pigheaded to look at the evidence."
>
> "Pigheaded! My son is being bused to a school with dumb students. It's as plain as the large nose on your face. Busing is bad news."

Heated discussions like the fictional one between Kay and Chris have been taking place in large and small towns across the country as people argue for and against the issue of busing children from neighborhood schools to other schools in order to achieve desegregation. How did Kay and Chris arrive at their conclusions? How did each become so convinced that he or she is correct? What do you think about school busing and how did you arrive at *your* conclusion?

UNDERSTANDING HYPOTHESIS TESTING

Research is an intellectual approach to an unsolved problem, and its function is to seek the truth.
—Leedy (1981, p. 7)

Much of our thinking is like the scientific method of **hypothesis testing.** A **hypothesis** is a set of beliefs about the nature of the world; it is usually a belief about a relationship between two or more variables. In order to understand the world around us, we accumulate observations, formulate beliefs or *hypotheses* (singular is hypothesis), and then observe if our hypotheses are confirmed or disconfirmed. Thus, hypothesis testing is one way of finding out the truth about the world. Formulating hypotheses and making systematic observations that could confirm or disconfirm them is the same method that scientists use when they want to understand events in their academic domain; thus, when thinking is done in this manner, it has much in common with the experimental methods used by scientists.

Explanation, Prediction and Control

There is a basic need to understand events in life. Nisbett and Ross (1980) believe that in our attempt to understand we often function as an "intuitive scientist." Like the scientist, we have our own theories about the causes of social and physical events. It is important to be able to explain why people react in certain ways (e.g., He's a bigot. She's tired after work.), to predict the results of our actions (e.g., If I don't study, I'll fail. If I wear designer clothes, people will think I'm sharp.), and to control some of the events in our environment (e.g., Since I want to have a good job in business, I'll have to do well in my accounting course.)

In order to understand the parallels between scientific and everyday thought, let's examine an example of scientific thought from a study by a clinical psychologist (H. Halpern, 1983). As a clinical psychologist, Halpern wanted to understand the variables that contribute to positive and negative attitudes towards homosexuality. As you probably know, some people believe homosexuality is a sin or a mental disorder; others believe it is a legitimate alternative lifestyle. How can we explain these differences in people's attitudes? H. Halpern formulated several hypotheses. He hypothesized that people who never had a close friendship with a homosexual will, in general, tend to have negative attitudes towards homosexuals. He also hypothesized that people with strong sex-role stereotypes (beliefs that certain activities and behaviors are appropriate for females, while others are appropriate for males) will have negative attitudes towards homosexuals. He also believed that persons from urban areas will tend to hold more positive attitudes towards homosexuals than those from rural areas.

If you've never thought about this topic, give it some thought now. What do you think about Halpern's hypotheses? If they were your own, how would you go about collecting the information that would confirm or disconfirm them? If your observations confirmed these hypotheses, then you would have, at least, a partial explanation of the way people feel towards homosexuals. You could use this information to predict someone's attitude. If you met a man from a rural area who had never met a homosexual and who believed in traditional sex-role stereotypes, what would you guess about his attitudes toward homosexuals? You would predict that they will not be favorable. Of course, sometimes you'll be wrong—he may even be homosexual himself—but, if the relationships among sex-role stereotypes, where a person lives, the lack of positive interactions with homosexuals and attitudes towards homosexuals were as hypothesized, it would allow you to predict the attitudes of people you've never met. This information could also be used to change attitudes toward homosexuals. You could provide opportunities for homosexuals to meet with other members of the community. You could attempt to change people's attitudes about traditional sex roles, and you could provide rural populations with some of the experiences of urban life. In this way, you could use your understanding of the concepts involved in improving attitudes towards homosexuals. (Of course, if you are interested in worsening attitudes towards homosexuals you could also use your information to provide experiences opposite to the ones just discussed. This section is not concerned with the issue of whether homosexuality is good or bad; it is simply being used as an example to compare and discuss the similarity between scientific research and everyday thought.)

Inductive and Deductive Methods

Sometimes a distinction is made between inductive and deductive methods of hypothesis testing (see the Development of Reasoning Skills chapter). In the **inductive method,** you observe events and then devise a hypothesis about the events you observed. To take a trivial example, you might notice that Joan, a pretty girl you know, seems to have many dates. Then you note that Minnie and Sue Ann, who are also pretty girls, also seem to have many dates. On the basis of these observations, you would hypothesize (invent a hypothesis) that pretty girls go out on many dates. In this way, you would work from your observations up to your hypothesis.

In the **deductive method,** you begin with a hypothesis that you believe to be true and then make systematic observations to see if your hypothesis is correct.

You might logically infer that since beauty is a valued asset for girls in our society, pretty girls will be popular and thus be asked out on many dates. After coming up with this hypothesis, you'd look around to find out which girls are pretty and then determine if they date often. You'd also want to compare them to their less comely friends to see if girls who are not pretty go out on fewer dates. When you begin with a hypothesis and then collect evidence that would confirm or disconfirm it, you are using the deductive method.

Although a distinction is usually made between these two types of reasoning, in real life they are just different phases of the hypothesis testing method. Often people observe events, formulate hypotheses, observe events again, reformulate hypotheses, and collect even more observations. The question of whether the observations or the hypothesis comes first is moot since our hypotheses determine what we choose to observe, and our observations determine what our hypotheses will be. It's like the perennial question of what came first, the chicken or the egg. Each process is dependent on the other for its existence. In this way, observing and hypothesizing recycle, with the observations changing the hypotheses and the hypotheses changing what gets observed.

If you are a Sherlock Holmes fan, you'll recognize this process as one that was developed into a fine art by this fictional detective. He would astutely note clues about potential suspects. For example, Sherlock Holmes could remember that the butler had a small mustard-yellow stain on his pants when it is well known that you don't serve mustard with wild goose. He would use these clues to devise hypotheses like, "the butler must have been in the field where wild mustard plants grow." The master sleuth would then check for other clues that would be consistent or inconsistent with this hypothesis. He might check the butler's boots for traces of the red clay soil that surrounds the field in question. After a circuitous route of hypotheses and observations, Sherlock Holmes would announce, "The butler did it." When called upon to explain how he reached his conclusion, he would utter his most famous reply, "It's elementary, my dear Watson."

For all of us, many of our beliefs about the world were obtained with the use of inductive and deductive methods, much like the great Sherlock Holmes. Do you see the parallels between the way Sherlock Holmes determined that "the butler did it" and the way Kay and Chris, in the opening paragraph of this chapter, decided if busing was beneficial or harmful? Think about the arguments made by Kay and Chris at the beginning of this chapter. Both of them gathered information, devised hypotheses about relationships, gathered more data and then processed the data into a conclusion about the truth of their hypotheses. Arthur Conan Doyle's fictional detective was invariably right in the conclusions he drew. Unfortunately, it is only in the realm of fiction that mistakes are never made. Let's examine the components of the hypothesis testing process to see where mistakes can occur.

Operational Definitions

An **operational definition** tells the reader how to recognize and measure the concept that you're interested in. For example, if you believe that hippies are dirty, you'll need to provide an operational definition for the concepts "hippies" and "dirty." How will I recognize a hippy when I meet one? You'd need to provide some statement like, "Hippies are people with long hair and sandals who play guitars, wear flowers, and oppose nuclear energy." You'll find that it is frequently difficult to provide good operational definitions for terms. I can think of several people who more or less fit this description, yet don't fit any other stereotype of hippies, and I know others whom I'd like to label hippy who eschew sandals, long hair, and flowers. Thus, this would seem to be an unsatisfactory operational definition. Suppose, for purposes of illustration, that this is our operational definition of hippies. You could then use this operational definition to classify people into "hippies" and "nonhippies" categories.

How would you operationally define "dirty?" Suppose you decided on, "hasn't had a bath or shower for 20 or more days." Once these terms are operationally defined, you could go around finding out whether hippies and nonhippies are clean or dirty. Operational definitions are important. Whenever you hear people talking about "punks," "our irresponsible youths," "knee-jerk liberals," "bleeding hearts," "red-necks," "reactionaries," "fascists," or "feminists," ask them to operationally define their terms. You may find that the impact of their argument is diminished when they are required to be precise about their terms.

In Halpern's study on attitudes towards homosexuals, how should he operationally define his terms? What is a negative or positive attitude towards homosexuals? He answered this question by using a scale consisting of statements about homosexuals. Respondents had to agree or disagree with statements like "Homosexuality is unnatural." Individual responses to these statements served as a way of measuring attitudes towards homosexuals in order to operationalize this concept. Another scale was used to measure sex-role steroetypes. He was still faced with the task of providing operational definitions for his other variables—the urban/rural distinction and the establishment of a close friendship with a homosexual. The urban/rural distinction was based on the size of the town in which respondents lived. He operationalized the close friendship with a homosexual variable by asking people if they had ever had such a relationship. Thus, by using operational definitions, he improved the precision of his study.

When you use operational definitions, you avoid the problems of ambiguity and vagueness. Try, for example, to write operational definitions for the following terms: love, prejudice, motivation, good grades, sickness, athletic, length, and growth.

Independent and Dependent Variables

A **variable** is any measurable characteristic that can take on more than one value. Examples of variables are gender (female and male), height, political affiliation (Republican, Democrat, Communist, etc.), handedness (right, left), and attitudes towards homosexuals (could range from extremely negative to extremely positive). When we test hypotheses we begin by choosing the variables we're interested in. In their argument over school busing, Kay and Chris were interested in the relationships among school busing, prejudice, and classroom performance. Kay argued that busing is beneficial because it reduces prejudice and improves academic performance. Chris' argument was opposite to Kay's: School busing is harmful because it increases prejudice and decreases school performance.

The variable that they're arguing about is busing. It is the one that they decided on before they collected their observations. In this case, they could decide to compare children who are bused with children who walk to their neighborhood schools. Busing is their **independent variable** because they decided on its measurement before they collected their observations. Any variable whose change (busing or no busing) is expected to affect the event that is being studied is called the independent variable. Ideally, if you want to know if busing *causes* changes in prejudice, you must be able to assign children at random to either the busing or no busing group. In this way, any other differences among the children (e.g., differences in socioeconomic status or sex or age or neighborhood of residence) should "cancel out" so that the two groups differ only in whether or not they are bused to school.

The behaviors they want to measure as they relate to busing are prejudice and school achievement. These are their **dependent variables.** The question they want to answer is: "Does children's prejudice and their academic performance *depend* upon whether or not they are bused?"

The next step in the hypothesis testing process is to define the varibles operationally. Suppose, we decide to define busing as riding a school bus two or more miles from a segregated neighborhood to an integrated school for at least a year and "not busing" as never having ridden a school bus. With these definitions we can decide which children will be in the "busing" group and which children will be in the "not busing" group. (Note also that with these definitions, children who have ridden a school bus less than a year or over distances less than two miles or who have not gone from segregated neighborhoods to integrated schools won't be studied.)

How did you define prejudice? Would you be happy with a definition that separated people into two groups—prejudiced and not prejudiced—or would you prefer a definition that measured the amount or degree of prejudice—a measure that allowed people to be measured as more or less prejudiced? Because I believe that prejudice is an attitude that exists in varying degrees, I'd prefer an operational definition that would allow me to quantify this variable. One way to operationalize this variable is to ask children how many close friends they have whose race differs from their own. In this way, the child who has no close friends of other races would be classified as more prejudiced than the child with one close other-race friend, and so on. Academic performance could be operationalized with grade point average. The higher the grade point average, the better the academic achievement.

It is important to think critically about operational definitions for your variables. If they are not stated in satisfactory terms, the conclusions you draw from your study may be wrong. In this example, the number of other-race friends a child has is a poor measure of prejudice. Suppose that the children who walk to school attend schools that are either 100% black or 100% white. These children may have very few other-race friends, not because they are prejudiced, but because they simply don't have opportunities to meet children of other races. If this is so, then you're not measuring prejudice, but some other variable, like the availability of other-race friends. Variables that we're not interested in, but affect our results, are called **extraneous variables.** They are extraneous to the purpose of our study.

Populations and Samples

In order to decide if Kay's or Chris' hypothesis about the effects of busing is correct, we need to decide which children we want to study. What we really want to know about is the effect of busing on all children in the United States. The group we want to know about is called a **population.** Since we obviously can't study every child in the United States, we'll need to study a subset of this population. A subset of a population is called a **sample.** How do we decide who will be in our study?

Biased and Unbiased Samples

We want our sample to be representative of our population. The problem then becomes one of finding a group of children that would be representative of all children in the United States. To be representative, the children in our sample would need to both female and male, from all socioeconomic levels, all intellectual levels, rural and urban areas, and so on. We need representative samples so that we can generalize our results. **Generalization** refers to using the results obtained with our sample to infer that similar results would be obtained from the population if everyone in the population had been measured.

Suppose that our sample is not representative of the population. Suppose we bus children from the Ozark Mountains and then use their scores on our measures of prejudice and grade point average to make conclusions about the effect of busing on all children in the United States. You would rightly be concerned about any conclusions drawn from this study. If you used only children from the

Ozark Mountains, you would have a *biased sample*. Because it is not representative or *unbiased*, you could not use it to draw conclusions about the population.

Another pitfall in sampling is the possibility of *confounding*. Suppose you study two groups of children—those who are bused and those who are not transported. The children in the bused group are all mentally gifted high achievers, while the children in the "not bused" group have all been classified as learning disabled. These groups differ in two ways. They differ with respect to the variable you're interested in (busing) and with respect to a second variable that you're not interested in (mental ability). If you found that the children who were bused had higher grades you wouldn't know if this were due to busing or the intellectual differences between the groups. Since you can't separate these effects, you have a confounded experiment.

Usually, scientists use *convenience samples*. They study a group of people who are readily available. The most frequent subjects in psychology experiments are college students and white rats. The extent to which you can generalize from these samples depends on your research question. If you want to understand how the human visual system works, college students should be useful as subjects. If, on the other hand, you want to understand sex-role stereotyping in adults, college students would not be a representative sample because college students tend to be less stereotyped than other adults. In this case, you could only generalize about college students.

Similarly, if you wanted to know how wild rats learn their way around in natural environments, laboratory rats who have spent their entire lives in small cages will not provide a satisfactory sample.

Sample Size

Given a thimblefull of facts, we rush to make generalizations as large as a tub.
—Gordon Allport (1954, p. 8.)

The number of subjects you include in your sample is called the *sample size*. Refer back to Kay and Chris' argument. What was their sample size? Kay used only one subject, her daughter. Chris also used only one subject, his son. (A *subject* is a person or animal or entity who participates in an experiment.) When scientists conduct experiments, they often use large numbers of subjects. If, for some reason, they cannot use a large number of subjects, they may need to be more cautious or conservative in the conclusions that they derive from their research. Although a discussion of the number of subjects needed in an experiment is beyond the scope of this book, it is important to keep in mind that for most everyday purposes, we cannot generalize about a population by observing how a few people respond.

We tend to ignore the importance of having an adequately large sample size when we function as intuitive scientists. If you asked one person from Little Town, Iowa how she felt about homosexuals and compared her response to one given by a resident of Chicago, would you consider this a fair test of the hypothesis that rural inhabitants maintain different attitudes towards homosexuals than their urban counterparts? I hope not. Everyone in Little Town or in Chicago doesn't think the same way about complex issues. People are variable in the attitudes they maintain.

The term *variability* is used to denote the fact that all people are not the same. Just by chance, you could have picked someone with unusual attitudes for either Little Town or Chicago. What we really want to know is whether people in Little Town are, on the average, more negative in their attitudes toward homosexuals than people in large cities like Chicago. To answer this question, we'd take a large *random sample* (a sample in which everyone in the population has an equal chance of being selected) of residents from rural and urban areas and compare the average attitudes from each group.

Suppose this happened to you:

After months of deliberation, you finally decided to buy a Chevrolet Citation. You found that both *Consumer Reports* and *Road and Track* magazines have given the Citation a good rating. The Citation is priced within your budget, and you like its racing stripes and "sharp" appearance. On your way out the door to close the deal, you run into a close friend and tell her about your intended purchase. "A Citation!" she shrieks. "My brother-in-law bought one and it's a tin can. It's constantly breaking down on the freeway. He's had it towed so often that the rear tires need replacing." What do you do?

Most people would have a difficult time completing the purchase because they are insufficiently sensitive to sample size issues. The national magazines presumably tested many cars before they determined their rating. Your friend's brother-in-law is a single subject. You should place greater confidence in results obtained with large samples than in results obtained with small samples (assuming that the "experiments" were equally good). Yet, many people find the testimonial of a single person more persuasive than information gathered from a large sample.

A few years ago, there was much excitement over the use of laetril, an extract from apricot pits, as a cure for cancer. Although the United States medical establishment found that it was worthless in the fight against cancer, many people continued to believe that it could be used as a cure. Suppose you read about someone who was diagnosed as having cancer, and this person then took laetril. Later this lucky individual recovered from her cancer. What can you conclude? Would you be willing to conclude that, at least for some people, laetril can cure or help to cure cancer? This conclusion is unwarranted. Some people recover from cancer while others do not. Just as people are variable in the beliefs and attitudes that they maintain, they are also variable in the way they respond to disease. With a sample size of one, we cannot conclude that the laetril contributed to her cure. Large-scale studies are needed that compare the survival rates of groups of people on laetril with groups of people who used other forms of cancer treatments to decide if laetril can be beneficial in the treatment of cancer. When these tests were conducted by the United States government, laetril was found to be worthless. It's easy to see how desperate cancer patients can be misled into believing results obtained with a very small number of people. People's willingness to believe that results obtained from a few subjects can be generalized to the entire population is called the **law of small numbers** (Tversky & Kahneman, 1971). In an experimental investigation of this phenomenon (Quattrone & Jones, 1980), college students demonstrated their belief that if one member of a group made a particular decision, then the other members of that group would make the same decision. This result was especially strong when the college students were observing the decisions of students from other colleges. Thus, it is easy to see how a belief in the law of small numbers can maintain prejudices and stereotypes. The actions of a single group member are indicative of the actions of the entire group. Have you ever heard someone say, "_____s (fill in your group) are all alike"? An acquaintance once told me that all Jamaicans are sneaky thiefs. She came to this conclusion after having one bad experience with a person from Jamaica. Expressions like this one are manifestations of the law of small numbers. When you collect observations about people and events, be sure to collect a large number of observations before you reach a conclusion.

DETERMINING CAUSE

Do you believe that children who are neglected become teenage delinquents?
Does jogging relieve depression?
Will a diet that is low in fat increase longevity?
Do clothes make the man?
Will strong spiritual beliefs give you peace of mind?
Does assertion training make you more assertive?

All of these questions concern a causative relationship in which one variable (e.g., neglect) is believed to cause another variable (e.g., delinquency). What sort of information do we need to determine the truth of causative relationships?

Isolation and Control of Variables

Stop and think for a minute about the way you would go about deciding if neglecting children causes them to become delinquent when they are teenagers. You could decide to conduct a long-term study in which you would divide children into groups—telling some of their parents to cater to their every need, others to neglect them occasionally, and still others to neglect their children totally. You could require everyone to remain in their groups, catering to or neglecting their children as instructed until the children reach their teen years, at which time you could count up the number of children in each group who became delinquents. This would be a good, although totally unrealistic, way to decide if neglect causes delinquency. It's a good way because this method would allow you to *control* how much neglect each child received and to *isolate* the cause of delinquency, since this would be the only systematic difference among the people in each group. It's unrealistic to the point of being ludicrous, since very few people would comply with your request to cater to or neglect their children. Furthermore, it would also be unethical to ask people to engage in potentially harmful behaviors.

In some experimental settings it is possible to isolate and control the variables you're interested in. If you wanted to know if grading students for course work will make college students work harder and therefore learn more, you could randomly assign college students to different classes. One class could be graded as pass or fail (no letter grades), while the other could use traditional letter grades (A, B, C, D, or F). At the end of the semester, both classes would take the same final exam. If the average final exam score in the class that received grades was *statistically significantly* higher than in the pass/fail class, we'd conclude that grades do result in greater learning. (See the Probability chapter for a discussion of significant differences.)

Can you see why it's so important to be able to assign students at random to either the graded or pass/fail class instead of just letting them pick the class they want? It is possible that the students who would pick the pass/fail class are less motivated or less intelligent than the students who would prefer to get grades. If they could pick their own class, we wouldn't know if the differences we found were due to the differences in grading practices or due to differences in motivation or intelligence, or some other variable between students in the two classes.

Let's return to the question of whether child neglect causes delinquency. Given the constraint that you cannot tell parents to neglect their children, how would you go about deciding if child neglect causes delinquency? You could decide to find a group of parents and ask each about the amount of care he or she gives to each child. Suppose you found that in general the more that children are neglected, the more likely they are to become teenage delinquents. Because you lost the control over your variables by not assigning parents to catering and neglecting groups, it is not possible, on the basis of this experiment alone, to conclude that neglect causes delinquency. It is possible that parents who neglect their children differ from caring parents in other ways. Parents who tend to neglect their children may also encourage drug use, or engage in other life style activities that contribute to the development of teenage delinquency. Because parents couldn't be assigned to groups, it would take many studies to establish conclusively this relationship.

Prospective and Retrospective Research

Consider a medical example: Some health psychologists believe that certain stressful experiences can cause people to develop cancer. If this were your hypothesis, how would you determine its validity? One way would be to ask cancer patients if they had anything particularly stressful happen to them just before they were diagnosed as having cancer. If the stress caused the cancer, it would have to *precede* (come first in time) the development of cancer. When experiments are conducted in this manner, they are called **retrospective experiments.** Retrospective experiments look back in time to understand causes for later events. There are many problems with this sort of research. As discussed in the memory chapter, memories are selective and malleable. It is possible that knowledge of one's cancer will change how one's past is remembered. Moderately stressful events like receiving a poor grade in a college course may be remembered as being traumatic. Happier events, like getting a raise, may be forgotten. It's even possible that the early stages of the cancer were causing stress instead of the stress causing the cancer. Thus, it will be difficult to determine if stress causes cancer from retrospective research.

A better method for understanding causative relationships is **prospective research.** In prospective research, you identify the causative factor when it occurs and then look forward in time to see if the hypothesized result occurs. In a prospective study, you would have many people record stressful life events when they occur (e.g., death of a spouse, imprisonment, loss of a job) and then see which people develop cancer. If the people who experience more stressful events are more likely to develop cancer, this result would provide support for your hypothesis.

Most of the research we conduct as intuitive scientists is *retrospective*. We often seek explanations for events *after* they have occurred. How many times have you tried to understand why a long-running marriage ended in divorce, or why a star rookie seems to be losing his touch, or why the underdog in a political race won? Our retrospective attempts at explanations are biased by selective memories and lack of systematic observations. (See the section on hindsight in the Development of Decision Making Skills chapter for a related discussion.)

Correlation and Cause

What you are about to read is absolutely true: As the weight of children increases, so does the number of items that they are likely to get correct on standardized tests of intelligence. In other words, heavier children answer more questions correctly than lighter ones. Before you start stuffing mashed potatoes into your children in an attempt to make them smarter, stop and think about what this means. Does it mean that gaining weight will make children smarter? Certainly not! Children get heavier as they get older, and older children answer more questions correctly than younger ones.

In the preceding example, the *variables* weight and number of questions answered correctly are related. An increase in one variable is associated with an increase in the other variable—as weight increases the number of questions answered correctly concomitantly (at the same time) increases. **Correlated variables** are two or more variables that are related. Because these are not true independent or dependent variables, just related variables, we can't infer that one causes the other to occur.

People frequently confuse correlation with cause. Consider the following example: Wally and Bob were arguing about the inheritance of intelligence. Wally thought about everyone he knew and concluded that since smart parents tend to have smart children, and dumb parents tend to have dumb children, intelligence is an inherited characteristic. Bob disagreed with Wally's line of reasoning, although he concurred with the facts that Wally presented. He agreed that if the parents score high on intelligence tests, then their children will also tend to score high, and if the parents score low on intelligence tests, then their children will also tend to score low. When two measures are related in this way, that is they tend to rise and fall together, they have a **positive correlation.** Although parents' intelligence and their children's intelligence are positively correlated, we cannot infer that parents caused their children (through inheritance or any other means) to be intelligent. It is possible that children affect the intelligence of their parents, or that both are being affected by a third variable that hasn't been considered. It is possible that diet, economic class or other life style variables determine intelligence levels, and since parents and children eat similar diets and have the same economic class, they tend to be similar in intelligence.

Let's consider a somewhat different example. Many people have taken up jogging in the belief that exercise will help them to lose weight. The two variables in this example are exercise and weight. I've heard people argue that because there are no fat athletes (except perhaps suma wrestlers), exercise must cause people to be thin. I hope that you can think critically about this claim.

It does seem to be true that exercise and weight are correlated. People who tend to exercise a great deal also tend to be thin. This sort of correlation, in which the tendency to be high on one variable (exercise) is associated with the tendency to be low on the other variable (weight) is called a **negative correlation.** Let's think about the relationship between exercise and weight. There are several possibilities: (1) It is possible that exercise causes people to be thin; or (2) It is possible that people who are thin tend to exercise more because it is more enjoyable to engage in exercise when you are thin; or (3) It is possible that a third variable, like concern for one's health, or some inherited trait, is responsible for both the tendency to exercise and the tendency to be thin. Perhaps there are inherited body types that naturally stay thin and also are graced with strong muscles that are well suited for exercise.

In summary, when considering the relationship between variables there are several possible explanations. Of course, it is also possible that they are unrelated or *not correlated.* Some examples of variables that are not correlated are typing speed and hat size, number of hairs on your head and grade point average, and height and reaction time on a driving test.

When variables are related or correlated they can either be positively correlated and vary together or they can be negatively correlated and vary so that when people are high on one variable, they will tend to be low on the other. Some positive correlations are: height and weight, number of churches and number of prostitutes in a city (both increase with increases in population), and the number of ice cream cones sold and number of reported rapes (both increase with increases in temperature). Some negative correlations are: amount of fluoride children consume and number of cavities they get, hours spent studying and number of courses failed. In understanding the relationship between two correlated variables, it is possible that variable A caused the changes in variable B (A→B), or the variable B caused the changes in variable A (B→A), or that both were caused by a third variable C (C→A) and (C→B).

An amusing anecdote of attributing cause to events that occur together was presented by Munson (1976):

> A farmer was traveling with his wife on a train when he saw a man across the aisle take something out of a bag and begin eating it. "Say, Mister," he asked, "What's that thing you're eating?
>
> "It's a banana," the man said. "Here, try one."
>
> The farmer took it, peeled it, and just as he swallowed the first bite, the train roared into a tunnel. "Don't eat any, Maude," he yelled to his wife. "It'll make you go blind!" (p. 277)

Illusory Correlation

Physicians, psychologists, and others who are faced with the task of diagnosing a patient's illness, must be able to observe symptoms and correlate them (decide if they are related) with particular disorders. They need to recognize that clusters of symptoms "go along with" certain disorders. Recent research has shown that professionals often believe that a correlation exists between a symptom and a disorder when, in fact, the symptom and disorder are not correlated. The term, **illusory correlation** has been coined for this phenomenon (Chapman & Chapman, 1967, 1969). It is one kind of error that diagnosticians make.

Professionals and nonprofessionals alike maintain beliefs about relationships in the world. These beliefs guide the kinds of observations they make and how they determine if a relationship exists between two variables.

Here is an example, similar to some actual research on illusory correlation (Mowrey, Doherty & Keeley, 1979). Suppose that you are a psychologist faced with the task of diagnosing a client. To make the problem somewhat easier, you're told that the correct diagnosis is either "depressed," "obese," or "feelings of inferiority." To help you make your diagnosis, you're given the patient's responses to Rorschach inkblots. Rorschach inkblots are symmetrical unstructured forms that can be perceived in different ways. A sample of a Rorschach-like inkblot is shown in Fig. 4.1.

Suppose that you are given the following responses from the patient: "I see a bowl in the picture and . . . it's filled with fruit. I can see part of a banana and some loose jelly-like stuff holding it all together." Which of the three diagnostic categories would you use for this patient? Would you guess that this patient is most likely depressed, obese, or feels inferior? Most people would diagnose this patient as obese because of the prevalent belief that obese people will perceive food in unstructured forms.

FIG. 4.1. A Rorschach-like inkblot similar to the ones used to investigate how diagnosticians decide that certain responses to unstructured forms are correlated with certain disorders. See text for explanation.

Of course, this is not a fair test, since you have very little information and no experience in diagnosing disorders. Similar experiments with psychodiagnosticians (people who make psychological diagnoses) have shown that they often believe that there are relationships between certain types of answers (e.g., food related) and certain diagnoses (e.g., obese) when in fact none exist (Chapman & Chapman, 1969). The psychodiagnosticians persisted in their belief in these illusory correlations even when faced with contradictory evidence. They believed that certain responses would co-occur with certain diagnoses, and they continued to maintain this belief even when the information they received did not support the relationship.

Let's try another example. Do you believe that you often see fat people overeating? Most people believe that they do; yet, research has shown that overweight adults tend to eat less in public places than normal-weight people. We expect to see overweight people overeating; and therefore, we believe that we do see the world according to our beliefs.

Beware of illusory correlations when you function as an intuitive scientist. This phenomenon works to maintain stereotypes (e.g., redheads are hot-tempered; Scots are cheap; women can't understand math; etc.). Our beliefs about relationships between variables guide the observations we make and the way we utilize this information to formulate conclusions.

Measurement

Sensitivity

When we measure something, we systematically assign a number to it for the purposes of quantification. Someone who is taller than you are is assigned a higher number of inches of height than you are. If not, the concept of height would be meaningless.

When we think as scientists and collect information in order to understand the world, we need to consider how we measure our variables. For example, suppose you believe that love is like a fever, and that people in love show fever-like symptoms. To find out if this is true, you could conduct an experiment, taking temperatures from people who are in love and comparing your results to the temperatures of people who are not in love. How will you measure temperature? Suppose that you decide to use temperature headbands that register body temperature with a band placed on the forehead. Suppose further that these bands measure temperature to the nearest degree (e.g., 98°, 99°, 100°, etc.). If being in love does raise your body temperature, but only raises it one-half of a degree, you'd never know this if you used headband thermometers. They just wouldn't be **sensitive** enough to register the small increment in body temperature. You would incorrectly conclude that love doesn't raise body temperatures, when in fact it may have. As far as I know, this experiment has never been done, but it is illustrative of the need for sensitive measurement in this and other situations.

Validity

The **validity** of a measure is usually defined as the extent to which it measures what you want it to measure. If I wanted to measure intelligence and measured the length of your big toe, this would obviously be *invalid.* Other examples of validity are less obvious. A popular radio commercial, touting the benefits of soup, points out that tomato soup has more Vitamin A than eggs. This is true, but it is not a valid measure of the goodness of tomato soup. Eggs, a generally healthy food, are not a good source of Vitamin A. Thus, the wrong comparisons were made, and the measure does not support the notion that soup is an excellent food.

How would you react to this claim: "The Baroness is a sleek new luxury car that will provide its owner with dependable transportation for many years to come. In fact, in a recent laboratory test, the Baroness went from zero to 60 miles per hour in 7 seconds flat, beating out the six other cars in the competition." Is the acceleration speed of a car a valid index of its dependability? Probably not. Even if the figure is accurate, it is not a valid measure of dependability. If you want to know about dependability, you'll want to know about the frequency of repairs, average number of miles the car can be expected to be driven before it gets turned into scrap metal, and how it performs on impact.

Convergent Validity

When several different measures all converge onto the same conclusion, the measures are said to have **convergent validity.** If, for example, you wanted to measure charisma—the psychological trait that is something more than charm that people as diverse as John F. Kennedy, Liza Minelli, and Laurence Olivier are said to possess, you'd need convergent validity for your measure. People who scored high on your charisma test should also be the ones who are selected for leadership positions and have other personality traits that are usually associated with charisma. If the class wallflower scored high on your test of charisma, you'd need to rethink the validity of your test.

People outside the laboratory also need to be mindful of the need for convergent validity. Before you decide that your classmate, Joyce, is shy because she hesitates to talk to you, you need to determine if she acts shy with other people in other places. If she frequently speaks up in class, you wouldn't want to conclude that she is a shy person because this inconsistency in her behavior would signal a lack of convergent validity.

Illusory Validity

Everyone complains of his memory and no one complains of his judgement.
—La Rochefoucauld

Both professionals and nonprofessionals place great confidence in their conclusions about most life events, even when their confidence is objectively unwarranted. Overconfidence in judgments is called **illusory validity.** In an experimental investigation of this phenomenon, Oskamp (1965) found that as clinicians were given more information about patients, they became more confident in the judgments they made about patients. What is interesting about this result is they were *not* more accurate in judgment, only more confident that they were right. Why do people place confidence in fallible judgments? There are several reasons why we persist in maintaining confidence in our judgments. A primary factor is the selective nature of memory. Consider this personal vignette: As a child, I would watch Philadelphia Phillies baseball games on television with my father. As each batter would step up to home plate, my father would excitedly yell, "He's going to hit a home run, I just know it!" Of course, he was usually wrong. (Phillies fans had to be tough in the 50s and 60s.) On the rare occasions when a Philly batter actually did hit a home run, my father would talk about it for weeks. "Yep, I knew as soon as he stepped up to home plate that he would hit a home run. I can always tell just by looking at the batter." In this instance, and countless others, we selectively remember our successful judgments and forget our unsuccessful ones. This tends to bolster confidence in the judgments we make.

A second reason for the illusion of validity is the failure to seek or consider disconfirming evidence. (See the Decision Making chapter for an additional discussion of this phenomenon.) Suppose that you have the job of personnel officer in a large corporation. Over a period of a year, you hire one hundred new employees for your corporation. How would you go about deciding if you're making good (valid) hiring decisions? Most people would check on the performance of the one hundred new employees. Suppose that you did this and found that 92% of the new employees were performing their jobs in a competent, professional manner. Would this bolster your confidence in your judgments? If you answered yes to this question, you forgot to consider disconfirming evidence. What about the people you didn't hire? Have most of them gone on to become Vice Presidents at General Motors? If you found that 100% of the people you didn't hire are superior employees at your competitor's corporation, you would have to revise your confidence in your judgmental ability.

Part of the reason that we fail to utilize disconfirming evidence is that it is often not available. Personnel officers don't have information about the employees they don't hire. Similarly, we don't know much about the person we chose not to date or the house we didn't buy. Thus, on the basis of partial information, we may conclude that our judgments are better than they objectively are.

Reliability

The **reliability** of a measure is the consistency with which it measures what it's supposed to measure. If you used a rubber ruler that could stretch or shrink to measure the top of your desk, you'd probably get a different number each time you measured it. Of course, we want our measurements to be reliable.

Researchers in the social and physical sciences devote a great deal of time to the issue of reliable measurement. Few of us even consider reliability when we function as intuitive scientists. When we decide if a professor or student is prejudiced, we often rely on one or two samples of behavior without considering if the individual is being reliably assessed.

Suppose that you learn that your friend Ricardo failed a college course which others easily passed. Could you conclude that his teacher is prejudiced? You'd need to collect many other observations of the same teacher to see how consistently or reliably Hispanic males fail his class. If there is an unusually high failure rate among Hispanic males (or whatever group you're interested in) in his class compared to their failure rate in other classes, then you'd have a strong case for the inference that the teacher is prejudiced.

SELF-FULFILLING PROPHECIES

Robert Rosenthal, a psychologist at Harvard University, and his colleague (Rosenthal & Fode, 1963) had their students train rats to run through mazes. Half of the students were told that they had rats that had been specially bred to be smart at learning their way through mazes, while the other half of the students were told that they had rats that had been specially bred to be dumb at this task. As you probably expected, the students with the bright rats had them outperforming the dull rats in a short period of time. These results are especially interesting because there were no real differences between the two groups of rats. Rosenthal and Fode had lied about the rats being specially bred. All of the rats were the usual laboratory variety. They had been assigned at random to each group. If there were no real differences between the groups of rats, how do we explain the fact that students who believed they had been given bright rats had them learn the maze faster than the other group?

The term **self-fulfilling prophecies** has been coined as a label for the tendency to act in ways that will lead us to find what we expected to find. I don't know what the students did to make the rats learn faster in the "bright" group or slower in the "dull" group. Perhaps the bright group was given extra handling or more food in the goal box. (When rats learn to run through mazes, they are given a food reward when they reach the goal box to keep them motivated.) Maybe the students given the "dull" rats dropped them harshly into the maze or were not as accurate in the records that they kept. Whatever they did, somehow, they influenced their experimental results so that the results were in accord with their expectations.

If self-fulfilling prophecies can influence how rats run through mazes, what sort of an effect will it have on everyday thinking? Earlier in this chapter, illusory correlations were discussed as the tendency to believe that events that you are observing are really correlated when you believe that they should be. Psychologists are becoming increasingly aware of the ways that personal convictions direct our selection and interpretation of facts. When you function as an intuitive scientist, it is important to keep in mind the ways we influence the results we obtain.

THINKING AS AN INTUITIVE SCIENTIST

One theme that has followed throughout this chapter is that everyday thinking has much in common with the research methods used by scientists when they investigate phenomena in their academic domains. Many of the pitfalls and problems that plague scientific investigations are also common in everyday thought. If you understand and avoid some of these problems, you will be a better consumer of research and a better intuitive scientist.

When you are evaluating the research claims of others or when you are asserting your own claims, there are several questions to keep in mind:

1. What was the nature of the sample? Was it large enough? Was it biased?
2. Are the variables operationally defined? What do the terms mean?
3. Were the measurements sensitive, valid, and reliable? Are the appropriate comparisons being made to support the claims?
4. Were extraneous variables controlled? What are other plausible explanations for the results?
5. Do the conclusions follow from the observations?
6. Are correlations being used to support causative arguments?
7. Is disconfirming evidence being considered?
8. How could the experimenter's expectancies be biasing the result?

If you scrutinize your own conclusions and those of others with these questions in mind, you should be able to defend yourself against invalid claims and improve your own ability to draw sound conclusions from observations.

CHAPTER SUMMARY

1. Much of our everyday thinking is like the scientific method of hypothesis testing. We formulate beliefs about the world and collect observations to decide if our beliefs are correct.

2. In the inductive method we devise hypotheses from our observations. In the deductive method we collect observations that confirm or disconfirm our hypotheses.

3. Operational definitions are precise statements that allow the identification and measurement of variables.

4. Independent variables are used to predict or explain dependent variables. When we formulate hypotheses, we want to know about the effect of the independent variable on the dependent variable(s).

5. When we draw conclusions from observations, it's important to utilize an adequately large sample size because people are variable in the way they respond. People are too willing to generalize results obtained from small samples.

6. In determining if one variable (e.g., smoking) causes another variable (e.g., lung cancer) to occur, it is important to be able to isolate and control the causative variables.

7. In everyday contexts, we often use retrospective techniques to understand what caused an event to occur. This is not a good technique because our memories tend to be selective and malleable and because we have no objective systematic observations of the cause. Prospective techniques that record events when they occur and then see if the hypothesized result follows are better methods for determining cause-effect relationships.

8. Variables that are related so that changes in one variable are associated with changes in the other variable are called correlated variables. Correlations can be positive as in the relationship between height and weight (taller people tend to weigh more, while shorter people tend to weigh less) or negative as in the relationship between exercise and weight (people who exercise a great deal tend to be thin, and those who exercise little tend to be heavy).

9. It is not correct to infer a cause relationship from correlated variables. It is possible that variable A caused variable B, or that variable B caused variable A, or that a third variable caused them both.

10. The belief that two variables are correlated when they are not (illusory correlation) is a common error in human judgment.

11. It is important that you use measurements that are sensitive, valid, and reliable or the conclusions you draw may be incorrect. Few people consider the importance of measurement issues when they draw everyday conclusions about the nature of the world.

12. Although many of our judgments lack validity, people report great confidence in them. This is called illusory validity.

13. Inadvertently, we may act in ways that will lead us to confirm or disconfirm hypotheses according to our expectations. These are called self-fulfilling prophecies.

Terms to Know:

You should be able to define or describe the following terms and concepts. If you find that you're having difficulty with any term, be sure to reread the section where it is discussed.

Hypothesis
Hypothesis Testing
Inductive Method
Deductive Method
Operational Definition
A Variable
Independent Variable
Dependent Variable
Extraneous Variable
Population
Sample
Generalization
Biased Sample
Confounding
Convenience Samples
Sample Size
Subject
Variability
Random Sample
Law of Small Numbers
Retrospective Research
Prospective Research
Correlated Variables
Positive Correlation
Negative Correlation
Illusory Correlation
Sensitive Measures
Validity
Convergent Validity
Illusory Validity
Reliability
Self-Fulfilling Prophecies

Be sure that you can answer the following questions:

1. How is everyday thinking like the experimentation used by scientists?

2. What is the difference between inductive and deductive methods? How are they used in a cyclical fashion?

3. Why do we need operational definitions?

4. What are hypotheses and how are they tested?

5. What are some mistakes that we can make when generalizing from a sample to a population?

6. Explain how confounding can lead to erroneous conclusions.

7. List three pairs of variables that you would expect to be positively correlated, three that you would expect to be negatively correlated, and three that you would expect to be uncorrelated.

8. Why can't we determine cause from correlated variables?

9. Why do people persist in believing in the validity of their conclusions even when their confidence is unwarranted?

10. Why is prospective research preferable to retrospective research?

11. We can be more confident in our conclusions when there is convergent validity. Why?

12. Explain why people sometimes believe that variables are correlated when, in fact, they are not.

13. How can experimenter biases affect the results obtained from experiments?

Exercises

Using the questions for evaluating research claims that are summarized at the end of this chapter, critically discuss each of the following:

1. According to Einhorn and Hogarth (1978), Benjamin Rush, a professor at the first medical school in the United States, believed that "blood-letting" (bleeding) of patients would cure a variety of illnesses. When his patients recovered from their illnesses, he would attribute their recovery to the practice of blood-letting. (Sometimes leeches were used to draw the blood.) When his patients died, he concluded that the nature of their illness was so severe that not even blood-letting could help them. Using your hypothesis testing skills, comment on Rush's observations and conclusions.

2. Whenever someone celebrates his or her 100*th* birthday, newspaper reporters ask him or her to reveal the secret of longevity. Suppose that you read in the newspaper that a 100 year old man attributed his long life to drinking a bottle of gin a day. Can you conclude that drinking gin will help you to live long?

3. Although research has shown that salt-free diets reduce blood pressure, Mike doubts that this is true. Mike's father has been on a salt-free diet for over a year and his blood pressure has remained high. What would you say to Mike about his conclusions?

4. Jim is very superstitious. He believes that when a black cat crosses his path, something bad happens. What would you tell Jim about his superstition?

5. You've probably heard a commercial that goes something like this, "Seven out of ten dentists recommend Chewsy Gum for their patients who chew gum." Comment on this commercial.

6. A conservative group of politicians attempted to persuade the local school board to eliminate its kindergarten program. A study conducted in a rural area of Montana showed that children who went to kindergarten did not score higher on an achievement test than children who did not attend kindergarten. How would you refute or prove their claim that kindergarten is a useless year?

7. Archie Bunker disapproves of feminists. He believes that they're manly, pushy, and aggressive. How would you (seriously) respond to Archie Bunker?

8. How would you decide if a new reading program should be implemented in your elementary schools?

9. Rosenthal & Jacobson (1968) told teachers that some of the children in their classrooms were ready to "bloom" intellectually. As you might expect, the children who were identified as bloomers did show large increases in intelligence. This is especially interesting in light of the fact that there were no real differences between the "bloomers" and other children. They had, in fact, picked the "bloomers" at random. What phenomenon discussed in this chapter can describe this result? How did it happen?

10. In a study by Pickren and Gamarra (1975, p. 188), the following relationship was found between histiocytes in lung tissues and people's smoking histories:

	Total Cases	*No. of Cases with Histiocytes*
nonsmokers	31	0 (0%)
former smokers	38	10 (27%)
smokers	43	40 (93%)

What can you conclude about the relationship between histiocytes and smoking history? Can you claim that smoking causes histiocytes? Why or why not? (Don't worry if you don't know what histiocytes are. It's not important in answering the question.)

11. A mad scientist taught his pet fly to "fetch" a small stick whenever a whistle was blown. The scientist then found that after he cut off the fly's wings, the fly didn't "fetch" the stick. He concluded that flies hear with their wings and that the fly had become deaf as a result of losing its wings. How would you convince the scientist that his experiment doesn't prove that flies hear with their wings?

12. Think about the television, radio, and magazine advertisements that bombard our daily existence. Collect some "choice" advertisements and question their claims and conclusions.

SUGGESTED READINGS

A good basic text on the topic of hypothesis testing is Leedy's (1981) *How to Read Research and Understand It.* It takes the perspective of a research consumer as opposed to that of the researcher. Three recommended books that discuss research methods are Drew's (1976) *Introduction to Designing Research and Evaluation,* Kerlinger's (1979) *Behavioral Research: A Conceptual Approach,* and Lewin's (1979) *Understanding Psychological Research.* All three are lucid texts that describe experimentation, correlation, and related research topics.

If you're interested in the development of scientific thinking through childhood and adolescence, see Siegler's (1978) chapter entitled "The Origins of Scientific Reasoning." It appears in an edited volume with other interesting chapters. The volume is Siegler's (Ed., 1978) *Children's Thinking: What Develops?*

A somewhat strange and iconoclastic book is *Against Method* by Feyerabend (1975). He argues against the use of scientific methods. Although this book is not easy reading, it is interesting. As an example that supports the notion that we don't need scientific methods, he argues that Galileo's views were eventually accepted, not on their scientific merit, but because Galileo "was clever in techniques of persuasion," wrote in Italian instead of Latin, and appealed to people who prefer new ideas to old ones.

The notion that we function as "intuitive" or everyday scientists is developed in *Human Inference: Strategies and Shortcomings of Social Judgment* by Nisbett and Ross (1980). This is an excellent text filled with interesting examples and concisely reviewed research on the way people utilize research principles in everyday life.

5 Understanding Probabilities (Likelihood and Uncertainty)

Contents

Probabilistic Nature of the World 120
Likelihood and Uncertainty 120
Degree of Belief 122
Odds 122
Using Probability 123
Implicit Use of Probability 124
Games of Chance 125
Computing Probabilities in Multiple Outcome Situations 126
Expected Values 132
Place Your Bets 132
Subjective Probability 135
An Experimental Example 135
Gambler's Fallacy 136
Frequency and Relative Frequency 137
Frequency Judgments 139
Base-Rate Biases 140
Posteriori Probabilities 143
Nonregressive Judgments 147
Statistical Abuse 148
On the Average 149
Precision 150
Significant Differences 151
Extrapolation 152
An Application of Probability Models 153
Extrasensory Perception 153

The theory of probabilities is nothing more than good sense confirmed by calculation.
—La Place

At a race track, everyone has a system. Some people buy predictions from professionals with colorful names like "Lucky Eddie," "Winner Al," and "Fabulous

Frieda," who set up small trailers outside of the race track. Others use the "horse's eye" technique to pick their winners. This method consists of inserting a pin in the eye of the horse that is pictured on the racing booklet. The pin passes through the names of several horses in the booklet which, as you might have guessed by now, are chosen for betting. There is also the "hot number" technique. If horse number 3 won the last race, then the horse that is assigned number 3 in the next race is the predicted winner. An interesting variation of this theme, one that is very common, is the "cold number" technique. If no horse with the number 7 has won the last several races, then the number 7 is predicted to win the next race, since it now seems more likely to occur. Of course, there is always the "favorite color" technique. This is a simple strategy that involves picking the horse or rider wearing one's favorite color. Serious bettors rely on hand-held racing calculators that can be purchased in toy stores. They "punch in" specific information about each horse, and the calculator will yield a prediction about the winner. Serious horse racing patrons carefully follow the careers of selected horses and attempt to subjectively combine the number of prior wins, the skill of the jockey, and other information deemed relevant to make their bets. Horse racing is a big business that has been growing rapidly in popularity. In order to place winning bets at the race track or in most other games, the bettor must take into account basic principles of probability.

PROBABILISTIC NATURE OF THE WORLD

It may seem obvious that the principles of probability are involved in horse racing and card games, but you may have never realized that probability plays a crucial role in almost all aspects of our lives. All medical diagnoses and treatment decisions are based on probability judgments, as are decisions made in business, law, sales, and research. Probability is the cornerstone of science. Very little is known with certainty. Because we live in a probabilistic world, good thinking will require an understanding of probability.

Likelihood and Uncertainty

If I flip a coin into the air and ask you to guess the probability that it will land heads up, you would say that the probability of a head is 50% (or .50). This means that the coin is expected to land heads up about half of the time. In statistical terms, **probability** *is defined as the number of ways a particular outcome (what we call a success) can occur divided by the number of possible outcomes.* It is a measure of how often we expect an event to occur *in the long run.* Success may seem like a strange word in this context, but you can think of it as the outcome you're interested in. In this case, a success is getting the coin to land heads up. There is only one way for a coin to land heads up, so the number of ways a success can occur in this example is 1. What are all the possible outcomes of flipping a coin in the air? The coin can either land heads up or tails up. (I've never seen a coin land on its edge, nor have I ever seen a bird come along and carry it off while it's flipped in the air, so I'm not considering these as possible outcomes.) Thus, there are two possible outcomes. To calculate the probability of getting a coin to land heads up, compute the number of ways a head can occur (1), divided by the number of possible outcomes (2), or ½, an answer you already knew. Since many people find it easier to think in percentages than in fractions, ½ is sometimes changed to 50%. (To change a fraction to a percent, divide the numerator by the denominator, then multiply by 100.)

Let's try another example. How likely are you to roll a 5 in one roll of a die? Since there is only one way for a 5 to occur, the numerator of the probability fraction is 1. A die is a 6-sided (cube) figure; thus there are 6 possible outcomes in one roll. The probability of rolling a 5 is ⅙, or 17%.

What is the probability of rolling an even number in one roll of a die? To find this probability, consider the number of ways a success can occur. You could roll a 2, 4, or 6, all possible even numbers. Thus, there are 3 ways a success can occur out of 6 possible outcomes, so the probability of rolling an even number is $\frac{3}{6} = \frac{1}{2}$.

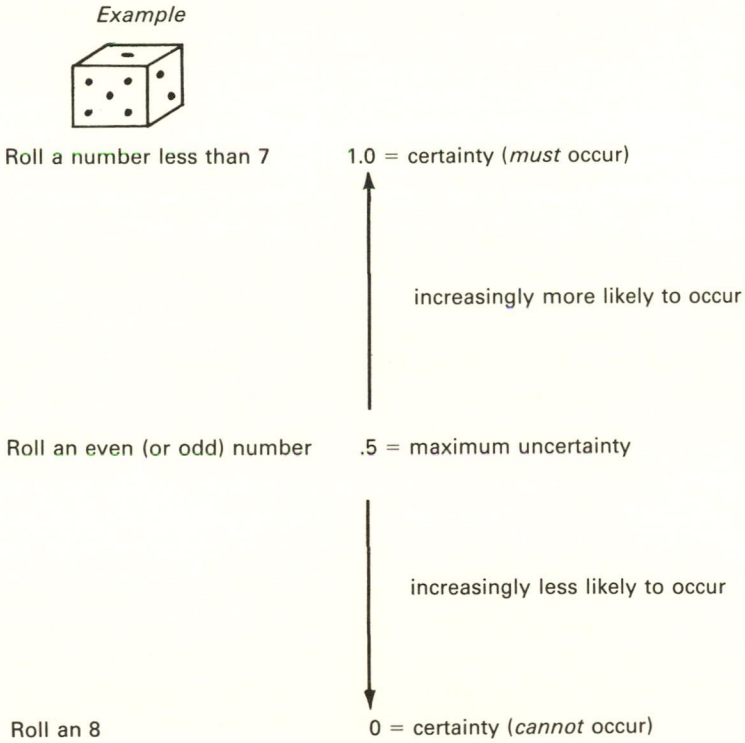

FIG. 5.1. Probability and likelihood.

What is the probability of rolling a whole number less than 7? If someone asked me to bet on this happening, I'd put up my house, my children, and my meager savings account to make this bet. In other words, I'd bet that this is extremely likely to happen. Let's see why. The number of ways a whole number less than seven can occur in one roll of a die is 6 (1, 2, 3, 4, 5, or 6), and the number of possible outcomes is 6. Thus, the probability is %, or 1. When a probability is equal to 1 (or 100%), it *must* happen; it is certain to occur.

What is the probability of rolling an 8 in one roll of a die? Again, I'd put up everything I own, but this time I'd bet against this occurrence. The number of ways an 8 can occur is 0. Thus, the probability of this occurring is 0; it *cannot* occur. This situation also reflects absolute certainty. Probabilities range from 0 (can never happen) to 1 (must happen), (or 0% to 100%). Probability values close to 0 or 1 represent events that are almost certain not to occur or almost certain to occur, while probabilities near .5 (50%) represent maximum uncertainty, because either outcome is equally likely, and thus there is no basis for predicting either one. This relationship is depicted in Fig. 5.1.

Degree of Belief

Probability is sometimes used to express how strongly someone feels about the likelihood of an outcome. For example, if you apply for a job and feel that the interview went well, you might assess the probability that you will be offered the job as 80%. This probability value was not mathematically derived by calculating the number of ways a success could occur divided by the number of possible outcomes. Instead, it indicates the *degree of belief* that the job will be offered. It suggests a moderate to high likelihood. If someone else interviewed for the same job and believed that his chance of being offered the job was 50%, it would be obvious that he was less confident about getting the job than you were.

The use of probability to express one's degree of belief in the likelihood of an outcome is particularly prevalent at election time. Political analysts will often attach probability values to the likelihood of a candidate's election. If a political analyst gives a candidate a 30% chance of winning, she is predicting that while the candidate might win, she believes that the candidate is more likely to lose. Probability values are handy ways of quantifying confidence in an outcome.

Odds

It is often convenient to discuss probabilities in terms of **odds.** If a friend gives you 3-to-1 odds that his school's championship tiddly-winks team will beat your school's tiddly-winks team, this means that if 4 games were played, he would expect his team to win 3 of them. Authorities on organized sports (announcers, sports page editors, and almost everyone else) usually express their degree of belief in the outcome of a sporting event in terms of odds. (Betting odds like those posted at race tracks and boxing matches refer to the amount of money that has been bet on each contender and, thus, have a different meaning from the one described here.)

© 1966 United Features Syndicate, Inc.

USING PROBABILITY

Without giving it much thought, we utilize probabilities many times each day. Let's start with one of the few examples where probability values are made explicit. Many people begin each day by reading the weather forecast in the morning paper. What do you do when you read that the probability of rain is 90% today? Most people will head off to school or work toting an umbrella, since they interpret this statement as, "It probably will rain." What this statement objectively means is that on 90% of the previous days when the weather conditions (atmospheric pressure, humidity, etc.) were like today's, it rained. A 90% probability of rain has nothing to do with how much it will rain, just how likely we are to get any rain.

The number of instances in which we are given explicit probability values that have been computed for us is relatively small. One area where this practice is growing is in the medicine inserts that are designed to help patients understand the risks and benefits of taking a particular drug. The Food and Drug Administration now requires that all oral contraceptive medications (birth control pills) be packaged with statistical information about the health risks associated with them. In order to arrive at an intelligent decision based on the information provided, potential oral contraceptive users must be able to understand the statistical summaries that are presented in the medicine inserts.

The following excerpt from an oral contraceptive packaged insert provides an example: "For women aged 20 to 44, it is estimated that about 1 in 2,000 using oral contraceptives will be hospitalized each year because of abnormal clotting. Among nonusers in the same age group, about 1 in 20,000 would be hospitalized each year" (Ortho Pharmaceutical Corp., 1979, p. 16). Although consumers can readily assess that clotting is more likely for pill users, this information is of little practical value unless an oral contraceptive consumer can decide if 1 in 2,000 is a large or small number, i.e., "Is it a danger to me if I am taking the pill?"

A recent experiment (Halpern & Blackman, in press) showed that most people find information like this to be relatively meaningless. Consider the following: Suppose you read that the risk of developing heart disease is 10.5 times more likely for oral contraceptive users than for nonusers. Most people will conclude from this information that oral contraceptives present a substantial risk of heart disease.

Suppose now that you are told that only 3.5 women out of 100,000 users will develop heart disease. You probably would interpret this sentence as meaning that there is little risk associated with oral contraceptive use.

A third way of presenting the same information is to convert it to a percentage. There is only a .0035% probability that oral contraceptive users will develop heart disease. Most people would now consider the risk associated with oral contraceptive use to be miniscule.

Which of these statements is correct? They all are. The only way they differ is the way in which the statistical information is presented. It is important to keep this in mind when interpreting statistical information.

Implicit Use of Probability

Although we are rarely given explicit, objectively determined probabilities to deal with, it is very frequent that we derive our own subjective estimates of probability to base decisions upon. There are numerous everyday examples in which people tacitly utilize rough estimates of probability. Most students use probabilities in deciding how to study for exams. It may surprise you to learn that some students put off studying until a few nights before the exam, even though they know that they can learn more if they keep up with their work. Suppose Geraldine has ten chapters to study for a final exam that she will have to take tomorrow. She can't possibly read all ten chapters in one night. She could try to cut down on her reading by concentrating on the chapters she believes that her professor is most likely to emphasize on the exam. Of course, if she's wrong, the results could be disastrous. If Geraldine decides to skip chapters 2 and 6 in her text, and the exam draw heavily from these chapters, she'll most likely fail the exam.

Every time you drive your car you make implicit probability estimates about what other drivers will no next. For example, accidents frequently occur when large trucks signal for a right hand turn from the left hand lane. Large trucks need the extra room to turn. Many drivers ignore the turn signal, thinking that the truck driver will probably continue straight, since he is in the left hand lane. Too often, a collision is the unfortunate result.

Games of Chance

Cards

We are in a country of people who love to play games. From Las Vegas to Atlantic City, and in all of the small towns in between, people spend countless hours and dollars playing games of chance, skill, and semi-skill. Card playing is a ubiquitous pastime, with small children playing "Fish" and "Old Maid," while their older counterparts play Canasta, Bridge, Poker, Pinocle, Black Jack, Hearts, and too many others to mention. The uncertainty inherent in card games adds to the pleasure of playing (although the comraderie and pretzels and beer also help).

Good card players, regardless of the game, understand and utilize the rules of probability. Let's apply the definitional formula for probability to card games. For example, how likely are you to draw an Ace of Spades from a deck of cards? The probability of this happening is $1/52$, or approximately 2%, since there is only one Ace of Spades and 52 possible outcomes. How likely are you to draw an ace of any suit from a full deck of cards? If you've been following the probability discussion so far, you'll realize that the answer is $4/52$, or 8%, since there are 4 aces in a 52-card deck. Some professional card players have worked out careful plans that will help them to change the odds of winning in their favor. A few people have reportedly been denied access to gambling casinos because their systems are so effective that the casino ends up losing money to them. This is especially true of Black Jack "counters." It is difficult to tell to what extent these stories are hype. (Professional gamblers often enjoy bragging about their winnings.) In any case, it is possible to improve the odds or probability of winning most card games if the player is willing to spend some time figuring the relevant probabilities and keeping track of the cards that have already been played. In determining the likelihood of getting an ace, a player needs to "count" the number of aces that already have been played. If all four aces have been played, then a good player will realize that there is no possibility of getting the desired ace. On the other hand, if half of the deck has been played and no aces have shown up so far, then the probability of now being dealt an ace is $4/26$—considerably higher than the earlier probability.

One of the biggest problems in "beating the house" is remembering which cards have been played. Top professionals have devised systems to help them remember. The most obvious system and cheapest mnemonic (memory) device is a pen and paper. This is usually not permitted in casinos. Elaborate counting methods often use body positions to keep track of played cards. The systems themselves are intricate and difficult to learn and use; and, while they may slightly improve a player's odds, they do not constitute a sure-fire scheme to quick riches. As you probably guessed, casino owners have responded to these schemes by tilting the odds back in their favor. Most Black Jack games now use several decks simultaneously, making it extremely difficult to count effectively.

Roulette

Roulette is often thought of as an aristocratic game. It is strange that it has gained this reputation, since it is a pure game of chance. Unlike most card games, there is no skillful way to play roulette. As you probably know, roulette is played by spinning a small ball inside a circular array of numbered and colored pockets. Eighteen of the pockets are red; eighteen are black; and two are green. Players can make a variety of bets. One possible bet is that the ball will land in a red pocket. What is the probability of this event? Since there are 18 red pockets out of 38 pocktes (possible outcomes), the probability of the ball landing in a red pocket is $^{18}/_{38}$. Since this is a number less than .5, we know that it will land in a red pocket slightly less than half of the time. Thus, if you kept betting on red pockets, you would lose slightly more often than you would win. Suppose now you bet on black pockets. Again, the probability would be $^{18}/_{38}$; and again, if you continue to bet on black pockets, you will lose more often than you win. Of course, sometimes you win, and at other times you will lose, but after many spins—in the long run, you will lose at roulette. The odds or probability of winning at any casino game are always favorable to the casinos, since this is how they make their money and stay in business.

Actually, there is one person who has been able to "beat" the roulette odds. One of my heros is Al Hibbs, a scientist at the Jet Propulsion Laboratory in Pasadena, California, where most of the work on the United States space program is done. When he was a student, he used his knowledge of probability to run his original stake of $125 up to $6,300 at the Pioneer Club in Reno. Here's how he did it: Hibbs knows that while every number in a roulette wheel should be equally likely to occur, all man-made devices have imperfections. These imperfections make some numbers more likely to occur than others. Hibbs and a friend recorded the results of 100,000 spins of a roulette wheel to find the numbers that occurred most often. Accordingly, they bet on these numbers. Unfortunately, none of us can duplicate his success, since the wheels are now taken apart and reassembled with different parts each day. Thus, while each wheel is still imperfect, the imperfections differ from day to day.

Computing Probabilities in Multiple Outcome Situations

Although it is relatively easy to understand that the probability of getting a head on one flip of a coin is ½, it is somewhat more difficult to know intuitively the probability of getting four heads in four flips of a coin. Let's figure it out.

On the first flip, only one of two possible outcomes can occur: a head (H) or tail (T). What can happen if a coin is flipped twice? There are four possible outcomes: a head on the first flip and a head on the second (HH); a head on the first flip and a tail on the second (HT); a tail on the first flip and a head on the second (TH); and a tail on the first flip and a tail on the second (TT). Since there are four possible outcomes and only one way to get two heads, the probability of this event is ¼.

A simple way to compute this probability is to represent all possible events with **tree diagrams.** On the first flip, either a H or T will land facing up. Let's depict this as follows:

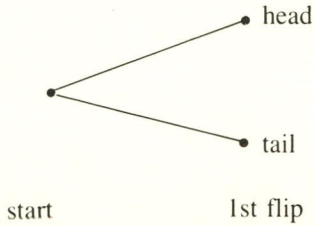

When you flip a second time, either a H on the first flip will be followed by a H or T, or a T on the first flip will be followed by a H or T. Outcomes from a second flip are added as "branches" on a tree diagram.

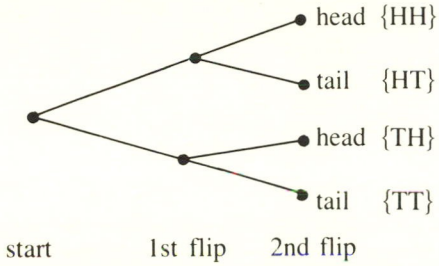

As you can see from this tree, there are four possible outcomes. You can use this tree to find out the probability of any other events. What is the probability of getting exactly one H in two flips of a coin? Since there are two ways for this to occur (HT) and (TH), the answer is ⅔, or ½.

Unfortunately, this method for calculating probabilities only works when the events (H or T) are equally likely. A more general way of computing probabilities is by multiplying the probabilities of each event. We can do this when the events are **independent.** Two events are independent when the occurrence of one of them does not influence the occurrence of the other. In this example, what you get on the first flip of a coin does not influence what you get on the second flip.

On the first flip of a coin, the probability of a head is equal to the probability of a tail, which is equal to

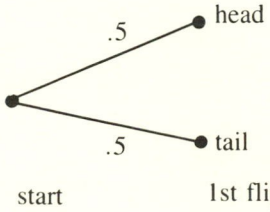

The probability of a head or tail on the second flip is still .5.

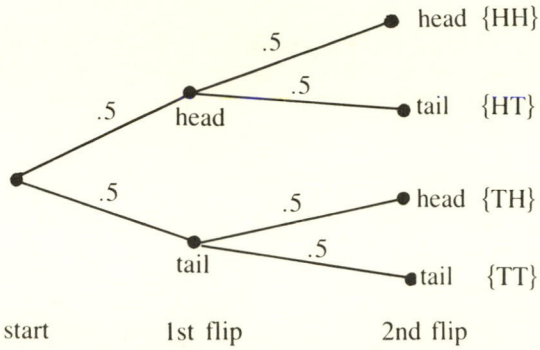

Thus, to find the probability of HH, you would multiply the values along the HH branch, .5 × .5 to get .25.

Tree diagrams are general ways of representing events that are useful in many situations. Let's extend this example. Suppose a man with a long handlebar moustache, shifty, beady eyes and a pinstripe suit stopped you on the street and asked you to bet on a coin flipping game. He always calls heads. On the first flip, the coin lands heads up. On the second flip, the coin lands head up. On the third flip, the coin lands heads up. When would you begin to suspect that he wasn't using a fair coin? Most people would get suspicious by the third or fourth flip. Calculate the probability of a fair coin (probability of heads = .5) landing heads up in three and four tosses.

To calculate the probability of three heads in three flips, you would draw a probability tree with three sets of "nodes" with two "branches" coming off each node.

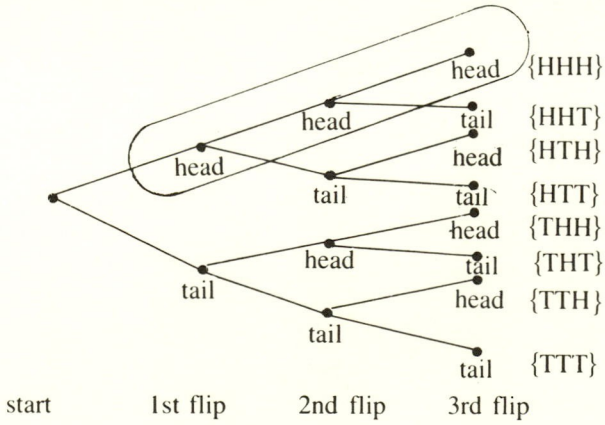

Since there is only one way to get 3 H's, multiply the probabilities along the HHH branch(circled above), which are .5 × .5 × .5 = .125. A probability of .125 means that if the coin is fair, it would, on the average, land heads up three times in a row 12.5% of the time. While this is unlikely to happen, most people would be willing to conclude that the coin is fair if it landed heads up three times in a row.

To calculate the probability of four heads in four flips, add another branch to the tree.

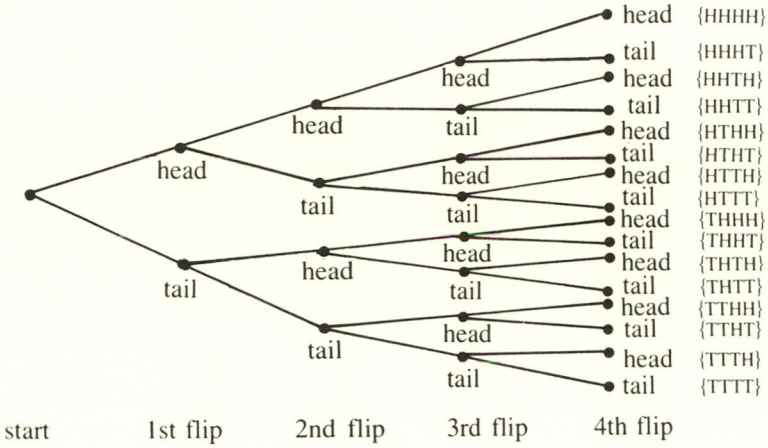

The probability of 4 H's is .5 × .5 × .5 × .5 = .0625; or about 6.25% of the time. As most of you already know, this is mathematically equal to $(.5)^4$, that is, multiplying a number by itself four times is the same as raising it to the fourth power. If you work this on a calculator with the ability to raise numbers to the fourth power, you'll get the same answer, 6.25%. While this is certainly a possible outcome, one that will sometimes occur, it is an unlikely outcome. In fact, it is so unlikely or unusual that most people would be willing to say that he is probably cheating by using a biased coin. For most scientific purposes, an event is considered "unusual" if it would be expected to occur by chance less than 5% of the time. (In probability jargon, this is less than .05.)

Let's get away from coin flipping, since this is an artificial example and use the same logic in a different context. I'm sure that every student has, at some time or other, taken a multiple-choice test. (Some students like to call them multiple-guess tests.) Most of these tests have five alternative answers for each question. Only one of these is correct. Suppose also that the questions are so difficult that all you can do is guess randomly at the correct answer. What is the probability of guessing correctly on the first question? If you have no idea which alternative is the correct answer, then you are equally likely to choose any of the five alternatives. Since the sum of all possible alternatives must be 1.0, the probablity of selecting each alternative is .20. One alternative is correct, and four are incorrect, so the probability of selecting the correct alternative is .20. A tree diagram of this situation is shown here.

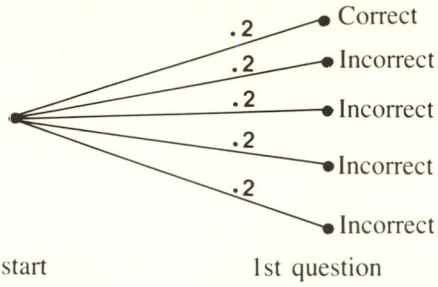

What is the probability of getting the first two multiple-choice questions correct by guessing? We'll have to add a second branch to a tree that will soon be very crowded:

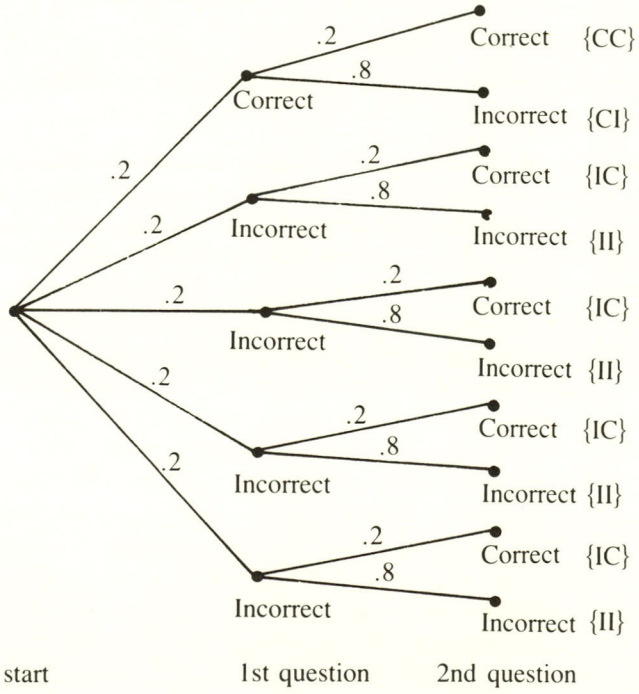

An alternative and much less tedious way to present the same information is:

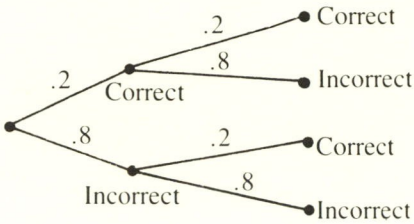

The probability of two correct questions by guessing is .2 × .2, which equals .04. That means that this would happen by chance only 4% of the time. Suppose we extend our example to three questions. I won't draw the tree, but you should be able to see by now that the probability is .2 × .2 × .2 = .008. This is so unusual that it would occur less than 1% of the time by chance. What would you conclude about someone who got all three of these questions correct? Most people (professors are people, too) would conclude that the student wasn't guessing, and that she really knew something. Of course, it is possible that the student was just lucky, but it is so unlikely that we would conclude that something other than luck was responsible for the outcome we obtained.

Let me point out a curious side to this kind of reasoning. Consider the plight of Sara. She took a fifteen question multiple-choice test in which every question had five alternatives. Sara got all fifteen questions wrong. Can you determine the probability of this happening by chance? I won't draw the tree diagram to depict this situation, but it is easy to see that the probability of being wrong on one question is .80; therefore the probability of being wrong on all 15 questions is $(.80)^{15}$. This is .80 times itself 15 times, which equals. .0352. Since this would happen by chance only 3.52% of the time, can Sara present the argument to her professor that something other than chance determined this unusual result? Of course, Sara can make this argument, but would you be willing to believe her if you were her professor? Suppose she argued that she must have known the correct answer to every question. How else could she have avoided selecting it in all fifteen consecutive questions? I don't know how many professors would buy her assertion that getting all 15 questions wrong demonstrates her knowledge, even though identical reasoning is used as proof of knowing correct answers when the probability of getting all the questions correct is about the same. (In this example, the probability of getting all 15 questions correct is $(.20)^{15}$, which is a number less than .0001.) Personally, if I were the professor, I'd give Sara high marks for creativity and for her understanding of statistical principles. I'd also point out to her that it is possible that she was both dumb *and* unlucky enough to guess wrong fifteen times.

Before going on to the next section, be sure that you understand how tree diagrams are used to compute probabilities and to consider all possible outcomes. I'll be returning to these diagrams later in this chapter. Once you learn how to use them, you'll be surprised at how many possible applications there are for tree diagrams.

EXPECTED VALUES

Place Your Bets

Which of the following bets would you take if you could only choose one of them?

1. The Big 12

It will cost you $1.00 to play. If you roll a pair of dice and get a 12, you'll win $24.00. If you roll any other number, you'll lose your $1.00.

2. Lucky 7

It will cost you $1.00 to play (same cost as above). If you roll a "lucky 7" with a pair of dice, you'll win $6.00. If you roll any other number, you'll lose your $1.00.

Stop now and select either 1 or 2.

Most people choose 1, reasoning that $24.00 if a 12 is rolled is four times more than they can win if a 7 is rolled, and the cost is the same for each bet. Let's see if this thinking is correct.

In order to decide which is the better bet, we need to consider the probability of winning and losing and the corresponding value of each. There is a formula that will take these variables into account and yield the **expected value** (EV) for each gamble. An expected value is the amount of money you would expect to win on each bet if you continued playing over and over. The formula for computing an expected value (EV) is:

$$\text{EV} = (\text{probability of a win}) \times (\text{value of a win}) + (\text{probability of a loss}) \times (\text{value of a loss})$$

Let's consider the EV for choice 1. We'll begin by computing the probability of rolling a 12 with one pair of dice. A tree diagram will help to determine the probability of this event. Begin by considering all possible outcomes on the first die. Because there are six sides to a cube and any one can land facing up, there are six possible outcomes. Each outcome is equally likely. One of these six outcomes *must* happen, so they must sum to 1.0. The probability of any one of them happening is $\frac{1}{6}$ (.167). What can happen with a second die? If you rolled a one on the first die, it would be followed by a 1, 2, 3, 4, 5 or 6 on the second die. This is true no matter what you rolled on the first die. A tree diagram of this is shown in Fig. 5.2.

As you can see in Fig. 5.2, there is only one way to roll a 12, and that is with a 6 on each die. The probability of this happening is $\frac{1}{6} \times \frac{1}{6} = \frac{1}{36} = .028$. Thus, we'd expect to roll a 12 about 2.8% of the time. What is the probability of *not* rolling a 12? Since we are certain that you will either roll a 12 or not roll a 12 (this covers all possible events), you can subtract .028 from 1.00. The proba-

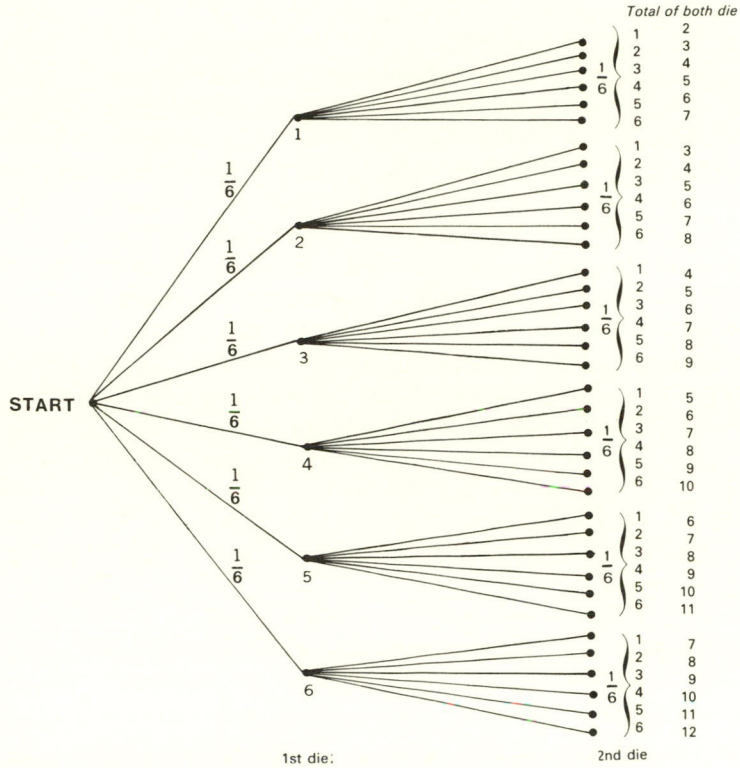

FIG. 5.2. A tree diagram depicting all possible outcomes from rolling a pair of dice.

bility of *not* rolling a 12 is .972. (You could also arrive at this figure, with some small rounding differences, by calculating the probability of each of the 35 other possible outcomes—each will be 1/36—and adding them together.) Using these probability values, the EV formula for choice #1 becomes:

$$\text{EV (Choice 1)} = (\text{Probability of a 12}) \times (\text{Value of a 12}) + (\text{Probability of } \textit{not} \text{ getting a 12}) \times (\text{Value of } \textit{not} \text{ getting a 12})$$

$$\text{EV (Choice 1)} = (.028 \times \$24.00) + [(.972) \times (-\$1.00)]$$

$$\text{EV (Choice 1)} = \$.672 - .972$$

$$\text{EV (Choice 1)} = -\$.30$$

Let's review what happened in this formula. If you rolled a 12, you'd win \$24.00, which is the value associated with this win. If you rolled any number other than a 12, you'd lose the \$1.00 you paid to play this game, thus −\$1.00 is the value associated with this loss. The probability of a win was multiplied by the value of a win. The probability of a loss was multiplied by the value of a loss. Then, these two products were added together. The EV of this bet is −$.30. This means that in the long run, if you continue playing this game many times, you could expect to *lose,* on the average, $.30 for every game played. Of course, on any single game, you'd either lose $1.00 or win $24.00, but after many, many games you would have lost an average of $.30 per game. If you played 1,000 games, making the same bet each time, you'd be $300.00 *poorer.*

How does this compare with Choice 2? To calculate the EV of Choice 2, we'll begin by computing the probability of rolling a 7. Refer back to Fig. 5.2. How many ways is it possible to roll a 7 with a pair of dice? You could get a 1 on the first die and a 6 on the second; or a 2 and a 5; a 3 and a 4; a 4 and a 3; a 5 and a 2; or a 6 and a 1. Thus, there are 6 possible ways to roll a 7 out of 36 possible outcomes. The probability of any one of these outcomes is $\frac{1}{6} \times \frac{1}{6}$, which equals $\frac{1}{36}$. Since there are six possible combinations, you would multiply $\frac{1}{36}$ by 6 (which is, of course, the same as adding it up 6 times). Thus, the probability of rolling a 7 with a pair of dice is $\frac{6}{36}$ ($\frac{1}{6}$ or .167). The probability of *not* rolling a 7 is 1 − .167, which equals .833. Now, we calculate the EV of Choice 2.

$$\text{EV (Choice 2)} = (\text{Probability of a 7}) \times (\text{Value of a 7}) + (\text{Probability of } \textit{not} \text{ getting a 7}) \times (\text{Value of } \textit{not} \text{ getting a 7})$$

$$\text{EV (Choice 2)} = (1.67) \times (\$6.00) + (.833) \times (-\$1.00)$$

$$= (\$1.002 - 8.33)$$

$$= \$.169, \text{ or approximately } \$.17$$

This means that if you continued to gamble on Choice 2, you would win an average of $.17 for every game played. Thus, after 1,000 games, you could expect to be $170.00 richer. Of course, as in Choice 1, you would never actually win this amount on any single game; this is what would result if you continued playing many, many games.

Choice 2 is the better choice because of the relatively high probability associated with rolling a 7. Seven has a high probability because there were six possible combinations that would add up to a 7.

There is a party game that is based on the principle that the more ways an event can occur, the more likely it is to occur. Suppose you get a random sample of 40 people together in a room. Estimate the probability that two of them share the same birthday. You may be surprised to learn that the probability is approximately .90. Can you figure out why it is so high? There are many, many ways that 40 people can share the same birthday. To figure out the exact probability, you would take all combinations of 40 people, two at a time, for each day of the year. Thus, we'd have to start with the combination of person 1 with person 2, then person 1 with person 3, and so on until person 1 is matched with person 40, then we'd begin again matching person 2 with person 3, 2 with 4, on until 2 is matched with 40. This whole process would have to be repeated until everyone of the 40 people is matched with every other one. This entire matching process would have to be repeated for each of the 365 days of the year. Since there are so many possible combinations of any 2 people sharing any birthday in the year, this "coincidence" is more probable than it may have seemed at first. The probability of two people sharing a common birthday is over .50, when there are 23 people and over .75 when there are 32 people (Loftus & Loftus, 1982). You can use this knowledge to make wagers at parties or at any gathering of people. It's a fairly good bet when the number of people is close to 40. Most people find it hard to believe that the probability is so high.

You can also use your knowledge of probability to improve your chances in other situations. Take, for example, Aaron and Jill, who have been arguing over who should take out the garbage. Their mother agrees to help them settle this matter by picking a number from 1 to 10. The one whose number comes closest to the one selected by their mother will win the dispute. Aaron goes first and picks "3". What number should Jill select to maximize her chances of winning? Stop now and decide what number she should select. The best number for Jill to pick is 4. If her mother was thinking of any number greater than 3, Jill would win with this strategy. Thus, she can change the probability of winning in what seems like a chance situation.

SUBJECTIVE PROBABILITY

We rarely deal directly with known or objective probabilities, such as the probability of rain on a given day or the probability of developing heart disease if oral contraceptives are taken. Yet, every day we make decisions using our best estimate of the likelihood of an event. **Subjective probability** refers to personal estimates of the likelihood of events. This term is in distinction from **objective probability,** which is a mathematically determined statement of likelihood about known frequencies.

Psychologists who have studied subjective probability have found that human judgments of probability are often fallible, yet we rely on them to guide our decisions in countless situations. Kahneman and Tversky (1972) have commented: "Subjective probabilities play an important role in our lives. The decisions we make, the conclusions we reach, and the explanations we offer are usually based on our judgments of the likelihood of uncertain events" (p. 430).

An Experimental Example

As a college statistics teacher, I can assert with some authority that without specific training in the laws of probability, people have naive beliefs about probability. To demonstrate this point, suppose that you could choose one of the following:

1. There are ten tickets in Box 1. One of them is the "winning ticket." You can close your eyes and pick one ticket from this box.

2. There are one hundred tickets in Box 2. One of them is the "winning ticket." You can close your eyes and pick a total of ten tickets, one at a time, returning each ticket to Box 2 before making the next selection. (Returning the tickets after each selection is called *replacement.*)

Did you make your choice? Cohen (1973) found that $\frac{4}{5}$ of the subjects who were asked to make this choice preferred taking the single draw from a box of 10 tickets. In fact, the probability of drawing the winning ticket is exactly the same in these two choices. The probability of a success is $\frac{1}{10}$ for Box 1 and $\frac{10}{100}$, which equals $\frac{1}{10}$, for Box 2. Overwhelmingly, people report that Box 1 seems like a better deal. Consider now a third choice:

3. There are ten separate boxes with 100 tickets in each. You may draw ten tickets from each of these boxes. Does this seem more likely to yield the winning ticket than the previous two choices?

Overwhelmingly, the subjects in Cohen's experiment preferred this situation to the earlier ones. Let's calculate the objective probability of drawing a winning ticket. As always, the probability of an event is equal to the number of ways a success can occur divided by the total number of possible outcomes. How many ways can a success occur? Since you would be selecting ten tickets from ten boxes, there are 100 ways a success can occur. Since there are ten boxes with 100 tickets in each, there are 1,000 possible outcomes. Thus, the probability of drawing the winning ticket is 100/1,000, which is equal to $\frac{1}{10}$, the identical objective probability for Choices 1 and 2. It seems clear that most people are poor at assessing probabilities. Furthermore, they are wrong in consistent ways. While terms like "probably" and "likely" are part of our everyday speech, few people can make accurate or even "ball-park" quantitative estimates of likelihood of the event they're discussing.

Gambler's Fallacy

The "Wheel of Fortune" is a popular game at fairs and amusement parks, and on television game shows. It consists of a large wheel which can be spun. The wheel is divided into many numbered sections, much like a roulette wheel. A rubber marker indicates the winning number.

Suppose that your friend, Gloria, decides to approach the Wheel of Fortune in a scientific manner. She sits at the Wheel of Fortune and records when each number comes up as the winning number. Suppose Gloria has recorded the following series of winning numbers: 3, 6, 10, 19, 18, 4, 1, 7, 7, 5, 20, 17, 2, 14, 19, 13, 8, 11, 13, 16, 12, 15, 19, 3, 8. After examining these numbers very carefully, she proclaims that a 9 has not appeared in the last 25 spins; therefore, she plans to bet heavily on number 9, since it is now much more likely to occur. Would you agree with her that this is a good bet?

If you responded, "Yes," you have committed a very common error in understanding probability. The Wheel of Fortune has no memory for which numbers have previously appeared. If the wheel had been built so that each number is equally likely to win, then it is equally likely on each spin, regardless of how frequently or infrequently it appeared in the past. People believe that chance processes like spinning a Wheel of Fortune should be self-correcting so that if an event has not occurred in a while it is now more likely to occur. This misconception is called **Gambler's Fallacy.**

Often, people will continue to believe in Gambler's Fallacy even after it has been explained to them. Students have told me that while they can understand on an intellectual level why Gambler's Fallacy must be wrong, on an intuitive or "gut" level, it seems that it ought to be right. Let's try another example.

Wayne and Marsha have four sons. While they really don't want to have five children, both have always wanted a daughter. Should they plan to have another child, since they are now more likely to have a daughter, given that their first four children were boys? If you understand Gambler's Fallacy, you'll recognize that a daughter is as likely as a son on the fifth try, just as it was on each of the first four. (Actually, since slightly more boys than girls are born, the probability of having a boy baby is slightly higher than the probability of having a girl baby.)

Frequency and Relative Frequency

Consider the following:

> Citing high housing costs, unemployment, and divorce among newlyweds, recent reports in the *New York Times* and *U.S. News and World Report* have proclaimed that more and more young adults are finding it necessary to live with their parents. Indeed, as the *Times* correctly reported, the number of people over 25 still living with their parents has jumped by 25 percent since 1970, to 4.3 million (Camer, 1983, p. 73).

Think carefully about this paragraph for a few minutes. Is there something wrong with the information it conveys? Obviously, there must be or I wouldn't have raised the question. Assuming that the numbers cited are correct, and there are more young adults living with Mom and Dad than there were in 1970, these figures neglect the fact that there are more young adults now than there were in 1970. According to Camer (1983, p. 73), "Since 1970, the proportion of young adults who haven't left the nest has only increased by 1 percent."

The figures cited in those prestigious news publications have failed to distinguish between frequency and **relative frequency.** Because there are more young adults now than in 1970, we could expect more of them to be doing almost anything, but if we want to talk about changing mores or patterns of behavior, relative frequencies are needed. Frequencies are obtained by counting the number of people that are doing what we're interested in. If you were in the housing business, this would be important to you, since you would know that more large houses are needed for the increased number of extended families. If, however, you are interested in social change, then you would want to compare the relative frequencies or number of people doing what you're interested in relative to (or divided by) the total number of people available. This formula should sound familiar to you, since it is the same one that was used to calculate probabilities. Relative frequencies are used to make probability statements. Thus, if you found that the relative frequency (or percent if you multiply this number by 100) hasn't changed since 1970, you would conclude that there have been no real societal changes with respect to the variable that you're studying. People frequently make erroneous judgments based on frequency data instead of relative frequency data (Estes, 1976). Here is an example of some of the research used to support this statement:

In a recent Miss America pageant, Miss California's name appeared in 20 polls in which spectators were asked to select the most likely winner. She won 11 of these polls. Miss New York's name appeared in 8 different polls. She won 5 of them. The event went down to the wire, with a final run-off between these West and East beauties. Given the information presented above, which one is more likely to win the key to Atlantic City?

Most people will predict that Miss California will win because she won 11 polls, while Miss New York only won 5. The frequency, or number of polls won, is the wrong comparison value, since they appeared in a different number of polls. What is needed is the relative frequency for each contestant.

$$\text{Relative frequency for Miss California} = \frac{\text{11 polls won}}{\text{20 polls entered}} = .55$$

$$\text{Relative frequency for Miss New York} = \frac{\text{5 polls won}}{\text{8 polls entered}} = .625$$

Thus, Miss New York is a better bet for those who wager on the outcomes of beauty pageants, since she won a greater proportion, or relative frequency, of the prepageant polls.

The confusion of frequency with relative frequency is a ubiquitous error. It is easier to spot in some contexts than in others. For example, this is an absolutely true statement: More people die in automobile accidents today than in 1928. Would you use this fact to conclude that the automobiles made today are not as safe as their 1928 counterparts? Most people would laugh at this statement, and realize there are many more drivers and automobiles today than there were in 1928. If, however, you read that there are 10.3 million people unemployed today compared to 7.6 million in 1970, would you realize that these numbers are not comparable, since there have been dramatic changes in the number of people between 20 and 65 in the intervening years? Whenever you are given data like this, decide whether the frequency or relative frequency is needed and then be sure that you are considering the correct one.

Frequency Judgments

The notion of frequency, or how often an event occurs, is inherent in the definition of probability. If an event is frequent, then its occurrence is highly probable. How do people determine the frequency of real-life events? Several researchers (Lichtenstein, Slovic, Fischoff, Layman, & Combs, 1978) have focused on the way people judge the frequency of lethal (deadly) events. They studied this by asking college students and members of the League of Women Voters to decide which of two possible causes of death is more probable for several pairs of lethal events. In order to understand their experiment and their results, let's try a few examples. For the following pairs of items, indicate which is the more likely cause of death, and then estimate how much more likely your choice is than the other event:

A.	asthma	or	tornado
B.	excess cold	or	syphilis
C.	diabetes	or	suicide
D.	heart disease	or	lung cancer
E.	flood	or	homicide
F.	syphilis	or	diabetes
G.	asthma	or	botulism
H.	poisoning by vitamins	or	lightning
I.	tuberculosis	or	homicide
J.	all accidents	or	stomach cancer

Researchers found that while, in general, people were more accurate as the differences in the true frequencies of occurrence between the events increased, they made a large number of errors in estimating the relative frequencies for the events. Their subjects overestimated the frequencies of events that occurred very rarely and underestimated the frequencies of those events that occurred very often. In addition, lethal events that had received a great deal of publicity (e.g., airplane crashes, flood, homicide, tornado, botulism) were overestimated, while those that were undramatic, silent killers (e.g., diabetes, stroke, asthma, tuberculosis) were underestimated. It seems that these events were more easily brought to mind and this biased judgments of their frequency. People's subjective or intuitive judgments of frequency are biased in very systematic ways. The authors conclude with a note of caution:

> . . . our society must often make judgments about hazardous activities for which adequate statistical data is lacking, such as recombinant DNA research or nuclear waste disposal. We suspect that the biases found here (overestimation of rare events, underestimation of likely events, and an undue influence of drama or vividness) may be operating, indeed, may even be amplified in such situations (Lichtenstein, Slovic, Fischhoff, Layman, and Combs, 1978, p. 577).

Answers to the questions about the probability of lethal events follow along with the true frequency of each event (rate per 1,000,000,000).

	More Likely	*Rate*	*Less Likely*	*Rate*
A.	Asthma	920	Tornado	44
B.	Syphilis	200	Excess Cold	163
C.	Diabetes	19,000	Suicide	12,000
D.	Heart Disease	360,000	Lung Cancer	37,000
E.	Homicide	9,200	Flood	100
F.	Diabetes	19,000	Syphilis	200
G.	Asthma	920	Botulism	1
H.	Lightning	52	Poisoning/Vitamins	.5
I.	Homicide	9,200	Tuberculosis	1,800
J.	All Accidents	55,000	Stomach Cancer	46,600

Base-Rate Biases

José has always wanted to be an actor. Accordingly, he plans to sell his worldly possessions and head for a career in the "Big Apple" (the loving nickname for New York). Suppose that you and José both know that only about 5% of all actors ever "make it" professionally in New York. José tells you not to worry, since 90% of those who *are* successful are tall and can sing and tell jokes well. Because he is tall, a good singer, and an hilarious comedian, he feels confident that he will soon be sending 8×10 glossy pictures of himself to his fan club members. Is José's optimism warranted? Exactly how likely is he to succeed? Before you continue, make a probability estimate for his chance of success. Remember, probabilities range from 0 to 1, with 0 meaning he will definitely fail and have to return home to Peoria, and 1 meaning he will definitely succeed on Broadway. Stop now and make a subjective probability judgment of his chance for success.

Can you think of a way of *objectively* finding his chance of success? In order to arrive at an objective probability, you'll need to know the percentage of those who *fail* and are tall, can sing, and tell jokes. Few people realize that they need to consider this value in assessing the probability of success. Suppose that 75% of those who fail have these attributes. The tree diagrams that were used earlier in this chapter can be used again to determine probabilities in this context. Let's begin at a start point and consider all possible outcomes. In this case, he will either succeed or fail, so we'll label the first branches "succeed" and "fail." As before, we'll put the probability of each event along the appropriate branch:

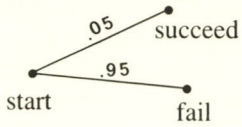

Notice that these two probabilities (.05 and .95) sum to 1.0, since they include all possibilities. One of these two possibilities *must* occur, so they will add up to 1.0 to indicate absolute certainty.

José knows that 90% of those who succeed are tall and can sing and joke. Let's add a second branch to the tree diagram, branching off from the succeed node, labeling the second branch tall/sing/tell jokes and *not* tall/sing/tell jokes.

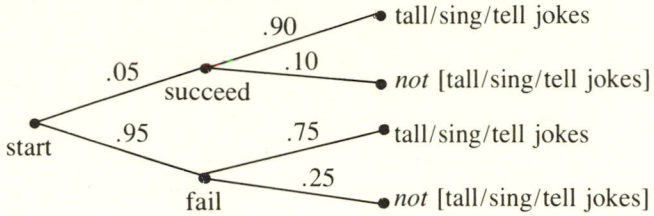

Note that since 90% (.90) of those who succeed are tall and can sing and tell jokes, 10% (.10) do not have these attributes, as the sum of all probabilities from a tree node must sum to 1.0.

Once the tree diagram is drawn, it is a simple matter to compute José's objective probability of success. As before, multiply along the branch you're interested in. In this case, we would multiply the values along each branch of the tree diagram:

Succeed/Tall/Sing/Tell Jokes	= .05 × .90 =	.045
Succeed/*Not* Tall/Sing/Tell Jokes	= .05 × .10 =	.005
Fail/Tall/Sing/Tell Jokes	= .95 × .75 =	.7125
Fail/*Not* Tall/Sing/Tell Jokes	= .95 × .25 =	.2375
		1.0000

To determine José's true chance of success, we need to divide the proportion who succeed and possess the attributes we're interested in by the total proportion who have these attributes.

$$\frac{\text{Proportion who Succeed/Tall/Sing/Tell Jokes}}{\text{Total Proportion who are Tall/Sing/Tell Jokes}} = \frac{.045}{.045 + .7125}$$

.045/.7575 = .059, or approximately .06, or 6%

Thus, José's chances for success are only slightly better (6% versus 5%) than they are for any unknown, aspiring actor.

Are you surprised to find that his chance of success is so low? Most people are. The reason that José has such a slim chance of becoming an actor is because so few people, in general, succeed. The probability value José obtained was close to the a priori, or **base rate,** of success among all aspiring actors. Since it was so low, José, and any other would-be Thespian, has a low chance for success. Research has shown that, in general, most people overestimate low base-rate probabilities and underestimate high ones.

Let's consider another and somewhat different example: Charlie is anxious to experience his first kiss. If he asks Louise to go to the movies with him, he's only 10% sure that she'll accept his invitation, but if she does, he's 95% sure that she'll kiss him goodnight. What are Charlie's chances for romance?

This problem differs from the last one in that we are now trying to determine the probability of two or more uncertain events. In the earlier problem, we wanted to *predict* one variable (success) from our knowledge of the other (tall/sing/tells jokes). This example is somewhat easier to work out since it has fewer steps. We'll start with a tree diagram that first branches into Louise accepts his date and Louise declines. A second branch will be drawn from the Louise accepts his date node indicating whether he gets kissed or not. Each branch should have the appropriate probability labels. Of course, if Louise declines his invitation, Charlie definitely won't get kissed. The branch from the "Louise declines" node is thus labeled 1.00 for "Charlie doesn't get kissed."

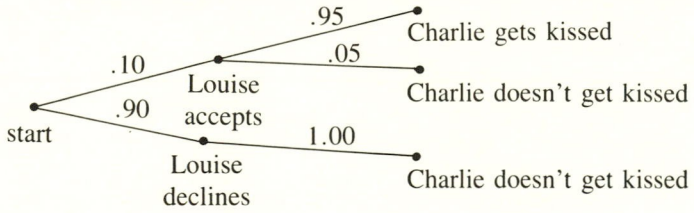

The probability that Louise will kiss Charlie goodnight is:

$$.10 \times .95 = .095$$

As in the previous example, the objective probability is closer to the low base rate of 10% than to the much higher secondary or subsequent rate of 95%.

Let's briefly try a third example. Suppose that 1% of all children become juvenile delinquents. Two sociologists have developed a test that can predict who will become a juvenile delinquent. It correctly predicts delinquency for 80% of all delinquents. Unfortunately, your daughter has been identified by her score on this test as a future juvenile delinquent. What is the probability that this prediction is correct? Since we are interested in predicting one variable (delinquency) with our knowledge of a second variable (test score), this problem is similar to José's problem presented earlier. As before, you'll need to know the probability that the test will incorrectly predict delinquency. Let's say that it is 10%.

Please stop now and work this problem before going on.

Your answer should look like this:

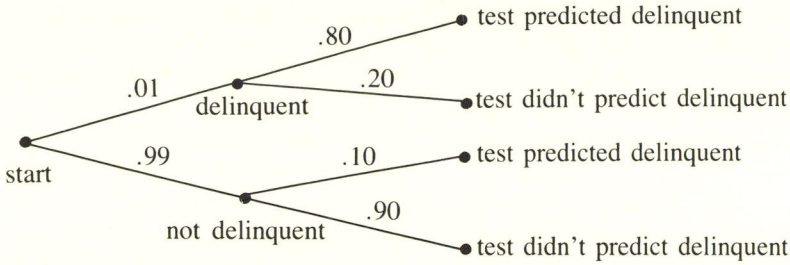

We'll need to compute the probabilities in each branch:

delinquent/test predicted delinquent	= .01 × .80 =	.008
delinquent/test doesn't predict delinquent	= .01 × .20 =	.002
not delinquent/test predicted delinquent	= .99 × .10 =	.099
not delinquent/test doesn't predict delinquent	= .99 × .90 =	.891
		1.000

As before, we'll need to form the appropriate ratio:

$$\frac{\text{proportion delinquent/test predicted delinquent}}{\text{total proportion test predicted delinquent}} = \frac{.008}{.008 + .099}$$

$$= .008/.107 = .07$$

That is, this test will correctly predict future delinquents about 7% of the time. Because of the low base rate for juvenile delinquency, a test like this one is of little value.

There are many diseases that occur with low base rates in the population. Medical test results must be interpreted in light of the relevant base rates for each disease. Medicine, like most other disciplines, is a probabilistic science, yet few physicians receive training in understanding probabilities. Failure to utilize base-rate information can lead to improper diagnoses. Doherty, Mynatt, Tweney, and Schiavo (1981) use the term "pseudodiagnosticity" to describe the way naive subjects (introductory psychology students) go about making diagnoses. Sixty out of 66 subjects in their experiment ignored base-rate information. They conclude that, "The tendency to ignore base rates is truly a robust phenomenon" (p. 167).

Posteriori Probabilities

Posteriori probabilities refer to probabilities that are based on previous occurrences. We use posteriori probabilities when we know something has happened and we need to determine its most likely cause.

It is possible to calculate posteriori probabilities using a somewhat intimidating-looking formula called **Bayes' Theorem.** If you find that mathematical formulas frighten you, you may want to take a few deep breaths before you go on. Working with Bayes Theorem is like anything else—it's easy once you know how to do it. Let's start with an example:

There are two warring street gangs who have been covering their neighborhood with ugly graffitti. The Dumbos are a mean group with 100 members, half of them female, half of them male. Their arch rivals, the Cows, have 200 members, 70% of them female. The police have captured a gang member who was defacing a building with graffitti. He refuses to tell them which gang he is from. Make your best estimate of his gang membership. This problem requires a posteriori probability analysis, since an event, namely the capture of a male gang member, has already occurred. We'll use Bayes Theorem to compare the probability that he's a Dumbo or a Cow.

Let's summarize the information we have so far:

Gang	*Number of Members*	*Proportion of Males*
Dumbos	100	.50
Cows	200	.30
	300 gang members	

What is the probability that the captured gang member is a Dumbo, given that we know he is a male?

$$P(\text{Dumbo/Male}) = \frac{P(\text{Dumbo}) \times P(\text{Male/Dumbo})}{P(\text{Dumbo}) \times P(\text{Male/Dumbo}) + P(\text{Cow}) \times P(\text{Male/Cow})}$$

In English, this reads, "The probability that he is a Dumbo, given that we know he is a male, is equal to the probability that he is a Dumbo times the probability that he is a male, given that we know that he is a Dumbo, divided by the same terms as in the numerator plus the probability that he is a Cow times the probability that he is a male, given that we know that he is a Cow."

The value for each of the terms in the equation can be found as follows:

P(Dumbo) = $^{100}/_{300}$ = ⅓ = .333, since ⅓ of the gang members are Dumbos (as usual, we take the number of ways a Dumbo can occur divided by the total number of possible outcomes).

P(Male/Dumbo) = .5 (read "the probability that he is a male, given that he is a Dumbo")

P(Cow) = 200/300 = 2/3 = .667

P(Male/Cow) = .30 (read "the probability that he is a male given that he is a Cow")

What we want to know is the probability that he is a Dumbo, given that we already know that he is a male. Using Bayes Theorem, we find that:

$$P(\text{Dumbo/Male}) = \frac{(.333)(.50)}{(.333)(.50) + (.667)(.30)}$$

$$= \frac{.167}{.167 + .200}$$

$$= \frac{.167}{.367}$$

$$= .455$$

Let's compare this figure to the probability that he is a Cow. This time, Bayes Theorem is:

$$P(\text{Cow/Male}) = \frac{P(\text{Cow}) \times P(\text{Male/Cow})}{P(\text{Dumbo}) \times P(\text{Male/Dumbo}) + P(\text{Cow}) \times P(\text{Male/Cow})}$$

Note that the denominator hasn't changed.

$$P(\text{Cow/Male}) = \frac{(.667)(.30)}{(.333)(.50) + (.667)(.30)}$$

$$= \frac{.200}{.367}$$

$$= .545$$

As you can see by comparing these two figures, it is more likely that he is a Cow than it is that he is a Dumbo.

The general notation for Bayes Theorem is:

$$P(E/A) = \frac{P(A) \times P(A/E)}{P(A) \times (A/E) + P(B) \times P(B/E)}$$

In English, this reads, "the probability of E, the event we're interested in, given that we know that A has occurred, is equal to the probability of A times the probability of A, given that we know E, divided by the numerator, plus the probability of the alternative, B, times the probability of B, given that we know E."

Subjective Probability Estimates and Bayes Theorem

How do people arrive at their own subjective probability estimate to decide if the gang member is a Dumbo or Cow?

Few people work through Bayes formula to make decisions, yet we make decisions of this sort quite often. Psychologists have studied whether people use the logic of Bayes formula on an intuitive level to adjust their probability estimates based on all of the information. In other words, are our subjective estimates of probability in accord with the objective ones predicted by Bayes formula?

In general, people do take into account the nature of the event that occurred (in the present example, the fact that the captured gang member was male) and will lower or raise their probability estimates when they should be lowered or raised, given the information about the event. However, there is a tendency to be too *conservative* in the amount they lower or raise their estimates. They don't change the probability estimates enough. Thus, if the probability of being a Dumbo is .333 and the probability that the gang member is a Dumbo, given that we know he is a male is .455, individuals should *raise* their estimate of likelihood of catching a Dumbo once they know that he is male. In general, people will increase their subjective probability estimates by saying that the new probability is greater than .333, but they won't increase it enough to get close to the .455 figure. Thus, people use posteriori information imperfectly and far too conservatively.

Astute readers will realize that the tendency to underutilize base rates and conservatism in the use of posteriori probabilities are related topics. For example, suppose that males comprised only 5% of the Cow's membership. Given this low base rate, do you think that most people would now predict that the captured gang member (a male) is a Dumbo? In fact, in examples like this one, most people do utilize base-rate information. However, subjective estimates of the probability that he is a Dumbo are considerably less than the ones that objectively determined by Bayes Theorem (see, for example, Manis, Dovalina, Avis, & Cardoze, 1980).

What can we conclude from this discussion? When people make subjective probability judgments, their judgments do reflect the available information about base rates and posteriori probabilities; however, their judgments fall short of the probability values determined with objective techniques such as Bayes Theorem.

Two social psychologists (McCauley & Jacques, 1979) have used Bayes Theorem to explain why conspiracy theories of presidential assassinations are so popular. Tom Bethell, a journalist for *The Atlantic Monthly* wrote that people believe that conspiracies were responsible for the killing of a president because "a lone assassin is too small and insignificant a cause to provide a satisfactory explanation for such large effects on policy and people as follows a president's death" (McCauley & Jacques, 1979, p. 638). In McCauley and Jacques' study, subjects were presented with questionnaires asking them to imagine one of the following news headlines: "Man Shoots, Kills President" or "Man Shoots at President, Misses." Subjects had to decide whether it is more likely that the man acted alone or was part of an organized group in each of these cases. Thus, in the jargon of Bayes Theorem, given that the event had occurred, did the man come from a group or did he act alone? McCauley and Jacques found that people were more likely to believe that a successful assassination was the result of a group conspiracy than the work of a lone gunman. People believe that conspiracies are more efficient and effective; therefore, they are more likely to be successful than an individual working alone.

Nonregressive Judgments

Harris is a new student at Rah-Rah State University. The average grade point average (GPA) for all students at Rah-Rah is 2.8. Harris is new to this college and has not yet taken any exams. Although we have no information about Harris specifically, what would be your best guess that his grade point average will be?

After his first set of midterm exams, Harris has a midterm GPA of 3.8. Given this new information, what would you now predict for Harris' GPA at the end of the school year? Most people readily answer the first question with 2.8, the average GPA for all students at Rah-Rah. This is a correct answer, as in the absence of any specific information, the average for all students, the population at Rah-Rah, is the best estimate for anyone.

Most people answer the second question with 3.80. Unfortunately, this is not the best answer. Although it is true that someone who scores high on midterms will also tend to score high on finals, the relationship is not a one-to-one or perfect relationship. In general, when someone scores extremely high on some scale, she or he will score closer to the average the second time. Thus, the best prediction for Harris' GPA at the end of the school year will be less than 3.8 and greater than 2.8. (The actual value can be mathematically determined, but the calculations are beyond the scope of this book.) This is a difficult concept to understand, because most people find it to be counterintuitive. Yet, it is true.

It may be useful to think about a sports example. Consider your favorite athletes. Although they may have a truly exceptional performance one day, most often they will perform closer to average, but still above average on other days. After all, no one bowls all perfect games or bats 1,000. Sports enthusiasts will recognize this principle as the "sophomore slump." Another example that may help to clarify the concept is an often used one about fathers' and sons' heights. In general, very tall fathers will have sons that are closer to average height (although still above average) than the fathers are. This phenomenon is called **regression toward the mean.** Mean is just another term for average—it is computed by adding up all the values you're interested in and dividing by the number of values. This is probably a concept that you learned about in the 7th grade.

Kahneman and Tversky (1973) studied what can happen when regression toward the mean is not understood by professionals. Israeli flight instructors were told that they should praise their students when they successfully performed difficult flight patterns and maneuvers and that they should criticize exceptionally poor performance. Based on what you've just learned about regression toward the mean, what, in general, should happen after a pilot performs extremely well? Subsequent maneuvers should be closer to average, or less than exceptional, since the performance moved or regressed toward the mean (average). Conservely, what should you expect to happen following very poor performance? Again, subsequent maneuvers should tend to be more average, or in this case, they would improve, although they may still be less than average. The Israeli flight instructors did not understand regression toward the mean and erroneously concluded that praise led to poorer performance and criticism improved it.

Desirability of Outcome

Suppose that you are waiting to find out if you've been accepted to law school. Do you think that the fact that you really want to be the next Perry Mason will influence how you assess your probability of acceptance?

For most people, the desirability of an outcome will influence its judged probability. In general, the true probability of an event will be overestimated if it is desirable and underestimated if it is undesirable. In experimental demonstrations of this effect, Morlock (1967) found that subjects required less information to decide that evidence was favorable to them than to decide that it was unfavorable. Halpern and Irwin (1973) found that college students would begin a problem-solving task by testing hypotheses that, if true, would earn them financial payoffs instead of testing alternative hypotheses that, if true, would cost them money. Furthermore, they would return to positive hypotheses even when they were given information that clearly showed that they were wrong. Nisbett and Ross (1980) have called the belief that the desired outcome is correct even after receiving evidence to the contrary the **perseverance phenomenon.** People tend to persevere in their optimistic prediction that events that are favorable to them are more likely to occur than unfavorable ones.

The implications that can be drawn from the perseverance phenomenon are clear. People tend to persevere in their belief that a preferred outcome is more likely to be true than a nonpreferred outcome. Evidence of this effect can be found in the thinking of some of our most respected scientists. In a large-scale study of NASA scientists, Mitroff (1974) found that many research scientists continued to believe that their hypotheses about outer space were correct, despite accumulating evidence that supported a rival hypothesis.

STATISTICAL ABUSE

There are three kinds of lies: lies, damned lies, and statistics.

—Disraeli

When we want to find out something about a group of people, it is often impossible or inconvenient to ask everyone in the group. The entire group of people we are interested in is called a **population.** Suppose you want to know if people who donate blood to the Red Cross are, in general, kind and generous people. Because you can't ask everyone who donates how kind and considerate she or he is, you would question a subset of the population, which is called a **sample.** A number calculated on a sample of people is called a **statistic.** ("Statistics" is also the branch of mathematics that utilizes probability theory to make decisions about populations.)

Statistics are found everywhere, from baseball earned run averages to the number of war casulaties. Many people are rightfully suspicious of statistics. A small book by Huff (1954) humorously illustrates many of the possible pitfalls of statistics. The book is entitled *How to Lie With Statistics.* In it, he rhymes the following message: "Like the 'little dash of powder, little pot of paint,' statistics are making many an important fact 'look like what she ain't" (p. 9).

On the Average

What does it mean to say that the average American family has 2.1 children? This number was computed by finding a sample of American families, adding up the number of children they have and dividing by the total number of families in the sample. This number could provide an accurate picture of American families, as most may have about two children, with some having more and others less, or it could be very misleading. It is possible that half of the families had no children and half had four or more children, thus misleading the reader into believing that most families had "about" two children, when in fact none did. This is like the man who had his head in the oven and feet in the freezer and reports that, on the average, he's quite comfortable. It is also possible that the sample used to calculate this statistic was not representative of the population—in this case, all American families. If the sample consisted of college students or residents in Manhattan, the number obtained would be too low. On the other hand, if the sample was taken in rural farm areas, the number obtained may be too high. When samples are not representative of the population, they are called **biased samples.** The statistics calculated on biased samples will not yield accurate information about the population.

Averages can also be misleading, since there are three different kinds of averages. Consider Mrs. Wang's five children. The oldest is a successful corporate executive. She earns $200,000. a year. The second is a schoolteacher who earns $25,000. a year. Child 3 is a waiter who earns $15,000. a year. The other two are starving artists, each earning $5,000. a year. If Mrs. Wang wants to brag about how well her children turned out, she could compute an arithmetic average, which is called the **mean.** The mean is what most people have in mind when they think about averages. It is the sum of all of the values divided by the total number of values. (Can you understand why statistics teachers are sometimes called mean teachers?) The mean income for Mrs. Wang's children is $250,000/5 = $50,000. Certainly, anyone who is told this figure would conclude that Mrs. Wang has very successful and wealthy children.

The reason that the mean income for Mrs. Wang's children was so high is because there is one extreme score that inflated this type of average. Averages are also called **measures of central tendency.** A second kind of measure of central tendency is the **median.** It is not affected by a few extreme scores. To compute the median, the values are lined up in ascending or descending order. The middle value is the median. For Mrs. Wang's children, this would be:

$5,000; $5,000; $15,000; $25,000; $200,000.

The middle value, or median, is the third value of $15,000. Thus, she could also claim that her children earn, on the average, $15,000. (When there is an even number of values, the median is equal to the mean of the middle two values.)

A third type of average, or measure of central tendency, is the **mode.** The word "mode" comes from the French meaning fashionable. It is really the most fashionable value. Mathematically, it is the number that occurs most often. Since two of Mrs. Wang's children earn $5,000, this is the modal income for her children. When there are no values that occur more than once, there is no mode. There also may be two or more modes.

Mrs. Wang can honestly claim that her children earn, on the average, $50,000 or $15,000 or $5,000. The point of this discussion is that you should be wary of average figures. To understand them, you need to know whether the average is a *mean, median* or a *mode*. Mrs. Wang could argue that her children are very rich or very poor, depending on which measure she uses. If you understand the distinction among these terms, you won't be fooled.

Precision

Suppose I tell you that a scientific survey was conducted on the length of workdays for office workers. Furthermore, this study found that the mean work day is 8.167 hours long. Does this sound impressive and scientific? What if I told you that most office workers work about 8 hours a day? Most of you would say,

© 1965 United Features Syndicate, Inc.

"I know that. Why did they bother?" The point is that we are often impressed with precise statistics, even when the precision is unwarranted.

Let me give you an example from a prestigious weekly news magazine. It is important that the magazine readers accept the articles as truthful and authoritative. About a year ago, a news magazine ran an article about the health hazards associated with dog droppings in New York City. To give the reader an idea of the magnitude of the problem, they presented the daily weight of New York City dog droppings, accurate to two decimal places. I have no idea how they arrived at that figure, nor do I even want to think about how they collected their data. I do know that they could not measure it that accurately. Of course, the impression that is presented with such precise statistics is that the news magazine is a carefully researched journal that can be trusted for the information it provides.

A more humorous example of overprecision comes from one of America's most famous authors, Mark Twain. He once reported that the Mississippi River was 100 million and 3 years old. It seems that 3 years earlier, he learned that it was 100 million years old.

Significant Differences

If you wanted to know the mean height of all women, you could select a sample of one hundred women, measure their height and compute the mean. Suppose you took another sample of one hundred women and computed their mean height. Would you expect the mean of these two samples to be exactly the same? No, of course not, since there could be expected to be small differences or fluctuations between these values. Each value was computed on different women, and each will yield a slightly different mean value.

If someone measured women who belong to sororities and found that their mean height is 5′5″ and then measured women who don't belong to sororities and found their mean height to be 5′4½″, would you conclude that sorority sisters are taller than nonsorority women? I hope not, because small differences between groups can be expected to occur just by chance, especially when the **sample size,** or number of people in the sample, is small.

If your college enrollment went from 15,862 to 15,879, would the administrators be justified in concluding that enrollment has increased? The answer to this question depends on many other variables. If the enrollment figure has been edging up slowly every year for the last 5 years, then these figures may represent a slight, but steady, trend. On the other hand, the relatively small increase could be due to chance fluctuations and may not represent a significant increase. Because of chance factors, it could just have easily gone down. Similarly, a change in the unemployment rate from 10% to 9.9% may be nothing more than random fluctuation, or it may be signaling the end of an economic quagmire, although you can be sure that at least some politicians will see it as a harbinger of a major economic recovery. You can expect that Democrats and Republicans will interpret these figures differently. There are statistical procedures to determine if a difference is likely to have happened by chance. If it is very unlikely to be a chance occurrence, it is called a **significant difference.**

Extrapolation

Extrapolation occurs when a value is estimated by extending some known values. For example, if we know the number of robberies committed in a community in January and March, we could extrapolate to find the number of robberies committed in February by taking the number midway between the January and March values. Similarly, we can extrapolate beyond the date we have to estimate future values. If the number of psychology majors over the last 5 years at Podunck University was approximately 150, 175, 200, 225, and 250, respectively, then most people would feel comfortable about the prediction that the number of psychology majors next year will be approximately 275.

Extrapolation can be wrong, and sometimes even ridiculous. An example of the latter was provided by Fischer (1970). The Census Bureau estimated that the size of the average American family increased from 3.54 to 3.65 in the decade between 1950 and 1960. If we assume that family sizes will continue to increase at the same rate, then we would find that the average American family in the year 2070 would have 228.52 persons. This is, of course, an inconceivable idea!

One journal that is dedicated to mocking scientific and statistical fallacies is the *Worm Runners Digest.* Have you ever wondered about the number of people who store back issues of *National Geographic* magazine? It seems as if no one ever throws them out. If we extrapolate the numbers of National Geographic magazines that people will store in their attics and garages over the next 100 years, the number is astronomical. Spoofs in *Worm Runners Digest* have offered theories about the dire consequences from the weight of so many *National Geographics.* It is easy to spot absurd examples of extrapolation, like this one. Keep in mind that virtually all extrapolated numbers are somewhat wrong, and that the assumption that trends will continue is often unwarranted.

By permission of Johnny Hart and Field Enterprises, Inc.

AN APPLICATION OF PROBABILITY MODELS

Extrasensory Perception

According to Gunther (1977), Vera Nettick (who is a real person) is a lucky lady. While playing a game of bridge, she was dealt a hand that contained all 13 diamonds. Breathlessly, she won a grand slam with the once-in-a-lifetime card hand. Any statistician will be quick to point out that every possible combination of cards will be dealt to somebody sooner or later. Thus, Vera Nettick's hand was no more unusual than any other card hand, although it certainly is more memorable. Can you guess how often such a hand would occur? Gunther (1977, p. 30) figured this out as follows:

> There are roughly 635 billion possible bridge hands. Of these, eight might be called 'perfect' hands, though some are more perfect than others. To begin with, there are four perfect no-trump hands. Such a hand would contain all four aces, all four kings, all four queens, and one of the four jacks. Any of these four hands would be unequivocally perfect, because no bid could top it. Slightly less perfect, in descending order, are hands containing all the spades, all the hearts, all the diamonds, and all the clubs. If there are eight of these perfect hands in a possible 635 billion, the statistical probability is that such a hand will be dealt once in every 79 billion tries, give or take a few.
>
> Now all we have to do is estimate how many games of bridge are played every year and how many hands are dealt in each game. Using fairly conservative estimates, it turns out that a perfect hand should be dealt to some lucky bridge player, somewhere in the United States, roughly once every three or four years.

Actually, Gunther's figures are too low, since new decks of cards are organized in ascending order by suits so that one or two "perfect" shuffles will produce "perfect" bridge hands (Alcock, 1981). (A perfect shuffle occurs when, following a "cut," there is a one-to-one interleaving of cards from each half of the deck.)

What happens when someone is dealt a "perfect" hand? If this happens in a parapsychology laboratory, the investigators conclude that the individual has **extrasensory perception** (ESP). ESP refers to the knowledge or perception of events through an "extra" sense and not through the usual ones that operate via our eyes, nose, mouth, and skin. The usual test of ESP utilizes a 25-card deck of Zener cards. Zener cards are five cards which portray either a cross, square, circle, star, or wavy lines. Zener cards are shown in Fig. 5.3.

To test for ESP, there is usually a "sender" who turns over the cards one at a time and attempts to transmit messages about the cards to a "receiver" in another room. Try to imagine that you are being tested for ESP. Suppose you decided always to say that the card being dealt is a star. Since five of the 25 cards

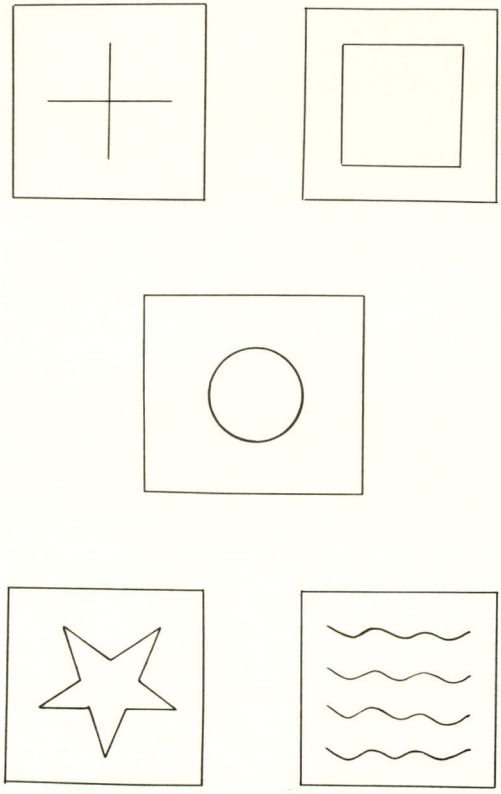

FIG. 5.3. Zener cards used to determine if someone has ESP.

are stars, you'd be correct five times. Is there some possibility that you'd be correct 10 or 15 times, just by guessing? Of course. Do you believe that Vera Nettick has ESP or that the hand she was dealt could be expected to occur just by chance?

All demonstrations of ESP rely on probability models. If an outcome is unlikely, then the ESP researchers claim that the subject has ESP. If many subjects are tested, you would expect that some would obtain results that are statistically unlikely.

CHAPTER SUMMARY

1. Since few things are known with certainty, probability plays a crucial role in many aspects of our lives.

2. Probability is defined as the number of ways a particular outcome (what we call a success) can occur divided by the number of possible outcomes.

3. We use probability values to indicate our belief in the likelihood of events with unknown frequencies.

4. Mathematically equivalent changes in the way probability information is presented can lead to dramatic changes in the way it is interpreted.

5. Tree diagrams are used to compute probabilities when there are multiple sequential events (e.g., two or more flips of a coin). When the events are independent, the probability of any outcome can be determined by multiplying the probability values along the tree "branches."

6. Expected values can be computed that will take into account the probabilities and values associated with a loss and a win in betting situations.

7. Subjective probabilities are our personal estimates of how likely events with unknown frequencies will occur.

8. Gambler's fallacy is the mistaken belief that random events are self-correcting so that if an event has not occurred in a while it is now more likely to occur.

9. A common probability error is the confusion of frequency with relative frequency. You need to consider the number of people in the population at the time the statistic was computed in order to make meaningful comparison about two statistics collected at different times.

10. Lethal events that are dramatic and have received much publicity are judged to be more frequent (likely) than silent killers. In general, people overestimate frequent events and underestimate infrequent ones.

11. There is a tendency to ignore base-rate information. Posteriori probabilities (after an event has occurred) also tend to be poorly understood and used far too conservatively.

12. Few people realize that if a person scores extremely high or low on one measure, he or she will tend to score close to average on the second measure. This is called "regression toward the mean."

13. If an outcome is desirable, we are more likely to believe that it will occur than if it is undesirable.

14. There are three measures of central tendency—the mean, median and mode. Each is computed with a different mathematical formula. In some cases, they can be highly discrepant.

15. When computing statistics, we take a subset (sample) of a population. If the sample is not representative of the population, it is called a "biased sample."

16. Many people erroneously believe that statistics that are expressed in precise numbers (e.g., many decimal places) are highly credible.

17. Extrapolation occurs when a value is estimated by extending a trend from known values.

Terms to Know:

You should be able to define the following terms and concepts. If you find that you're having difficulty with any term, be sure to reread the section where it is discussed:

Probability
Odds
Tree Diagrams (or Probability Trees)
Expected Value
Subjective Probability
Objective Probability
Gambler's Fallacy
Relative Frequency
Base-Rate Biases
Posteriori Probabilities
Bayes Theorem
Regression Toward the Mean
Perseverence Phenomenon
Population
Sample
Statistic
Biased Samples
Measures of Central Tendency
Mean
Median
Mode
Sample Size
Significant Difference
Extrapolation
Extrasensory Perception

Be sure that you can answer the following questions:

1. How certain can we be about the occurrence of an event if its probability is 0? .2? .5? .9? 1.0?

2. Explain how Al Hibbs was able to "beat the house" at roulette.

3. What is the logic of tree diagrams?

4. What principle explains why the probability of 40 people sharing a common birthday is as high as .90?

5. Explain Gambler's Fallacy. What is fallacious about it? Ask your friends what they would expect on the next flip of a fair coin that has landed "heads up" on the last five flips.

6. When people were asked to judge the frequency of lethal events, what kinds of errors did they make?

7. If a disease is very rare, how optimistic can we be about devising a test that will detect it? Why?

8. If a student gets the highest grade in his class on a psychology exam, what grade would you predict that he will get on the midterm? What is the name of the principle you used to make this prediction?

9. Explain why the Israeli flight instructors believed that praise led to poorer performance and criticism improved performance. What is a better explanation of these results?

10. How do human probability judgments compare to those obtained with Bayes Theorem?

11. How does the desirability of an event influence our estimates of its probability?

12. How can biases in sampling lead to wrong results?

13. Demonstrations of ESP depend on statistical notions of probability. Explain the position taken in this chapter that unusual results are bound to occur sometimes just by chance and do not necessarily support an ESP interpretation.

Exercises

Apply what you've learned about probability to answer the following problems:

1. If each of the letters in the word "PROBABILITY" were thrown separately into a hat and one letter is drawn from the hat, what is the probability that it is a vowel?

2. Your friend is willing to give you 5:2 odds that the Phillies will beat the Dodgers. Convert these odds to a probability value.

3. What is the probability of drawing a picture card (Jack, Queen, or King) from a full deck of cards?

4. In a party game called "Spin the Bottle," the players form a circle with a bottle at the center. A spinner spins the bottle and then kisses the person to whom it points. Although five people are playing, the bottle has pointed to Marlene on each of its three spins. What is the probability of this occurring by chance?

5. Professor Aardvark gives such difficult exams that students can only guess at the answers. What is the probability of getting all 5 questions on his True/False test correct by guessing? What is the probability of getting all 5 wrong?

6. Rubinstein and Pfeiffer (1980) have suggested that instead of reporting weather forecasts in terms of the probability of rain, a more useful index would be the Expected Value (EV) of rain. Suppose the weather forecaster knows that there is a 30% probability of 5 inches of rain and a 70% probability of no rain on a given day. What is the EV for rain?

7. Comment on the following: Today, over 47 million homes have air conditioning, while only 23 million homes had air conditioning a decade ago.

8. In one survey, 10 out of 12 people preferred the taste of Crunchies corn cereal to that of Munchies, Flakies or Hefties. Another survey found that 6 out of 7 people preferred the new, improved taste of Crackles to that of Munchies, Flakies or Hefties. Both Crunchies and Crackles will soon be available in supermarkets. Which cereal is more likely to be preferred by the cereal-eating public?

9. Officials at the suicide prevention center know that 2% of all people who phone their hotlines actually attempt suicide. A psychologist has devised a test that can identify 80% of all future suicides. Unfortunately, this test incorrectly predicts that 5% of those

who don't commit suicide will. If you get a positive identification from a caller on this test, what is the probability that he would actually attempt suicide?

10. Suppose that your friend belongs to two "singles" clubs. The Suaves have 500 members; 60% of them are good dancers, and 40% of them can't dance. The other club, the Chics, have only 100 members; 95% of them are good dancers, and 5% can't dance. You saw her at a party with a terrific dancer. Was he more likely a Suave or a Chic?

11. Every student in Mr. Weasel's class kept a record of the number of books read over a 3-month period. The data are: 15, 5, 8, 12, 1, 3, 1, 7, 21, 4. Compute the mean, median, and mode for these numbers. Which one seems best?

SUGGESTED READING

The classic in the misuse of probability and statistics is Huff's *How to Lie with Statistics* (1954). You'll find this small paperback both entertaining and instructive. Another book on this topic that also maintains an informal style is Campbell's *Flaws and Fallacies in Statistic Thinking* (1974). A chapter in Kahane's *Logic and Contemporary Rhetoric,* 3rd Ed. (1980) also presents examples of statistical abuse.

The computation of probability and expected value are discussed in one chapter of Copi's *Introduction to Logic* (1978). A psychological approach to expected values can be found in Slovic and Lichtenstein's (1968) article, "Relative Importance of Probabilities and Payoffs in Risk Taking." This article is somewhat more advanced than the usual textbook coverage of these topics. Rubinstein and Pfeiffer's excellent text *Concepts in Problem Solving* (1980) contains an easy-to-read section on computing probabilities using tree diagrams and expected values.

If you're interested in chance and are lucky, or even if you're not, you'll *probably* enjoy Gunther's *The Luck Factor* (1977). This is an enjoyable book, filled with vignettes about randomness, probability, and people's notions about them. Alcock's *Parapsychology: Science or Magic?* (1981) reviews probability interpretations of ESP, as does an interesting article by Ayer (1965) entitled "Chance."

The psychologist who is most noted for his research on the distinction between frequency and relative frequency data is Estes. A somewhat advanced treatment of this topic appears in his journal article (1976) "The Cognitive Side of Probability Learning." If you found the section on the ways people judge the frequency of lethal events interesting, you'll enjoy reading *Acceptable Risk* by Fischhoff, Lichtenstein, Slovic, Derby, and Keeney (1981). In their book, the authors describe the variables that people consider when deciding whether the risk associated with an event (e.g., X-rays, nuclear accident, motorcycle riding) is low enough to be considered acceptable.

Summaries of the literature on subjective probabilities can be found in the three following sources: Tversky and Kahneman's (1974) article "Judgment Under Uncertainty: Heuristics and Biases"; Hogarth's (1980) *Judgement and Choice: The Psychology of Decision;* and Nisbett and Ross' (1980) *Human Inferences: Strategies and Shortcomings of Social Judgment.* The Nisbett and Ross work interprets much of the literature on subjective probability in a social psychology framework. A diverse collection of papers on probability (some of them are advanced readings) can be found in Kyburg and Smoker, Eds., (1980) *Studies in Subjective Probability.*

6 Development of Problem Solving Skills

Contents

Anatomy of a Problem 161
Stages in Problem Solving 163
  Incubation 163
Insight 164
Well-Defined and Ill-Defined Problems 165
Problem Solving Strategies 166
  Representing Problems 167
  Means-Ends Analysis 182
  Working Backwards 184
  Simplification 185
  Generalization and Specialization 188
  Random Search and Trial-and-Error 189
  Rules 189
  Hints 190
  Split-Half Method 192
  Brainstorming 193
  Contradiction 194
  Restating the Problem 194
  Analogies and Metaphors 195
  Consult an Expert 198
  Select the Best Strategy 198
Problem Solving Problems 199
  Functional Fixedness and Mental Set 199
  Misleading and Irrelevant Information 201
  World View Constraints 201
  Mechanization 202

Problems are our most important product.
—Beardsley

Suppose you're driving alone at night on a long, dark stretch of freeway that is infrequently traveled when you suddenly hear the familiar "thump-thump" of a very flat tire. You pull onto the shoulder of the road and begin the unpleasant task of changing a tire, illuminated only with the light of the moon and a small flashlight. Carefully, you remove the lug nuts and place them in the hubcap by the roadside. A speeding motorist whizzes past you, hitting the hubcap and scattering the lug nuts across the dark freeway and out of sight. Here you sit, a spare tire in one hand, a flat tire propped against the car, and no lug nuts, on a dark night on a lonely stretch of freeway. To make matters worse, a cold rain is beginning to fall. What would you do?

One of my students told me that this incident actually happened. He went on to elaborate that the flat tire occurred alongside a large mental institution near our college. While the hapless motorist sat pondering his problem, he attracted the attention of several "residents" of the institution, who gathered near the motorist along the chain link fence that separated them. One resident offered this solution to the motorist's problem: Remove one lug nut from each of the other three tires and use them to attach the spare. Each tire should hold securely with three lug nuts until the motorist reaches a gas station. The grateful motorist thanked the institution resident and then asked, "How'd you think of such a good solution to this problem?" The resident replied, "I'm not dumb, I'm just crazy!"

I don't know if this exchange ever really occurred, although I've had several students tell me that they've heard the story, too. In any case, virtually everyone agrees that the resident offered a good solution to the motorist's predicament. Why was it so difficult for the motorist to solve the problem, yet upon hearing

Reprinted by permission: Tribune Company Syndicate, Inc.

the solution, it seemed so easy and so obvious? How did the resident come up with such a good solution?

ANATOMY OF A PROBLEM

Consider this mundane problem: Keith has to catch a 9:00 A.M. plane for Philadelphia, and he's already a little late. The *freeway route* to the airport is the quickest, except when the traffic is heavy. The traffic is almost always heavy with commuters during the morning rush hour. There is a *back roads route* that might be a good one, if the road along the river isn't flooded. The road is frequently closed because of flooding after heavy rains. As you can probably guess by now, it rained last week. The *surface street route* is the longest. If Keith chooses this route, he may miss his plane. Of course, if he spends too much time pondering this problem, he'll surely miss his plane. Which route should he take?

In their classic book, Newell and Simon (1972) have conceptualized all problems as being composed of the same basic parts or structures. Their idea is that problems, like people, can be understood by reducing them to their anatomical parts. According to this view, the **anatomy of a problem** can be thought of as having a starting or **initial state** (Keith's home) and a final or **goal state** (the airport). Hayes (1978) uses this framework when he asks: "What is a problem? . . . The problem is the gap which separates where you are from where you want to be" (p. 177). All of the possible solution **paths** from the initial state to the goal state comprise the **problem space.** In more general terms, all possible alternative solutions to a problem are called the problem space. In solving a problem, people search through the problem space to find the best path from the initial state to the goal; that is, they consider the alternatives that would lead to the goal and select the best one.

In addition to an initial state, a goal state, and the paths connecting them, there are *givens* or information and rules that place constraints upon the problem. The givens are the knowledge needed to reach the goal. They can be explicitly stated or implicitly assumed. Two implicit givens in the problem presented earlier were the knowledge that Keith would drive a car to the airport and that he would take either the freeway route, back-roads route, or surface-street route. When solving a problem, the given information is transformed into a solution. This anatomy or framework for understanding problems has proven useful in understanding the process of problem solving. We are all faced with countless problems, and surely know one when we see one. Yet, like most of the topics in this book, the word "problem" remains a difficult one to define. Polya (1962) has offered the following definition: "Solving a problem means finding a way out of a difficulty, a way around an obstacle, attaining an aim that was not immediately understandable." The anatomy of the airport problem is schematically shown in Fig. 6.1. We'll return to the airport problem later in the chapter as different problem-solving strategies are considered.

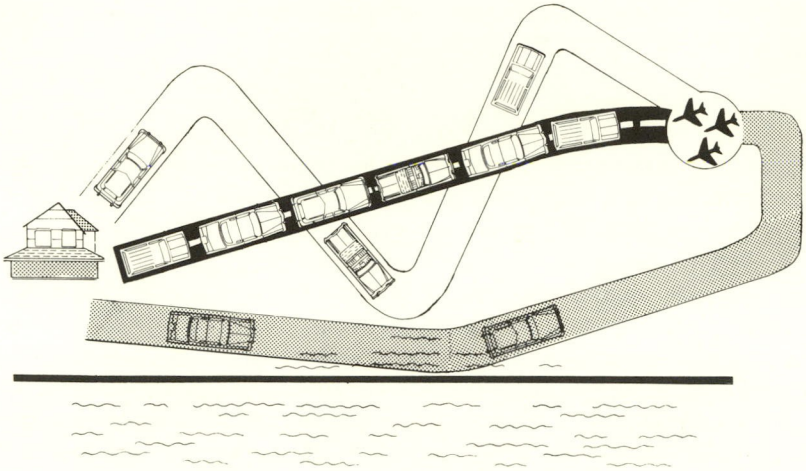

FIG. 6.1. The anatomy of the airport problem. *Givens:* Keith will drive to the airport. He will take one of these routes. He must take the fastest route.

Problems differ in difficulty. In the airport problem, the difficulty lies in choosing which of the three paths (routes) would get Keith to the goal in the shortest time. In the lug nut problem the difficulty was in generating any solution path. The initial state was a spare tire and no lug nuts; the goal state was a spare tire attached to the car securely enough to drive the car. The problem was the apparent absence of paths to the goal.

Consider Rubik's cube as a difficult problem. The goal for a Rubik's cube is to align each small colored square so that each of the six sides of the cube will be a uniform color. This is a prohibitive problem since there are millions of combinations of possible moves (paths to the goal). The "trick" is to determine which combination of moves will lead to the goal. In this sort of problem, the difficulty lies in reducing the number of possible paths so that only potentially correct ones will be chosen. Newell and Simon (1972) calculated that the average 40-move chess game has 10^{120} paths. This is a number greater than the national debt! Perhaps this is why we view great chess masters with such awe. They have the knowledge to avoid blind paths (bad moves) that won't lead to the goal (winning) and to select the best combination of moves.

Although problem solving, decision making, and creativity are discussed in separate chapters in this book, there is considerable overlap among these topics. Many decisions are involved in solving a problem, and generating satisfactory solution paths often requires considerable creativity. The division among these topics is for ease of presentation. All of the chapters in this text are interrelated in that they represent somewhat arbitrary ways of "cutting up the thinking pie." The information presented in the other chapters will also contribute to your understanding of problem solving.

STAGES IN PROBLEM SOLVING

In 1926 Graham Wallas examined anecdotal accounts of creative scientists and concluded that problem solving progresses in a series of stages. Although there is disagreement among psychologists as to whether all problem solving is done in qualitatively different stages, a brief review of the hypothesized stages may prove useful to problem solvers.

The first stage is **preparation or familiarization.** This includes the time spent in understanding the nature of the problem, the desired goal, and the givens. This is a crucial part in problem solving since a correct solution cannot be generated without an adequate understanding of the problem. The second stage is the **production** stage. During this stage, the problem solver produces the solution paths that define the problem space. **Judgment or evaluation** is the third stage. During this stage, individuals evaluate the solution paths in order to select the best one. The fourth stage is a strange one that may or may not occur, depending on the problem. Sometimes when we can't find a solution path, we stop working on the problem. The period when we're not actively considering the problem is called the **incubation stage.** There are many reports from famous scientists that a solution came to them during the incubation phase—seemingly "out of the blue." Because of the fascination incubation holds for most people, it deserves separate consideration.

Incubation

The idea of an incubation phase is attractive to most people. It represents one of the few instances when we may get something for nothing. An oft cited example of incubation comes from the writings of the famous French mathematician Poincare (1929):

> Then I turned my attention to the study of some arithmetical questions apparently without much success and without a suspicion of any connection with my preceding researches. Disgusted with my failure, I went to spend a few days at the seaside, and thought of something else. One morning, walking on the bluff, the idea came to me, with just the same characteristics of brevity, suddenness and immediate certainty, that the arithmetic transformations of indeterminate ternary quadratic forms were identical with those of non-Euclidean geometry (p. 388).

Have you ever had the experience of working unsuccessfully on a problem, then having the solution come to you sometime later when you were not consciously thinking about it? If so, then you have experienced incubation effects first hand. The term incubation suggests a mother hen sitting on great ideas that are about to hatch.

Incubation is a poorly understood phenomenon. Because it can't reliably be expected to occur, the contribution of "time outs" to finding solutions is often downplayed. If your employer found you sitting with your feet propped on your desk, gazing out the window, she is unlikely to be pleased to learn that you were "incubating" on company time. A familiar experience is having a correct answer come to someone immediately after turning in an exam or paper. This is most likely the result of incubation. It's a good idea to work well ahead of deadlines to allow ample time for incubation effects to occur. We don't know how people are able to produce solutions during time-outs. There is no evidence that people continue to work on the problem at an unconscious level, although some people have suggested that this is how incubation effects occur. Most likely the time-out period serves to dissipate fatigue and allow individuals to get out of *sets* or ruts in their thinking processes so that they can view the problem from a different perspective.

Herbert A. Simon (1977), the Nobel Prize winning psychologist, has attempted to explain incubation as due, in part, to selective forgetting. He suggested that when we are working on a problem we rely on a relatively small number of concepts held in a limited capacity short-term memory. (See the Memory chapter for a detailed discussion of this concept.) When we're not working on a problem, the information held in short-term memory is quickly forgotten. If this information was not productive for discovering a solution, then having forgotten it will be beneficial to finding a good solution. Simon regards scientific discovery as a form of problem solving. He goes on to say that selective forgetting may be one of the processes that underlie the incubation effect, famous examples of which are Galileo's discovery of uniform acceleration, Newtonian notions of gravity, and Einstein's theory of relativity.

It is a good idea to put aside a problem that you're having difficulty with and return to it at a later time. This is especially good advice during an exam. At least you'll be sure of getting credit for the easier problems, but watch your time limits carefully so that you can correctly finish as many problems as possible in the allotted time. (Of course, it's also a good idea to work on the problems worth the most points first to maximize your exam score.)

INSIGHT

Did you ever have the solution to a problem come to you "in a flash?" Sudden knowledge of the solution is called **insight** or the *Aha! experience*. It is metaphorically referred to as a light bulb in the head that is suddenly switched on. Interestingly, the earliest studies of insight were conducted with chimpanzees, not humans (Köhler, 1925). It seems that when chimpanzees are confronted with problems such as reaching food that can only be obtained by putting two sticks together to form a rake, a period of seemingly random behavior is followed by what appears to be sudden insight into the problem.

Insight experiences are common. I have found them to occur frequently in the statistics classes that I teach. Often students will ponder over a problem or listen attentively to a lecture, then suddenly they'll break into a broad grin and exclaim, "Now I understand." A law school student once told me that she spent the first three-fourths of her first year in law school in an intellectual fog. She really felt that she understood very little about the basic concepts. Then, something "clicked" and she suddenly understood the concepts of the legal principles. It's as if a little light went on that illuminated the concepts. Her insight paid off into a successful legal career.

It should be noted that the insight follows a period of concentrated effort. Few would deny that thinking about a difficult problem is work. Yet somehow this work pays off in an insightful solution. A review of the problem-solving strategies presented later in this chapter provide some thinking guides that serve to direct the thinking processes in ways that will maximize insightful solutions.

WELL-DEFINED AND ILL-DEFINED PROBLEMS

Problems come in all shapes and sizes. Consider the following two problems:

1. The parallelogram problem (after Wertheimer, 1959).

Some time back in fifth or sixth grade, you learned that in order to find the area of a rectangle you should multiply the height by the length. Now you are given the following parallelogram that is 4″ long and 2″ high. What is its area?

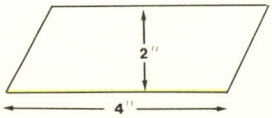

2. Write a poem expressing the joy you feel when spring flowers bloom.

Do these problems seem qualitatively different to you? The parallelogram problem has a single correct answer. Have you figured it out? Wertheimer suggests that the correct answer lies in **perceptual reorganization,** or seeing the problem in a new way. The new way consists of seeing the parallelogram in terms of a rectangle and two triangles. Thus, the parallelogram becomes:

Once the problem is restructured this way, it is only a short leap to figure out that the area of the parallelogram can be found with the same formula for the area of a rectangle since the two triangles can be fit together so that a new rectangular figure is formed with a 4″ length and a 2″ height. In the present example, the area of the parallelogram is 2″ × 4″ = 8 square inches. There is no other correct answer. The goal (correct answer) is **well defined,** as is the path to the goal.

Writing a poem is a different sort of problem. The goal (a poem) is **ill defined,** as there are many forms a poem can take. There are countless ways to write a poem. The greatest difficulty in this case lies in evaluating the quality of the end product.

Most of the problems that confront people outside of the laboratory are ill defined in that the problem solver must evaluate how well the goal has been attained. Other examples of ill-defined problems are: creating a way to increase sales for a business; finding more time to study; writing a clear easy-to-read textbook; saving money for college tuition; building a better mousetrap; de-escalating the nuclear arms race, and improving the environment. In ill-defined problems, the goal may be vague or incomplete, which makes the generation of solution paths difficult and their evaluation even more difficult.

One of the best ways to approach ill-defined problems is to make the goal explicit. It is usually possible to state the goal in several different ways for ill-defined problems. For example, the problem of increasing sales can be re-identified as the problem of increasing profits since the real goal is to find ways to make more money. When asked in this form, the problem changes from its initial conceptualization. Solution paths can now include ways to cut losses, reduce inventories, or collect bad debts. The best way to approach ill-defined problems is to specify the goal or goals in objective terms so that solution paths can be considered.

Sometimes the distinction between well-defined and ill-defined problems blurs. Consider again the problem of getting Keith to the airport on time. If the problem is selecting among the three routes, it is well defined, but if other solutions are possible, e.g., fly to the airport, take a different plane from a nearer airport, take the subway, then the problem becomes somewhat more difficult to define.

PROBLEM SOLVING STRATEGIES

Solving problems can be regarded as the most characteristically human activity.
—Polya (1962)

There are several strategies that can be used in a systematic manner to help you solve problems. Although no single strategy can guarantee perfect solutions every time, learning how to use several different strategies can give you direction and confidence when presented with a new problem. Schoenfeld (1979) found that many mathematicians and scientists claimed to use specific strategies and rules when solving problems in their academic disciplines. Many of the scientists and mathematicians believed that their students would solve problems better if they learned some basic skills for attacking problems. In addition, several researchers have found that instruction in general problem solving skills can improve problem solving ability (e.g., Klein & Weizenfeld, 1978; Wickelgren, 1974).

Representing Problems

The best way to solve a problem is to devise the best representation. This forces the problem solver to be explicit about the desired goal and to plan carefully the steps necessary to reach the goal.

The representation of a problem is often a good index of how well it is understood (Greeno, 1973, 1977). A good representation will contain all of the relevant information or givens and display the relationships among the givens in a way that will facilitate progress toward the goal. Of course, when you begin solving a problem it is difficult to determine which of the possible solution paths will ultimately lead to the goal. The givens need to be transformed in ways that will generate solution paths. In the jargon of problem solving, the givens are transformed into solution paths with **operations.** Every time an operation is applied, the problem space changes. Different representational systems can be thought of as strategies or "plans of attack." Let's try some examples of ways to represent problems.

Write It Down

All problems are initially represented in your head. It is a good idea to get the paths and goals on paper or into some other concrete form. This will reduce the memory load and allow you to view the problem visually. The simplest example of the aid provided by a pencil and paper is a straightforward multiplication problem. Solve the following problem *without* writing anything:

$$\begin{array}{r} 76 \\ \times\ \underline{89} \end{array}$$

Of course, you would consider this a ridiculous request since it is a simple problem with paper and pencil and a difficult one to perform in your head because of the memory demands. Whenever there are several facts to keep track of, it is a good idea to use a paper and pencil.

Draw A Graph Or Diagram

"A bear, starting at point P, walked one mile due south. Then he changed direction and walked one mile due east. Then he turned again to the left and walked on mile due north, and arrived exactly at the point P he started from. What was the color of the bear?" (Polya, 1957, p. 234).

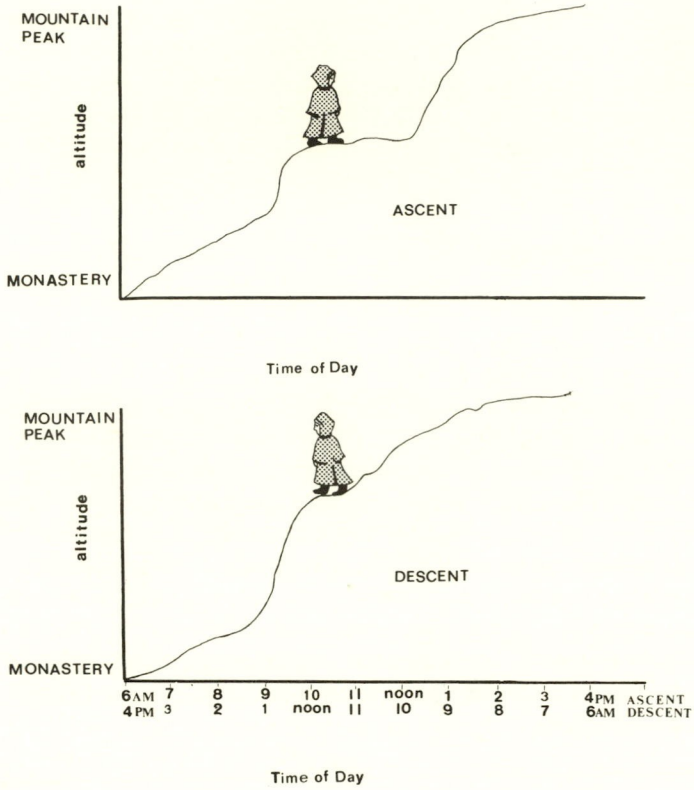

FIG. 6.2. Graphs of the monk's ascent and descent. The graphs can take any shape since the monk can rest as often as he wishes.

Does this problem seem strange or even impossible to you? If you draw a simple "map" of the bear's route, it will be a pie-shaped wedge. Where on earth is this possible? Think about a globe. Did you just say "Why, of course, point P must be the North Pole" to yourself? Once you realize that you're at the North Pole, this problem becomes trivial. The bear must be white, since only polar bears live at the North Pole.

Consider the following problem:

A venerable old monk leaves the monastery at exactly 6 A.M. to climb a winding mountain trail to the solitude of the mountain peak. He arrives at exactly 4 P.M. After spending the night in sleep and prayer, he leaves the mountain peak at exactly 6 A.M. and arrives at the monastery at exactly 4 P.M. There are no constraints on the speed at which he walks. In fact, he stops several times along the way to rest. Is there some point on the mountain trail that he passes at exactly the same time each day?

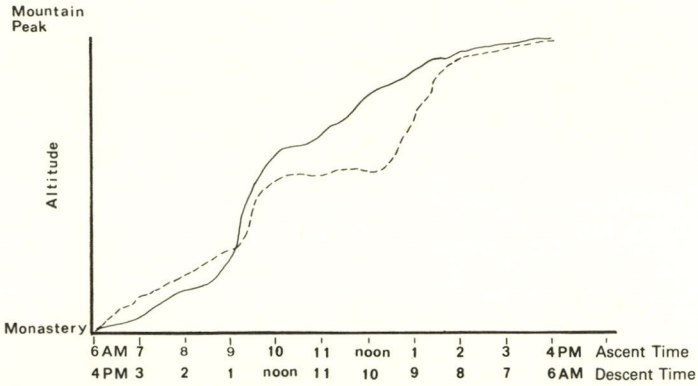

FIG. 6.3. By superimposing the ascent and descent graphs, it is easy to see that there must be some place at which the graphs intersect. Thus, there must be a place on the mountain trail that the monk crosses at the same time on each day.

Stop and think about this problem for a moment. Does it seem like a difficult one? There are two ways to consider this problem that will make the answer seem simple, but before you go on, decide how you would go about solving this problem, then solve it.

One solution is to draw a graph of the monk's ascent and descent. The graph can take any shape since you know nothing about his hourly progress. The graphs of the ascent and descent should appear as in Fig. 6.2.

Now, superimpose the two graphs and see if there must be some point where the graphs intersect. If there is, then there is some time when the monk passed the same point at the same time on each day. This is shown in Fig. 6.3.

Drawing a graph provides a clear picture of the results. Actually, an easier way of solving this problem involves changing the representation and restating the facts in the problem in an equivalent, but different, form. Assume two people traverse the same mountain path at the same time on the same morning. If one starts at the monastery and the other starts at the mountain peak, both leaving at 6 A.M. and both arriving at their opposite destinations at 4 P.M., it is obvious they must meet somewhere along the path no matter when each chooses to rest and reflect. Thus, with a change in representation, a difficult problem can become trivial.

Drawing a graph is often an excellent strategy for solving problems. Several years ago, I taught a laboratory course in experimental psychology. In that course, college students were required to conduct experiments, gather data, and interpret their data in a meaningful way. Although the students were taught the statistical methods needed for data analysis, I found that when they graphed their results they obtained a much better understanding of the phenomenon they were investigating. They were able to use their experimental results to formulate

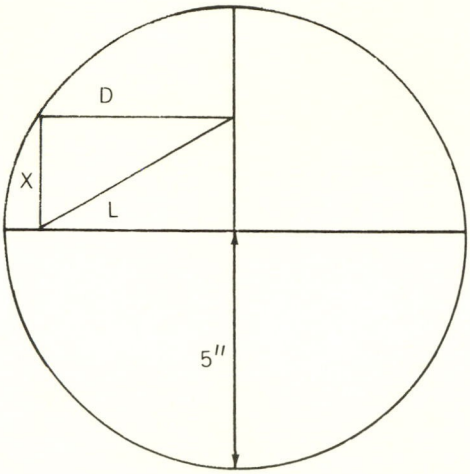

FIG. 6.4. Using only the information given in this figure, can you determine the length of line L? (Problem adapted from Köhler, 1969.)

sound conclusions since they understood the nature of their findings. The students found that a simple graph was a more valuable tool for comprehension than the elaborate statistical procedures that they were required to use.

Graphs and other kinds of diagrams are especially useful comprehension strategies in mathematical and scientific problem solving. For example, a common problem in undergraduate statistics courses requires finding the area between two points under a certain kind of curve called a "normal" or "bell-shaped" curve. This can be a difficult or confusing problem for students, but it becomes easy if they draw the curve and shade in the area they want to find. In fact, I don't give my statistics students the algebraic rules for finding the appropriate area. Students find it easier to figure it out for themselves from the diagrams they draw.

Graphs and diagrams are also useful in solving spatial problems. The blueprints of architects and engineers are their problem-solving tools. Problems in geometry and trigonometry usually require carefully labeled diagrams for their correct solution.

Consider the geometry problem that was posed by Köhler in 1969. You are given only information in Fig. 6.4 and the fact that the radius of the circle is 5 inches. Can you find the length of line L in inches?

One of the reasons that this is a difficult problem is that in the pictorial representation line L appears most saliently as the hypotenuse of two right triangles, the triangle with sides LDX, and the triangle with the other two sides defined by the intersecting horizontal and vertical radii. How can you change this diagram so that the solution can be obtained?

Consider the information given. Since the only length given in this diagram is the radius of the circle, it is likely that this will be needed in solving the problem.

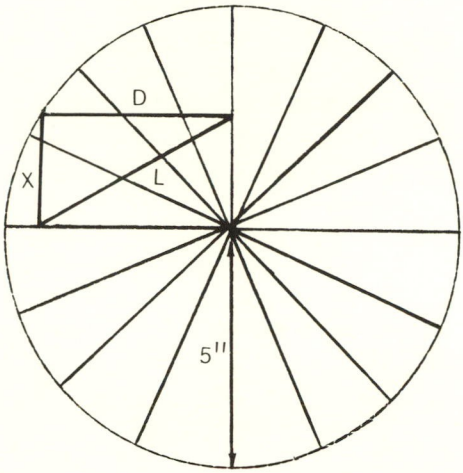

FIG. 6.5. Additional radii have been drawn in over Figure 6.4 as an intermediate step toward the solution. Can you use the additional radii to find the length of line L?

Try drawing in additional radii around the circle as shown in Fig. 6.5. Does this help to suggest the solution?

Look carefully at the quadrant containing L. Can you find another line equal in length to L? If you think of L as the diagonal inside a rectangle with sides D, X, and the unlabeled sides formed by the intersection of the horizontal and vertical radii, the other diagonal in the rectangle must be the same length as L. The other diagonal must be the radius; thus line L, like the radius is also 5″ long. Although the initial representation of the problem was somewhat misleading, a solution was found with the appropriate operations.

Of course, there was no way of knowing at the outset that moving the radii around the circle would lead to the answer. It was obvious, however, that the answer would depend on the radius in some way, since it was the only measurement given, and the goal was to find the length of line L. The operations used to transform the givens into solution paths involved the knowledge you brought with you to the problem. If you did not know that the two diagonals in a rectangle must be equal, then you could not have solved the problem. Good problem solvers utilize a solid knowledge base that is built up over a lifetime of educational experiences—ones that are accumulated both inside and outside of the classroom. The best strategy for solving problems is to know a great deal about a great many topics.

Let's try another example in which graphs or diagrams will simplify the search for a solution path.

In order to save money and their sanity, Melvin, Brock, Marc, and Claire decide to form a babysitting cooperative. They agree to babsit for each other's children with the understanding that when one of them stays with another's children, the recipient will repay the sitter with an equal number of babysitting hours. They decide to tally babysitting hours at the end of the month. During the month, Melvin sat with Brock's children 9 hours, Marc sat with Melvin's children 3 hours and Claire stayed with Melvin's children 6 hours. Marc babysat 9 hours with Claire's children and Brock babysat 5 hours with Claire's children. Which of these people has 12 hours of babysitting time due to him or her?

A good diagram of the relationship among these four people is clearly needed. The relevant givens will involve the four people and the number of hours owed to each. Let's start with the first sentence, "Melvin sat with Brock's children 9 hours." Thus, Brock owes Melvin 9 hours of babysitting at the end of the month. The operation being used is the transformation of number of hours spent babysitting into number of hours owed to each sitter. A simple diagram of this relationship is:

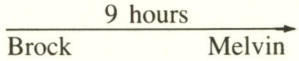

The next sentence translates into "Melvin owes Marc 3 hours and Melvin owes Claire 6 hours."

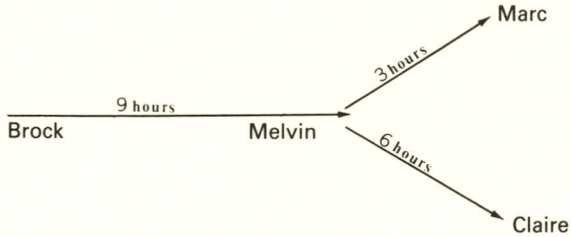

Then, changing the third sentence so that it reflects what is owed, Claire owes Marc 9 hours and Claire owes Brock 5 hours.

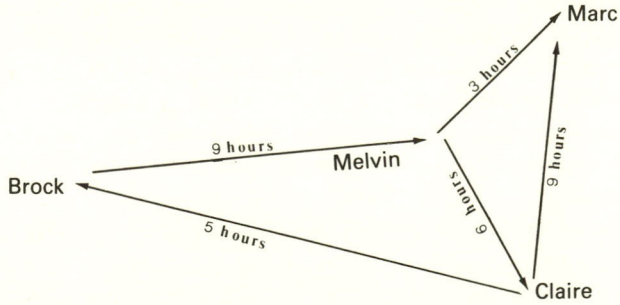

It is easy to see from this diagram that only Marc is owed 12 hours of babysitting, 3 hours from Melvin and 9 hours from Claire. A diagram of the hours owed is essential in finding the solution to this problem.

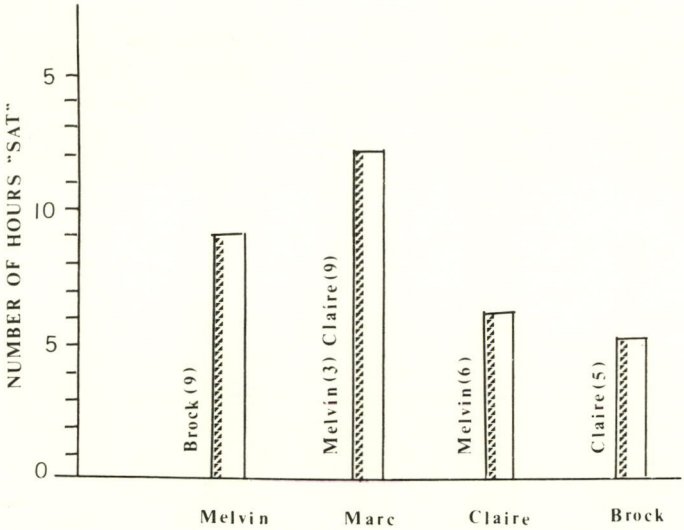

FIG. 6.6. Alternative form of representation for solving the co-op problem.

There are several other ways of representing the information in the babysitting co-op problem that will display all of the essential relationships, and thus also give the correct answer. When a colleague (Dr. Susan Nummedal at California State University, Long Beach) posed this problem to her students, she found that they devised a variety of representations to solve the problem. One student used a simple bar graph to keep track of the number of hours sat by each participant. This representation is shown in Fig. 6.6.

Other students used a variety of table formats. One listed the number of hours "gave" as a positive number and "received" as a negative number since it was owed. Another student split the information into "sitter" and "sat for" categories, then filled in a table of information summing across the columns for the total number of "sat for" hours for each participant, and summing down the rows for the total number of "sitter" hours for each participant. These representations are offered in Tables 6.1 and 6.2.

TABLE 6.1
A Table Format for Representing the Information in the Babysitting Co-op Problem

	Gave	*Received*	*Total Due*
Melvin	+9	−3, −6	0
Marc	+3, +9		12
Claire	+6	−9, −15	−8
Brock	+5	−9	−4

TABLE 6.2
An Alternative Table Format That Can Be Used to Represent the Information in the Babysitting Co-op Problem

		Sitter				*Total Number of Hours Sat For*
		Melvin	*Marc*	*Claire*	*Brock*	
Sat For	*Melvin*		3	6		9
	Marc					0
	Claire		9		5	14
	Brock	9				9
Total Number of Hours Sat		9	12	6	5	

As the babysitting co-op problem demonstrates, there are often many ways of representing a given problem. As you work through the problems in this chapter, try a variety of representations. A good representation will present all of the relevant information in a way that it can be readily understood and assimilated. Good representations provide the necessary solution paths to the goal.

Try A Hierarchical Tree

Hierarchical trees are branching diagrams. They are most frequently used to assess mathematically the probability or likelihood of uncertain outcomes. In this context they are called decision trees. (See the Probability chapter for the use of decision trees in determining probabilities.) Hierarchical trees or tree diagrams can be useful aids in the context of problem solving. (As stated earlier in this chapter, the distinction between problem solving and decision making is somewhat artificial in that they are closely related concepts.)

If the problem you're working on is fairly complex, with each possible solution path requiring subsequent additional paths, a hierarchical tree or tree diagram should be considered.

Here is a classical problem first presented by Duncker (1945). Although the problem is a medical one, no specialized knowledge is needed to solve it.

> A patient has an inoperative tumor deep within her stomach. The problem is to devise a way of treating the tumor with X-rays without damaging the healthy tissue that surrounds the tumor on all sides. Stop and think for a few minutes how you would go about solving this problem.

Most of Duncker's subjects went about reaching a solution in several steps. Although a variety of solutions were attempted, the best solution is to use several weak rays, each coming from different places outside the body, focused so that they would meet and summate at the tumor site. In this manner, the healthy

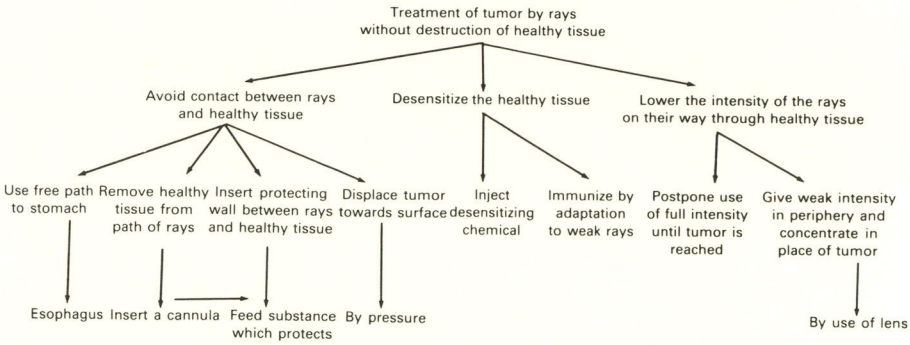

FIG. 6.7. A hierarchical three diagram of one subject's attempted solutions to Duncker's X-ray problem. (After Duncker, 1945.)

tissue won't be hurt by the weak rays and the tumor will receive a high level of radiation. This solution was formulated from a broader category of solutions that included having each ray grow stronger as it reached the tumor.

One subject's search for solution paths is shown in Fig. 6.7 in a hierarchical tree diagram. Note that the goal is explicitly stated at the top of the tree. General broad strategies are listed one level below the goal, with more specific ways of satisfying each strategy on lower levels.

Tree diagrams are particularly useful when the given information has a natural hierarchical organization. For example, all living things are classified into a hierarchical organization by biologists. If you ask a child if a bee is an animal, he will probably respond that it isn't an animal because it is an insect. This problem can be made clear to him by drawing a biological classification tree like the one shown in Fig. 6.8.

Another example of using trees to solve problems is the familiar use of family trees. Estate lawyers, who often face a tangled web of family relationships, need to be able to determine the relations among family members in order to handle wills and estate taxes. Multiple spouses, cohabitation, step-children, half-siblings, and out-of-wedlock births can make the difficult matter of inheritance a legal nightmare. A carefully drawn family tree that places each member on the appropriate generation branch is an invaluable aid in solving tangled inheritance claims.

Make A Matrix

A **matrix** is a rectangular array of facts or numbers. It is really just a fancy word for a chart. When the givens in a problem can be broken down into categories, a matrix may be a good method of representation. Consider the problem posed by Whimbey and Lochhead (1982):

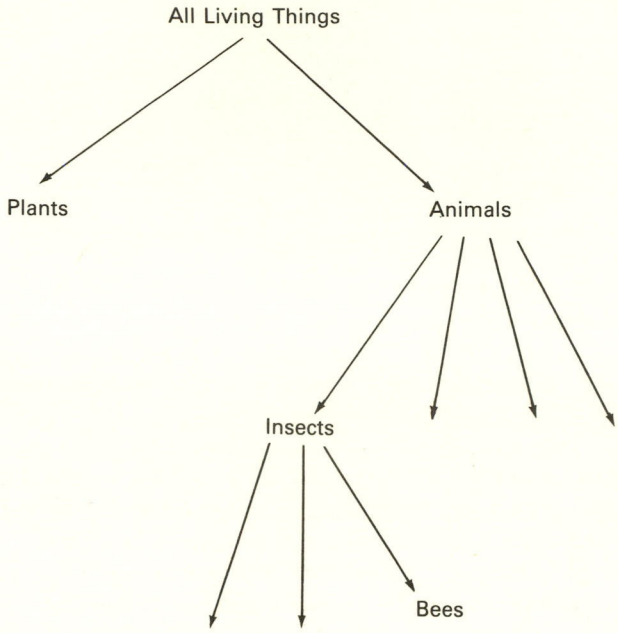

FIG. 6.8. A hierarchical three diagram that can be used to answer the question, "Are bees animals?"

Three men—Fred, Ed and Ted—are married to Joan, Sally and Vickie, but not necessarily in that order. Joan, who is Ed's sister, lives in Detroit. Fred dislikes animals. Ed weighs more than the man who is married to Vickie. The man married to Sally breeds Siamese cats as a hobby. Fred commutes over 200 hours a year from his home in Ann Arbor to his job in Detroit. Match up the men with the women they married. (p. 67)

What are the categories of information given in this problem? The givens concern husbands and wives. Set up a three-by-three matrix and fill in as much of it as you can with the information:

	Joan	*Sally*	*Vickie*
Fred			
Ed			
Ted			

Since Joan is Ed's sister, she cannot be his wife, so fill in a "NO" in the Joan–Ed cell of the matrix. Skip the next two statements for the time being and go on to the statement that Ed weighs more than the man married to Vickie; therefore Ed is not married to Vickie. Ed must be married to Sally. So far the matrix appears as below:

	Joan	*Sally*	*Vickie*
Fred		NO	
Ed	NO	YES	NO
Ted		NO	

Peruse the problem for more clues. Have you found the important one? Fred lives in Ann Arbor and Joan lives in Detroit; therefore, we'd conclude that they are not married. Since Fred is not married to Joan or Sally, he must be married to Vickie. Who's left for Ted? Joan must be married to Ted.

The completed matrix:

	Joan	*Sally*	*Vickie*
Fred	NO	NO	YES
Ed	NO	YES	NO
Ted	YES	NO	NO

Let's try another example. This problem is from a delightful book by Phillips (1961) called *My Best Puzzles in Logic and Reasoning*. This one should seem easier since you are now familiar with the technique.

> "My four granddaughters are all accomplished girls." Canon Chasuble was speaking with evident self-satisfaction. "Each of them," he went on, "plays a different musical instrument and each speaks one European language as well as—if not better than—a native."
>
> "What does Mary play?" asked someone.
>
> "The cello."
>
> "Who plays the violin?"
>
> "D'you know," said Chasuble, "I've temporarily forgotten. Anno Domini, alas! But I know it's the girl who speaks French."
>
> The remainder of the facts which I elicited were of a somewhat negative character. I learned that the organist is not Valerie; that the girl who speaks German is not Lorna; and that Mary knows no Italian. Anthea doesn't play the violin; nor is she the girl who speaks Spanish. Valerie knows no French; Lorna doesn't play the harp; and the organist can't speak Italian.
>
> What are Valerie's accomplishments?

Stop now and work on solving this problem. Don't go on until you've actually worked through this problem.

You'd begin by realizing that since the relevant information is categorical, a matrix is a good form of representation. There are four granddaughters, musical instruments, and languages. Thus, the matrix can be set up as:

Granddaughter	*Musical Instrument*	*Language*
Mary	Cello	
Valerie		
Lorna		
Anthea		

Since most of the information we have is negative, let's list the possible combinations of granddaughters, instruments, and languages.

Granddaughters	*Musical Instruments*	*Languages*
Mary	Cello	Spanish or French or German
Valerie	Violin or Harp	Spanish or Italian or German
Lorna	Violin or Organ	French or Italian or Spanish
Anthea	Harp or Organ	Italian or German or French

Since the girl who plays the violin speaks French, this must be Lorna. Anthea is the organist who speaks German. This means that only Mary can speak Spanish. The only combination left for Valerie is the harp and Italian.

Admittedly, these are artificial problems, not much like the ones we encounter in real life. Let's consider a more practical application of the matrix form of problem representation.

There is considerable controversy over the issue of vitamin C as a deterrent for the common cold. How would you decide if vitamin C prevents colds? Most probably, you'd give vitamin C to some people and not others and count the number of colds in each group. Suppose you found the following results: 10 people who took vitamin C did not catch a cold; 4 people who took vitamin C caught a cold; 8 people who didn't take vitamin C didn't catch a cold and 6 people who didn't take vitamin C caught a cold. What would you conclude?

Since we have categories of information (took or didn't take vitamin C and caught or didn't catch a cold) a matrix displaying the appropriate values will help us to understand the givens.

		Vitamin C		
		Took Vitamin C	*Didn't Take Vitamin C*	
Cold	*Caught a Cold*	4	6	Total number who caught a cold 10
	Didn't Catch a Cold	10	8	Total number who didn't catch a cold 18

By examining every cell of the matrix, you can determine if vitamin C prevented colds. To see if vitamin C worked, you need to consider how many of those who caught a cold had taken vitamin C. The answer is 4 out of 10, or 40%. You also need to consider how many of those who didn't catch a cold had taken vitamin C. The answer is 10 out of 18, or 55.5%. Few would be willing to conclude from these data that vitamin C helped to prevent colds. (Research concepts are discussed more fully in the Thinking as Hypothesis Testing and Probability chapters.) The point being made here is that by representing the information in a matrix, the results can be more easily understood.

Manipulate Models

It is often a good idea to make a concrete representation for abstract problems. I'm sure that you've seen an architect's model for a planned complex like a shopping center, office building, or college campus. The miniature buildings and walkways are not made because architects love doll-sized buildings. Although they are often made to communicate architectural plans to others who are not skilled at reading blueprints, the miniature models also help the architect solve problems. With the movable parts, she or he can move the buildings to find the best way to place them before construction begins.

Let's try a problem where making a model will help in finding a solution. The problem I want you to solve has an interesting history. It was originally known as the Missionaries and Cannibals Problem with the cannibals as the "bad guys." In response to possible racist overtones, other versions have made the missionaries the "bad guys" (they converted the cannibals against their will). A later version calls the two groups Hobbits and Orks since there is no racial identification with either mythical group:

There are two groups of beings on a mythical planet in a far away galaxy: they are Hobbits and Orks. One day three Hobbits got lost while exploring the homeland of the Orks. The Hobbits could get home safely if they could cross the river that separates their two homelands. The Orks agreed to help the Hobbits cross the river, but the only boat they had could hold only two beings at a time, and the Hobbits could not let themselves ever be outnumbered by the Orks or the Orks would eat them.

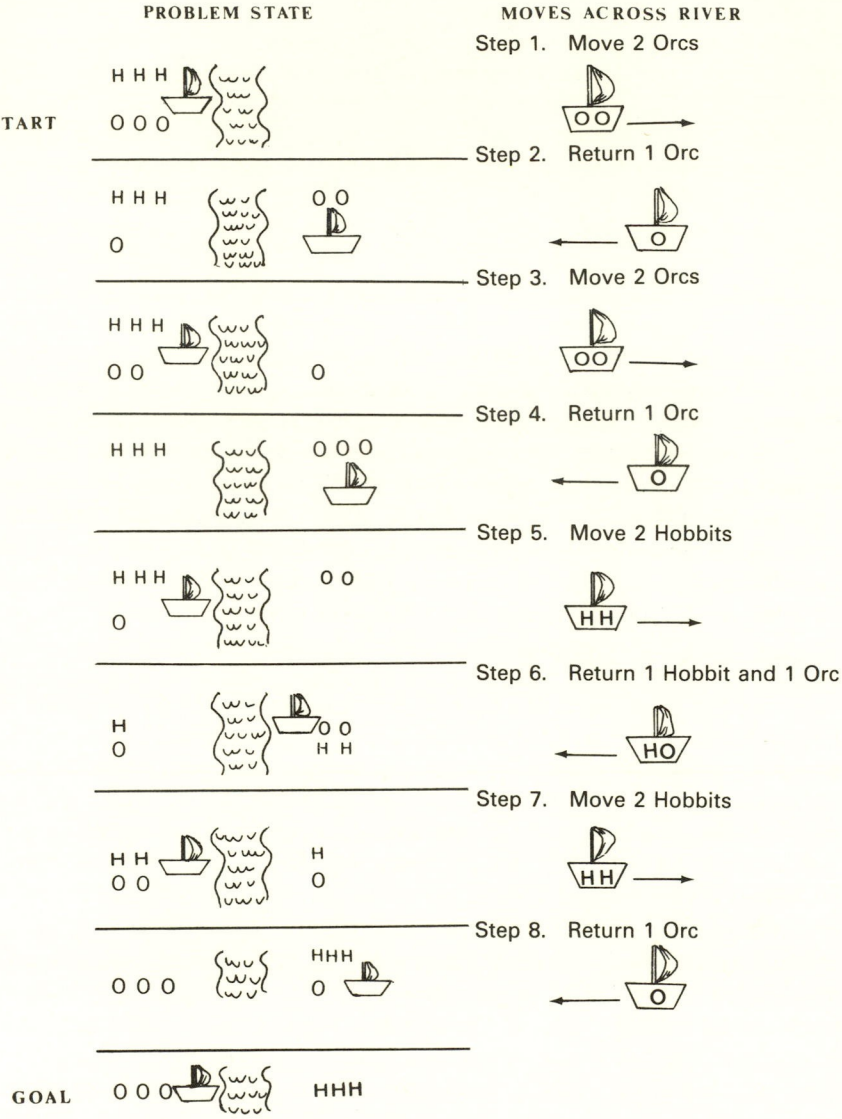

FIG. 6.9. Steps needed to move three hobbits across the river using a boat that will hold only two beings without allowing the orks to ever outnumber the hobbits.

Your problem is to figure out a sequence of moves that will carry all three Hobbits to the other side of the river and return all three Orks on their own side. The constraints are that only two beings can fit in the boat at one time, and if at anytime the Orks on one shore outnumber the Hobbits, you'll have to start over. An empty boat cannot travel across the river since it needs someone to row.

This would be an impossible problem to solve without some external form of representation. Use some small objects to represent the Hobbits and Orks and move them across an imaginary river. Three large paper clips for the Hobbits and three small paper clips for the Orks will work well. You'll have to imagine that you are transporting them in a boat. Be sure to write down all of your moves. Plan to take as long as 10 to 15 minutes to solve this problem. As you work toward the solution, be aware of how you're thinking about the moves. Don't go on until you've worked through the problem.

The complete sequence of moves needed to move the Hobbits is shown in Fig. 6.9. One of the greatest difficulties with this problem is the need to move all three Orks across the river, a situation that is not desired, in order to move the Hobbits without allowing them to become outnumbered. Problems of this sort have come to be known as **detour problems** because the path to the goal is not a direct linear one. Intermediate steps are required that seem directly opposite to the goal—in this case moving all three Orks to the opposite side of the river when the desired goal is to have all of them on the side from which they originated. It is important to recognize that the route to a goal will often involve detours. As a more realistic example, consider Leon's goal to become very wealthy. One solution path to the goal may involve going deeply into debt in order to finance his education. While going deeply into debt is seemingly antagonistic to becoming wealthy, it may be a necessary detour. Be sure to consider solution paths that involve detours when faced with difficult problems.

Select the Best Representation

It's a good idea to utilize an external form of representation (e.g., paper and pencil) whenever there are more than a few givens that need to be manipulated. The immediate or working memory span can quickly become overloaded. An external form of representation will help to alleviate this problem. Experimental results or almost any other pattern of numbers should always be graphed.

If your problem is mathematical or spatial, a diagram is likely to be helpful. Diagrams can help to disentangle any situation in which the givens have many complex interrelationships. Diagrams can make important relationships explicit, a fact that can often lead directly to the goal. Hierarchical trees are a natural form of representation when the material itself forms a hierarchically arranged structure. Matrices are likely to be useful when the givens can be grouped into categories for meaningful comparisons. "Mock-ups" or miniature models can aid in problem solving when movement and placement of the givens determine the solution. Often the way a problem is represented can mean the difference

© 1983 Field Enterprises, Inc. Courtesy of Field Newspaper Syndicate.

between a solution or a nonsolution (Posner, 1973). If you find that one form of representation isn't fruitful, try a different one.

Means-Ends Analysis

Most often progress toward the goal is not made along a single well-paved road. When the goal is not immediately attainable, we often need to take detours or break the problem down into smaller problems, called **subproblems,** each with its own goal, called a **subgoal.**

Like all of the strategies for solving problems, selecting and utilizing subgoals requires planning. The procedure by which people select subgoals and use them to progress toward the goal is called **means-ends analysis.** This is a general, often powerful method for problem solving. The problem is first broken down into subgoals. Operations that will move the problem solver closer to a subgoal are then used. An operation should reduce the distance between the problem solver's current state and the subgoal. In this manner, the problem solver will move closer and closer to the goal. Work through the following examples in order to clarify this concept.

The first step in means-ends analysis is to enumerate appropriate subgoals and to select the most promising one. Suppose that during a game of chess you decide that a good subgoal is to put the opposing king in check. The goal, of course, is to win the game, but it will be necessary to work toward subgoals to attain the goal. Putting the opposing king in check is the "end" that you're working towards. You now need to select the "means" for obtaining that end, hence the term "means-ends analysis." In order to achieve your subgoal, you determine the current state and identify any difference between where your pieces are and where you want them to be. Operations would be selected that would reduce this difference, and place the opposing king in check. Suppose no single move can achieve this subgoal. The means-ends analysis procedure would recycle, this time selecting a smaller subgoal, perhaps moving another piece out of the way. The constant recycling of these two processes—setting subgoals and reducing distances—will allow you to make progress toward the goal.

A favorite problem of psychologists that can be used to demonstrate means-ends analysis is the Tower of Hanoi problem. (I have no idea how it got this

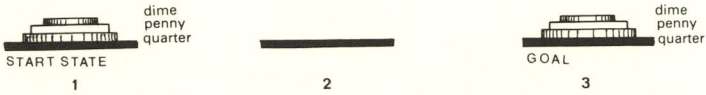

FIG. 6.10. Start state and goal for the Tower of Hanoi problem. Use the strategy of means-ends analysis to solve this problem.

name.) You can easily work this problem using any three coins of different sizes (a quarter, penny, and dime will work well) and three small sheets of paper. Stack the coins with the smallest on top and largest on the bottom on one sheet of paper. The task is to move the coins from the first piece of paper to the third so that they will be in the same size order. You may move only one coin at a time. All three pieces of paper may be used in solving the problem. Write down all of the moves you make in solving this problem. The initial and goal states are shown in Fig. 6.10.

In a means-end analysis of the Tower of Hanoi problem, one obvious subgoal is to get the quarter on the third piece of paper. Since this cannot be done immediately because the dime and penny are on it, a second subgoal needs to be considered. A second subgoal is to end up with the penny on the quarter. This can be accomplished when the penny is on the second paper and the quarter is on the third paper. This subgoal cannot yet be pursued since the dime must be moved first. In this manner, subgoals or ends are considered along with the means to accomplish them. A complete solution with all of the moves is shown in Fig. 6.11.

Means-ends analysis is a general strategy that is applicable in a wide variety of problems. There is a general purpose computer program called the **General**

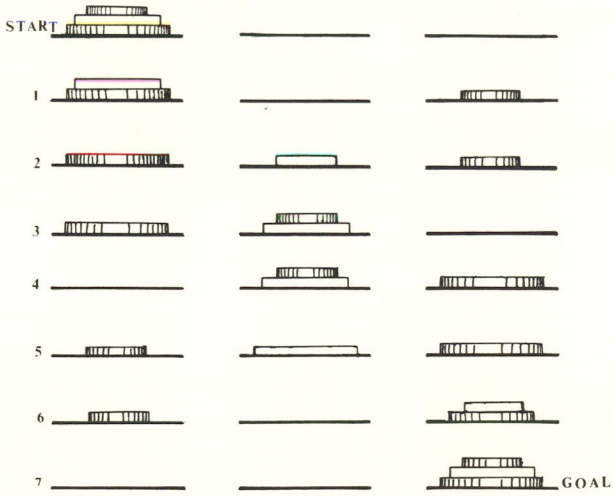

FIG. 6.11. Solution to the Tower of Hanoi problem. Notice how subgoals are planned and obtained in reaching the goal.

Problem Solver that was developed in 1972 by Newell and Simon. The program is given specific information about the problem to be solved, for example, a proof in geometry. The General Problem Solver uses this knowledge and the means-ends analysis strategy to solve the problem. With a little practice with this strategy, people can also become general problem solvers.

Working Backwards

Means-ends analysis is a **forward-looking strategy** which means that all of the planning is done by considering operations that move you closer to subgoals and, ultimately, the final goal. Sometimes, it is a better strategy to plan operations by

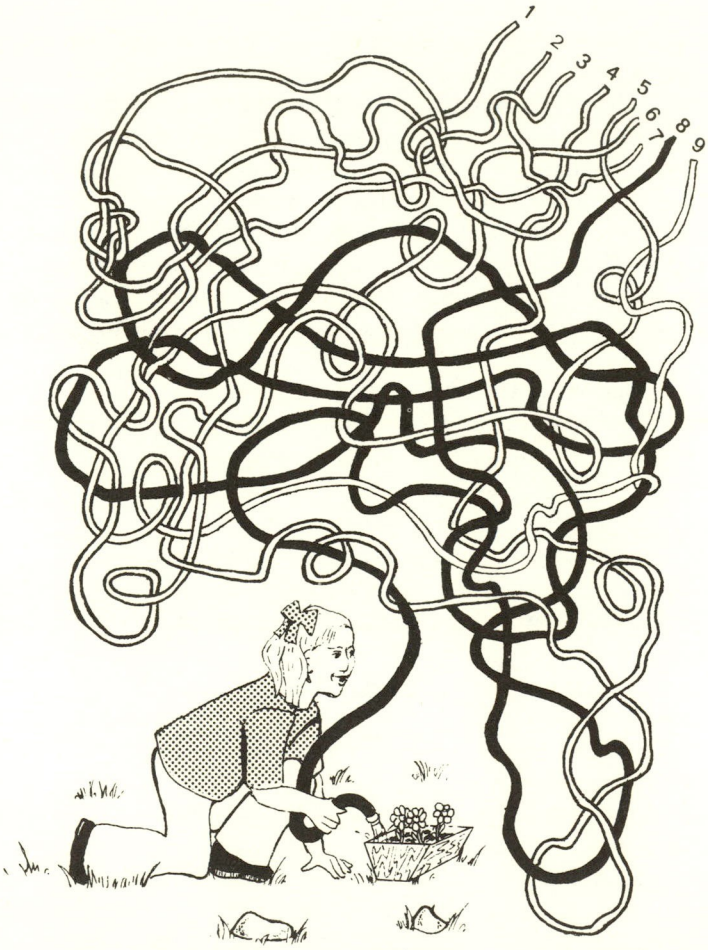

FIG. 6.12. Working backwards is a good strategy when there are fewer paths from the goal than from the start.

working backwards from the goal to your present or initial state. The simplest example of this can be found in the paper and pencil mazes that many children love to solve.

Some of these mazes have several possible paths leading away from the start box and only one correct path ending in the goal box. Even young children realize that they can solve the maze more quickly if they work the maze backward, beginning from the goal and drawing their path to the start box. An example of this type of maze is shown in Fig. 6.12.

Working backward is a good strategy to use whenever there are fewer paths leading from the goal than there are leading from the start. Of course, mazes aren't the only situation when working backward is a good strategy. Consider the following problem. "Water lilies on a certain lake double in area every twenty-four hours. From the time the first water lily appears until the lake is completely covered takes sixty days. On what day is it half covered?" (Fixx, 1978, p. 50).

The only way to solve this problem is to work backwards. Can you solve it? If the lake is covered on the 60th day and the area covered by the lilies doubles every day, how much of the lake is covered on the 59th day? The answer is half. Thus, by working backward, the problem is easy to solve. A forward-looking strategy with this problem will insure insanity.

It is often a good idea to combine forward and backward strategies. If you are faced with the task of solving proofs in geometry and trigonometry, a combination of forward and backward strategies may often prove most useful. You can start from the goal, transforming expressions on each line and then alternate operations between the start state and the goal until the solution path meets somewhere between the two.

Simplification

Problems that are difficult to solve are often complex in nature. A good way to approach such problems is to strip away as much of the complexity as possible in order to reduce it to a simpler form. Often, the best form of representation can perform the task of simplification since it will allow you to "see" the solution in an efficient way. Some authors call **simplification** the planning strategy. I believe that this terminology is misleading since most of the general problem-solving strategies require planning.

Suppose you are faced with the classic cat-in-the-tree problem. According to common folklore, cats can climb up trees, but not down. (There is no more truth to this than to the notion that elephants are afraid of mice.) Suppose that you are faced with the task of retrieving a cat from the top branch of a 10-foot tall tree. The only ladder you have is 6 feet long. You'll need to place the base of the ladder three feet from the trunk of the tree to steady it. Will you be able to reach the cat?

FIG. 6.13. The cat-in-the-tree problem. Once the information is drawn in a diagram format, it is easy to see that it is a simple geometry problem. (See text for details.)

Like most problems, a good way to approach this problem is to diagram the given facts. A diagram of this problem has been drawn in Fig. 6.13. Once the information is presented in a diagram format, it is easy to perceive the problem as a simple geometry problem: What is the hypotenuse of a triangle whose two other sides are 10 feet and 3 feet long? At this point, you'd need to rely on previously acquired knowledge about triangles to recognize and solve this problem. When the topic is thinking, there is no substitute for a good education to provide the foundation and raw materials for thought.

The formula for finding the hypotenuse of a right triangle is:

$$a^2 + b^2 = c^2$$

Substituting the appropriate values in the above equation:

$$\begin{aligned} 10^2 + 3^2 &= c^2 \\ 100 + 9 &= c^2 \\ 109 &= c^2 \\ \sqrt{109} &= c \\ 10.4 &= c \end{aligned}$$

FIG. 6.14. If the cat-in-the-tree problem is changed so that the unknown value is how high a 6-foot ladder will reach if it is placed 3 feet from the trunk, a different answer is obtained. (See text for details.)

Thus, the ladder would need to be 10.4 feet long to reach the top. But wait, could you redraw the problem using the information given to find out if you could still use the 6 foot ladder to reach the cat? See Fig. 6.14 for a slightly different diagram of the problem.

The same formula can be used, but now the unknown is not the hypotenuse, but another one of the sides of the right triangle.

Rearranging the terms will yield:

$$a^2 + b^2 = c^2$$
$$a^2 = c^2 - b^2$$
$$a^2 = 6^2 - 3^2$$
$$a^2 = 36 - 9$$

$$a^2 = 27$$
$$a = \sqrt{27}$$
$$a = 5.2$$

Thus, the top rung of the ladder will touch the tree 5.2 feet above the ground. Will you be able to reach the cat? Draw yourself near the top rung of the ladder. If you are over 5 feet tall you should have no trouble reaching the cat if you are standing on the top or second rung. In fact, you won't even have to reach up.

Simplification is a good strategy when the problem is abstract or complex or contains information that is irrelevant to finding a solution. Often, simplification will work hand-in-hand with selecting the optimal form of representation since a good representation will often simplify a problem.

Generalization and Specialization

When confronted with a problem, it is sometimes helpful to consider it as an example of a larger class of problems (**generalization**); or to consider it as a special case (**specialization**).

The form of problem representation that is most compatible with the generalization and specialization strategy is the tree diagram. Most goals can be classified as both a subset of a larger category and as a heading for a smaller one. Let's work an example to clarify what this means. As a furniture designer, you are given the problem of designing a chair that will be especially well suited for reading. How would you go about solving this problem?

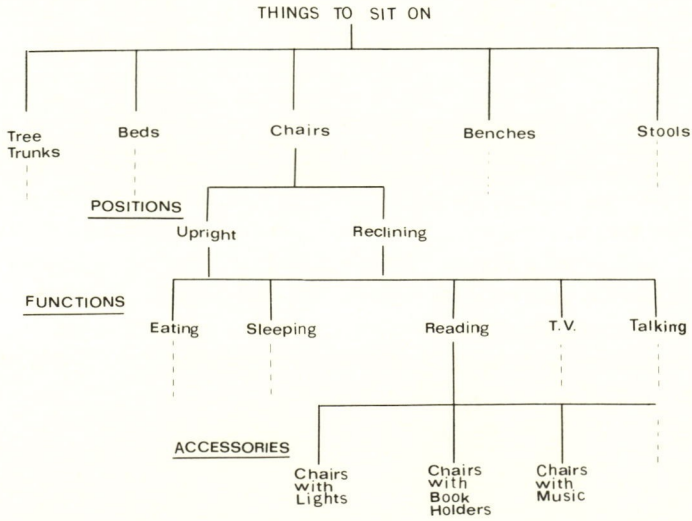

FIG. 6.15. Possible tree diagram for problem of designing a chair for reading.

As you probably realized, this is an ill-defined problem. The difficulty is largely centered on evaluating which of several possible chairs will best satisfy the goal. Use a tree diagram to classify chairs, in general, and "chairs for reading" in particular. Although there are many possible diagrams, one example is presented in Fig. 6.15.

I hope that you worked through this problem and drew your own tree diagram. As you can see in Fig. 6.15 thinking about "chairs for reading" as a subset of the category "chairs" can help you to incorporate other features of chairs in your design while custom tailoring the chair with some of the possibilities that are unique to "chairs for reading."

Thus, the process of generalization and/or specialization can help you to consider your problem from both broad and narrow perspectives.

Random Search and Trial-and-Error

Recall that the anatomy of a problem consists of a start or initial state, a goal, and solution paths leading from the start state to the goal. One strategy for searching among possible solution paths is **random search.** While this probably seems like a nonstrategy or "un-strategy," in some cases it will work quite well. When there are very few possible solution paths, random search will lead to the goal in a short time. A truly random search would mean that there is no systematic order in which the possible paths are explored and no memory for paths already tried. A systematic **trial-and-error** search through the problem space (contains the paths, goal, and start state) is preferable. *Trial-and-error* search is best applied to well-defined problems with few possible solution paths. Simple, short anagrams are good candidates for these search methods. Unscramble the following letter to form an English word.

THA

Since there are only six possible orders for these three letters (THA; TAH; HTA; HAT; ATH; AHT), trying each one until a solution is found is fairly straightforward and simple strategy. If you used a truly random search, you would not keep track of which letter orderings you used and would repeat some until the correct order was found. Systematic trial-and-error is almost always superior to random search, although only slightly better when there are very few possibilties.

Both trial-and-error and random search are poor strategies when the number of possible paths increases, because of the sheer number of possible combinations. Often, in larger problems, it is helpful to eliminate some of the paths and then search among a smaller subset with a trial-and-error strategy.

Rules

Some kinds of problems, like series problems, depend on **rules.** Once the underlying principles are established, the problem is solved. Most problems in mathematics and the physical sciences follow rules. Look back at the Tower of Hanoi problem presented earlier in the section on Means-Ends Analysis. The solution is quite easy once the rule that "a larger circle should never be placed on top of a smaller circle" was discovered. A good way to discover rules is to look for patterns in the givens or subgoals. Problems requiring rule-discovery are often used on tests of intelligence.

Complete the following pattern:

ABBACCCADDDDA------

This is a fairly simple series problem. The next six letters are EEEEEA. Certain patterns are common in problems of this sort. To detect them, count the number of repeating symbols, look across the series for repetitions at long intervals, try simple additions and subtractions, etc. This is not a trivial problem since the decoding of enemy war messages during World War II was a major factor contributing to our victory. The United States and British governments employed many professional decoders whose job it was to find rules that could be used to decipher German and Japanese military messages.

Suppose for a minute that there is intelligent life in outer space, and that they are also wondering about us. How would they let us know that they exist? Some scientists, science fiction authors, and members of the general public believe that they would make their presence known by sending messages. No one believes that these messages would be in English, or Chinese, or Samoan or any other Earth language. They would send messages in their own native tongue or native whatever if they don't have tongues. How would we on Earth recognize such messages? The United States military has decided that if we are being sent messages from outer space the one distinguishing characteristic of these messages would be a rule-governed "grammar" or patterned repetition. As strange as this may seem, the military does monitor outer space for anything that seems like a patterned communication. So far, they haven't received any and we can continue to believe, for the time being at least, that we are the most intelligent beings in space (or that the more intelligent beings do not want us to know they are out there, or that they can't reach us).

Hints

Hints are additional information that is given after an individual has begun to work on a problem. Often the hint provides additional information that is important to your solution. Sometimes a hint will require that you change the way you have been approaching the problem. A common example of the use of hints is the "hot-cold" game played by children. An object is hidden in a room. The child who is "it" wanders around the room while the other children yell "hotter" if she is moving closer to the hidden object and "colder" if she is moving away from the hidden object. In this problem, the child who is "it" should take one

FIG. 6.16. The two-string problem. How could you reach both strings at the same time? (After Maier, 1930.)

small step at a time continuing in the same direction when the hint is "hotter" and trying a slight change in direction when the hint is "colder."

Research on the way people use hints has shown that general hints like "think of new ways of using objects" don't facilitate the problem solution (Duncan, 1961). The more specific the hint, the greater the benefit derived from it.

One of psychology's favorite problems is the two-string problem. Imagine walking into a room with two strings hanging from the ceiling. The strings are too far apart for you to reach both at the same time, yet your task is to do exactly that. This situation is depicted in Fig. 6.16.

The best solution to the two-string problem involves setting one string in a swinging motion, usually by tying a heavy object to the end of one string to serve as a weight, so that the problem solver can reach the string as it swings toward him. When researchers provided hints for the problem solver by pretending to accidentally bump against one string to get it swinging, most of the problem solvers hit upon this solution, but few were consicously aware that they utilized this hint (Maier, 1931).

In one experimental investigation of how people use hints, researchers had subjects learn pairs of words so that if the experimenter said one word, the subject would respond with its pair. (This is called *paired-associates* learning.) One of the pairs that the subjects learned was "candle-box." After learning the list of paired-associates, subjects were given Duncker's (1945) candle problem, which involved affixing a candle to a wall by using a box as the candle holder (see p. 10). Did this hint help them to solve this problem? In general, their performance on this task was improved only if they were told by the experimenter to think about the pairs of words they had learned as a problem-solving aid (Weisberg, DiCamillo, & Phillips, 1978). They did not spontaneously use this hint to solve the problem, most likely because they were unaware that it was a hint. Recent research has confirmed these results with other types of problems (Perfetto, Bransford, & Franks, 1983). In general, it seems that hints are helpful only when the problem solver perceives the hint as a possible solution aid.

Good problem solvers will seek out hints. Gathering additional information can be thought of as hint-seeking behavior. It is usually a good strategy to get all of the information that you can about your problem. The additional givens will help to structure the problem space and provide direction so that solution paths may be found more easily.

Split-Half Method

The **split-half method** is an excellent search strategy when there is no a priori reason for selecting among a sequentially organized set of possible solution paths. Suppose, for example, that there is a stoppage in the plumbing system that prevents water from coming out of your kitchen sink. The stoppage is somewhere between the place where your pipes connect with the other pipes on your street and your kitchen faucet. How would you search for the pipe stoppage while making as few holes as possible in the pipe?

In this example, the solution (the place where the pipe is stopped) lies somewhere along a linear route. The best way to search in this problem is the split-half method. Since this problem requires that you break the pipe each place you search, you want to search as efficiently as possible. Begin halfway between the street connection and your kitchen sink. If you find that water can still run freely at this point, you know that the stoppage is between this point and your sink. If this happens, look again half-way between this point and your kitchen sink. If the water is still running freely at this point, then you'll know that the stoppage is closer still to the sink and you'll look again midway between that point and your sink.

Suppose that on your first attempt you find that the water is not running at this point. Then the stoppage must be between the street and this midpoint. Your next search would be midway between the current search point and the street connection. In this manner, you would continue searching until the stoppage is found. This is a good method anytime you have a similar problem, such as trying to locate a break in the electrical wiring in your home or auto.

You can use the split-half method to play a party game called "Guess Your Age." (I made this game up.) Your friends can pretend to be any age. You can guess the age of anyone between 0 and 100 with only 7 guesses. How would you do it? Begin with the age that is midway between 0 and 100, which, of course, is 50. The player would have to respond by telling you if the age she is thinking of is older or younger than 50. Thus, she would respond with "younger" or "older." Suppose that she responds, "younger." What age should you guess next? You'd pick the age midway between 0 and 50, which is 25. Suppose she now responds, "older." Your third guess should be halfway between 25 and 50. Since we're only concerned with whole numbers, your next guess would be 38. If she now responds younger, you'd guess 32, since this number is midway between 25 and 38. If the next response is older, you'd guess 35 (midway between 32 and 38). If the response is younger, you'd guess 33. At this point you know that she is pretending to be either 33 or 34. Thus, any age can be guess with at most seven guesses. Try this method out with some friends. It will be good practice in using the split-half strategy. Consider this strategy whenever there are several possible equally likely solutions.

Brainstorming

The best way to have good ideas is to have lots of ideas.
—Linus Pauling

Brainstorming is fun. It was originally proposed by Osborn (1963) as a method for group problem solving, but it's also useful for individuals working alone. Brainstorming is useful in generating additional solution paths and thus should be considered whenever the difficulty involves finding solution paths.

The goal of brainstorming is to produce a large number of possible solutions. Problem solvers are encouraged to think up wild, unusual, imaginative ideas and to write them all down, no matter how silly they seem. The underlying principle is that the greater the quantity of ideas, the greater the likelihood that at least one of them will be good. In order to foster creative use of imagination, rules include no criticism or ridicule, even when the ideas may appear ridiculous. Judgments about the worth of the ideas is deferred until a later evaluation phase. Sometimes parts of the various ideas are combined or refined to improve upon them.

Brainstorming can be done in large or small groups or alone. After the brainstorming session, the list of possible solutions can be perused to find ones that will solve the problem in light of the problem constraints, which often include financial and time limitations and/or ethical considerations.

Brainstorming was used effectively by a food manufacturer faced with the problem of finding a better way to bag potato chips. The problem solvers (corporate executives) were asked to think up the best packaging solution they had ever seen. Someone said that bagging wet leaves was the best packaging solution he had ever seen. If you attempt to bag dry leaves they crumble and don't fit into trash bags well, but if you hose them down before bagging them you can use fewer bags and fill them more easily with less empty space in each bag. Following this lead, they tried wetting potato chips and then putting them into bags. The result was disastrous—the potato chips dried into tasteless crumbs. But, this idea ultimately led to the popular potato chip that comes stacked in a can. The identical chips are formed from a potato mixture that is cooked into chip-shaped molds. In this manner, a wild and not-too-good initial solution was parlayed into a highly successful solution.

Contradiction

The method of **contradiction** works by showing that "the goal could not possibly be obtained from the givens, since it is inconsistent with the givens" (Wickelgren, 1974, p. 109). A simple example of the use of contradiction is the problem of finding out if it is snowing given that you're indoors and a large overhanging roof prevents you from looking up. If it is snowing, then there will be snow on the ground, so look down to solve this problem. If you find that there is no snow on the ground, then by the method of contradiction, you can conclude that it is not snowing.

Contradiction can be used in a variety of contexts. You may want to know if a democratic country is politically conservative or liberal. Given that all liberal candidates were recently elected, the country cannot be conservative (assuming, of course, that conservative candidates were running for the election, their political views were well known, etc.).

Suppose you are given the following mathematical problem to solve:

$x^5 = \sqrt[5]{x}$

Does $x = 10861$?

I am guessing that you don't know how to take the fifth root of a number. How would you solve this problem? Suppose you specialize this problem and try the special case where $x = 1$. One raised to any power is 1 and any root of 1 is 1. Since $X = 1$, it cannot also equal 10861; thus, by the method of contradiction, the answer is "no."

Wickelgren (1974) suggests that contradiction is a good strategy when the population of alternative goals is small or when alternative goals can be classified and thus reduced to a smaller number of mutually exclusive possibilities.

Restating the Problem

Restating the problem is a most useful strategy for ill-defined problems. In well-defined problems the goal is usually explicitly stated in unambiguous terms which leave little room for restatement.

Consider the problem that faces virtually every adult I've ever met: "How can I save money?" Countless families around the world shop in discount markets, eat peanut butter sandwiches and spend their Saturday evenings at home in an attempt to solve this problem. Suppose you restate this problem so that it becomes, "How can I have more money?" Additional solutions would now include finding a better paying job, marrying a rich man or woman, investing in high-paying stocks, winning the Irish Sweepstakes, etc. Whenever you are faced with an ill-defined problem, try to restate the goal. This is often a very good strategy since a different goal will have different solution paths. The greater the number of solution paths you have to consider, the more likely you are to obtain the goal.

Analogies and Metaphors

Gick and Holyoak (1980) ask, "Where do new ideas come from?" Many scientists and mathematicians respond that their ideas or solutions to problems come from recognizing **analogies** and **metaphors** drawn from different academic disciplines (Hadamard, 1945). In fact, it seems that the most common form of inference is made by noting similarities (analogies and metaphors) between two or more situations. Like hints, the analogy must be recognized as relevant in the problem being considered and then modified for the particular situation.

Consider the following problem:

> A small country fell under the iron rule of a dictator. The dictator ruled the country from a strong fortress. The fortress was situated in the middle of the country, surrounded by farms and villages. Many roads radiated outward from the fortress like spokes on a wheel. A great general arose who raised a large army at the border and vowed to capture the fortress and free the country of the dictator. The general knew that if his entire army could attack the fortress at once it could be captured. His troops were poised at the head of one of the roads leading to the fortress, ready to attack. However, a spy brought the general a disturbing report. The ruthless dictator had planted mines on each of the roads. The mines were set so that small bodies of men could pass over them safely, since the dictator needed to be able to move troops and workers to and from the fortress. However, any large force would detonate the mines. Not only would this blow up the road and render it impassable, but the dictator would then destroy many villages in retaliation. A full-scale direct attack on the fortress therefore appeared impossible. (Gick & Holyoak, 1980, p. 351)

To help you solve this problem, I'll also give you a hint. The solution is analogous to one discussed earlier in this chapter, although the context is entirely different. Stop for a few minutes and attempt to work on this problem. Think about the problems presented earlier.

The solution to this problem is analogous to the one used in the inoperable stomach tumor problem. In that problem (Duncker, 1945), the best solution involved sending weak rays through the body simultaneously from several different points so that they would converge on the tumor. Similarly, the army could be divided into small groups that would attack the fortress from all sides. Did you recognize that these problems were essentially similar in form and could be solved with the same solution?

Gordon (1961), originator of a group called "Synectics," has presented guidelines for the use of analogies in solving problems. The term "Synectics" was taken from the Greek. It means joining together of different and apparently unrelated elements. Gordon suggests that we consider four different types of analogies when faced with a problem:

1. **Personal Analogy**

If you want to understand a complex phenomenon think of yourself as a participant in the phenomenon. For example, if you want to understand the molecular structure of a compound, think of yourself as a molecule. How would you behave? What other molecules would you want to attach yourself to? Get away from reliance on scientific notations and actually pretend to be a molecule bouncing in a compound. You may see relationships from this perspective that you were blind to when acting as a scientist.

2. **Direct Analogy**

Compare the problems you're working on with several problems in other domains. According to Gordon, this method was used by Alexander Graham Bell: "it struck me that the bones of the human ear were very massive indeed, as compared with the delicate thin membrane that operated them, and the thought occurred that if a membrane so delicate could move bones relatively so massive, why should not a thicker and stouter piece of membrane move my piece of steel. And the telephone was conceived" (Gordon, 1961, p. 41).

A particularly fertile area for analoges is biology, where many solutions to biological problems have been evolving since the first life form appeared on Earth. When a Synectics group was faced with the problem of devising a bottle closure that could be used with glue or nail polish, the analogy they used was the biological closure of the anus (rectum). Apparently, this solution worked quite well. (You can think about this the next time you use a bottle of LePage's mucilage.)

3. **Symbolic Activity**

This solution strategy utilizes visual imagery. Its goal is to get away from the constraints of words or mathematical symbols. Students who utilized imagery to visualize the tumor problem and the fortress problem were most likely to notice spontaneously that the two problems were analogous. If you work on generating a clear image of a problem, you may "see" a solution that had been overlooked.

4. **Fantasy Analogy**

In your wildest dreams, what would you want of a solution? An example of this is to image two small insects that would automatically zip your jacket or a silk worm that would spin silk rapidly to keep you warm when the temperature drops. These are *fantasy analogies.*

Analogies and metaphors are useful problem-solving strategies; however, difficulties can arise when analogies are misapplied. Consider this problem posed by DeBono (1967b, p. 7):

> Place three bottles upright on a table or on the floor. Position them so that each bottle forms the corner point of a triangle of equal sides. The distance between the bases of any two bottles should be slightly more than the length of a knife.
>
> Using only [the] four knives, construct a platform on top of the bottles. No part of any knife may touch the ground. The platform must be strong enough to support a full glass of water.

The solution to this problem involves forming a triangle by interweaving three of the knives. The fourth isn't used. Now that I've told you how to solve the three bottle problem, try this one (DeBono, 1967b, p. 31):

> This time use only two bottles. Place these upright, their bases separated by the length of a knife handle added to the length of a knife.
>
> Using only [the] four knives, erect between the two bottles a bridge which will support at its center the weight of a full glass of water. The ends of the bridge rest on the tops of the bottles. No part of any knife may touch the ground.

Stop now, and work on this problem.

The solution entails interweaving the four knives so that they form a square area with only two of the knives resting on a bottle. This is a difficult problem to solve. An analogy can be used from the earlier problem, but it needs to be adjusted so that each knife is no longer resting on a bottle. You can use the analogy of folding the tops of a carton by sliding the corner of the fourth side under the corner of the first one. People often find that the *change* in the way the second problem is solved is a source of difficulty. DeBono (1977b, p. 37), concludes,

> There is a limit to the usefulness of re-examining old experiences in this way. Sometimes it is more efficient to approach the problem as a fresh one than to spend a long time seeking a parallel in past experience. It depends on how similar the other problems are, but that depends on how good one is at detecting similarities. . . .

Consult an Expert

If at first you don't succeed, try, try, again. Then quit. No use being a damned fool about it.
—W. C. Fields (quoted in Teger, 1979, p. XIV)

Often in life, we don't have to solve problems alone. Sometimes, the best way to solve a problem is to let experts do it for us. People seek accountants for help with their tax problems, attorneys for their legal problems, physicians for their health problems. We elect officials to handle the problems of running our country and rely on military experts to wage wars. These people became experts in their field by obtaining the appropriate knowledge in their subject area, and through repeated applications of this knowledge to real-world problems. Consulting an expert is often an excellent solution strategy. Their greater experience and knowledge will allow them to solve many problems in their area of expertise much more efficiently than a novice. If you decide to consult an expert, the problem becomes: (1) how to know somebody who is an expert; and (2) how to select which "expert" to use. Once you've passed these hurdles, your problems still aren't over. You need to be sure that the expert has all of the facts and has considered all of the relevant alternatives. Listen carefully to the expert's analysis of the risks and alternatives, but make the decision yourself. An expert is a problem-solving aid, not the solution.

Select the Best Strategy

Fourteen different strategies have been presented as aids in problem solving. When confronted with a problem, how do you know which to use? It is important to keep in mind that these strategies are not mutually exclusive. It will often be best to use them in combinations. The best strategy or strategies depends on the nature of the problem. After all, if you are taking an exam, you could be expelled if you consult the paper of an "expert" student sitting next to you.

Along with each strategy, I presented some guidelines for its appropriate use. In general, a few higher level "strategies for selecting strategies" include:

1. If the problem is ill defined, try to restate the goal or the problem.
2. When there are very few possible solutions, a trial-and-error approach will work well.
3. If a problem is complex, try simplification, means-ends analysis, and generalization and specialization.
4. When there are fewer paths leading away from the goal than there are from the start state, work backwards.
5. If you can gather additional information, do it. Look for and utilize hints.

6. If there is an ordered array of equally likely alternatives, try the split-half method and seek rules.

7. If the problem is a lack of possible solution paths, brainstorm to generate alternative solution paths.

8. Problems in mathematics and logic are especially amenable to a solution by contradiction.

9. Use of analogies and metaphors and consulting an expert are widely applicable to all sorts of problems.

10. Remember that these are only guidelines to solving problems. The best way to be an expert problem solver is to solve lots of problems.

PROBLEM SOLVING PROBLEMS

Functional Fixedness and Mental Set

Recall the two-string problem presented earlier in this chapter. The task was to grasp simultaneously two strings that hung from the ceiling. The correct solution involved setting one string into motion, perhaps by tying a heavy object like a pair of pliers to its end to serve as a weight. One reason why this was such a difficult problem is **functional fixedness.** Subjects were fixated or "stuck" on the usual function of a pair of pliers and have difficulty thinking of them as having a different function.

Another example of functional fixedness was presented in the Introduction (Chapter 1). In a classic problem, subjects were asked to attach a candle to the wall so that it could be burned, using only a box of thumbtacks and some matches. Subjects had difficulty thinking of the box as a candle holder since they saw it in terms of its usual function—a container for thumbtacks.

Functional fixedness is one kind of **mental set.** I think of these terms as "ruts in one's thinking." They are predispositions to think and respond in certain ways. To demonstrate how powerful some sets can be, work on the nine-dot problem in Fig. 6.17. Stop now and work on this problem.

FIG. 6.17. The nine-dot problem. Using no more than four straight lines and without lifting your pencil from the paper, draw a line through all nine dots.

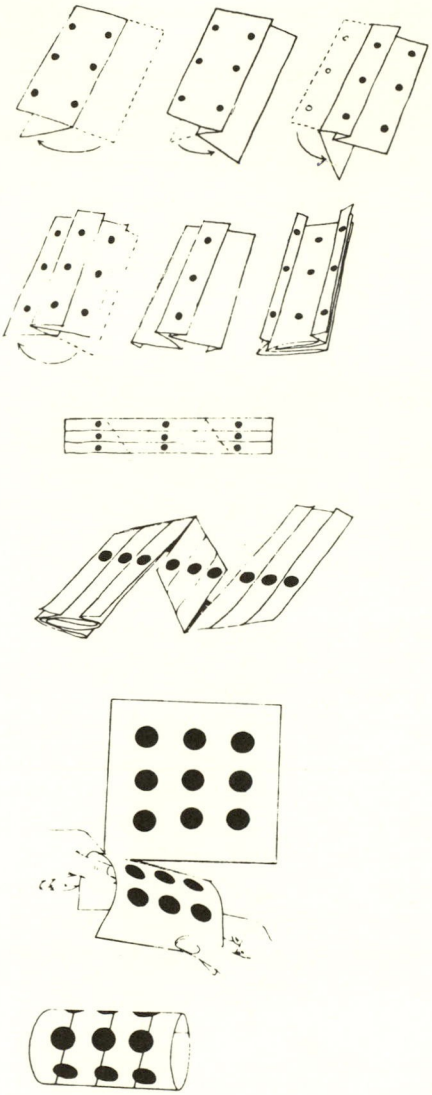

One possible solution is to fold the paper as indicated so that the dots line up in a straight line.

It is also possible to roll up the puzzle and draw a spiral through the dots, and otherwise violate the two-dimensional format.

FIG. 6.18. Two possible solutions to the nine-dot problem. (from Adams, J. L. (1979). *Conceptual blockbusting*. N.Y.: W. W. Norton, pp. 25–26).

The difficulty posed by the nine-dot problem comes from a perceptual set imposed by the square arrangement. Most people attempt to solve the problem by staying within an imaginary boundary formed by the outer dots. In addition, most people attempt solutions in which the line goes through the center of each dot.

There are several solutions to the nine-dot problem. Each of them involves *breaking-set* in some way. Two solutions (Adams, 1979, pp. 25–26) are presented in Fig. 6.18. A few other more exotic solutions, including one submitted by a 10-year-old girl, which consists of one very fat line drawn through all nine dots can be found in Adams' (1979) gem of a book, *Conceptual Blockbusting*. The set of staying within the rectangular area is pervasive and difficult to break. Strategies that get you to view problems in novel ways, like the personal analogy strategy, are good ways to work on set-breaking solutions.

Misleading and Irrelevant Information

My father used to love this riddle:

> Suppose you are a bus driver. On the first stop you pick up 6 men and 2 women. At the second stop 2 men leave and 1 woman boards the bus. At the third stop 1 man leaves and 2 women enter the bus. At the fourth stop 3 men get on and 3 women get off. At the fifth stop 2 men get off, 3 men get on, 1 woman gets off and 2 women get on. What is the bus driver's name?

Could you answer this question without rereading the problem? The bus driver's name is, of course, your name since the riddle began, "Suppose you are a bus driver." All of the information about the rest of the passengers was irrelevant. Often information that is irrelevant to the problem serves to mislead problem solvers down dead-end paths.

To avoid being misled by information, be clear about the goal state. Simplification will sometimes help in separating the relevant from the irrelevant givens.

Let's try another example:

> If you have black socks and brown socks in your drawer mixed in the ratio of 4 to 5, how many socks will you have to take out to make sure of having a pair of the same color?" (Fixx, 1978).

Think about this problem. What is relevant? What is irrelevant? The answer is three socks since any two must match if there are only brown and black socks. The information about the ratio of socks is irrelevant and misleading. Imagine yourself actually picking socks from a drawer and this problem will be easier to solve.

World View Constraints

Often we fail to solve problems because of the **world view constraints** placed on us by our social class, nationality, or political views. Consider the following problem:

A ball 1 inch in diameter falls into a 3 inch length of pipe that is 1 ⅛ inch in diameter. The pipe is firmly affixed to the concrete pavement. It is extremely important to remove the ball. You and some friends are faced with this task. All you have is some fine wire and your collective abilities to solve this problem. What do you do?

Most people approach this task by attempting to bend fine wire into tweezers to pluck it up. A better solution is to urinate into the pipe so that the ball will float to the top. This probably never occurred to you since it is not an acceptable thought for most people in our society. Although this has never been verified, it would probably be an easier task for people in other societies where urination is not considered as private an act as it is in our society.

Mechanization

Using jars with the following capacities, measure the amount of water desired. (After Luchins, 1942)

	Jug A	*Jug B*	*Jug C*	*Desired*
1	14	163	25	99
2	18	43	10	5
3	9	42	6	21
4	20	59	4	31
5	23	49	3	20

Stop now and solve these five problems. Keep a record of how you went about solving them.

The first four problems can be solved by filling Jug B, then filling Jug A from it once and then filling Jug C from it twice. The water left in Jug B will be the desired amount. In algebraic terms, it's B-A-2C.

Look at how you solved the fifth problem. Did you use this formula? Most people do although it's much simpler to fill Jug A, then pour from it into C to get the answer. People overlook the simpler solution because their approach to the problem has become mechanized. You can guard against this by rethinking occasionally about the way you are solving a problem. **Mechanization** can be helpful in that it saves solution times when we don't have to stop and rethink each problem, but it can also blind us to better solutions.

CHAPTER SUMMARY

1. All problems can be conceptualized as being composed of "anatomical" parts that include a start state, a goal state and paths leading from the start to the goal. This entire structure is called the problem space.

2. It is common to divide the problem solving process into four stages: preparation or familiarization; production; judgment or evaluation; and incubation. Incubation is an optional stage that does not always occur.

3. Problems can be classified along a continuum ranging from well defined to ill defined. Well-defined problems have explicit paths and goals. Ill-defined problems are subject to multiple interpretations.

4. An invaluable aid in solving problems is to utilize an external form of representation. The best representation to choose will depend on the problem type.

5. Fourteen different strategies for approaching problems were presented. Often several will be used together in solving a problem. General guidelines were offered for the appropriate use of each.

6. There ar four common sources of difficulty that problem solvers encounter. Functional fixedness refers to the failure to utilize items in unusual ways. Mental set refers to the predisposition to respond to any situation in a fixed way. Misleading and irrelevant information can "derail one's trail of thought" and can lead you down blind paths. The constraints imposed upon us by our society cause us to view problems from our own narrow experiences. Mechanization refers to the rote unthinking applications of previous solutions without stopping to think about improving our strategies.

Terms to Know

You should be able to define or describe the following terms or concepts. If you find that you're having difficulty with any term, be sure to reread the section where it is discussed.

Anatomy of a Problem
Initial State
Goal State
Solution Paths
Problem Space
Preparation or Familiarization Stage
Production Stage
Judgment or Evaluation Stage
Incubation
Insight
Well-Defined Problems
Ill-Defined Problems
Perceptual Reorganization
Operations
Hierarchical Trees
Matrix
Detour Problems
Subproblems
Subgoal
Means-Ends Analysis
General Problem Solver
Working Backwards
Forward-Looking Strategy

Simplification
Generalization
Specialization
Random Search
Trial-and-Error
Rules
Hints
Split-Half Method
Brainstorming
Contradiction
Restating the Problem
Analogies and Metaphors
Personal Analogy
Direct Analogy
Symbolic Activity
Fantasy Analogy
Functional Fixedness
Mental Set
World View Constraints
Mechanization

Be sure that you can answer the following questions:

1. Identify and explain the "anatomical" parts of all problems.

2. What are the four stages in problem solving? How does each stage contribute to the solution?

3. Give an example of a well-defined and an ill-defined problem. In general, how do they differ?

4. How are external forms of representation (e.g., graphs, diagrams) helpful in solving problems?

5. Explain how the General Problem Solver is able to solve a wide variety of problems.

6. Compare and contrast the fourteen problem solving strategies presented in this chapter. Provide an example when each might be used.

7. How does each of the problem-solving problems relate to the anatomical parts of a problem? For example, irrelevant information causes people to consider solution paths that don't lead to the goal. How do the other problem solving problems interfere with obtaining a direct route to the goal?

8. There are good and bad aspects to mechanization. What are they?

Exercises

Try out the problem solving skills you've learned in this chapter.

1. A frog fell into a five-foot deep well and needs to begin the arduous task of hopping out. Every hour he jumps two feet, but then slides back one foot. How long will it take him to get out of the well? (*Hint:* draw a diagram.)

2. Irvin has begun a jogging program. He jogs 2 miles north, then turns right and jogs 3 miles, then heads left 1 mile, then turns and jogs 2 miles to the right, then he jogs 3 miles south, and finally 5 miles west. How far is he from his starting point? (*Hint:* draw a map.)

3. You agree to be a contestant on a silly television show. There are 24 gift boxes lined up in four rows of six boxes each. One of these boxes contains the grand prize (a weekend in San Bernardino, California). You can ask your television host any question that has a "Yes" or "No" answer. What questions would you ask him? How many questions would you need to definitely identify the box containing the grand prize? (*Hint:* Use the strategy that works best with an organized array of equally likely choices.)

4. There are four dogs sitting in front of their dog houses. The dogs, in left to right order, are Pizza, Tiger, Lady, and Sancho. Based on the information given below, figure out which dog eats Crunchy Blend dog food.

1. Pizza lives in a blue dog house.
2. The dog who lives in a red house eats Yummies.
3. Sancho eats Butcher Boy dog food.
4. Lady lives next to the dog with the green house.
5. Tiger lives next to the dog who eats Crunchy Blend.
6. The dog in the white house is next to the dog who eats Butcher Boy.
7. The dog who eats medium rare steak is farthest away from the dog who eats Butcher Boy.

(*Hint:* Use the form of representation that is recommended when the givens are taken from categories of information.)

5. Solve the following anagrams:

CRA	ETA
NIK	NTU

(*Hint:* Use the strategy that is recommended for problems with few solution paths.)

6. Design an automobile that can drive across land and water.

7. Using Fig. 6.19, place the cowboys on their horses so that they can ride properly. (After Scheerer, 1963). (*Hint:* You will have to break set to answer this problem.)

FIG. 6.19. Can you figure out how to place the cowboys on their horses so that they could ride them properly? (From Scheerer, M. Problem solving. © 1963 by Scientific American, Inc. All rights reserved. (Solution is presented on p. 207, see Fig. 6.21.)

FIG. 6.20. The notched checkerboard problem. (After Wickelgren, 1974, p. 29.)

8. Using only six short sticks, arrange them to form four equilateral triangles. (*Hint:* This problem will also require that you break a mental set.)

9. The notched-checkerboard problem: "You are given a checkerboard and 32 dominoes. Each domino covers exactly two adjacent squares on the board. Thus, the 32 dominoes can cover all 64 squares on the checkerboard. Now suppose two squares are cut off at diagonally opposite corners of the board (see Fig. 6.20). Is it possible to place 31 dominoes on the board so that all of the 62 remaining squares are covered? If so, show how it can be done. If not, prove it impossible" (Wickelgren, 1974, p. 29). (*Hint:* Specialize and consider which squares can be covered by each domino.)

10. The Jealous-Husbands Problem: "Three jealous husbands and their wives, having to cross a river at a ferry, find a boat. However, the boat is so small that it can hold no more than two people. Find the simplest schedule of crossings that will permit all six people to cross the river so that no woman is left in company with any of the men unless her husband is present. It is assumed that all passengers on the boat unboard before the next trip and that at least one person has to be in the boat for each crossing." (Reed, 1982, p. 308). (*Hint:* This problem is directly analogous to another one solved in this chapter.)

11. A favorite problem of Newell and Simon's (1972) is this cryptarithmetic problem:

$$\begin{array}{r} D\ O\ N\ A\ L\ D \\ +\ G\ E\ R\ A\ L\ D \\ \hline R\ O\ B\ E\ R\ T \end{array}$$

The problem is to substitute a digit (0 through 9) for each letter so that the letters follow the usual rules of addition. (*Hint*: D = 5.) I'll demonstrate the first step:

$$\begin{array}{r} 5\ O\ N\ A\ L\ 5 \\ \underline{G\ E\ R\ A\ L\ 5} \\ R\ O\ B\ E\ R\ 0 \end{array}$$

I'll give you a second hint: R must be an odd number. Complete this problem.

12. Complete the following letter series. (This problem has been used in intelligence tests for English school children.)

OTTFFSS---

What are the next three letters? (*Hint:* Thinking about repeating sequences of letters will lead to blind paths.)

13. An anxious mother wants to send a T-square (a rigid drafting instrument) to her son in college. The T-square is 13″ long. Unfortunately the express mail service won't accept any packages more than 12″ long. How was she able to send the T-square by express mail. (No, she didn't cut or fold it. *Hint:* Draw boxes around an imaginary 13″ T-square.)

14. Show that the following mathematical formula is true:

$$4 + X^3 \div X^2 + 1 \neq 6$$

(*Hint:* Consider special cases and contradiction.)

15. A penny gum machine is filled with red and white gumballs. There is no way of knowing the color of the next ball. If Mrs. Jones wants to be sure of getting a matching pair of gumballs, how many pennies *must* she be prepared to spend (Gardner, 1978)? (*Hint:* This problem is analogous to another one presented in this chapter.)

16. Find problems of your own and apply the strategies you've learned in this chapter.

SUGGESTED READINGS

There are many excellent books and articles on problem solving. My personal favorites are Adam's (1979) delightful little book, *Conceptual Blockbusting: A Guide to Better Ideas* and Gardner's (1978) *Aha! Insight*. They provide many examples of clever solutions to problems.

A classic in the field or problem solving is Rubinstein's (1975) text *Patterns of Problem Solving*. This text is heavily mathematical and requires serious concentration. His co-authored undergraduate text (Rubinstein & Pfeiffer, 1980), *Concepts in Problem*

FIG. 6.21. Solution to the problem shown in Fig. 6.19. This is a difficult problem because it requires that we break a mental set by rotating the horses 90° to a vertical position and switching heads for each horse. (From Scheerer, M. Problem solving. © 1963 by Scientific American, Inc. All rights reserved.)

Solving is highly recommended. Another classic is Wickelgren's (1974) text *How to Solve Problems*. Like Rubinstein's 1975 book, this is not easy reading because of its heavy reliance on mathematics.

Hayes' (1981) *The Complete Problem Solver* and Whimbey and Lochhead's (1982) *Problem Solving and Comprehension* (3rd Ed.) are easy-to-read, interesting books in this area. Both are written for undergraduate audiences. If you don't have enough problems in life, you can always purchase books filled with them. Virtually every bookstand has several to choose from. Some thought provoking problems can be found in Phillips' (1961) *My Best Puzzles in Logic and Reasoning*. Fixx, the author of *The Complete Book of Running*, has written several delightful books filled with problems to solve. I especially recommend his 1978 book *Solve It!*

Polya's (1957) book *How To Solve It* gives helpful advice about understanding problems, devising plans, carrying them out, and then looking back. If you'd like some empirical evidence that people can, in fact, improve the way they solve problems by learning general strategies, see Klein and Weizenfeld's (1978) journal article, "Improvement of Skills for Solving Ill-Defined Problems," and Schoenfeld and Herrmann's (1982) journal article, "Problem Perception and Knowledge Structure in Expert and Novice Mathematical Problem Solvers." Schoenfeld and Herrmann found that after college students took a general problem solving course they demonstrated a marked improvement in their problem solving performance.

7 Decision Making

Contents

Making Sound Decisions 210
Decision Making Among Trained Professionals 212
Pitfalls and Pratfalls in Decision Making 213
  Failure to Seek Disconfirming Evidence 214
  Availability Heuristic 216
  Representativeness Heuristic 219
  Belief in the Law of Small Numbers 220
  Wishful Thinking (Pollyanna Principle) 221
  Entrapment 222
Uncertainty and Risks 223
  Assessing Risks 223
Elimination by Aspects 225
Multidimensional Comparisons 225
Preparing a Worksheet 228
  Defining the Problem 228
  Generating the Alternatives 229
  Listing the Considerations 229
  Weighting the Considerations 230
  Weighting the Alternatives 231
  Calculating a Decision 232
  Dilemmas in Decision Making 235
Postdecision Commitment and Evaluation 236
  Cognitive Dissonance 236
  Hindsight and Forethought 237

Six doctors in white hospital coats approach your bed. No one is smiling. The results of the biopsy are in. One doctor explains that the cells were irregular in shape; they appeared abnormal. It is possible that the tumor was not clearly malignant, but not clearly normal either. They probably removed the entire tumor. It's hard to be certain about these things. You have some choices. You could leave the hospital this afternoon and forget about this unpleasant episode, except for semiannual checkups. There is an above-average chance, however, that some abnormal cells remain and will spread and grow. On the other hand, you could choose to have the entire area surgically removed. While this would be major surgery, it would clearly reduce the risk of cancer.

How do you decide what to do? Your first response is probably to ask the doctors what they recommend. But if you do, it's likely that you won't receive a consensus of opinion. Often physicians disagree about the best way to treat a disease, especially a controversial one like cancer. It is possible that some will believe that the risk of cancer is small enough to warrant the wait-and-see decision, while others believe that immediate surgery is the best decision. Ultimately the decision is yours.

Of course, not all decisions are a matter of life and death. We are constantly making minor decisions without much thought, such as what to wear, what to eat for breakfast, which pen to buy, and when to go to sleep. Everyone is faced with a lifetime of decisions, and some of them have major and far-reaching consequences. In this chapter we are concerned with life's major decisions. Major decisions include medical decisions like the one at the beginning of this chapter, whether to marry, whom to marry, if and when to have children, what kind of occupation to choose, where to live, how to spend your hard-earned dollars, etc. These are all personal decisions. Most of us will also be required to make professional and business decisions like when to increase your company's inventory, whether to invest in a new invention, how to negotiate a contract, which party to support during political upheaval, and how to increase profits. In this chapter you will learn about decision-making skills designed to help you make sound decisions. To accomplish this, we look at the kinds of decisions made by professional decision makers, examine common pitfalls and fallacies in the decision making process, consider the risks involved and develop a strategy or plan that you can always use when faced with a major decision.

MAKING SOUND DECISIONS

The decision making process is stressful. Ask anyone you know who has recently made an important decision and you will undoubtedly be told about sleepless nights, loss of appetite, irritability, and generalized feelings of anxiety. Autobiographical and biographical accounts of decision making stress can be found in the books written by and about several past presidents. Theodore C. Sorensen (1965) in his book, *Kennedy,* tells of the stress John Kennedy faced during the Berlin blockade crisis, and a book written by Richard M. Nixon before his presidency, appropriately titled *Six Crises* (1962), tells about the stress caused by his early political decisions. It is not surprising that many people will avoid making decisions whenever possible. Although avoidance is one way of handling stressful decisions, it is seldom a good way. In most cases, avoiding a decision is, in fact, making one without any of the benefits of a carefully thought out consideration of the problem.

A decision always involves two or more competing alternatives of action. Usually each alternative has several pros and cons associated with it. The decision maker has to choose the "best" alternative. Although decision making starts with the awareness that a problem exists, it differs from traditional problem solving in that there is no single correct solution. The difficulty lies in judging which alternative is best. Usually decisions have to be made with missing information and involve guesses and predictions about future events. In the medical scenario at the beginning of this chapter, the best decision must take into account the likelihood of developing cancer at some time in the future. When you decide which stock to invest in, you must consider what the economy will be like in the years to come. Similarly the decision whether or not to have children requires that you think about what your life will be like with children who don't even exist yet.

Decision making is an active process. The decision maker takes responsibility for her or his own future. After all, you are in the best position for determining how you want to spend your life and how you should make the business and professional decisions that will ultimately reflect on you. Good decision makers get the good jobs and make favorable decisions about their personal lives as well. Although many famous instances of good decisions (profitable investments, successful army maneuvers) and bad decisions (Watergate, the U.S. attempt to rescue American hostages in Iran) come to mind, it is important to realize that a decision is judged to be good or bad after the fact. For example, most Americans would have agreed that President Carter made a wise decision to rescue American hostages in Iran if it had been successful and no lives were lost. However, since it failed and eight Americans were killed, it is now seen as a bad decision.

Often, we will never know if the best decision was made. If you are a college senior who must decide between a lucrative career in accounting or more personally rewarding career as a high school English teacher, you may never be sure if you picked the better option since you can only speculate about the career you didn't select. Robert Frost, the famous American poet, captured this feeling in his poem about a traveler who comes to a fork in the road. The traveler can never know about "the path not taken."

Before a decision can be made, the individual must realize that a problem exists and that there are several possible solutions to the problem. Let's consider an example with which many of you will be able to identify. Joan is taking several demanding college courses. She also needs to supplement her income by working part time and has family obligations as well. Her free time is virtually nonexistent. Joan has a problem. She must decide how to juggle all of these commitments while still having some time left for herself. Joan has to realize that a problem exists. Too often this first step is missed and inertia sets in. People will continue doing what they have been doing without contemplating ways to improve a difficult situation. A clear definition of the problem is the first step in successful decision making. Simply stated, the problem is that Joan has too many responsibilities and this is making her feel anxious and stressed. The best solution will give her more time for herself while still allowing her to fulfill her responsibilities. Since these are essentially conflicting goals, the best decision will probably involve a compromise that will only partially satisfy each. It is not likely that she will find a course of action that will allow her to fill her days with leisure activities while maintaining high grades, earning money, and caring for her family.

The objective criteria for a good decision are that it is feasible and that it will, at least, help to solve the problem. Some possible good decisions for Joan include finding a higher paying job so she would need to work fewer hours, beginning a more efficient study program and visiting her family less frequently. You may be surprised to find that with a little effort several possibilities occur to you that you might otherwise never have considered.

If you've seen the movie "Star Trek II: The Wrath of Khan" you've seen a popularized version of the need to define clearly the problem. In the opening scene, an attractive pointy-eared Vulcan is facing a serious problem. A sister spaceship has wandered into neutral territory and has sent a distress signal. If she does not go in to save them they will perish; if she does she risks enemy attack. She nervously decides to follow them and is immediately apprised that her starship is under attack. We soon learn that this is a computer simulated drill designed to test the decision making skills of future starship commanders and that only one person has made the correct decision in this drill. Of course, it is Captain Kirk. The question of interest is whether he decided to attempt to save the sister ship and thus risk attack of his own spaceship or whether he decided to sacrifice the crew of the sister ship to save lives on his own spaceship. It seems that Captain Kirk did neither. Later we find out that he redesigned the computer problem so that he would have additional choices with more favorable outcomes. For him, the problem was "how to change contingencies in a mock drill." For others, the problem had been "how to save the sister starship without being attacked." Captain Kirk made a superior decision because he defined the problem in a unique way. The point being made here is that often there are alternative ways of formulating what the problem is, and some will result in more favorable outcomes than others. Different formulations will lead to different solutions.

DECISION MAKING AMONG TRAINED PROFESSIONALS

It seems logical that one way to understand how good decisions are made is by studying professional decision makers—doctors, judges, research scientists and others who routinely make important decisions that affect society.

In recent years a comprehensive series of experiments by several leading psychologists has revealed an interesting fact about the decisions made by trained professionals. They are often wrong. Moreover, they are wrong in predictable ways. This finding is of great concern because it is the professional decision makers in our society who determine, for example, whether a tissue sample is malignant, whether an individual has committed a crime, and whether a certain level of radiation is harmful. Because the unfortunate consequences of wrong decisions by professional decision makers are painfully obvious, an examination of the types of errors they make is an important initial step toward correcting them.

Perhaps the most intriguing finding regarding decision making errors by professionals is that their wrong intuitions are shared by laymen. It seems that despite the many years of education they receive, professionals make the same kinds of mistakes that are made by people without their specialized education. While physicians learn medicine and lawyers learn jurisprudence, few are being trained in the essential skills of decision making. Not even those trained in formal disciplines such as logic and probability theory are free from certain flaws in thinking.

A **fallacy** is an error or mistake in the thinking process. If a bad decision is made, then something went wrong in the decision making process. An example of common thinking fallacies among trained professionals can be found in research conducted by Smedslund (1963). He presented trained nurses with a deck of cards which supposedly contained information gleaned from the files of 100 patients. Each card indicated whether a patient had a particular disease and whether a particular symptom was present or absent in the patient. Thus, there were four possible combinations for each patient. The patient (1) has the disease and has the symptom; (2) does not have the disease and does not have the symptom; (3) does not have the disease but has the symptom; (4) has the disease but does not have the symptom. The task for the nurses was to determine if there is a relationship between the symptom and the disease. Overwhelmingly, the nurses concluded that there was a symptom-disease relationship, basing their decisions largely upon the fact that 37 patients had both the disease and the symptom and 13 had neither the disease nor the symptom. They tended to ignore the 33 cases in which the symptom was present without the disease and the 17 cases in which patients had the disease, but not the symptom. These trained nurses routinely ignored half of the available information. The correct decision should have been that there was no relationship since there were numerous instances of the disease without the symptom and the symptom without the disease. Decision making errors like the one described here are prevalent in the everyday thinking of people from all walks of life. We need to examine common decision making fallacies since a skilled decision maker will need to know what to avoid as well as what to do.

PITFALLS AND PRATFALLS IN DECISION MAKING

A pitfall is a danger or difficulty that is not easily avoided. If you've ever spent long afternoons at the beach, you've probably seen bratty kids creating pitfalls. They dig holes in the sand and cover them with newspaper so that unsuspecting sun lovers will fall into them. The word "pratfall" needs no formal definition for fans of the original *Saturday Night Live* television series. Chevy Chase became famous for his frequent pratfalls on this television program. He's been described as "the comedian who falls down a lot." The American Heritage dictionary defines pratfall as "a fall on the buttocks." Put these terms together and you will realize that unless common pitfalls in decision making are avoided, the decision maker will slip and fall on the part of the anatomy that is featured on blue jeans commercials without reaching the best decision. Let's examine some of the common fallacies or pitfalls in decision making.

Failure to Seek Disconfirming Evidence

Suppose you have a friend who is always working on cross-word puzzles, anagrams, mazes, and other similar problems from puzzle books. He corners you one day with the following problem:

> I'm going to give you a series of numbers. This series conforms to a simple rule. You have to figure out what the rule is. The way to do this is by coming up with your own series of numbers. I'll tell you whether or not your own series conforms to this rule. You can give me as many series of numbers as necessary to discover the rule. When you believe that you know the rule, tell it to me and I'll let you know if you're right.

Reluctantly, you agree to participate. You are given the following number series:

2 4 6

Stop right now and think how you would go about generating other number series that conform to the same rule as this one.

This problem was actually presented to many subjects in an experiment conducted by Wason (1960, 1968). He found that most people had difficulty with this task. Suppose that you believe that the rule is "any continuous series of even numbers." To test this rule most subjects would try series like "14, 16, 18." The experimenter would respond that this series conforms to the rule. To be certain most subjects would try again with another series, "182, 184, 186." Again the experimenter would respond affirmatively. Confidently, the subject would announce the rule, "Any continuous even series of numbers." The experimenter then informs the subject that this is not the correct rule.

Typically, subjects will try again, this time thinking up a new rule that will describe the correct number series. Suppose, this time the subject decides to try out the rule "the middle number is halfway between the other two." Now the subject asks about the series "50, 100, 150." The experimenter answers that this series is correct. The subject tries again "1006, 1007, 1008" and is told that this also conforms to the rule. Even more confident this time, the subject announces that the correct rule is "the middle number is halfway between the other two." The experimenter tells him that this is not the correct rule.

Have you discovered the correct rule by now? It is "numbers in increasing order of magnitude." After almost an hour of working on this problem one of Wason's subjects came up with this rule: "The rule is that either the first number equals the second minus two, and the third is random but greater than the second, or the third number equals the second plus two, and the first is random but less than the second." You can imagine how this poor subject felt when he was told that this rule was incorrect.

Why is this problem so difficult? In all of the sample number series I've given and most of the ones people actually try, the number series conform to the rule they have in mind. There is an infinite number of possible number series that conform to the correct rule, "numbers in increasing order of magnitude." What subjects should have done is try out series that would *disconfirm* the rule they were trying out. For example, if you believed that the correct rule is "any continuous series of even numbers" you should try the series "1, 2, 4." If the experimenter tells you that you are correct, then you know that the rule "any continuous series of even numbers" must be wrong.

The tendency to seek information that agrees with the ideas we have is called **confirmation bias.** We have a bias or predilection to look for confirming information. Another interesting example of the confirmation bias or failure to seek disconfirming evidence is discussed in the chapter on the Development of Reasoning Skills.

What are the implications of the bias to seek confirming evidence on decisions making? Suppose someone confronts your best friend with "the opportunity of a lifetime." A dynamic saleswoman offers him the chance to invest in a new corporation that will manufacture and sell small computers. It sounds good, but he's unsure. Prudently he decides to do some investigating. He checks out ten computer companies that are listed on the New York Stock Exchange. He finds that IBM is a large profitable corporation. If he had only invested in IBM when it was just being formed, he'd be a rich man today. He can already imagine himself lighting cigars with $10 bills. What advice would you give your friend?

Hopefully, you would point out to him that he only looked for evidence that supports the decision to invest in the corporation since only substantial corporations are listed on the stock exchange. He also needs to seek evidence that would disconfirm this decision. He should find out how many small computer corporations *have* gone bankrupt and how many *have not* gone bankrupt in the last 10 years. He also should attempt to estimate the future market for small computers.

Another real life (nonlaboratory) example can be drawn from medical decision making. Imagine a young physician examining a sick patient. The patient is complaining of a high fever and sore throat. The physician must decide on a diagnosis from among a myriad of possible diseases. The physician decided that it may be the flu. She asks the patient if he feels "achey all over." The answer is "yes." The physician asks if the symptoms began a few days ago. Again, the response is "yes." It should be clear to the reader that the physician should also be seeking evidence that would disconfirm the flu diagnosis. She should also ask about patterns of symptoms that are not usually associated with the flu, like a rash or swollen joints.

The confirmation bias is a pitfall in decision making. Wason claims that it is prevalent in the thoughts and research of scientists. In fact, a large scale study of NASA scientists showed a strong confirmation bias (Mynatt, Doherty, & Tweney, 1978). We all need to be trained to seek and examine data that are inconsistent with the ideas we are considering.

Availability Heuristic

A **heuristic** is any "rule of thumb" that we use to solve problems. It won't always give us the right answer, but it is a helpful aid. Psychologists usually distinguish between *heuristics* and *algorithms*. An **algorithm** is a procedure that will always yield the correct answer if you follow it exactly. Let's try a simple example from mathematics to clarify these terms. Remember the procedures you learned in solving long division problems. Given a problem like $176\overline{)7010}$, you were first told to estimate about how often 176 would "go into" 701, since it is unlikely that you ever learned the 176 tables. You might estimate it to be about 4 times. The problem thus far would look like this:

$$\begin{array}{r} 4 \\ 176\overline{)7019} \end{array}$$

You would check out this estimate with the appropriate multiplication.

$$\begin{array}{r} 4 \\ 176\overline{)7019} \\ \underline{704} \end{array}$$

oops, too large!

You would soon realize that 4 was too large and would probably try 3. This procedure is a heuristic. It is a guide or aide to help you find the correct answer, but it doesn't always work perfectly as seen in the above example. On the other hand, an algorithm always leads to the correct answer. If you want to find the area of a rectangle that is 3 feet long and 2 feet wide you will always get the correct answer if you use the formula: length $\times$ width, or in this case, 3 ft $\times$ 2 ft = 6 square feet.

Heuristics or "rules of thumb" are frequently used by a decision maker without the realization by the decision maker that they're being used. **Availabili-**

ty is one such heuristic. The term was coined by two prominent psychologists, Daniel Kahneman and Amos Tversky (1973; Tversky & Kahneman, 1974), who have conducted numerous experiments on human decision making. In order to understand the availability heuristic, consider the following questions:

1. Are there more words in the English language that begin with the letter K or have the K in the third position?
2. Would you expect the 1980 census to show that there are more librarians or farmers in the United States?
3. Are there more deaths due to homicide or due to diabetes-related diseases?

If you answered the first question like most people, you believe that there are more words that start with the letter k than there are words with k in the third position. In answering this question most people find that they can think of more words that start with "k" (kite, kitty, kill, kiss, kick, key, king, know, knife, koala, kidney) than have "k" in the third position (make, take, like, lake). In the jargon of psychology, words starting with the letter "k" are more available than words with "k" in the third position. That is, they come to mind more easily. If you answered "words that start with 'k,'" you were wrong. According to Kahneman and Tversky, the English language contains many more words with "k" in the third position than in the first position. It is just more difficult to think of them because it is easier to retrieve words from memory by the first letter than by the third.

Your answer to the second question probably depends on whether you live in an urban or rural area. Most city dwellers believe that there are more librarians than farmers in the United States. After all, few city dwellers have ever met a farmer while they probably know, or at least know of, several librarians. Actually, there are many more farmers in the United States than there are librarians. This is another example of how the use of the availability heuristic can lead to the wrong decision.

Most residents of large cities probably believe incorrectly that there are more deaths due to homicide than to diabetes. The reason for this is not difficult to understand. Pick up any newspaper or watch television news on any day and there is likely to be a report of one or more homicides. While you may know only a few people who have diabetes and may not know personally anyone who has been murdered, you've heard or read about many homicide victims, so there seems to be more of them.

The availability heuristic can have serious negative consequences on the kinds of decisions we make. Its influence can best be understood with an example:

A psychologist must decide whether he should recommend that a patient be admitted to a mental institution. The patient claims that he hears sinister voices telling him repeatedly to kill his girlfriend. In deciding whether the patient will act on his impulse, the psychologist is likely to consider the frequency with which other patients who are similar to the one being considered commit violent crimes. Because the commission of a violent crime is a highly salient event, cases in which this outcome occurred are more available (more easily brought to mind) than cases where the patient quietly improved. The availability advantage of one type of outcome over another leads to serious decision making biases. In this case, the psychologist is ignoring the fact that very few disturbed patients ever commit crimes of violence. Of course the frequency or likelihood of the crime cannot be the only consideration in deciding whether to recommend that a patient be admitted to a mental institution. Even if a violent crime would be committed by only 1 in 100 similar patients, the consequences are so severe that the psychologist may decide that the patient should be admitted even if he is unlikely to act on his impulses because the crime itself is so heinous.

Although the availability heuristic can lead to poor decisions, it can, under certain circumstances, be a valuable decision making aid. Very few cases of Toxic Shock Syndrome were reported before 1978. As soon as the relationship between Toxic Shock Syndrome and tampon use in menstruating women became widely publicized, there was a dramatic increase in the number of reported cases. The most likely explanation for this dramatic increase is that the diagnosis became available for physicians. For most U.S. physicians, Toxic Shock Syndrome was one of the many illnesses that they studied back in medical school, and therefore was not a diagnostic category that was easily available for them to use. The publicity surrounding Toxic Shock Syndrome helped many women receive a correct diagnosis.

The availability heuristic is frequently seen in other medical examples. It is not unusual for a pediatrician whose own children suffer from severe allergies to be especially vigilant about possible allergic reactions in his patients. This may or may not be a good thing. The best physician is one who has a broad scope of experience with a large variety of illnesses so that he has a large number of medical diagnoses available to him.

Prejudice and stereotypes may also exist, at least in part, because of the human tendency to utilize readily available information. While prejudice and stereotypes are discussed more fully in the chapter on the Development of Memory Skills, it is easy to see how availability plays a role in establishing and maintaining them. If a minority person is convicted of a heinous crime, many people will distrust other members of the same minority. The thousands of honest hard-working minority persons are forgotten or overlooked. Their existence is overshadowed by the salient criminal.

Availability has been carefully studied in the laboratory by research psychologists because it plays a role in decisions that are made in a wide range of settings. In another experiment by Tversky and Kahneman (1974), groups of college students were given one of the two following arithmetic problems:

$$8 \times 7 \times 6 \times 5 \times 4 \times 3 \times 2 \times 1 = ?$$

or

$$1 \times 2 \times 3 \times 4 \times 5 \times 6 \times 7 \times 8 = ?$$

The college students examined either the first or second row of numbers for 5 seconds. Their task was to estimate the product since 5 seconds was not enough time to solve the problem. Students who were given the first problem, the one beginning with large numbers, estimated the product to be 2,250. Students who were given the second problem, the one beginning with small numbers, estimated the product to be 512. The correct answer is 40,320. Thus, when the problem began with large numbers the estimated answer was large compared to the problem that began with small numbers. The estimate differences between the ascending and descending series demonstrates that judgments were systematically biased toward the most readily available information.

Representativeness Heuristic

Suppose that a young man in a pin stripe suit, black shirt and white tie comes up to you and asks if you'd like to make some money by betting on whether a coin lands on "heads" or "tails." You look at him dubiously. He explains that it's really quite simple. He'll flip one coin six times. All you have to do is bet on the pattern of head and tails that will result from six tosses of a coin. Although there are many sequences possible, you decide to concentrate on three of them. Using the letters "H" to represent heads and "T" to represent tails, which of the following three outcomes would you bet on?

H–T–H–T–T–H
H–H–H–T–T–T
H–T–H–T–H–T

If you responded like most other people, then you selected the first series of heads and tails, probably because it seemed more similar to a random or chance pattern of heads and tails. In fact all three series are equally likely. Any series of heads and tails taken six at a time is as likely to occur as any other. The above example demonstrates the belief that an outcome of a random process should look like or be representative of randomness. Since our common sense notion of randomness is that of a process without a pattern, we tend to think that H–T–H–T–H–T is not as likely to occur from six tosses of a coin as a more random-looking series. This, however, is not true.

Of course, you're more likely to get approximately equal numbers of heads and tails after many coin flips than you are to get mostly or all heads or mostly or all tails because there are more possible patterns that yield these outcomes. For example, there is only one pattern of outcomes that will correspond to 6 heads (H–H–H–H–H–H), while there are many ways to get 3 heads and 3 tails in 6 flips of a coin (e.g., H–H–H–T–T–T; H–T–H–T–H–T; T–T–T–H–H–H;

H–T–H–T–H–T; etc.). Each series or pattern of heads and tails is equally likely. The concept of probability and likelihood is discussed in chapter 5.

To clarify the **representativeness heuristic** (Kahneman & Tversky, 1972), let's try another example. Suppose you get a letter from an old friend from whom you haven't heard in many years. He tells you that he is the proud father of six children—three girls and three boys. After trying to consider what life is like with six children, you then wonder about their birth order. Which of the following orders do you think is more likely (with "G" standing for girl and "B" standing for boy):

B–B–B–G–G–G
or
B–G–G–B–G–B

If you've followed the discussion so far, you will realize that although the second series appears to be more representative of a random process, they are, in fact, equally likely.

Another bias that is similar to the representative heuristic and that also affects the decisions we make is a unwarranted **belief in the fairness of the laws of chance.** Suppose for the moment that you are as likely to have a boy child as you are to have a girl child. (Actually slightly more boys than girls are born.) Then about half of all births should be girls and half boys. You and your spouse have had three boys. Are you now more likely to have a girl for your fourth child? If you answered "yes" to this question, you were wrong. The chances of your having a girl for your fourth child are still 50–50, the same as they have been for each birth. This common decision-making error is known as **gambler's fallacy.** It is the erroneous belief that if an event has not recently occurred, then it is now more likely than if it had just occurred. *Gambler's fallacy* is discussed more fully in the Understanding Probabilities chapter.

Belief in the Law of Small Numbers

What would you conclude if you read the following hypothetical research report in the newspaper? Five elderly people participated in a research project designed to help them improve their ability to remember everyday occurrences. The treatment for each subject consisted of eating one watermelon a day. After 2 months, four of the five elderly subjects showed substantial memory improvement. Would you be willing to conclude that, at least for some elderly people, memory can be improved by eating watermelon? Certainly not! While there are several problems in drawing any conclusion from this study, the point that is relevant here is that the **sample size** is too small to demonstrate the effect of watermelon on memory. Sample size refers to the number of people in an experiment. For most purposes, five people is too few to allow a meaningful conclusion about a phenomenon as variable as memory in the elderly.

The belief in the law of small numbers has been studied by Tversky and Kahneman (1971). They found that a group of research psychologists held this erroneous belief. It is wrong to believe that small samples (small numbers of people or whatever is being studied) will be similar to each other and to the group we are interested in learning more about. Information obtained from small samples is not as reliable as information obtained from large ones. If 500 elderly people had participated in the experiment and 400 of them improved, then it would be reasonable to conclude that the treatment (in this hypothetical example, watermelon) facilitated memory in the aged. This conclusion is not warranted when four out of five elderly show memory improvement.

Let's try another example of how the belief in the law of small numbers can lead to poor decisions. Common wisdom and Dear Abby both strongly suggest that two people should know each other quite well before deciding to get married. Suppose, however, that you have a friend who is anxious to get to the altar. He has had two dates with "Princess Charming" and on the basis of these two evenings he is certain that he wants to spend the rest of his life with her. He is exhibiting a belief in the law of small numbers. The eager groom-to-be has observed the woman's behavior twice and believes that the rest of their life together will be like these two dates. If you counsel him to take his time and get to know her better, you are, in effect, telling him to take a larger sample of their time together before making the marriage decision.

Wishful Thinking (Pollyanna Principle)

Quite often people will overestimate their chances for success or the likelihood of a desired outcome. Halpern and Irwin (1973) found that when participants in an experiment wanted an event to occur (they would win money), they believed that it was more likely to occur than when its occurrence would have been unfavorable (they would lose money). It seems that humans are an optimistic species. The tendency to believe that pleasant events are more likely than unpleasant ones is a manifestation of **wishful thinking,** the idea that if we want something to happen it will. This has also been called the *Pollyanna Principle* in honor of the protagonist of a 1913 novel who always found something to be happy about, no matter how bleak the situation.

A large fast food hamburger chain is basing a promotional gimmic on wishful thinking. The corporation that made golden arches an integral part of American life is offering a game that pays off with large sums of money. Some lucky Big Mac hamburger consumer will match up small game coupons for the grand prize. A blitz of television advertising shows lucky burger eaters exclaiming over the money they've won. Apparently, the lure of winning must sell more hamburgers, or it would have been discontinued. It must be assumed that people grossly overestimate their chance of winning the prizes. The actual estimated probability of winning the grand prize is less than a million to one. As required by law, these odds are posted (in fine print) on the posters that announce the game, yet they are routinely ignored and thought to be more favorable than they actually are. Few of us can appreciate astronomical odds like this one. You're probably more likely to find a needle in a haystack. Yet, because of wishful thinking, many people will line up for hamburgers and a chance to win.

Optimism is certainly a wonderful human trait, except when it distorts the decision making process. Good decisions rely upon realistic assessments of likelihood, not optimistic ones. Failure to consider seriously unpleasant outcomes can lead to disastrous consequences. Currently, seismologists (people who study earthquakes) are predicting that a major earthquake will occur in Southern California within the next 50 years. Few people will be prepared, however, if an earthquake occurs because they are duped by wishful thinking. Most believe that a major earthquake won't occur, or alternatively, if it does, it will be "somewhere else." Random "person on the street" interviews shown on television reveal that the Polyanna Principle is alive and well and living in Southern California.

Entrapment

Suppose you were offered the opportunity to bid on a one-dollar bill. You and some friends can make bids, and the highest bidder will pay the amount bid and get $1.00 in return. The only hitch is that *both* the highest bidder and second highest bidder must pay the amount they bid, but only the highest bidder will receive the dollar bill in return. Suppose that you agree to play and that you continue to raise your bid until you have offered 80 cents. Now a friend bids $1.00. What do you do? You will probably decide to bid $1.05 for the $1.00 since you'll certainly lose $.80 unless you continue to increase your bid. Shubik (1971) has found that people will continue to bid amounts over $1.00 to win the dollar bill in an attempt to keep their losses at a minimum in this game.

What has happened in this game is **entrapment,** a situation in which an individual has already invested money, time, or effort and decides to continue in this situation because of the initial investment. People commonly fall prey to entrapment. Consider Fred's decision about his automobile. He has already replaced the muffler, brakes, and ignition system when he finds out that his car needs a new transmission. Since he has already invested so much money into his car, he feels "trapped" into replacing the transmission instead of buying a new car. Or consider another common example. Everyone has had the frustrating experience of calling on the phone for some information and being put on "hold." After listening to the irritating strains of "elevator music" for several minutes, you need to decide whether to hang up or continue waiting. Many people continue to wait because of the time they've already invested.

Making decisions in light of previous investments requires that the individual consider why the investment has been so high. Since Fred has been "pouring money'' into his car for some time, it is likely that it will continue to need repairs and thus the purchase of a new automobile is probably the better choice if it is financially feasible. If you've waited on ''hold'' for several minutes it is likely that the secretary or whomever you were waiting for has forgotten about you. Eventually he or she may notice that you are still on the line, but it is probably best to hang up and call again. On the other hand, if you have been waiting a long time for a bus it should be more likely that one will come along. You need to consider the other alternatives in deciding if you should continue waiting—the cost and availability of other means of transportation, time constraints, etc.

UNCERTAINTY AND RISKS

Murphy's Law: Anything that can go wrong, will.
Comment on Murphy's Law: Murphy was an optimist.

Decision making always involves uncertainty. The decisions that we make have implications for the future and the future inherently involves unknowns.

Research on how people typically deal with uncertainty has shown that the usual response is to ignore it (Hogarth, 1980). Although this may reduce the immediate complexity of a decision, it is obviously a maladaptive procedure that could lead to catastrophic results.

It is possible to reduce the number of unknowns in any situation. This will almost always involve some work by the decision maker, but if the decision is an important one it will be time well spent. Let's consider a common example. Most of us will purchase several automobiles in our lifetimes. For a majority of Americans, this will represent the second largest expenditure that they will make, exceeded only by a home purchase. The quality of this decision can be improved with a little research. You can determine what automobile variables are important to you and gather relevant data about each car you are considering for possible purchase.

Almost any decision can be improved with a little research. For example, if you are uncertain about the safety of nuclear plants, an afternoon at the library reading both pro and con materials should allow you to make a much more informed decision about this important issue.

Assessing Risks

The decision maker must always be aware of the risks associated with taking or not taking a particular course of action. If you live in an apartment near a college campus, you are well aware of the ''joys'' associated with apartment hunting. Rental units are often in short supply in college communities and are priced in a range that strains the typical student's budget. Students may find themselves considering an apartment that lacks the amenities they were hoping for at a price that is really above their income. The risk associated with turning the apartment down is that they might not find another apartment within walking distance to the college campus. The risks associated with renting the apartment must also be considered. What if they find that they really can't afford to keep up the monthly rental payments? The decision maker has to decide which risk is greater and the likelihood of each occurring. Obviously, both risks need to be assessed very carefully and additional alternatives considered. Perhaps a cheaper apartment can be found in another section of town with good public transportation to campus or perhaps a roommate can be found to share the rent.

A poignant example of failure to assess adequately risks can be found in an analysis of the United States military actions just prior to the attack on Pearl Harbor. Admiral Kimmel, Commander in Chief of Naval Operations in the Pacific, had received several warnings from Washington that a Japanese attack in the Southwest was possible. He decided to downplay the probability of an attack on Pearl Harbor since he believed that other naval sites were more likely targets. Quite by accident and almost an hour before the attack, two army privates spotted on a radar screen large unidentified aircraft flying towards Pearl Harbor. Realizing that these could be Japanese bomber planes, they reported the presence of the unidentified aircraft to the Army's radar center. Let's consider the plight of the officer on duty at the radar center. The United States was not at war with Japan. He had never received the recent warning that a Japanese attack was imminent. He had to decide whether the unidentified objects on the radar screen belonged to the United States or Japan. There were costs and risks associated with either choice. If he had erroneously decided that they were Japanese planes, he would have been responsible for recalling personal "leaves" for large numbers of servicemen and women and creating havoc and panic on the military base. There were also large financial costs involved in preparing for antiaircraft maneuvers. Since he assessed the possibility of a Japanese attack to be low, he told the two privates to forget about the objects detected by radar. He decided that they were probably the Army B-17's that were expected to arrive some time that day. With the unfortunate benefit of hindsight, it is clear that he failed to assess adequately the risks associated with each decision. The result was the worst naval disaster in the United States history with over 2,000 lives lost. Even though he believed that an attack was unlikely (wishful thinking), he should have realized that the risks were too great to justify his decision. Decisions made under extreme risks need careful scrutiny and not an off-hand dismissal. In this case the risks associated with deciding that the planes belonged to the United States were many times greater than those associated with the decision that they were Japanese bombers.

Research has shown that the Pearl Harbor scenario is not unusual. Whenever extreme risk is associated with a course of action, there is a tendency to minimize the unfavorable consequences (Janis & Mann, 1977). This is sometimes called

biased discounting. It is the bias or predilection to discount or reduce perceived risk or its probability. Thus, the radar officer could bolster his decision to ignore the unidentified objects by rationalizing either that even if they were Japanese bomber planes they probably would not do much damage or it was extremely unlikely that they were Japanese aircraft.

ELIMINATION BY ASPECTS

Let's return to the earlier problem of deciding which automobile to buy because it is a decision that most of us will make several times. With so many automobiles on the market, where do you begin? Most people begin decision-making processes of this sort with a strategy known as **elimination by aspects,** although few people know it by this name (Tversky, 1972). An individual who is concerned about unemployment in the United States car industry would begin by considering only cars that are manufactured in the United States. In this instance, the aspect under consideration is the place in which the automobile is manufactured. Autos that are not made in the United States are eliminated from further consideration. At this point, most people will decide what features (or aspects) of automobiles are important to them. Suppose that you are on a limited budget and therefore cost is an important feature to you. You would probably determine the cost of various models of Fords, Plymouths, Chevrolets, and other U.S. autos. Models that cost more than your price ceiling would be eliminated. Let's suppose further that frequency of repair is another important variable. Of course, no one can tell you how frequently the car you choose will need repair, but you can reduce some of the uncertainty associated with this variable by finding out how often other models similar to the ones you are considering have needed repair in the past. This information is available in consumer periodicals in every library. If one or more models that you are still considering is judged as "worse than average" on the frequency of repairs, then presumably these would be eliminated from further consideration. The elimination by strategy would be recycled repeatedly until the decision maker is left with a few possible models from which to choose. Typically, small and seemingly insignificant differences will come into play to complete the process—e.g., "I'm tired of shopping," or "Let's take this one," or "The dealer will include at no extra cost furry dice to hang from the rear view mirror if I buy this model," or "I can drive this one home today."

MULTIDIMENSIONAL COMPARISONS

The overwhelming majority of decisions involve **multidimensional comparisons.** The concept of multiple dimensions is best understood with an example adapted from research conducted by Tversky (1969). Think for a moment about how you would decide which one of three students should be admitted to a university. Most likely you would want to know something about the intelligence of these three applicants. You learn that Student A's (Anne's) high school grade average (on a scale from 0 to 100) is 92, Student B's (Bruno's) is 85, and Student C's (Clarence's) is 81. If you only considered intelligence, you would decide that Anne should be admitted since she appears to be most intelligent. In this case, you have made only a **unidimensional comparison.** Although scores on intelligence can range from low to high, it is only one dimension. Most people would object to considering only intelligence in determining who is best suited for a university education. Certainly other variables like emotional stability and sociability (the ability to get along with others) are important considerations. Suppose you are now given additional information about the three applicants. You're told that Anne's rating on emotional stability is 71 (also on a scale from 0 to 100), Bruno's is 93, and Clarence's is 80. Given this additional information, would you switch your choice to Bruno or Clarence?

Stop now and decide who you would select at this point.

What would you decide if you now learned that the sociability score (also on a scale from 0 to 100) for each prospective student is: Anne, 89; Bruno, 73, and Clarence, 96? A summary table of this information appears below:

Dimensions	*Anne*	*Bruno*	*Clarence*
Intelligence	92	85	81
Emotional Stability	71	93	80
Sociability	89	73	96

If you based your decision on information about intelligence, emotional stability, *and* sociability, then your decision involved multidimensional comparisons. If any student had scored highest on all of the dimensions, the task would be easy; however, this is rarely true. Tversky, who conducted this experiment, found that subjects used more than one of the relevant dimensions when making decisions of this sort. In other words, people take into consideration which comparisons are most important and the distances among applicants on each dimension.

Transitivity

How can we determine when subjects are utilizing multidimensional comparisons? The answer to this question involves the mathematical concept of **transitivity.** Somewhere back in elementary school you learned that

if A > B (A is greater than B)
and B > C (B is greater than C)
then A > C (A is greater than C)

Applying transitivity to decision making is straightforward. If you considered only intelligence as the criterion for university admission, then you would have ranked the applicants:

Anne > Bruno (Anne is preferred over Bruno)
Bruno > Clarence (Bruno is preferred over Clarence)

Thus, your first choice for admission would be Anne (she has the "most" intelligence), then Bruno, then Clarence. If you had to choose between Anne and Clarence, you would select Anne, since Anne > Clarence by the rules of transitivity. This demonstrates transitivity in decision making and may seem obvious and logical.

If after receiving the information about emotional stability and sociability you are asked to choose between Anne and Clarence, you might look at the composite information and combine what you've learned about the three candidates overall and select

Anne > Clarence

and when choosing between Clarence and Bruno you might select

Clarence > Bruno

Suppose that you are now asked to choose between Anne and Bruno. If the decisions were transitive, then you would select Anne > Bruno. Many people, however, would find the difference in emotionality scores too large to ignore (Bruno has 93, Anne has 71) and decide

Bruno > Anne

This preference for Bruno over Anne represents intransitivity (a violation of transitivity). Whenever intransitivity occurs, experimenters infer that multidimensional comparisons have been made. Thus, it is not necessarily true that logical or good decisions obey the mathematical principle of transitivity. (Note: It is possible for a set of decisions to obey the law of transitivity even when multidimensional comparisons have been made. If one applicant scored highest on all dimensions, a second was consistently in the middle, and a third was always lowest, decisions would still be transitive. However, only when decisions are intransitive, can experimenters assert that multidimensional comparisons were made.)

PREPARING A WORKSHEET

Researchers have found that the best way to make an important decision involves the preparation and utilization of a decision worksheet. The purpose of a worksheet is to *optimize* decision making. Psychologists who study **optimization** compare the actual decision made by a person to a theoretical "ideal" decision to see how similar they are. Proponents of the worksheet procedure believe that it will yield optimal (best) decisions. Although there are several variations on the exact format that a worksheet can take, they are all similar in their essential aspects. Worksheets require defining the problem in a clear and concise way, listing all possible solutions to the problem, listing the relevant considerations that will be affected by the decision, determining the relative importance of each consideration, and mathematically calculating a decision. The end product of the worksheet procedure is a single numerical summary of each possible solution or alternative. The alternative with the highest number of points emerges as the best decision.

Since most important problems are multifaceted, there are several alternatives to choose from, each with unique advantages and disadvantages. One of the benefits of a pencil and paper decision-making procedure is that it permits us to deal with more variables than our immediate processing ability would allow. On the average, we can keep about seven ideas in our mind at once (Miller, 1956). A worksheet can be especially useful when the decision involves a large number of variables with complex relationships.

Let's consider the worksheet procedure with a realistic example for most college students: "What will I do after graduation?" A hypothetical student, Evan, has several postgraduation opportunities. He is contemplating the following: (1) a job in a large fashionable department store where he will train to be a buyer; (2) a teaching position in an inner city school, probably a 5th or 6th grade class; (3) a graduate school degree in business administration; (4) a law school degree; and (5) a year off to "bum around" Europe. A decision-making worksheet will be very important in helping him choose the best alternative.

Defining the Problem

The first step is the realization that a decision needs to be made. A decision-making worksheet begins with a succinct statement of the problem that will also help to narrow it. Thus, the problem for Evan becomes "What will I do after graduation that will lead to a successful career?" If Evan words his decision this way, he has already decided that his decision will involve long-range goals and not immediate ones. It is important to be clear about this distinction because most often long-range goals will involve a different decision than short range ones. Thus the options of attending graduate or law school are really statements about working in business or as a lawyer and not decisions about school per se.

Generating the Alternatives

The next step is to write out in separate columns across the top of the worksheet all possible alternatives that could solve the problem. You'll need a large sheet of ruled paper because it would make no sense to cut the worksheet process short because you ran out of space on your paper. It is important that you don't evaluate the alternatives at this stage; however, this is not the place for fiction either. If you are tone deaf, this is not the time to fantasize about a career in the opera. Allow room for two columns under each alternative which will be used later for calculations. Thus far, Evan's worksheet would look something like this:

What Will I Do After College That Will Lead to a Successful Career?

Alternatives	Dept. Store buyer	Teacher—inner city school	Graduate School—Business	Law School	"Bum" in Europe for a year

Evan notices while drawing up his worksheet that these alternatives are not all mutually exclusive. There's no reason why he can't decide to travel around Europe for a year and then select a career goal; besides, a vacation in Europe is not a long-range plan and the decision currently being made is for life career goals. He decides at this point to erase the fifth alternative since it seemed to require a separate decision from the other four. He also remembers at this point that his father always hoped that Evan would want to run the family-owned lumber business after his graduation from college. Although this is not an appealing idea to Evan, he substitutes it as an additional choice since the rules for this step of the process do not allow for evaluation.

Listing the Considerations

The decision Evan makes will have multiple effects. His feelings about making a personal contribution to society, his income and his future life style, his parents' and friends' opinions of him, the quality of his workday and many other variables are at stake. If Evan were married with children, the impact of each decision on his spouse and children would also need to be considered. At this point Evan should cover the alternatives and list on the left-hand side of his worksheet the considerations or variables that will be affected by his decision. The worksheet would now look like this. (See Table 7.1.)

Before proceeding, Evan should now put the worksheet away and mull over the problem: the alternatives and the considerations. Often people find that in the course of worksheet preparation they think of new alternatives and discover which considerations are important to them. It is also a good idea to ask other people you trust if they can think of additional alternatives and considerations.

TABLE 7.1
What Will I Do After College That Will Lead to a Successful Career?

Alternatives	*Dept. Store Buyer*	*Teacher—Inner City School*	*Graduate School—Business*	*Law School*	*Run Family Lumber Business*
considerations					
Desire to Help Society					
Income					
Parents' Opinions					
Friends' Opinions					
Interest in the Work					

Be sure, however, that you don't let other people make the decision for you. Suppose that Evan's friend suggests that Evan seriously pursues his interest in music and becomes a jazz musician. In addition, Evan thinks up several additional considerations which he lists on his worksheet. He also decides that since he is planning for his future, he should realistically consider his chances for success at each alternative. The worksheet now looks like this. (See Table 7.2.)

Listing all relevant considerations is an important part of the worksheet process. Janis and Mann (1977) believe that poor decisions often result from failures to think through all of the relevant considerations. They suggest that considerations be listed under four categories—gains and losses for self, gains and losses for significant others, self-approval and disapproval, and social approval and disapproval, to avoid overlooking important considerations.

Weighting the Considerations

It is almost always true that the considerations are not equally important to the decision maker and therefore need to be weighted accordingly. A five-point scale in which 1 = of slight importance, 5 = of great importance, and the numbers 2, 3, 4 reflect gradations of importance between these end points can be used to quantify the relative importance of each consideration. Weighting considerations is a personal matter. It is likely that each of us would assign weights somewhat differently. If Evan felt that his desire to help society was moderately important to him he would rate it a "3." Similarly, if he believed that income was more than moderately important to him, but less than "of great importance" he would rate it a "4." The appropriate weightings are placed alongside each consideration.

Weighting the considerations is an important part of the worksheet process. After assigning numbers (the weights) to each consideration you should stop to survey the weights. If Evan rated "friend's opinions" with a larger number than "parents' opinions," this reflects how he feels about their relative opinions. This is a good way to clarify which considerations are most important to you.

Weighting the Alternatives

Now is the time to think carefully about each alternative and determine how well each satisfies the considerations listed. The alternatives will be weighted using the numbers −2, −1, 0, +1, and +2. A positive number indicates that it is favorable or "pro" the consideration with +2 indicating that it is highly favorable and +1 indicating that it is somewhat favorable. A negative number will be used if an alternative is incompatible with or "con" a consideration, with −2 indicating that it is highly incompatible and −1 indicating that it is somewhat incompatible. Zero will be used when an alternative is neither favorable nor unfavorable to a consideration.

We'll use Evan's worksheet to demonstrate how to weight alternatives. First, Evan has to contemplate how becoming a department store buyer will satisfy his desire to help society. Certainly it won't hurt society, but it probably won't help it either. Evan believes that while it may create additional jobs in related industries (fashion, sewing, etc.), this is not really what he had in mind when he thought about helping society; therefore, he rates it a zero on this consideration. This number is placed under "Department Store Buyer" in the left hand column on the first row. Subsequent ratings will be placed directly below this number. If he does eventually become a buyer for a large department store, he probably will earn a satisfactory income. He certainly won't be rich, but it will be enough money to allow him to live comfortably; therefore, he gives it a +1. Both his parents and friends will consider it to be a moderately good job, so he rates it a +1 on both these considerations. He believes that it should be very interesting work and rates it a +2 on "interest in the work." It should be a moderately prestigious occupation and thus rates a +1 in this category. Unfortunately, it probably won't offer much employment security because department store sales

TABLE 7.2
What Will I Do After Graduation That Will Lead to a Successful Career?

Alternatives	*Dept. Store Buyer*	*Teacher—Inner City School*	*Graduate School—Business*	*Law School*	*Run Family Lumber Business*	*Jazz Musician*
Considerations						
Desire to Help Society						
Income						
Parents' Opinions						
Friends' Opinions						
Interest in the Work						
Prestige of Occupation						
Employment Security						
Amount of Vacation and Free Time						
Likelihood of Success						

TABLE 7.3
What Will I Do After College That Will Lead to a Successful Career?

Alternatives		*Dept. Store Buyer*	*Teacher—Inner City School*	*Graduate School—Business*	*Law School*	*Run Family Lumber Business*	*Jazz Musician*
Considerations							
Desire to Help Society	(3)	0	+2	0	+1	0	0
Income	(4)	+1	−1	+2	+2	0	−1
Parents' Opinions	(2)	+1	0	+1	+2	+2	−1
Friends' Opinions	(3)	+1	+2	0	+1	−1	+2
Interest in the Work	(5)	+2	+2	+1	0	−1	+1
Prestige of Occupation	(1)	+1	−1	+2	+2	−2	+1
Employment Security	(3)	−1	−2	0	+1	+2	−2
Amount of Vacation and Free Time	(2)	−2	+2	−2	−2	+1	+2
Likelihood of Success	(5)	+1	+1	−1	−1	+2	−2

are tied to the economy, which seems to fluctuate erratically; he therefore rates it −1 on "employment security." A department store buyer is required to work a fixed 40-hour or more work week with only a few weeks a year for vacation, thus rating a −2 on vacation and free time. He notes that he is moderately likely to succeed as a department store buyer, so he rates it +1 on this consideration.

It is usually necessary to gather more information at this stage of the decision-making process. Evan may need to phone the local school district to find out what the median salary is for school teachers. He also might seek the advice of his college advisor to determine if he has the math skills needed to succeed in business administration.

Each alternative is rated in similar manner by thinking how well it satisfies the objectives of each consideration. When he completed weighting the alternatives, Evan's worksheet looked like this. (See Table 7.3.)

Calculating a Decision

If you have carefully followed the worksheet procedure this far, you've realized that it requires numerous decisions before even coming close to yielding the one you want to make. By now Evan has decided what type of decision he's making (long range), listed all the alternatives and all the considerations that he believes to be necessary, decided how important each consideration is to him and how well each alternative satisfies the objectives of each consideration.

There are three different strategies for calculating a decision at this point. They are overall assessment, dimensional comparison, and the "2/3 Ideal Rule." Each utilizes a different criterion for selecting the best decision from a worksheet.

Overall Assessment

An **overall assessment** is obtained by determining how well each alternative satisfies the considerations taken as a whole or overall. This is calculated by multiplying the weight previously assigned for each consideration by the value assigned to how well an alternative satisfies that consideration. For example, Evan has rated his desire to help society a "3" and the department store buyer alternative a "0" on this consideration. The first cell of the worksheet is $3 \times 0 = 0$. This result, 0, is placed in the right hand column under "department store buyer." Continuing down to the next consideration, we see that Evan rated Income as "4" and the department store buyer alternative "+1" on income. Since $4 \times 1 = 4$ he would place a "4" in the right hand column below department store buyer and next to "Income." This procedure is repeated for each alternative. The right hand column for each alternative is then added yielding a total score for each alternative. This is demonstrated in Table 7.4.

Perusal of the worksheet will now show that based on an overall assessment, the alternative with the highest total score is "Teacher—Inner City School." You will also notice that the alternative to become a department store buyer obtained a fairly high score that was close to the winning alternative. Thus far, it seems that Evan should seriously be thinking about a career as a teacher.

Dimensional Comparison

In a **dimensional comparison** strategy each consideration (the "dimensions") is examined to find which alternative has the highest score. For example, if "Desire to help society" is examined, you will see that "Teacher—Inner City School" had the highest rating among all the other alternatives; therefore, it

TABLE 7.4
What Will I Do After College That Will Lead to a Successful Career?

Alternatives		*Dept. Store Buyer*		*Teacher— Inner City School*		*Graduate School— Business*		*Law School*		*Run Family Lumber Business*		*Jazz Musician*	
Considerations													
Desire to Help Society	(3)	0	0	+2	6	0	0	+1	3	0	0	0	0
Income	(4)	+1	4	−1	−4	+2	8	+2	8	0	0	−1	−4
Parents' Opinions	(2)	+1	2	0	0	+1	2	+2	4	+2	4	−1	−2
Friends' Opinions	(3)	+1	3	+2	6	0	0	+1	3	−1	−3	+2	6
Interest in the Work	(5)	+2	10	+2	10	+1	5	0	0	−1	−5	+1	5
Prestige of Occupation	(1)	+1	1	−1	−1	+2	2	+2	2	−2	−2	+1	1
Employment Security	(3)	−1	−3	−2	−6	0	0	1	3	+2	6	−2	−6
Amount of Vacation and Free Time	(2)	−2	−4	+2	4	−2	−4	−2	−4	+1	2	+2	4
Likelihood of Success	(5)	+1	5	+1	5	−1	−5	−1	−5	+2	10	−2	−10
			18		20		8		14		12		−6

would "win" on this consideration and get one point. Looking at "income" you will see that both "Graduate School-Business" and "Law School" were assigned +2 on this dimension. In the event of ties each of the winning tied alternative is awarded one point. If each consideration is examined in a similar manner, the following number of considerations won for each alternative will result:

Number of Considerations Won

Dept. Store Buyer	*Teacher Inner City School*	*Graduate School—Business*	*Law School*	*Run Family Lumber Business*	*Jazz Musician*
1	4	2	3	3	2

As seen above, the alternative "Teacher—Inner City School" scored highest among the alternatives on four considerations. Thus, the results of the dimensional comparison strategy agree with the overall assessment results. Notice that both "Law School" and "Run Family Lumber Business" won three considerations each, yet scored fairly low on the overall assessment.

2/3 Ideal Rule

The **"2/3 Ideal Rule"** was suggested by Carkhuff (1973). It requires the decision maker to calculate an overall assessment total for a perfect or ideal alternative. If an ideal alternative were added to Evan's worksheet, it would rate +2 on each consideration since it would be highly favorable to each consideration. A total overall score for an ideal alternative can be arrived at by adding all of the consideration weights and multiplying the total by 2 as seen below:

$$3 + 4 + 2 + 3 + 5 + 1 + 3 + 2 + 5 = 28$$
$$28 \times 2 = 56$$

The reasoning behind the 2/3 Ideal Rule is that a best alternative may not be good enough if it fails to measure up to 2/3 of an ideal solution. Thus, according to this rule a minimally acceptable alternative would score an overall 37.5 ($2/3 \times 56 = 37.5$). If you turn back to the completed worksheet you'll see that the highest total was for the teacher alternative and it rated, by the overall assessment method, a 20 (considerably less than the 37.5 required by this rule). Evan has several choices at this point. He can disregard the 2/3 Ideal Rule (which is likely if he is pleased with the decision to become a teacher), or he can expand and recycle the process by generating additional considerations and alternatives until he reaches a consensus with all three calculating procedures.

The "2/3 ideal rule" is based on the idea that some alternatives are "good enough" while others are not. Searching for alternatives that are good enough is called **satisficing** (Marsh & Shapira, 1982; Tversky & Kahneman, 1981). Satisficing refers to terminating the decision making process when an alternative that is "good enough" to satisfy most of the important considerations is found.

Dilemmas in Decision Making

The decision maker will often encounter dilemmas in calculating a decision. It is not unusual for two or more alternatives to have exactly the same high score or for one alternative to obtain the highest total with the overall assessment and a different one with the dimensional comparison. This can always be remedied by generating additional considerations and repeating the process until an alternative emerges as best. It is also possible to combine two or more alternatives. For example, Evan could become a buyer in a department store and volunteer to tutor children on weekends. This would allow him to realize his desire to help society while maintaining the benefits of the buyer alternative. Sometimes the decision maker will abandon the worksheet before it's completed because the process helped to clarify the issues and led directly to a decision without the calculations.

Certainly, the worksheet procedure requires a great deal of work, as its name implies. You might be wondering if there is any evidence to suggest that it's worth the extra effort—that it actually leads to better decisions. Yes, there is. In a study by Mann (1972), he randomly selected 30 high school seniors (15 females and 15 males) from a college preparatory program to participate in an experimental investigation of the worksheet procedure. He taught them how to prepare a worksheet that would help them make decisions about college. The procedure he used was similar to the one presented here, but not identical to it. He also employed a "control group" of 20 students who were not taught the worksheet procedure. Mann contacted the students approximately 6 weeks after they notified the colleges about their decision concerning which college they planned to attend. The group that had received worksheet training (the experimental group) had less postdecision stress and anxiety and were happier about the decisions they made than the control group. Mann also reported that they had considered possible unfavorable consequences of their decision more carefully than the control group. Thus, if something does go wrong they will more likely be prepared for it than those in the group without worksheet training.

Additional evidence that supports the validity of the worksheet procedure comes from a study by Wanous (1973). He conducted an experiment to study the employment decisions of telephone operators. One group of prospective telephone operators was shown a film that portrayed both the positive and negative aspects of the job while a control group was shown the standard training film that stressed only the positive aspects. All subjects in both groups decided to accept the employment offer to become telephone operators. One month later, subjects who had viewed the "balanced" presentation reported that they were happier with their decision than the other telephone operators who had viewed the standard one-sided film. In addition, significantly fewer subjects from the experimental group were thinking about quitting their job than from the control group. In a similar vein, Janis and Mann (1977) reported several studies in which the worksheet procedure has been utilized in health decisions (e.g., elective surgery) with beneficial outcomes.

POSTDECISION COMMITMENT AND EVALUATION

The decision making process doesn't end with the decision. Once a course of action has been selected, the decision maker must make detailed plans to carry it out and needs to remain committed to the decision. However, if a major change occurs in the evaluation of the consideration, then the process should be repeated. For example, if Evan were unexpectedly offered a lucrative contract to become a jazz musician, he would be wise to reconsider this alternative. Success at this alternative would now seem much more likely and a large income would be assured. Decision making is not a static process. Our major life decisions will have to be reconsidered whenever the major variables change.

Cognitive Dissonance

Most of the time, people find that they are pleased with their decisions. This finding has been of considerable interest to research psychologists. Leon Festinger (1957), a famous research psychologist, proposed a theory to explain this phenomenon. It is called the theory of **cognitive dissonance.** It is based on the idea that people like their beliefs, attitudes, and actions to be consistent, and when they are not consistent an unpleasant internal state arises—dissonance. Dissonance needs to be reduced. If you believe that it is wrong to smoke marijuana and you attend a party where you smoke marijuana, you will feel uncomfortable because your actions and beliefs are not in agreement. They are not consistent with each other. In order to reduce the discomfort of cognitive dissonance, the unpleasant internal state, you will generally change your beliefs and conclude that you did the right thing since "marijuana probably isn't so bad after all." In general, the theory of cognitive dissonance has received considerable experimental support. In one study (Brehm, 1956) subjects rated the desirability of several gifts (e.g., toaster, coffeemaker). They were then asked to choose between two gifts that they had rated as equally desirable. After a decision had been made, subjects rated the rejected gift as being much less desirable than the one they chose. The theory of *cognitive dissonance* would have predicted this result since subjects would now believe that they must like the selected object much more than the rejected one in order to maintain consistency. It seems that once a decision is made the alternatives that were not selected will seem much less attractive than the one that was.

The theory of cognitive dissonance can be applied in a number of situations. It can be used to explain the famous fable *The Fox and the Sour Grapes*. The story goes something like this: A hungry fox spies grapes hanging high overhead. After repeated unsuccessful attempts to reach them, he decides that they were probably sour and walks away. Like the human subjects described in this section, he downplayed the desirability of the object he didn't obtain.

The theory of cognitive dissonance only applies when a conscious decision has been made. If you were coerced in some way, there would be no dissonance. Suppose that you were required to write an essay on some topic that you are opposed to, like the inferiority of a racial or ethnic group, or why drugs should be available to elementary school children. If you were coerced into doing this, there would be no need to change your attitudes to keep them consistent with this behavior. However, if you voluntarily decided to write such an essay, then cognitive dissonance theory would predict a change in your attitude toward the position you took in the essay. This is a major theory in social psychology that explains why people are usually satisfied with the decisions they make.

Hindsight and Forethought

The term **hindsight** is probably not a new one for you. After a decision has been made and the relevant events occur, well meaning friends will often tell you they could have predicted the consequences of your decision. If you have ever been divorced (or have exchanged confidences with someone who has), there were probably several acquaintances who claimed to have known all along that, "he (or she) was no good for you." Events appear different with the benefit of hindsight. Forethought is the opposite of hindsight. There should be fewer unfortunate consequences if decisions are carefully thought out *before* they are made.

In experimental investigations of hindsight, most participants erroneously believed that they could have predicted the consequences of historical and personal decisions before they occurred. In our earlier analysis of the Pearl Harbor disaster, it seemed obvious that the only possible decision was to assume that the aircraft belonged to the Japanese. It should be remembered that we analyzed the disaster with the full knowledge of the ensuing events. Hindsight occurs only when poor or wrong decisions have been made. It is seldom that good decisions are analyzed after the fact. Forethought and hindsight are qualitatively different. At the time of the decision (forethought) there is doubt and deliberation, but following the unfavorable consequences of the decision (hindsight) there is often a great sense of certainty that the future should have been predicted more accurately.

An example of the power of hindsight occurred in 1974 when an editorial in a Eugene, Oregon newspaper called upon the local prison warden to resign. A "convicted murderer, bank robber, and all-around bad actor" had been given a 4-hour pass to leave the state penitentiary (Fischoff, 1975). Instead of returning, he kidnapped and murdered an Oregon couple. With the benefit of hindsight, that is with the full knowledge of the result, does it seem that the warden should have known that this would happen? Given the disasterous outcome it was a wrong decision, but was the result obvious or even likely before the pass was granted? The convict had been a model prisoner before the pass was granted. Do you think that the warden should have been required to resign?

Hindsight is of little value in the decision-making process. It distorts our memory for events that occurred at the time of the decision so that the actual consequence seems to have been a "foregone conclusion." Thus, it may be difficult to learn from our mistakes. Retrospective (after the fact) review, on the other hand, can be a valuable aid in improving future decisions. Unlike hindsight, it does not involve a faulty reconstruction of the information available at the time of the decision so that the consequence appears obvious.

It is a good idea to determine what went wrong if a poor decision has been made. Look for the kinds of fallacies discussed earlier in the chapter. If you can find the weaknesses in earlier decisions, you'll know what to watch out for in subsequent ones. With practice and hard work you can actively plan for your future and make good decisions that will affect your whole life.

CHAPTER SUMMARY

1. Decision making is an active process that begins with a clear definition of the problem.

2. Even trained professionals commonly commit decision making fallacies.

3. There is a robust tendency for people to seek information that will confirm the decision that they're considering and to avoid information that will disconfirm their decision.

4. People often rely on heuristics or "rules of thumb" to help them make decisions. The availability heuristic or reliance on events that are readily thought of is a common decision making heuristic.

5. Because of the widespread but erroneous belief that the laws of chance are self-correcting, many people believe that "random-looking" sequences of outcomes are more probable than orderly sequences of outcomes.

6. Unwarranted optimism and the willingness to generalize from small samples can also lead to poor decisions.

7. People often fall prey to entrapment. They find it difficult to reverse their decision after having invested large amounts of time or money.

8. Risky decisions require special care. There is often a tendency to downplay the likelihood of a disastrous outcome.

9. Some decisions are made by eliminating alternatives until only one or two choices remain.

10. Important decisions can be optimized by preparing a worksheet in which alternatives and considerations are listed and weighted in a table format.

11. People are most often satisfied with the decisions that they make, possibly because cognitive dissonance works to maintain consistency between actions and beliefs. Thus, we reason that if we decided on a course of action it must have been the best one.

12. After the consequences of a decision have occurred, there is a great sense of certainty that the consequences should have been obvious. Hindsight is a ubiquitous phenomenon that distorts how we perceive the information that was available before the decision was made.

Terms to Know:

You should be able to define or describe the following terms and concepts. If you find that you're having difficulty with any term, be sure to reread the section where it is discussed.

Fallacy
Confirmation Bias
Heuristic
Algorithm
Availability Heuristic
Representativeness Heuristic
Gambler's Fallacy
Law of Small Numbers
Sample Size
Belief in the Fairness of Chance
Wishful Thinking
Entrapment
Biased Discounting
Elimination by Aspects
Multidimensional Comparisons
Unidimensional Comparison
Transitivity
Optimization
Overall Assessment
Dimensional Comparison
2/3 Ideal Rule
Satisficing
Cognitive Dissonance
Hindsight

Be sure that you can answer the following questions.

1. Describe some experimental studies that support the validity of the worksheet procedure.

2. What are heuristics? How do they differ from algorithms? Describe two examples of heuristics. Are they necessarily bad?

3. List and describe the steps in preparing a decision worksheet.

4. How does the theory of cognitive dissonance explain why people are usually satisfied with the decisions they make?

5. Explain how the "elimination by aspects" strategy can be applied to deciding where to live.

6. What should a decision maker do if one alternative "wins" by the overall assessment method and a different one "wins" by the dimensional comparison method?

7. How can the "failure to seek disconfirming evidence" lead to wrong decisions in research?

8. Justify all of the effort involved in making a worksheet.

9. How could a decision worksheet be a valuable aid to people in psychotherapy?

10. How does the mathematical concept of transitivity apply to decision making? If your friend was deciding which university to attend and told you that she preferred Ohio State over Penn State, and Penn State over California State, but preferred California State over Ohio State, what could you conclude about her decision?

11. Why can we be more confident about results obtained from experiments with a large sample size than those with a small sample size?

Exercises

Try out the decision making skills you've learned in this chapter.

1. Think of a major decision that you will be facing in the near future. Use the worksheet procedure to help you reach a decision.

2. Study a major political decision that was made in the last 25 years (e.g., The Bay of Pigs decision, Watergate, President Ford's decision to pardon Nixon). Look for the role that fallacies and heuristics played. Analyze the decision. Would you have made the same one? If not, what would you have done?

3. Look for instances of the confirmation bias, availability heuristic, representativeness heuristic, belief in the law of small numbers, wishful thinking, cognitive dissonance, hindsight and gambler's fallacy in the everyday decisions made by yourself and others around you.

4. Reread the hospital scenario presented at the beginning of this chapter. Based on what you've learned about how to make sound decisions, what would you do if you were the protagonist in this story?

5. Try out some of the examples presented in this chapter on your friends (e.g., the ascending number series, the multiplication series, the information about a symptom and disease, the head-tail sequence). If they make the usual errors explain to them why the errors occurred and how to avoid these errors in the future.

SUGGESTED READINGS

A comprehensive and moderately easy-to-read coverage of the decision-making process can be found in a book appropriately named *Decision Making* by Janis and Mann (1977) and in *A Practical Guide for Making Decisions* by Wheeler and Janis (1980). Both have an extensive section on the worksheet procedure as does *The Art of Problem-Solving* by Carkhuff (1973). A variation on the worksheet procedure is presented in *Practical Reasoning in Natural Language* by Thomas (1977).

Several excellent papers on heuristics and biases appear in a volume edited by Johnson-Laird and Wason entitled *Thinking: Readings in Cognitive Science* (1977). A book that is fun to read because the examples of decision strategies are humorous and current is *Decisions Decisions: Game Theory and You* by Bell and Caplans (1976). An interesting multidisciplinary approach can be found in *Making Decisions: A Multidisciplinary Introduction* by Hill et al. (1979). This book begins with the problem of "What to do with dear Aunt Sarah?" It discusses the ethical, economic, psychological, and philosophical problems that a family is faced with in planning the future of an aging aunt. A collection of interdisciplinary papers appears in *Decision Making: An Interdisciplinary Inquiry* edited by Ungson and Braunstein (1982).

Readers with a serious interest in learning more about decision making will find a comprehensive review of the literature in *Judgment and Choice* by Hogarth (1980). Advanced treatments of the topic can be found in *Human Judgment and Decision Making: Theories, Methods, and Procedures* by Hammond, McClelland and Mumpower (1980), *Human Judgement and Decision Processes* edited by Kaplin and Schwartz (1975) and *Decision Methodology* by White (1975). A collection of papers dealing with a variety of topics in the field of decision making can be found in *Cognitive Processes in Choice and Decision Behavior* edited by Wallsten (1980).

If you're interested in learning more about the theory of cognitive dissonance, you can consult *A Theory of Cognitive Dissonance* by Festinger (1957). Some of the experimental literature on cognitive dissonance appear in a volume edited by Festinger called *Conflict, Decision and Dissonance* (1964). A classic study of dissonance with a group of people who believed that the world would end on a given day and their reactions when it didn't appear in *When Prophecy Fails,* Festinger, Riecken, and Schacter (1956).

8 Memory

Contents

Acquisition of Knowledge 243
Learning and Memory 244
Human Information Processing 245
  Acquisition 247
  Retention 250
  The Constructive Nature of Memory 251
  Retrieval 257
Marijuana 261
Emotions and Memory 263
  Periodic Review 263
  Anxiety and Stress 264
  Repression 265
Metamemory 267
Mnemonics 268
  Mnemonic Principles 274

Many years ago I read a story about a beautiful young woman who made an interesting deal with the Devil. She agreed to sell her soul to him. In return, he promised that she would spend her old age in complete happiness. The Devil kept his promise. When the woman grew old, she became totally senile. Her old age was spent in the memories of her youth, visiting with friends who had long since died, totally oblivious to life around her. The memory of this story has stayed with me for a long time. I wonder if she would have made this deal if she had known that her happiness would be bought with senility and would consist of a life among her memories. I would like to be able to tell you who wrote this story and give you the title, so that you can read it for yourself, but I can't. I've forgotten where I read it. While I believe that I can remember accurately many of the details of the story, I can't remember where I read it.

ACQUISITION OF KNOWLEDGE

Ulric Neisser (1982), a cognitive psychologist, has asked, "What do we use the past for?" (p. 13). This may seem like a strange question, but a good way to begin our quest to understand memory is by examining its function. According to

Neisser, we use the past to define ourselves. If you are a fan of the soap operas, you'll recognize this as one of their favorite themes. Soap opera plots often involve memory loss (amnesia) for one of the protagonists. The usual sequence of events consists of a sudden blow to the head of a leading man or woman followed by a peculiar loss of memory in which the identity of family members is forgotten. While this is rare in real life, it does point out the essential role of memory. It tells you who you are, where you're from, and where you're going. Try to imagine what life would be like if you had no memory. For most of us, this is a frightening thought. Our memories are our most valuable possession. I don't know anyone who would sell the memories he or she has accumulated over a lifetime, no matter how much money was offered. Life without memory is unfathomable.

All intelligent systems (e.g., humans, computers, dogs, cockroaches) have the ability to learn and remember. These abilities play a crucial role in all of our lives. Most importantly, they are inevitable consequences of living. For humans, the ability to learn and remember well often determines the quality of life, economic status, and sometimes even survival. Because the ability to think clearly depends, in large part, on how well we can utilize past experiences, memory is a central topic in developing thinking skills. In this chapter, we consider current views of how memory works, why forgetting occurs, and ways to improve memory.

LEARNING AND MEMORY

The relationship between learning and memory involves the passage of time. Let's clarify this with an example. It is reasonable to expect that during a college career, students will take many, many exams. When you finish reading this section of the book, you should be able to answer a question like: "What is the relationship between learning and memory?" If you write the correct answer on an exam, your professor will infer that sometime before the exam you learned the relevant material and that you remembered it. Learning and memory are always *inferred.* No one can ever observe you learning or remembering. These activities are inferred from some behavior. A friend can watch you while you move your eyes across the lines of print that appear in a book propped up in front of you, but she can't *see* you learn. In the example presented here, writing the correct answer on an exam is the behavior that allows the inference that learning and memory have occurred. Learning and memory are **hypothetical constructs,** hypothetical terms that have been made up to help psychologists study and understand the mind and, thus, they have been called "convenient fictions." Learning and memory are like perception, motivation, thirst, sex drives, hallucinations, and many other terms in that they have no physical reality. They are only known by inference, and they are helpful in understanding the processes of the mind.

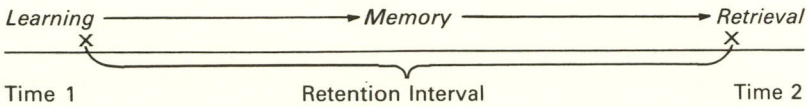

Example:

Learning	*Memory*	*Retrieval*
Study your textbook	During the retention interval (time between learning and retrieval) you engage in other activities—e.g., eat dinner, sleep, eat breakfast	Answer exam question correctly

FIG. 8.1. A time-line depicting the relationship among learning, memory and retrieval.

Learning and memory are usually inferred together. If I ask you why RED CHINA had been a problem for the Reagans, and you answer correctly, then I will infer that you learned and remembered that Nancy Reagan obtained very expensive red-rimmed china for the White House. If you are unable to answer this question, then either: (1) you never learned the facts in question; or (2) you learned them, but forgot them.

The Time Line

The relationship between learning and memory is a *temporal* one (time-based) and is depicted on the time line in Fig. 8.1. Something happens at Time 1 that we call learning. Following Time 1 is an interval which can be as short as a few thousandths of a second or as long as a lifetime. Retention of information during this time interval is attributed to memory, but indexed by retrieval. At Time 2, (some time after Time 1), the individual exhibits some behavior, like correctly answering an exam question, that allows us to infer that the material was both learned and remembered.

HUMAN INFORMATION PROCESSING

The term "learning" has gone out of style in psychology. Part of the reason that the terms have changed is that we have changed the way we think about these topics. We have borrowed from the most modern technology of each time period to create a model of how the mind "must" work. Early in this century, when indoor plumbing became widely available, some psychologists suggested that the mind must work like a plumbing system with thoughts traveling through conduits or pipes (this could irreverently be referred to as the "your mind is like a toilet" metaphor). Later, when large switchboards were developed that could transmit telephone calls to many centers at once, this served as the model of the mind.

Currently, the most advanced technology we have is the computer, and many psychologists have been quick to point out parallels between humans and computers. Like a computer, we take in information, process it, and send information out. Thus, the term **Human Information Processing** (HIP) refers to the idea that humans and computers have many functional similarities. These are shown in more detail in Fig. 8.2

Many psychologists believe that if we think about humans as information processors, similar in function to highly sophisticated computers, then we can use this metaphor to understand human memory and thought. It is important to point out here that they're using the computer as a **model** of human thought processes. A model is an "as if" statement—that means think about the human mind *as if* it were a computer. Many people find a computer model of human thought processes objectionable, but it is important to note that no one believes that the neurons, blood vessels, and brain tissue of the human brain is similar to the *hardware* (electronic registers) of the computer! The simile that your mind is like a computer applies only to the processes both go through in understanding and in solving problems. Proponents of the HIP view say that the human information processing model has proven useful in understanding memory and thinking. Those opposed to it point out that there are too many differences—people are emotional, machines are not; people are adaptable, machines are rigid; peo-

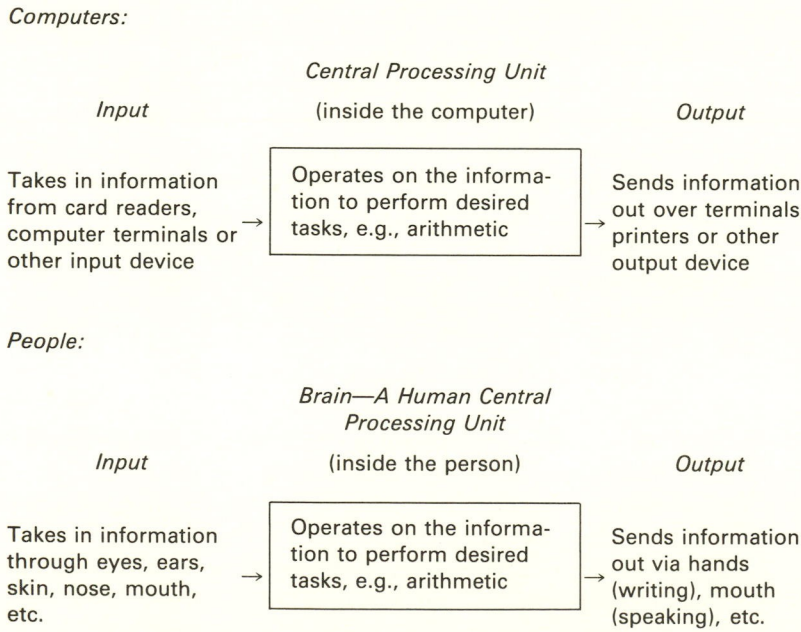

FIG. 8.2. Human Information Processing Model. Computers are used as an analogy for understanding human thought and memory processes.

ple can create other people and machines, machines cannot. Although these differences are important enough to cause some researchers to abandon this model, it has been a dominant theme in recent research on human memory.

Because our ability to think is viewed as similar to the computer's ability to process information, the first stage of this process is usually called *input* or **acquisition,** to keep it consistent with computer terminology. The term "learning" is nowadays usually reserved for a particular theory of how we learn, called conditioning, which won't be discussed here.

The interval between acquiring some information and the time when you remember it is called the **retention interval.** The act of remembering something is called **retrieval.** In order to understand memory, we'll examine each of these three components of human information processing in turn.

Acquisition

A poster of Farrah Fawcett-Majors in a red bathing suit sold over twelve million copies, thus becoming the best-selling poster of all time. One spin-off of this success story is the marketing of Farrah look-alike dolls, clad in a similar red bathing suit, that is "recommended for girls over three years old."

Unless you already knew this, you have just acquired new information. You can answer questions that you couldn't answer a few moments ago. You are a changed person.

We are surrounded every moment by more information than we could possibly acquire. Stop some friends some time during the day and ask them to close their eyes. Ask them questions about the room they're in (like which pots are on the stove, if they're in the kitchen) or the book they're reading (like how wide the margins are or what is shown on the book cover) or the person they're with (like does a friend part her hair on the side or down the middle). You'll be surprised how much of this potentially available information is not known. We are selective in the information we acquire.

Attention

One of the primary determinants of what we know is what we attend to. Think back to the last time you were at a large, noisy party with people standing around in small groups talking to each other.

Imagine that you're standing with two acquaintances discussing the weather. There are several small groups of people standing nearby who are also carrying on conversations. If someone near you, but not talking to you, mentions your name or something of interest (e.g., "Did you hear the latest news about Debbie and Stanley . . .?"), this will attract your attention. If, however, the same person standing at the same distance from you, speaking in the same voice is discussing tree blight, you probably would never notice, unless you have a special interest in tree blight. Think about what will happen to the conversation about the weather that you've been engaged in. If your answer is "Nothing," you're correct. When you switched your attention to the more interesting conversation, you lost the original conversation. If, at this point, the person who has been talking to you suddenly stops and asks, "What do you think about it?", you'd have to give an embarrassed explanation, since you would have no knowledge of her conversation.

The scenario described here is called the **Cocktail Party Effect.** Most people can think of an episode where something similar to this has happened to them. It demonstrates several basic properties of attention.

1. *If you don't pay attention, you won't acquire information.* Let's consider the scenario a little more closely. When you were attending to the weather conversation, you knew very little or nothing about the other conversations around you. When you switched your attention to the more interesting conversation, you could not say what was happening in the weather conversation. Thus, attention will be a major concept in what gets remembered, since it determines what gets into the human information system.

2. *There are limitations on your ability to process information.* All of the conversations going on around you are not processed. Your attentional processes determine what will get into the system and what will not. You simply cannot carry on several conversations at the same time.

3. *There are individual differences in what is attended to.* If you had no interest in "the latest news about Debbie and Stanley," but found the weather fascinating, then you would not have switched your attention and could have responded with more than a sheepish grin to the question, "What do you think about it?"

Experimental Studies. Researchers, of course, don't go to cocktail parties to study attention. (They go for other purposes.) The *Cocktail Party Effect* is studied in the laboratory with a technique called **dichotic listening.** In the dichotic listening technique, subjects wear headphones similar to the ones that come with stereo equipment. Different messages are heard over each earphone. You can try this out for yourself, to see what it's like, by getting two friends to stand on either side of you and having them read aloud, simultaneously, from different books. Try attending to only one message. How much did you remember from that message? How much did you remember from the message you weren't attending to?

When experiments like this were conducted in laboratories under controlled conditions (e.g., volume was controlled and subjects were required to repeat the message to which they were attending to be certain that they really were attending to the appropriate message), researchers found that little was remembered from the nonattended message, although subjects could recall gross properties like whether the voice changed from a man's to a woman's and when there was no message at all (Cherry, 1953; Moray, 1959; Treisman, 1964). The gist or theme of the nonattended message was lost, whereas subjects could remember a great deal of the message to which they were attending.

If you're interested in knowing more about memory so that you can improve your own, then you'll have to pay attention to attention. Many people complain that they forget the names of people soon after they've been introduced. It is likely that they never paid attention to the name at the time of introduction. When meeting someone, it is a good idea to repeat the person's name aloud to be certain that you've heard it correctly and to be certain that you've paid attention. It's been said that a good politician remembers names. This is also true of successful salespeople, teachers, waiters, and waitresses. Even if you'll never be a politician, salesperson, teacher, or waiter or waitress, it is a good social skill that is well worth the effort.

In case you're unimpressed with the rule that unless you attend to something you won't know it, let's try a demonstration. Most people will admit that they like money and have worked hard to earn it and have spent it countless times. In Fig. 8.3 there are several drawings of a penny. Only one is correct. If you're like most people, you won't be able to recognize the correct penny because you never attended to its details. To find the "correct" answer, check it with a real penny, but be certain that you attend to all of the details carefully. If you're still dubious, try drawing a telephone dial from memory. Few people find that they know which numbers and letters go together, yet we've all dialed telephones thousands of times. The moral is simple: Without attention there will be little memory.

FIG. 8.3. Fifteen drawings of a U.S. penny. Which one is correct? (From Nickerson and Adams, 1979.)

The need to pay attention in school should be obvious. John Holt, a respected educator and author of the book *How Children Fail* (1964) believes that many children fail in school because they don't pay attention. Think about how your mind sometimes seems to wander when reading textbooks or during lectures. Most students are not even aware when they're not paying attention. It should be obvious by now that in order to develop better memory skills, you will also have to develop attentional skills.

Retention

The term "retention" is sometimes used synonymously with memory. Unfortunately, this term suggests that memory is like a vast storage tank or library where memories are stored. This notion of memory is wrong. Some psychologists believe that there are three basic "types" of memory which are differentiated on the basis of the length of the retention interval and the amount of information they can retain.

The first type of memory does not conform to the usual notion of memory. It refers to retention intervals that are less than 1 or 2 seconds long. When we see something, the image persists on the retinas of our eyes for a very brief period of time. As this "memory system" is so closely tied to our sensory systems, it is called **Sensory Memory.** You can demonstrate sensory memory for yourself. Go into a dark room with a lit flashlight and wave it in a circular path until you see a streak of light trailing behind the flashlight. The streak is your sensory memory of the light. A demonstration of this was used effectively in the movie "Star Wars." Long rods of light, presumably the weapons of the future, were waved during the combat scenes. The streaks, lagging behind the rods were your eyes' memory of where the light had been. Persistence on the sensory receptors is also true for hearing, touching, smelling, and tasting. We won't be considering sensory memory here because it is so closely tied to sensory functioning that there is probably little that we can do to improve it.

The second memory system covers retention intervals from about 2 seconds to somewhere between 30 seconds and 1 minute. Since this is a relatively short time period it is called **Short-Term Memory.** All the rest of memory, from 1 minute to a lifetime is called **Long-Term Memory.**

Many people feel that memories that last only a matter of seconds are not only quantitatively but also qualitatively different from memories that are older. Think of looking up a telephone number in the phone book for a friend you've just met. You find the number, "876-7317," and repeat it to yourself as you walk across the room to dial. If you get a busy signal or if someone interrupts you with a question, or if you trip over the cat, the number is forgotten and you need to look it up again. This certainly seems qualitatively different from the process you go through in remembering your own phone number and those of your close friends and family whose phone numbers you've known a long time. Furthermore, while you can remember one new phone number as you walk across the room, you can't remember two new 7-digit numbers (try it—you'll find that there are too many digits). Compare this with your memory for items you already know. Think of all the words you know, all of the people you can recognize, all of the book plots you can remember. It seems as if your long-term memory is limitless in the number of items it can retain. Despite the intuitive notion that the distinction between short-term and long-term memory is useful, some psychologists prefer the idea of one memory system.

Whether there are one, two, or three memory systems is not as important for a thinking course as understanding what happens to the information stored in memory and what we can do to improve the ability to remember.

Many of the popular notions people hold about memory are wrong. For example, in a story by the famous mystery writer Agatha Christie, the witness to a crime had her memory of it "covered over" by a series of events that followed the crime so that she was unable to remember what happened. As the years passed and the witness grew old, the distracting and confusing information was forgotten until only the "true" memory remained. This notion of how our memory works makes for great fiction, but is a wrong account of what psychologists have learned about memory.

The Constructive Nature of Memory

Prior Knowledge

Your ability to learn and remember new material depends on what you already know. You certainly wouldn't take an advanced course in nuclear physics if you never had a basic course in physics. However, you probably never realized that *prior knowledge*, the information you already know, influences how you think and how you remember new information in almost any context.

Stereotype and Prejudice. An interesting experimental demonstration of the idea that prior knowledge influences what people will remember was conducted by two psychologists, Snyder and Uranowitz (1978). Two groups of college students served as subjects. Students in both groups read the same story about a woman named Betty. The story contained information about her life. Among the information presented was the fact that she occasionally dated men. Up to this point, everything was the same for the students in both groups. After reading the story, one group of students was told that Betty had become a lesbian, while the other group of students was told that she was leading a heterosexual life-style. The question of interest was whether this would influence what they remembered about Betty's life story. One week later, all of the students returned to the laboratory to answer questions about the story they had read. They were asked many questions. The critical question was:

In high school, Betty:
(a) occasionally dated men
(b) never went out with men
(c) went steady
(d) no information provided

Can you guess the results of this experiment? The group of students who were told that Betty is now a lesbian were much more likely to "remember" (b) as the correct answer than the group of students who were told that Betty is a heterosexual. The students who had been told that Betty is a lesbian believed that they remembered something that hadn't occurred. Their prejudices and beliefs about lesbians caused them to remember events that never transpired.

In an experiment designed to determine how sex role stereotypes influence memory (Halpern, in press), high school students were given dull, boring stories to read about the life of a main character who was either a male ("David") or a female ("Linda"). The events described in the story were those commonly engaged in by both women and men. Female high school students who read stories with Linda as the protagonist remembered the story better than other female students who read the same story with David as the protagonist, whereas male high school students remembered the story better when David was the protagonist. It seems that high school students were able to identify with the main character when his or her sex was the same as their own, and this resulted in better memory for the details of the story.

Our beliefs about lesbians, women, men, and other groups, especially racial and ethnic groups, exert strong influences on what we will remember about members of these groups.

Experiments like the ones just described have important implications for understanding the nature of prejudice. Let's return to the earlier example and suppose that Betty was a real person whom you knew while growing up. There may be many things that you can remember about Betty. You now learn that she is a lesbian. Suppose further that you have a stereotype of lesbians as women who drive trucks, crush beer cans with one hand, and hate all men. Because this stereotype, like most, contains very little truth about any hypothetical "average" lesbian, you would be forced either to change your stereotype or to change what you remember about Betty. It seems that it is our memories that change while the stereotype resists change. You might selectively remember information like the fact that she always liked to play basketball and forget other information about Betty that is inconsistent with your stereotype, like the fact that she also liked to cook and plant flowers.

Inference and Distortion

Memory is malleable. What we remember changes over time. When our knowledge and experience change, our memories also change (Bartlett, 1932). There are additions made to memories so that we remember events that never occurred and deletions made so that we forget other events that did. At your next high school or college reunion get together with friends to remember old times. You may be surprised to find that the same events are remembered differently by each of you, and each will have memories that others don't have.

Eyewitness Testimony

Seeing is believing, or at least most people believe it is. Nowhere is this adage held as strongly as in our legal system. Very often eyewitness testimony, the testimony of someone who saw a crime being committed, is the determining factor between a conviction and an acquittal. Defendants with credible, plausible alibis have been convicted by an eye witness's identification. Should we be placing so much faith in the accounts given by eye witnesses?

If we use the theoretical framework provided earlier, then recall of the event depends on acquisition, retention, and retrieval. Information can never be recalled correctly unless it was attended to at the time it occurred. This would not seem to be a problem if we're interested in memory for a crime, since it would seem to demand our attention. In fact, witnesses and victims fail to notice many important details because of a narrowing of attention that occurs under stress. If there is a gun or other weapon used during the crime, then the victim focuses on the weapon. Other details that are needed for correct identification, like whether the assailant had a moustache, may go unnoticed (Loftus, 1979).

There are many alterations of the memory of the event that occur during the retention interval, which in this case is the time between the crime and the recollection of it at trial. Discussions of the crime after it occurred can be incorporated into memory so that the individual may honestly believe that he is recalling the crime, while what he is recalling is a discussion of the crime.

Events that occur at retrieval can also influence memory. For example, the way a question is asked can lead to a particular answer. The legal system has recognized this possibility and consequently doesn't allow an attorney to ask his "own" witness "leading" questions. The "line-up" is another example of the way retrieval events can influence what is remembered. Suppose you are in a 24-hour convenience store at night, when a tall, Oriental man bursts in and holds up the cashier at gunpoint. Five days later you're asked to come to the police station to identify the assailant from a line-up. The line consists of one old woman, a 14-year-old white man, two young black men, and one tall Oriental man. The chances of selecting the Oriental man are obviously greater than if the line-up contained five different tall Oriental men. Furthermore, we also know that cross-racial identification tends to be poorer than intra-racial identification (the idea that "they all look alike"), so unless you too are Oriental, this hapless man is even more likely to be "remembered" as the robber. Since events that occur during the retention interval influence recall, the line-up can actually hinder recall. Once a person is selected from the line-up as the assailant, he will look even more familiar at the trial. The victim may, indeed, be remembering him, but he may look familiar because he was seen in the line-up.

A notorious example of the fallibility of human memory was seen in a highly publicized case involving a Catholic priest who was positively identified as an armed robber by several different witnesses. The trial ended abruptly when a much younger and taller man confessed, offering details of the crime that could only have been known by the real robber, since they were never publicized. *The witnesses had not lied.* Each honestly believed that he or she remembered seeing the priest as the robber. It is important to realize that while memory can sometimes be astonishingly accurate, it can also be astonishingly wrong.

Meaningfulness

Information that is highly meaningful will be remembered better than information that has little meaning to you. To demonstrate this, look at A, B, and C in Fig. 8.4 for a few seconds, then cover the figure and reproduce them from memory. Try this now.

You probably remembered some parts of the figures shown in Fig. 8.4, but didn't remember them perfectly. Suppose I now tell you that Fig. 8.4A is a soldier walking his dog behind a picket fence (Do you see the dog's tail and the end of the soldier's rifle?), and that Fig. 8.4B is a washerwoman scrubbing the floor (Do you see her water bucket and the bottoms of her shoes?). If you recognized Fig. 8.4C as a bear behind a tree, then you drew it more accurately than if it seemed more like abstract art. Making the figures meaningful will enhance how well they are remembered. You can test this with friends by telling them what the figures are, uncovering them briefly, and then comparing how much your friends remembered to your own drawings.

Your elementary school teachers recognized the role that meaning plays in memory when they told you to "read for meaning." It seems that comprehension and memory go together and anything that improves comprehension will also improve memory. In a clever demonstration of this, two psychologists (Bransford & Johnson, 1972) presented college students with the following passage to read. Read it for yourself and then see how much you can remember.

> The procedure is actually quite simple. First you arrange things into different groups depending on their makeup. Of course, one pile may be sufficient depending on how much there is to do. If you have to go somewhere else due to lack of facilities that is the next step, otherwise you are pretty well set. It is important not to overdo any particular endeavor. That is, it is better to do too few things at once

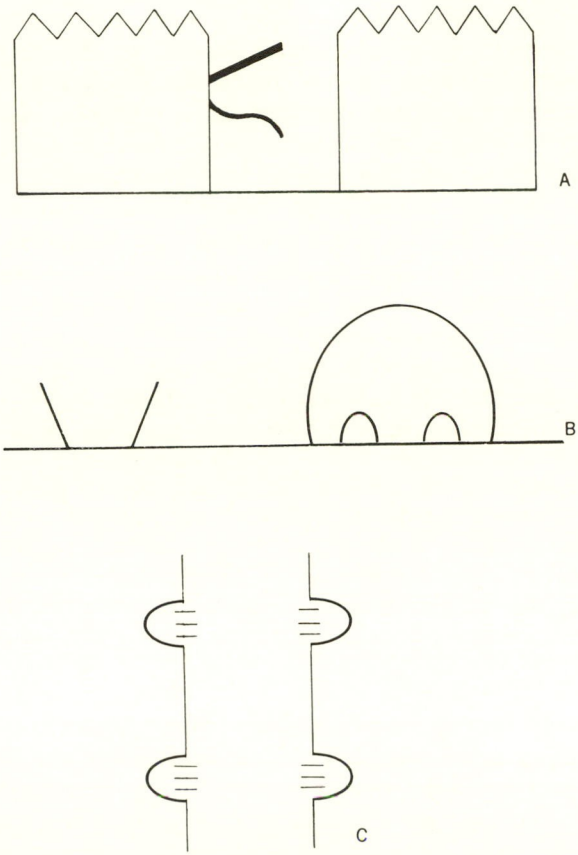

FIG. 8.4. A demonstration of the effect of meaningfulness on memory. Look at these figures for a few seconds, then cover them and reproduce them from memory. (Figures A and B are adapted from Osgood, 1953. Figure C is adapted from Hanson, 1958.)

than too many. In the short run this may not seem important, but complications from doing too many can easily arise. A mistake can be expensive as well. The manipulation of the appropriate mechanisms should be self-explanatory, and we need not dwell on it here. At first the whole procedure will seem complicated. Soon, however, it will become just another facet of life. It is difficult to foresee any end to the necessity for this task in the immediate future, but then one never can tell.

You probably did not remember very much of this passage. I also doubt that you found it very understandable.

I'd like you to read the passage again, this time keeping the title "Washing Clothes" in mind. It should seem much more memorable because the title provided a context or a framework for understanding the passage.

We seldom remember anything verbatim, that is in the exact words that were spoken or read. Most of our memory is for **gist** or interpretation of the meaning of the message. If a student ever answered an examination question with the exact words I had spoken in class or the student had read from the text, I'd be worried. I'd think that the student probably didn't understand the material and hadn't learned it in a meaningful way. Let's try another demonstration of the influence of meaningfulness on memory. Read and remember the following passage (Bransford & Johnson, 1973).

Watching a Peace March From the Fortieth Floor

The view was breathtaking. From the window one could see the crowd below. Everything looked extremely small from such a distance, but the colorful costumes could still be seen. Everyone seemed to be moving in one direction in an orderly fashion, and there seemed to be little children as well as adults. The landing was gentle, and luckily the atmosphere was such that no special suits had to be worn. At first there was a great deal of activity. Later, when the speeches started, the crowd quieted down. The man with the television camera took many shots of the setting and the crowd. Everyone was very friendly and seemed glad when the music started.

What did you remember from this passage? Most people forget the sentence starting with, "The landing was gentle . . . ." Most people who read this try to understand what it is saying about a peace march. The "landing sentence" is incomprehensible in this context, so it is often forgotten. When college students were told that the title was "Space Trip to an Inhabited Planet," the "landing sentence" was almost always remembered. Thus, what people remember depends on the meaning that is extracted.

Meaningfulness can account for some individual differences in memory. Have you ever wondered how a good poker or pinochle or chess player is able to remember which cards have been played or which moves have been made? In a classic study of chess players' memories for the positions of chess pieces on a board, deGroot (1966) found that chess masters could remember chess positions that actually occurred in a game after looking at the board for only 5 seconds. Novice chess players had much more difficulty in remembering where the chess pieces had been. Does this mean that really good chess players have extraordinary memories? To answer this question, deGroot placed the pieces randomly on the board and asked master and novice players to view the board for 5 seconds and then recall the positions of the pieces. In the random placement condition, both groups performed about the same. It seems that the master players remembered more than the novices only when the board positions were highly meaningful to the chess masters and consequently were remembered quite accurately.

It seems likely that good card players remember which cards have already been played because each hand is highly meaningful to them. For example, John Moss (a pseudonym for the author of *How to Win at Poker,* 1950) describes a series of possible hands that a player can be dealt along with several possible cards that could be drawn. It would be easy for him or another poker shark to remember a "four of diamonds in the hole with a four of hearts, six of diamonds and ace of spades exposed." He could remember this as a single familiar hand, while a novice player would have to remember four separate cards. For the good players, this hand would represent a single *chunk* in memory. Reducing a large number of items to a single item to be remembered is called **chunking.** (No, it is not a brand of Chinese food.) It is a subtle and ubiquitous memory process. It allows us to recall whole sentences instead of words and whole words instead of letters. As material becomes increasingly meaningful, we can reduce the number of items that need to be remembered. Master chess players and card players seem to have this memory advantage.

The notion that meaning is important in memory will be raised again, later in this chapter, when we consider strategies for improving memory.

Retrieval

What is your mother's maiden name? Unless you happened to be sitting here thinking about your mother's maiden name, the name seemed to "pop" into your mind. The answer must have been stored in some way that allowed it to be retrieved with a simple question. In fact, it seems almost impossible *not* to remember your mother's maiden name, when you are asked this question. Who was Gerald Ford's Vice Presidential running mate during his bid for the Presidency in 1976? For many people, this is a difficult question to answer. (The answer is Robert Dole.) Certainly you once knew the answer, but over the years, it has been forgotten. Forgetting or retrieval failure can be frustrating experiences for everyone. How can we understand the retrieval process when it works so well sometimes and so poorly other times?

Forgetting

One of the major theories of forgetting is that events interfere with each other in memory. This is called the **Interference Theory of Forgetting.** Suppose that you are studying French and Spanish in college. You'd probably find that you get them confused because what you've learned about one language "interferes" with what you've learned about the other. In general the more similar two events are (or in this case languages), the more interference there will be. By knowing this, can you think of a way to reduce interference and improve memory? In the example just given, one way would be to take the courses in different semesters to minimize the interference, or at least one course early in the morning and the other in the evening. By keeping the French and Spanish courses as separate as possible, you can reduce some of the interference.

Sleeping

It should seem likely that if interference is a cause of forgetting, then if we can eliminate the interference we can improve memory. This was the goal of a study that was conducted in 1924 (Jenkins & Dallenbach). The experimenters had two subjects learn several lists of nonsense syllables (e.g., zev, bip, kuz) which they were asked to recall following a retention interval that ranged from 1 to 8 hours. After learning the list of nonsense syllables, they would either go about their usual activities or they would go to sleep. At the end of the retention interval, the subjects were required to recall as many of the nonsense syllables as they could remember. If they were asleep, the experimenter would wake them and ask them to recall the list. In general, no matter how long the retention interval lasted, the subjects remembered more syllables when they were asleep during the retention interval than when they were awake. Although this study employed only two subjects, it lent strong support for the *Interference Theory of Forgetting*. (This study differs from some classroom situations that you might have experienced in that the subjects went to sleep after, not during the learning process.)

You may be wondering whether it is possible to learn while you're asleep. This seems like a great idea—you could painlessly learn all of the subjects you find to be tedious and difficult. Despite frequent magazine advertisements for "sleep learning" and a popular Walt Disney movie that claimed that sleep learning is possible, the answer is no. It is possible for you to learn while drowsy, but still awake; it is not possible to learn while asleep. Numerous investigations have shown that only information presented while subjects are still awake will be retained (e.g., Bruce, Evans, Fenwick & Spencer, 1970).

Retrieval Cues

Did you ever smell a particular perfume and remember someone you knew who used to wear it?

Perfume commercials would have us believe that the memory of your perfume will keep you constantly on his (or her) mind. Have you ever heard a song on the radio and then thought about the time you first heard it? ("They're playing our song.") Where did these memories come from? Something in the environment acted as a retrieval cue so that the memory was brought into conscious awareness.

Let's try a demonstration of the powerful effect retrival cues can have on memory. Below is a list of words I'd like you to read through. Go through the list once at a rate of approximately one word per second, or have someone read them aloud to you. See how many words you can remember.

Winter
Green
Foot
Pencil
Sweater
Jupiter
Chicago
Bible
French
Violin
Lunch
Russia
Collie
Spaghetti
CHiPs
Newsweek

Stop now; cover the above list and see how many of the list items you can recall in any order. Be sure to try this exercise before you go on. Don't look back at the list when you are finished.

If you didn't remember all 16 words, I'd like you to think about the items you forgot. What happened to them? Are they permanently lost or could you remember them with the proper retrieval cues?

Here is a list of cues. See how many of the "forgotten" words you can recall.

A season of the year
A color
A part of the body
A writing instrument
An article of clothing
A planet
A name of a city
A type of book
A language
A musical instrument
A meal
A country
A breed of dog
A food
A television show
A magazine

Certainly you can remember many more of the items on the list with the appropriate retrieval cues, and this improvement can't be attributed simply to guessing. Generating your own cues while you are trying to learn something in order to facilitate recall is one good way to improve memory. The cues interact with information in memory to make it more accessible so that it can be more readily remembered.

Organization

"Clean up your room!" I don't think that there is a person alive who hasn't heard (or spoken) these words. The idea that "you'll never be able to find anything in this mess" may also apply to how you store information in memory, although the similarity between memory and a messy room is obviously a gross oversimplification. Organization, however, does make it easier to find a pair of socks that match and easier to retrieve information from memory.

I'd like to demonstrate this point with two lists of words. Read one list, at a rate of approximately one word per second, cover the list and write down as many of the words as you can remember, then repeat this process with the second list.

Girl
Heart
Robin
Purple
Finger
Flute
Blue
Organ
Man
Hawk
Green
Lung
Eagle
Child
Piano

Stop now, cover the above list, and write down as many words from this list as you can remember.

Now read the next list, cover it, and then write down as many of the words that you can remember from this list.

Green
Blue
Purple
Man
Girl

Child
Piano
Flute
Organ
Heart
Lung
Finger
Eagle
Hawk
Robin

Stop now, cover the above list and write down as many words from this list as you can remember.

Undoubtedly, you recalled correctly more words from the second list than from the first. You may not have realized that the lists were identical except for the order in which the words were presented. You might expect that you did better the second time because you had a chance to practice the words once, and this was some help. This is true. The additional time spent studying the words can partially account for the improvement in recall. But, most of the improvement on the second list came from the organization provided by presenting words in categories. Research has shown that when lists of words are presented in categories, recall of material was two to three times better than when the same word list was randomly presented (Bower & Clark, 1969). When words are presented in random order, as in the first list, recall is improved when subjects have enough time to generate their own categories (Bousfield, 1953).

You can apply this memory principle by organizing material that you need to learn. If you are learning a classification system for a biology course or the properties of metals for a course in science, study one group or category at a time. See how the groups relate and note similarities and differences within and between categories. Impose a structure or organization on the material to be learned. Interrelate the items so that they become coherent.

MARIJUANA

Students frequently ask about the effect of marijuana on memory. I'll present the answer before I discuss the topic. *Marijuana definitely affects memory.* While this may seem like a straightforward and simple question and answer, the more pertinent questions like how much does it affect memory, when, and what quantity of marijuana is needed to get this effect are much more difficult to answer. It is important to keep in mind that marijuana is an illegal drug, although the severity of laws governing possession, sale, and cultivation vary from state to state. Marijuana is also in widespread use among middle-class Americans, especially college students and young adults. It has been estimated that marijuana is the second largest cash crop in California, although there is no way to verify this claim.

Results of laboratory conducted marijuana studies may be somewhat misleading since they use carefully controlled amounts of tetrahydrocannabinal (THC), the active ingredient in marijuana. There are no controls on street marijuana since it is an illegal drug. (The Food and Drug Administration which carefully monitors all food and drug contents has no jurisdiction over illegal drugs.) According to laboratory research, if you went to a party and got "high" or "stoned" on marijuana, you may have some trouble remembering events that occurred just before getting high. It is also likely that you would have difficulty remembering what happened at the party while you were high if you tried to recall it the next day, after the effects of the drug had worn off (Darley, Tinklenberg, Roth, Hollister, & Atkinson, 1973).

We also know that it takes longer to respond to an event while you are high than when you are not. I believe that this is the most important finding from the marijuana research. What does this suggest about driving while high? Don't do it! If a child or other person ran out in front of your car, it would take you longer to put your foot on the brake if you were high than if you were not. The additional time needed to react could mean the difference between life or death. There are massive media campaigns in almost every city to discourage drunk drivers, while there is little attention paid to stoned drivers. This warning applies not only to driving an automobile, but also to operating other potentially dangerous equipment like drills, power lawn mowers, and chain saws.

What about the long-term effects of marijuana use? This question is difficult to answer because we are talking about an illegal drug, so long-term users are hesitant to volunteer for experiments. I have had students who are regular marijuana users report that they have difficulty concentrating; however, this is a small biased sample, and other students have reported that they have no difficulty concentrating. Studies done in other countries where marijuana is legal provide a more encouraging picture of the effects of long-term marijuana use on memory. In these countries, some people in professional positions admit to long-term marijuana use. It is impossible to derive conclusive statements from testimonies like these since the amount of use was never monitored and the professionals who report long-term marijuana use may be atypical in their response to marijuana. There is no evidence that marijuana use will cause you to take "harder" drugs or that it will shrink your brain or make you go crazy.

There are many variables that will determine the type of effect marijuana will have on any individual. First time users may respond differently from long-term users. Dose size is important, and this is never carefully controlled in street drugs like marijuana. Purity is also an important factor. I know someone who bought a very expensive ounce of oregano believing it to be marijuana. (Smoking hot oregano is O.K. on pizza.) There are also individual differences in the amount of THC that is absorbed into the body, which differences are only partially dependent on the amount of marijuana smoke inhaled and exhaled. Thus, it is very difficult to predict marijuana's effects.

There has been a marijuana initiative on the ballot in California every year since 1972. Other states have attempted to pass similar measures. Few voters know the facts about marijuana use. I've only presented its effects on remembering and responding here, since this is a text on thinking. Other physiological responses to marijuana need to be considered before you can cast an intelligent vote on the marijuana issue.

EMOTIONS AND MEMORY

One of the major criticisms of drawing parallels between the way humans think and remember and the way computers do is that human emotion is an integral part of the human process, and there is no computer counterpart for emotion. There are several ways that emotions influence our ability to think and remember.

Periodic Review

Most people over 30 years of age have heard the question, "Where were you when you heard that President Kennedy was shot?" This was a favorite topic of conversation for many years. It was often the opening line for a couple on their first date (before it was replaced with "What's your sign?"), and remained a favorite theme for English term paper assignments. Emotionally charged events, both negative and positive, are often rehearsed, while everyday events are largely ignored. This periodic review may make the event seem more memorable, but in fact you may be remembering your own account of the event rather than the event itself.

An interesting example of the way **Periodic Review** influences memory for an emotional event can be found in an autobiographical account by the world famous developmental psychologist, Jean Piaget. He remembered most clearly the following:

> I was sitting in my pram, which my nurses was pushing in the Champs Elysees, when a man tried to kidnap me. I was held in by the strap fastened around me while my nurse bravely tried to stand between me and the thief. She received various scratches, and I can still see vaguely those on her face. Then a crowd gathered, a policeman with a short cloak and a white baton came up, and the man took to his heels. I can still see the whole scene, and can even place it near the tube station. (Piaget, 1962, footnote, pp. 188)

Piaget's childhood and early adulthood passed with the memory of the attempted kidnapping. Later, the former nurse wrote to his parents to say that she had been converted to the Salvation Army. She wanted to confess her past sins and return the watch she had been given as a reward for saving their baby's life. She had made up the entire episode. Piaget's vivid memory of the event was really a memory of the stories he had been told about it. "Many real memories are doubtless of the same order" (Piaget, 1962, p. 188).

Anxiety and Stress

"The horror of that moment," the King went on, "I shall never, never forget!"
"You will though," the Queen said, "if you don't make a memorandum of it."
—Lewis Carroll

What is the influence of extremely negative emotions on memory and thought? If you suffer from severe test anxiety you already know the answer to this question. Almost everyone becomes somewhat anxious before a test. A moderate amount of anxiety may actually improve performance; however, extreme anxiety adversely affects recall and clear thought. People who become overwhelmed with anxiety during tests find that they can't concentrate while they are preparing their response to the questions. Sometimes they even have difficulty reading the questions.

Consider how you feel when you are excited, angry or afraid. Your heart rate accelerates; your face may become flushed or pale; your stomach seems to tighten; and you may begin to perspire. Simple well-learned tasks, like tying your shoes, won't be affected much by extreme emotions, but difficult tasks like answering exam questions will. A graph of the relationship between level of stress or arousal and efficiency of performance is shown in Fig. 8.5.

Students who suffer from extreme test anxiety often report that instead of thinking about the questions on the exam, their minds are occupied with thoughts of impending failure. It seems that, among other things, negative emotions generate extraneous thoughts so that the individual finds himself unable to concentrate on the task he's supposed to be working on. Most colleges and universities have counseling centers to help students who suffer from extreme test anxiety. One of the best ways to prevent or reduce test anxiety is by establishing a personal history of successful test taking. If you practice the strategies for improving memory, you may be able to reduce test anxiety to a more manageable level. The adage "nothing suceeds like success" is appropriate here.

In a test of the effect of stress on memory (Baddeley, 1972), servicemen were told that it may be necessary to crash land the plane in which they were traveling. To make this seem real, they were asked to fill out forms indicating who would get their personal property in the event of death. They were then told that they would need to take a test to see how well they remembered their emergency instructions. The men were told that this might be needed for their heirs to collect the insurance in the event of their death. Thus, the men were given a test with the belief that they might soon crash and die. They made many more mistakes under

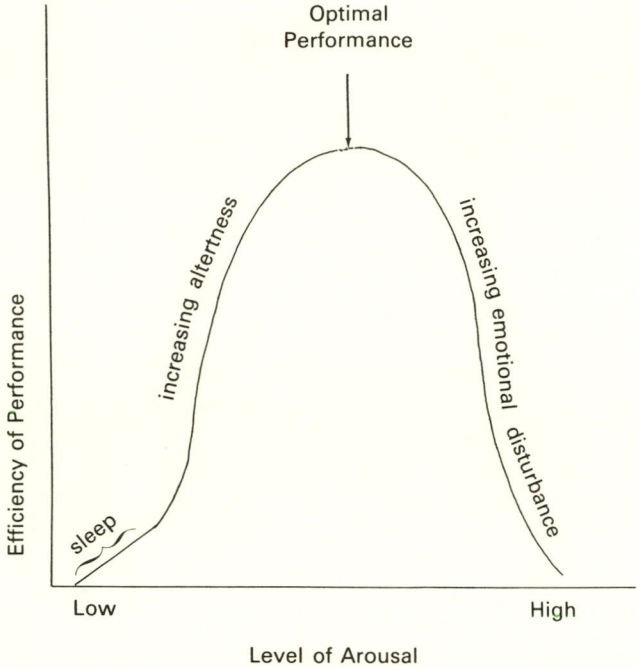

FIG. 8.5. The relationship between level of arousal and efficiency of performance is an "inverted U shaped" curve.

these stressful conditions than a control group that took the same test without stress. (Psychologists have to wrestle with the ethical problems in research of this sort. Is such research justifiable on the grounds that countless lives can be saved if we understand how memory and thought functions change under stress and if we can use this knowledge to improve performance?)

Rape victims and other victims of violent crime often report similar memory lapses, although usually for memory of the event itself. They would like to be able to recall the event clearly because it would be helpful in apprehending their assailant and because it might be therapeutic. It is not unusual for victims to blame themselves for their attack (I should have been more careful; I should have known better, etc.) and then blame themselves for their inability to recall it in detail. If they knew that memory failures were normal under these circumstances, then at least some of the self-blame could be alleviated.

Repression

Sigmund Freud, the father of a major branch of psychological thought, called **psychoanalysis,** believed that highly emotionally charged events are forgotten because if they were remembered we would be flooded with overwhelming emotions that we might not be able to handle. According to Freudian theory, the traumatic event is **repressed** unconsciously (without our awareness) and can be remembered only with appropriate *psychotherapy*. Psychotherapy is a general term that refers to the use of the principles of psychology to alleviate emotional problems or mental disorders. (The term psychoanalysis has two meanings. It refers to Freud's theories about psychology and to the form of psychotherapy he developed.)

Recently, Gordon Bower (1981) reiterated how the emotions experienced during psychotherapy can trigger memory for previously forgotten events. As an example, he used the case of Sirhan Sirhan, the man who assassinated Robert Kennedy in Los Angeles in 1968. Sirhan had no memory for the emotionally charged event. To help him remember, Bernard Diamond, a forensic psychiatrist (a lawyer who is also a psychiatrist) placed Sirhan under hypnosis. "Under hypnosis, as Sirhan became more worked up and excited, he recalled progressively more, the memories tumbling out while his excitement built to a crescendo leading up to the shooting. At that point, Sirhan would scream out the death curses, 'fire' the shots, and then choke as he reexperienced the Secret Service bodyguard nearly throttling him after he was caught. On different occasions, while in a trance, Sirhan was able to recall the crucial events, sometimes speaking, other times recording his recollections in automatic writing, but the recall was always accompanied by great excitement" (Bower, 1981, p. 129).

The case of Sirhan Sirhan demonstrates **State-Dependent Memory;** events that occur in one emotional state are remembered best when the individual is in the same emotional state. Imagine a couple undergoing psychotherapy for marital problems. When they are happy they seem to remember the good aspects of their marriage, but when they are unhappy the bad memories from their marriage predominate. Can you understand how psychotherapy can help someone remember emotional events? The therapist can induce a particular mood by the kinds of questions she poses. Suppose further that the husband, we'll call him Michael, saw his father hit his mother when he was very young. This can be a frightening and confusing experience for a child; and later in life Michael is unable to recall this event. His therapist can ask him questions about other frightening experiences that occurred during his childhood that he is able to remember, thus making Michael's mood similar to the one he experienced when the forgotten event occurred. The congruity between his present emotional state and the one he was in when the event occurred can facilitate recall. Thus, a skilled therapist can help Michael remember his father's deed. The therapist could also use this knowledge to help Michael understand why he is afraid to show anger toward his wife. Successful retrieval of his memory, which has been hidden since Michael's childhood, could aid Michael in improving his relationship with his wife.

I'd like to end this section with a note of caution about a topic I raised earlier—hypnosis. It may have been useful in helping Sirhan Sirhan to remember the events surrounding the murder of Robert Kennedy, but it can also produce inaccurate recall. Memory is not a permanent unchanging storage of information, and what is remembered can be influenced by subtle suggestions made during hypnosis. Six states now bar witnesses who have been hypnotised from testifying at trials because their memory may have been altered during hypnosis. On the other hand, some police departments feel that hypnosis is a valuable tool for obtaining information that would not be available without its use. A prudent conclusion about hypnosis is that while it may make some memories more accessible for recall, they are not necessarily accurate ones. The use of hypnosis as a memory aid is likely to remain a major controversy for many years.

METAMEMORY

The term **metamemory** refers to one's personal knowledge of his or her own memory system. It seems that much of the difference between good and poor learners can be attributed to metamemory. Bransford (1979) has summarized this: ". . . (E)ffective learners know themselves what they need to know and do in order to perform effectively; they are able to monitor their own levels of understanding and mastery. These active learners are therefore likely to ask questions of clarification and more efficiently plan their study activities. Such activities are quite different from passivelv accepting (yet *momentarily* actively processing) the particular information that a person or text presents" (p. 248).

This quote from Bransford brings up the important concept of active learning. Very little, if anything, can be learned passively. This general rule supports the research that was cited earlier demonstrating that sleep learning is not possible. You need to actively deal with material if you want to remember it. Good learners know when they understand the material and when they do not understand it; poor learners don't seem to notice the difference. Good learners know what they have to do to facilitate learning. For example, they may spontaneously link new information to information previously learned or think of possible applications for the new material they are learning. As you read this paragraph, you may be applying this learning "device" by noting the similarity of this concept with one you learned in the section entitled organization, that imposing additional organization on material by activities like these will result in improved comprehension.

An interesting study (Whimbey, 1976) has shown that students who are having academic problems in college approach their text assignments differently from good students. The less successful college students read difficult material straight through without seeming to notice when they didn't understand the material and without rereading the difficult sections. Good students know these strategies. Most importantly, Whimby found that he could improve performance for the poorer students by teaching them how to organize the material and how to become aware of what they were understanding and what they weren't. Too often college students and others believe that they know some material because they've read or heard it. They're surprised to find that they can't answer basic questions about the material they supposedly knew.

MNEMONICS

In a recent episode of the popular children's television show, Sesame Street, Bert and Ernie, two lovable muppets, discussed an intriguing memory phenomenon. Bert noticed that Ernie had tied a piece of string around his finger to help him remember something. In fact, Ernie tied string around each of his eight fingers (apparently muppets have eight fingers) to be really sure that he didn't forget. After some prompting from Bert, Ernie recalled that the string was supposed to help him remember he should buy more string, as they had run out of string.

Although this example is humorous, it illustrates some fundamental assumptions and problems encountered by humans (and muppets) in dealing with their memory. The wide range of activities from tying a string around one's finger to the more elaborate procedures presented later are called **mnemonic devices.** "A mnemonic device is a technique (often referred to as a memory trick) for organizing information so that it can be more easily remembered" (Loftus & Loftus, 1976, p. 64). Mnemonics relate to the ways that information is processed so that the material that is being learned is easily recalled. Norman (1976, p. 131) has said ". . . they teach the user to pay attention and to learn how to organize." Mnemonics can be used to optimize memory. Many students use mnemonic devices to prepare for exams and some of the techniques are so common that we usually don't think of them as mnemonics.

During the summers when I was in college, I worked as a waitress at a resort in the Catskill Mountains of New York. The resort had a night club with the usual array of singers, dancers, jugglers, and animal acts. (The kitchen help was not allowed to attend the night club, so, of course, we would sneak in often.) One particular act that amazed me was a memory act by Harry Lorayne. He went around the audience recalling people's names. His memory seemed limitless. I was also surprised at how much the audience enjoyed his performance and that an amazing memory would qualify as a night club act. Harry Lorayne later wrote two books on this topic (Lorayne, 1975; Lorayne & Lucas, 1974). The mnemonic principles he used are presented here along with several others.

The mnemonics are based on a few simple memory principles. They all force you to pay attention to the items to be remembered. They provide a meaningful context for unrelated items. The user is required to organize the material and to use the mnemonic as an efficient retrieval cue. Thus, from what you've already learned about memory earlier in this chapter, you can see that mnemonics are not mere theatrical tricks. They work because they represent applications of basic principles of memory. There are five basic types of mnemonics—keywords and images, rhymes, places, first letters and narrative stories. Each will be discussed in turn.

Keywords and Images

The following demonstration was presented as an anecdote by Donald Norman (1976, p. 134). I have used it as a class demonstration many times, and students are always surprised at how well it works. The use of this mnemonic depends on first learning **keywords** which serve as "hooks" for information that is learned later. In this case, the keywords are in the form of a simple poem to learn. Spend a minute or two learning this poem:

One is a bun,
Two is a shoe,
Three is a tree,
Four is a door,
Five is a hive,
Six are sticks,
Seven is heaven,
Eight is a gate,
Nine is a line, and
Ten is a hen.

Do you have this memorized? If not, go over the poem again.

Now, I'm going to present a list of words to be remembered. You have to form an image or association between the listed items and the items in the poem you just learned. For example, the first item on the list is ashtray. Image an ashtray with a bun in it, since the bun was the first item in the poem. You could imagine something like a large hamburger bun sitting in a dirty ashtray. Read the items on the list one at a time, allowing enough time to form an image.

1. ashtray
2. firewood
3. picture
4. cigarette
5. table
6. matchbook
7. glass
8. lamp
9. shoe
10. phonograph

Now, cover the list of words and answer the following questions:

What is number eight?
What number is cigarette?

If your experience was like the one Norman described or the ones my students report, then you've been surprised to find that the answers were easily available.

In this case you learned a list of rhyming keywords and then used imagery to relate the words to be learned to the keywords. Research has shown that images are best when they're interacting (e.g., the bun is *in* the ashtray and not just next to it) (Bower, 1970), and when they are vivid and detailed (the bun that I was imaging was a hamburger bun and the ashtray was glass) (Bower, 1972).

A more sophisticated keyword system is the **phonetic system.** It can be used to remember words or numbers. The basic principle is to associate a consonant sound with a digit. It is an old system, developed by Loisette in 1896.

Consider the following pairing of digits with consonants sounds.

Digit	*Consonants*
0	S or Z or soft C
1	T or D or TH
2	N
3	M
4	R
5	L
6	SH or J or CH or soft G
7	K or hard G or hard C or Q or NG
8	F or V
9	B or P

How do you use this keyword system? Notice that vowels are not assigned to digits. They are supplied as needed to make up words. Suppose your friend moves to a new home and you need to remember her new phone number. You could repeat it over and over again, hoping that by rehearsal the number would eventually be learned, or you could use the phonetic system. It's important to remember here that we're interested in the *sound* of words and not the spelling. Suppose your friend's new phone number is 641-7132. Try to transform this into words with the phonetic system. How about changing 641 into ShiRT, 71 into CaT, and 32 into MaN. As you can see, the vowels are added to make words, but can easily be deleted when you need use to phone your friend.

Once you have learned the phonetic alphabet you can use it to remember any sequence of numbers. You could finally learn your social security number, student identification number, bank account number, and all of the other numbers that haunt our lives. The advantage of this technique comes from transforming the numbers, which are abstract and therefore difficult to remember, into a comprehensive unit. The obvious disadvantage is that it requires some preliminary work in order to learn the phonetic system; however, once it's learned, it's yours to use for life.

Images can also be used alone (without keywords). They are especially advantageous when you want to remember names and faces. This is the technique that Harry Lorayne (1975) uses. Change the names you want to remember to a concrete noun; pick out a distinctive feature of the face and image the two as interacting. He suggests that you pay special attention to cheeks, lips, facial lines, forehead, nose, eyebrows, and eyes. For example, if you meet Ms. Silverstein and you notice that she has wide-set eyes, you could image a silver beer mug (a stein) between her eyes. Mr. Dinter could be changed to dinner and an entire dinner could be imaged on his large forehead. Try this at the next party you attend. You'll find it fun, and you may surprise yourself with your new abilities.

A keyword mnemonic system has been developed especially for learning a second language (Atkinson, 1975). Suppose you are learning French and are faced with the following three vocabulary words with their English translations to learn:

French	*English*
homme	man
étoile	star
legume	vegetable

Students begin by generating their own keywords. The keyword should *sound like* the foreign vocabulary word. Thus, for the word homme, I'd generate "home," for étoile, I'd use "a towel," and for legume, I'd use "lagoon."

The second step makes use of imagery by linking an image of the keyword with the correct translation of the foreign word. I'd visualize a man standing in front of a large home, a towel with a star painted on it, and vegetables floating in a lagoon. When the foreign words homme, étoile and legume are encountered, students would then automatically recall the images and retrieve the correct translations.

Atkinson claims that as facility with the foreign language develops the need to remember the images diminishes and students can extract the intended meaning without the use of imagery. Students who are taught to use this method consistently recall more correct English translations than students who use the usual rote rehearsal method of repeating the words until they "stick." Furthermore, this method seems to work best when students generate their own keywords and images. The need for active participation in learning is a general rule.

We also use rhymes to help us remember. For example, there are few people who haven't heard:

I before E, except after C

or

Thirty days hath September, April, June and November

Answer this question quickly. What letter comes after N? Most people find that they need to repeat that portion of the alphabet (l,m,n,o,p) to answer this question. Like rhymes, the rhythm established in songs help to deter forgetting.

Rhymes are useful when order is important because mistakes in order will usually destroy the rhyme. Notice that the first keyword poem I presented relied on keywords, images, and rhymes (one is a bun, etc.). This is an especially easy mnemonic to use, probably because several mnemonic devices are employed in the same poem to guard against forgetting.

Method of Places

Before I describe how "places" works as a mnemonic device, I'd like you to remember my back-to-school shopping list. Read the list through slowly once, then see how many items you can recall.

Pencils
Ruler
Notebook
Marking pens
Compass
Tape
Paper
Scissors
Sharpener
Reinforcements
Tablet
Glue

How many items on this list did you remember?

Now I'll show you how the **Method of Places** (or Method of Loci) could improve your recall for this list. Pick a familiar route, like the one from your house to school. Now imagine each of the items on this list placed somewhere along this route. The pencils could be very tall and form a fence around your front lawn, the ruler could be sitting across your car, the notebook could be the Stop sign at your corner, etc. Try this now with the back-to-school shopping list just presented. Once the images are formed, you should be able to remember every item by "mentally walking through" your route and noticing the items you've imaged along the way.

I once went to an introductory lesson for a very expensive memory improvement course. The Method of Places was the demonstration they used to convince potential students that the course was valuable. For months afterward, I received letters in the mail asking me if I "forgot" to send my money and to register for their course. The expensive (there are no cheap ones) memory improvement courses teach the same methods presented in this chapter. They have no magic secrets that are unavailable in the psychology literature.

The Method of Places has an interesting history that was described by an English historian (Yates, 1966). According to the story, it was first used by a Greek poet named Simonides. He had been paid by a rich nobleman to chant a lyric poem at a banquet. (There were no televisions or video games or Pac-people to provide entertainment in ancient Greece.) He used half of the poem to praise the nobleman who hired him; the other half of the poem was devoted to the twin gods, Pollux and Castor. The nobleman was outraged by this because he wanted the entire poem to consist of praise of himself. Angrily, he told Simonides that he would only pay him half the amount they had agreed upon. Simonides could collect the rest of the money from the twin gods he had praised. Later that evening, in the middle of dinner, a messenger told Simonides that two men were waiting outside to see him. When he went outside, no one was there. During his absence, the roof caved in on the nobleman and his banquet guests, who were crushed beyond recognition. Simonides was able to help the relatives claim the appropriate bodies by remembering where they had been sitting at the banquet table. He mentally "walked" around the table, using imagery to remember where each guest had been sitting. It seems that the invisible callers had paid well for their half of the poem. This is reportedly the first use of the Method of Places.

The Greeks, who were famous for giving long speeches from memory, have left us with many tips on how to best use this method. For example, the same route can be used repeatedly for different lists (Ross & Laurence, 1968). They also suggested that the places should not be too much alike (e.g., don't use only Stop signs along your route) and that they should not be too brightly lit (or there will be glare) nor too dimly lit (or the objects will be difficult to see). This is a good method to use when events need to be remembered in a particular order, since the route can be mentally traversed forward or backward.

First Letters

First letter mnemonics are probably most commonly used in preparing for tests. To use this technique, take the first letter of each term to be learned, insert vowels and other letters if necessary, and make a word. When you need to remember the list, you recall the word you formed and then use each letter as a retrieval cue for each item on the list. Many of us learned to remember the names of the Great Lakes as HOMES (Huron, Ontario, Michigan, Erie, and Superior). If you never learned this before, you'll never forget it again.

The first letter mnemonic organizes unrelated terms into a single word. You already know how important good organization is for memory. I can remember using this technique when I was a college student. The class had been told to be prepared to answer a long essay question during an in-class exam. There were six points that I wanted to make in the essay, and I wanted to be sure that I included all of them. I took the first letter of each of the points, made up a word using these letters and used this word to help me remember all of the points for the exam. (It worked well.) This technique is also especially useful when you have to speak in front of people without notes. Select one word that can stand for each point you want to make and use the first letter of each word to form a single, retrievable word. Even though good speeches may appear unrehearsed, good speakers practice with techniques like this one. It helps them to present their speech in a confident and professional manner.

Narrative Stories

The **Narrative Stories** mnemonic method was demonstrated by Bower and Clark (1969). They presented college students with lists of words to remember. The students were told to remember the words by constructing a narrative story that contained all of the words in the list. In addition, they were told to visualize the story they were constructing. The students were given 12 different lists, each containing ten words. They remembered an average of over 90% of the 120 words (recall followed each list). A control group of college students, who were given the same lists of words to remember, but were not given the narrative stories instructions, remembered an average of less than 20% of the 120 words. Surprisingly, the students rarely intruded a nonlist word that was part of the story into their recall.

Two sample stories from Bower and Clark's (1969) study are presented here. The list words are typed in capital letters.

> A LUMBERJACK DARTed out of a forest, SKATEd around a HEDGE past a COLONY of DUCKs. He tripped on some FURNITURE, tearing his STOCKING while hastening toward the PILLOW where his MISTRESS lay.

> A VEGETABLE can be a useful INSTRUMENT for a COLLEGE student. A carrot can be a NAIL for your FENCE or BASIN. But a MERCHANT of the QUEEN would SCALE that fence and feed the carrot to a GOAT.

Mnemonic Principles

Mnemonic devices can be powerful aids for memory. They are also somewhat paradoxical since it seems that to remember better you need to remember more. Consider the narrative stories mnemonic just presented. To use this method, you are required to remember not just the words in the list, but an entire story as well. The first letter mnemonic requires that you remember the new word you created with the first letters as well as each of the words. The keyword systems require that you learn a keyword system like the phonetic alphabet system, and the rhymes present you with a song or poem to be learned. They each necessitate work. Acquiring a good memory means working at it, but it is work that pays off in life long dividends.

Let's try to develop a mnemonic that could help you to remember the five types of mnemonics. First, let's review what they are: keywords and images, rhymes, method of places, narrative stories, and (first) letters. While you could use the method of places and image each of these terms along a route or weave them into a narrative story, or associate them with a keyword or make up a poem, my choice for a list like this one is the first letter mnemonic. Start by listing the first letter of each term: K, R, M, NS, L. You can modify the first letter technique by using each letter to begin a word in a sentence, since incorporating these letters in a single word may be difficult. Try it. The sentence one of my students came up with is "Kind round men never sing lyrics." Use imagery also to aid recall. Imagine a round (fat) man with a kind face who doesn't sing well. Make your images detailed and vivid. If you're asked to recall the five mnemonic devices, you can list each one, and by remembering the name of each, all of the information you've learned about them should also be easily retrieved.

Many people find it difficult to remember how to spell the word "mnemonics." How about Memory Never Explains MONey and Ice Cream Sandwiches? Be sure to think about your mnemonic device. You should never have difficulty spelling this word correctly again.

There are many practical applications for mnemonics. I don't suggest that you commit your weekly grocery shopping list to memory when a pen and pencil would do as well. There are, however, countless other areas where they can be invaluable. For example, you could try the Method of Places for subject areas like history and the social sciences where knowing the correct sequence of events is crucial to understanding them. For example, it is difficult to understand what happened during World War II without knowing the sequence of events that preceded it. Harry Lorayne's imaging technique for associating names and faces can be valuable when you start a new job and need to learn many new names. Formulas in chemistry and math can be learned with the phonetic alphabet system. Good students have always used mnemonics to improve their exam performance. Everyone should make the effort. You'll find that memory improvement will help you to achieve, whatever the goal.

CHAPTER SUMMARY

1. The human information processing approach uses a computer analogy to understand human memory.

2. Like a computer, people acquire, retain, and retrieve information.

3. It is important that people attend to information that they want to learn.

4. Our memories are *not* perfect true "copies" of events that have occurred. Prior knowledge, subsequent knowledge, stereotypes, and meaningfulness of the material all influence what will be remembered.

5. Memory can be improved with appropriate retrieval cues and good organization.

6. Marijuana has been found to be detrimental to memory, although long-term users report that it has had little effect on their professional lives.

7. Emotions like anxiety and stress can either improve memory because of periodic review or hinder memory because of the distractions they provide.

8. Mnemonics improve recall because they utilize the basic memory principles of attention, organization and chunking. The mnemonics presented were keywords and images, rhymes, method of places, narrative stories, and first letters. (Remember: Kind Round Men Never Sing Lyrics.)

Terms to Know:

You should be able to define or describe the following terms and concepts. If you find that you're having difficulty with any term, be sure to reread the section where it is discussed.

Hypothetical Constructs
Human Information Processing (HIP)
Model
Acquisition
Retention
Interval
Retrieval
Cocktail Party Effect
Dichotic Listening
Sensory Memory
Short-Term Memory
Long-Term Memory
Gist
Chunking
Interference Theory of Forgetting
Periodic Review
Psychoanalysis
Repression
State-Dependent Memory
Metamemory
Mnemonic Devices
Keywords
Phonetic System
Method of Places (Method of Loci)
First Letter Mnemonics
Narrative Stories

Be sure that you can answer the following questions:

1. What is the relationship between learning and memory? (You should have expected this question.)

2. Why are learning and memory called hypothetical constructs?

3. The Human Information Processing Model is predicated on the idea that people and computers are similar in many important ways. What are the similarities? What are some important *differences* between humans and computers that weaken the model?

4. Name and explain some basic properties of attention. Why is it an important concept in memory?

5. Three different types of memory were discussed in your text. Name and briefly describe each. Be sure to give the appropriate retention interval for each type of memory.

6. How can stereotypes and prejudices influence what we remember? Describe an experimental study that supports this view.

7. What does it mean to say, "memory is malleable."

8. How did the experiment in which recall for nonsense syllables was better after sleeping than after remaining awake provide support for the Interference Theory of Forgetting?

9. What is the effect of marijuana on memory?

10. There are several ways that emotions can affect memory. How can they improve memory? How can they diminish it?

11. What were the results of the research that tested servicemen's memory for emergency information under extremely stressful conditions? Why is it important to know this?

12. How can the concept of state-dependent memory be used to explain why some events that normally aren't available can be recalled during psychotherapy?

13. How can the development of a good *metamemory* improve your academic performance?

14. How do mnemonic devices work? List and describe five different types of mnemonics.

Exercises

Try out the memory skills you've learned in this chapter.

1. If you are currently learning a second language, use the keyword technique for second language learning (Atkinson, 1975) to learn your foreign vocabulary for the next month. You may find that it's fun to change the way you usually study, and you may be able to improve your memory for the foreign language terms.

2. Learn the phonetic alphabet system and use it to remember the important numbers in your life. B. F. Anderson (1980) suggests that you use this system to astound your friends. The next time you're at a party, go around the room assigning different 4-digit numbers to each person there and demonstrate that you can remember each person's number at the end of the evening or at any time in the future. You can do this by giving each person the 4-digit number that translates into her or his name. Thus, Katharine would be given the number 7142 (KTHRN in the phonetic number alphabet); Robert would be given 4941 (RBRT); and Charles would be given 6450 (CHRLS).

3. Now that you understand the importance of attention for memory and thought, try to become aware of the times when your attention wanders from a task. With some effort, you can learn to pay attention. You may be surprised at all that you've missed. The next time you take a walk, notice the colors of the flowers, the shades of raindrops, the

expressions of children. Some believe that artists attend to these things that most of us miss.

4. Organize your notes so that topics that belong together are placed near each other. Divide your study material into units that can be studied in one block of time. Look for the structure in the material you're learning and interrelate the items so that you can "see the whole picture."

5. Go to your local courthouse and see part of a trial. (Traffic court works well for this purpose.) What are some possible memory biases in the testimony given by eyewitnesses?

6. Use the mnemonics described in this chapter to help you prepare for exams. Be sure that you understand the material you're learning.

7. There are many popular memory games. For example, one game involves planning for a trip. Each person tells what she or he will pack and must also remember what the previous players are packing. Use imagery so that for each item you can visualize it along with the person's face who named the item. You'll be sure to win first prize, unless someone else in the room is also using an imagery mnemonic.

8. Be aware of common notions of memory that are presented in books, on television and in movies. Most show memory as a passive storage tank that can be accessed with the appropriate tools. Few present the view that memory is dynamic and changes as the individual changes. Discuss these topics with friends and family to see what they think about memory.

9. Try to remember something that happened to you in your childhood and then compare that memory with the account given by a parent or older child you were with at that time. Compare the similarities and discrepancies in your memories. What are some principles that you've learned in this chapter that could account for the differences?

10. Learn how to generate your own retrieval cues. Loftus (1980) suggests that if you go to the supermarket without a shopping list, you can remember what items are needed by going through categories such as dairy, spices, meats, and cleaning supplies. You can use categories as retrieval cues in a variety of situations. Did you ever have the frustrating experience of knowing that you have to call someone, but don't remember who? Try to recall by systematically going through categories—family, friends from school, employer, etc.

SUGGESTED READINGS

There are several good books that discuss the memory phenomena presented here. I recommend Klatsky's (1980) *Human Memory: Structures and Processes* (2nd Ed.), Baddeley's (1976) *The Psychology of Memory,* and Zechmeister and Nyberg's (1982) *Human Memory: An Introduction to Research and Theory* for easy-to-read, comprehensive reviews of most of these topics. You may also find the book *Memory: Surprising New Insights Into How We Remember and Why We Forget* by E. Loftus (1980) to be an interesting account of some of the more intriguing aspects of memory, but you should realize it is not intended for a college audience; and you may find her treatment of some of the topics to be too simplistic. E. Loftus is also the author of several other excellent texts in this area of memory. If your interest was piqued by the section on eyewitness testimony, then I suggest that you read her 1979 book entitled *Eyewitness Testimony,* which is a pleasant meld of memory theory, research and law.

The leading text in the area of *Human Information Processing* is one by that name (2nd Ed., 1977) by Lindsay and Norman. It can serve as a fascinating introduction to this field. It was written with a student audience in mind.

There are several good accounts of mnemonic devices. A collection of articles with extensive commentary on this and related topics was compiled by Norman in *Memory and Attention: An Introduction to Human Information Processing* (2nd Ed., 1976). As the title implies, it also contains a section on attention, which deals largely with theories and models of attention. A detailed and influential study of mnemonics was published by a Russian, Luria. His book, *The Mind of a Mnemonist* (1968) provided an in-depth account of a man with a "supernormal" memory.

The mnemonist Harry Lorayne has written two books which have also been popular in this area. They are *The Memory Book* (1974) by Lorayne and Lucus and *Remembering People* (1975) by Lorayne. An interesting account of some research on the Method of Places and other memory phenomena is presented by Crovitz in *Galton's Walk: Methods for the Analysis of Thinking, Intelligence and Creativity* (1970).

Two excellent books with sections on memory for prose passages are Bransford's *Human Cognition: Learning, Understanding and Remembering* (1979) and Clark and Clark's *Psychology and Language* (1977). One of the original classics in this area with a contemporary viewpoint is Bartlett's *Remembering: A Study in Experimental and Social Psychology* (1932).

If you're interested in memory for everyday events, then you'll want to consult Neisser's (1982) edited volume *Memory Observed,* Gruneberg and Morris' (1979) edited volume *Applied Problems in Memory,* and Seamon's (1980) *Human Memory: Contemporary Readings.*

9 Intelligence

Contents

The Nature of Intelligence 282
The Measurement of Intelligence 285
The Intelligence Quotient (IQ) 285
Sample Test Items 288
Standardization 289
Is There Bias in Intelligence Testing? 290
Culture-Reduced Tests 293
Stability 295
Validity 295
Sex Differences in Intelligence 295
Learning to Be Intelligent 298
Increasing IQ Scores 298
A Paradox 298
Development of Intelligence 299
Piagetian Model of Intelligence 300
Piagetian Tasks 302

"The problem is really quite simple. If you'd only listen to me, I'm sure that you could understand it." Ms. Miller, the junior high school teacher was becoming frustrated with Johnny's parents. She went on, "We can't place Johnny in the academic preparatory program because he just isn't smart enough. I know that he does well in school, but his intelligence tests show that he just isn't very bright.

How can he do so well, then? That's easy to answer. Johnny is an *overachiever*. This means that he does well in school because he works hard and is well motivated.

What do I mean by saying that he's achieved more than he's able to achieve? I just explained it to you."

The conference continued this way for fifteen minutes, Johnny's parents arguing that he has already demonstrated the ability to perform academically and Ms. Miller reiterating her position that Johnny's intelligence tests show that he isn't intelligent and that his good grades are the result of his overachievement. Finally, Johnny's parents left, vowing to take the matter up with the School Board.

"What do you expect," Ms. Miller fumed out loud to no one in particular. "The parents are as dumb as their child."

While a scenario exactly like this one may never have taken place, intelligence tests have played a subtle but crucial role in most of our lives. It should be obvious that a term like *overachiever* should never be interpreted the way Ms. Miller in the opening scenario interpreted it since it is a logical impossibility to achieve more than you are able to. What terms like *overachiever* and *underachiever* mean is that the intelligence test failed to predict how a particular student would perform in school. In Johnny's case, the test underestimated his scholastic ability. The test was wrong and so was Ms. Miller's interpretation of the results. In this chapter, we examine issues like this one and see how intelligence is measured. Specific theories of intelligence are considered, as well as current controversies that involve the notion of race and sex differences in intelligence. Finally, we look at attempts to teach students how to become intelligent.

THE NATURE OF INTELLIGENCE

Intelligence is one of the most controversial topics in psychology. It is a basic topic in thinking since intelligence is the "stuff" of thought. You can conceptualize intelligence as the raw material from which thoughts are made. It is difficult to imagine a context in which intelligence isn't manifested or needed. The term intelligence is used commonly in everyday language. We all know who, among our friends and acquaintances, has it and who hasn't (although our friends and acquaintances may disagree with our assessment of them). Most people believe that they are at least about average or above average in intelligence (Brim, 1966). (If you've already read the chapter on Understanding Probability, then you should realize that this is mathematically absurd since about half of the population must be below average.)

I hope that you weren't expecting a definition of intelligence, because there is little agreement about what it does or should mean. Think for a minute about your own definition of intelligence. A dictionary won't be much help, since dictionaries define difficult multifaceted concepts like intelligence with a few simple words. When Robert Sternberg (1982), a psychologist known for his research on understanding the concept of intelligence, asked people to list the characteristics of an intelligent person the following answers were frequently given: "reasons logically and well," "reads widely," "keeps an open mind," and "reads with high comprehension." Most people share these intuitive notions of intelligence.

Sternberg's (1981) own definition of intelligence is concerned with the way people approach novel tasks. He believes that little can be learned about intelligence by watching someone perform well-learned tasks. For example, if you are already proficient at long division, then analyzing your performance on long division problems won't reveal much about your intelligence. If, however, you are totally unfamiliar with long division problems, then examining the way you go about solving them and the kinds of answers you formulate will reveal a great deal about your intelligence. Thus, the ability to handle novel tasks and situations is a key element in Sternberg's definition. Sternberg (1981) has said: "It is not merely the ability to learn and reason with new concepts but the ability to learn and reason with new *kinds* of concepts. . . ." intelligence is in large part the ability to acquire and reason with new conceptual systems" (p. 4).

An Example

Sternberg (1981) calls novel tasks **nonentrenched tasks.** These are tasks that are totally unfamiliar, and thus can be used to understand the nature of intelligence. One such task is a *projection task.* Individuals who work on projection tasks are required to make predictions about what will be true in the year 2000. If this task seems strange, don't worry, since nonentrenched tasks should be very different from the other kinds of tasks you've encountered in the past.

Consider the following example (adapted from Sternberg, 1981).

> Four types of persons live on the planet Kyron.
> A *plin* is a person who is born a child and remains a child throughout her or his life span.
> A *kwef* is a person who is born an adult and remains an adult throughout her or his life span.
> A *balt* is a person who is born a child but becomes an adult during the course of her or his life span.
> A *pros* is a person who is born an adult but becomes a child during the course of her or his life span.

This task involves using the above information to answer questions about what is true in the year 2000. A person can be described as she or he physically appears:  (a child) or  (an adult) or with one of the four terms: plin, kwef, balt or pros. The physical description is always correct since it merely reflects what is physically true when you make your observations. However, verbal descriptions that are made in the present may be wrong since they require an implication about the future appearance of a person. For example, if you describe a person as a plin in the present you are saying that he now appears as a child, and that you expect him to also appear as a child in the year 2000. Your belief about the future appearance is only a guess that may be right or wrong. When you make verbal descriptions in the year 2000, there is no longer any uncertainty since you would know at that time both the physical appearance in the present and in the year 2000. Thus, verbal descriptions made in 2000 must be correct since there is no longer any uncertainty.

To make these problems even more complicated, sometimes you will be given information that is inconsistent. For example, suppose that a person is born a kwef and is a plin in the year 2000. If a person were born a kwef, we would be certain that he was an adult at birth. If he is a plin in 2000, then we would also be certain that he was born a child and remained as a child in 2000. Since these two pieces of information are inconsistent (he could not appear as both a child and an adult at birth), you would have to select I (for inconsistent) as the correct answer. These problems will become clearer as we proceed with some examples. Be sure to work through each example since most people find that this is a difficult task.

Example 1: A person is born a plin and is a plin in the year 2000.

You now need to select an answer that reflects what is true in the year 2000. The person is described as a plin at birth (born a child and expected to be a child in 2000) and in 2000, thus the physical description in 2000 is the small stick figure. You'd indicate your answer by circling the small stick figure below.

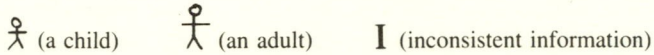

Example 2: A person is born a plin and is an  in 2000.

Circle the correct answer:

plin balt I

The verbal description plin signifies that the person was born a child and was expected to remain a child. In the year 2000, he appeared as an adult, thus the correct answer is balt (someone who is born a child and becomes an adult). The verbal description at birth was wrong since he grew into an adult instead of remaining a child.

Example 3: A person is born an  and is a kwef in 2000.

Circle the correct answer:

You should have circled the large figure since the kwefs are adults in the future and this person is an adult in 2000.

Example 4: A person is born a  and is a kwef in 2000.

Select the correct answer:

In this example, the person is born a child, but described verbally as a kwef (born an adult and remains an adult) in 2000. This is not possible. The correct answer is I for inconsistent information.

Example 5: A person is born a  and is a  in 2000.

Select the correct answer:

balt plin pros

Since the person is described physically as a child at birth and as an adult in 2000, the correct verbal description is balt (born a child, becomes an adult).

If you were able to solve these problems (most people find them difficult), then you had to think in a new way. The idea of some adults growing into children is, to say the least, novel. Another example of Sternberg's non-entrenched tasks is presented at the end of this chapter.

The definitions of intelligence that we've considered so far include the "person-on-the street's" notions of intelligence, which includes traits like common sense and open-mindedness, and one expert's opinion that the ability to master new kinds of tasks constitutes intelligence. Another definition of intelligence was offered by E. G. Boring, a psychology historian: "intelligence is what the tests test" (1923, p. 35). The "tests" he was referring to are, of course, intelligence tests. The way psychologists have measured intelligence has had a direct effect on the way they have come to think about intelligence.

The Measurement of Intelligence

As you can imagine, the measurement of intelligence has proven to be a difficult task. The underlying idea is that intelligence exists, and since it exists, it exists in some quantity (in each individual), and since it exists in some quantity, it can be measured. The only difficulty with this line of reasoning is: "How?"

There is an obvious need to be able to quantify or measure intelligence. Historically, intelligence tests were designed for a very practical reason. In the early part of this century, the French government realized the need to know which children should get regular classroom instruction and which should get remedial or accelerated instruction. Alfred Binet and Theodore Simon were given the job of designing a test that could be used to place children in the appropriate educational setting. Modern day intelligence tests are still used for this purpose.

Binet and Simon soon realized that the type of question that an intelligent 4 year old can answer correctly is very different from the type of question that an intelligent 8 year old can answer correctly. Thus, they devised a test with items that varied in difficulty for each age level.

THE INTELLIGENCE QUOTIENT (IQ)

Binet and Simon introduced the concept of **Intelligence Quotient (IQ)** in their tests for the French educational system. It has remained the yardstick by which intelligence is measured. Let's see how it is determined.

Intelligence tests were developed with six questions at each age level which the "average" child at that age level could answer correctly. Testing for each child would begin at an easy level, probably a few years below her or his chronological age, so that the child could answer all six questions at that level correctly. Suppose a 10 year old child was administered the test. The test administrator might decide to begin with the six questions geared for 6 years olds. Suppose a hypothetical 10 year old, Richard, answered all six of these questions correctly. He would be given six years of **Mental Age (MA)** credit to signify that, thus far, he has performed on an intellectual or mental level that is equivalent to the average 6 year old. Richard would then be asked the next six questions that correspond to the seven year level. Suppose he answered four of these correctly. For every question he answered correctly, he would get 2 months of MA credit. Thus, the four correct answers would give him an additional 8 months of MA credit. Thus far, his MA is calculated by adding:

	6 years	(for answering all 6-year questions correctly)
+	8 months	(for answering 4 of the 7-year questions correctly)
MA =	6 years, 8 months	

The tester would continue by asking him the six questions that an average 8 year old should be able to answer. Richard answered three of these correctly, thus giving himself an additional 6 months of MA credit. His total MA so far is:

	6 years, 8 months	
+	6 months	(for answering 3 of the 8-year questions correctly)
MA =	7 years, 2 months	

Richard went on to answer correctly two of the six questions at the 9-year level. This gave him four more months of MA credit:

	7 years, 2 months	
+	4 months	(for answering 2 of the 9-year questions correctly)
MA =	7 years, 6 months	

He was then unable to answer any of the questions at the 10-year level, at which point the tester terminated the session.

Richard's mental age score of 7 years, 6 months means that he performed intellectually like an average 7 1/2 year old child. If Richard were 5 years old, we'd want some way to express the fact that he had performed much better than an average 5 year old; similarly, we want some way to express that he had performed worse than an average 10 year old. The Intelligence Quotient is an algebraic way to convey this information. It is computed with the following formula:

$$IQ = \frac{\text{Mental Age (MA)}}{\text{Chronological Age (CA)}} \times 100$$

Expressing this equation in words: IQ is equal to mental age divided by chronological age (age in years and months expressed as a decimal) times 100. We multiply by 100 in this formula to eliminate decimals (or fractions). Let's try this with Richard's score.

$$IQ = \frac{7.5 \text{ years}}{10 \text{ years}} \times 100$$

$$IQ = 75$$

If Richard were 5 years old, then

$$IQ = \frac{7.5 \text{ years}}{5 \text{ years}} \times 100$$

$$IQ = 150$$

Consider the case if Richard were 7.5 years old:

$$IQ = \frac{7.5 \text{ years}}{7.5 \text{ years}} \times 100$$

$$IQ = 100$$

As you can see whenever MA > CA (mental age is greater than chronological age), then IQ > 100.

Whenever MA < CA (mental age is less than chronological age), then IQ < 100.

and

Whenever MA = CA, then IQ = 100.

Thus, an "average" child (who, as we discuss later in this chapter, doesn't exist) should expect to obtain a mental age score that is nearly identical or close in value to her or his chronological age.

The IQ formula doesn't translate well when measuring adult intelligence. Suppose that you're 25 years old and you answer the same number of questions correctly as your 50 year old mother. How would your IQ compare to that of your mother's? If you've been following the calculations, it's easy to see that you would end up with an IQ that is double the one your mother would receive. While this may seem like a good idea to you now, it is surely not one that you would endorse as you grew older. Consequently, the IQ formula is not used for measuring adult intelligence. For adults, an IQ = 100 is an "average" score and, in general, IQs greater than 100 signify better than average intelligence, and IQs less than 100 signify less than average intelligence.

Approximately 50% of all people will score between 90 and 110. A total of 80% of all people will obtain IQs between 80 and 120. The few who score above 120 are labeled superior in intelligence, while those who score below 80 are labeled mentally defective.

Sample Test Items

The tests designed in France by Binet and Simon have been revised many times. The most popular revision was undertaken by Lewis Terman, a psychologist at Stanford University. Terman's revision of the earlier intelligence test is commonly referred to as the Stanford-Binet. Another popular battery of intelligence tests was written by David Wechsler. He authored two separate tests, the Wechsler Intelligence Scale for Children (WISC) and Wechsler Adult Intelligence Scale (WAIS) designed for adults from 16 to over 75 years of age. Wechsler's intelligence tests yield three IQ scores—one based on Verbal test items, one based on Performance test items, and one based on all of the test items, called Full Scale IQ. Following are some test items written to be similar to the ones found in the WAIS (Jensen, 1980, pp. 144–145). Unfortunately, it is not appropriate (it may even be illegal) to publish actual items from intelligence tests because if test takers knew the question in advance, IQ scores would be artificially inflated.

Verbal Test Items

1. At what temperature does water freeze?
2. Who wrote *The Republic?*
3. Why is gold worth more than copper?
4. How many inches are there in 3½ feet?
5. If six men can finish a job in 3 days, how many men would be needed to finish it in 1 day?
6. In what way are sperm and ovum alike?
7. Repeat a series of digits after the test administrator recites them. For example, a test taker would hear "8175621" and then repeat the digits either in the same order they were given or in reverse order.
8. Explain the meaning of strange.
9. Explain the meaning of adumbrate.

Performance Test Items

Test takers are asked to:

10. Translate the numerals 1 to 9 into code symbols (e.g., 1=└┘, 2=┴, 3=/\, etc.)
11. Tell what is missing from familiar objects or scenes (e.g., a clock without hands).
12. Use wooden cubes painted red and white to duplicate a design shown on cards.
13. Arrange a series of cartoons into a logical sequence.
14. Assemble jigsaw puzzles.

The actual test items vary in difficulty and are presented in increasing difficulty within each type of test. The IQ score that an individual receives is determined by calculating how many questions she or he answered correctly relative to the average person in the *standardization group*.

As you can see from these items, intelligence is measured with a variety of questions. The general knowledge verbal questions tap information that most people would be expected to learn as a member in our society. Some of the more difficult ones, like "Who wrote The Republic?" would obviously favor those with a good academic background. Abstract reasoning about the nature of supply-and-demand is needed to answer the question "Why is gold worth more than copper?" The ability to use numbers as well as the knowledge that there are 12 inches in one foot is needed to answer the fifth question. The answer to question number 6 is difficult because the differences between sperm and ovum may be more salient than their similarities. Of course, you also need to know what these terms mean. Repeating a series of digits forward or backward requires good memory skills. If you have already learned the memory aids (mnemonics) discussed in the memory chapter, you can go off the top of the scale on this question. The eighth and ninth questions are standard vocabulary questions.

The performance items are more difficult to categorize. Since most of the tests are timed, speed is an important factor in determining performance IQ. Changing numerals to code symbols involves a careful balance of speed and accuracy in order to finish as many numeral to code transformations as possible with few errors. Question 11 tests your knowledge of common objects. The ability to duplicate designs is a spatial ability. Arranging a series of cartoons in a logical sequence requires the test taker to generate hypotheses about the actions depicted. It's necessary to be able to see a whole object from its parts, a spatial ability, to put jigsaw puzzles together.

Standardization

You have probably wondered about the hypothetical "average" person I've been referring to. Who is average? This is one of the few questions posed in this book that is easy to answer: no one. The average person is a statistical abstraction. Intelligence tests are developed by presenting large numbers of people with potential test items and selecting for use in future tests only those items that a majority of people in the group answered correctly. This method of selecting test items for intelligence tests is called **standardization.** The characteristics of the people in the group that is used to standardize test items will have an effect on which items get selected for inclusion in the test. This is one area of controversy in intelligence testing. Let's consider in more detail how standardization can influence intelligence tests.

Let's begin this topic with an extreme example. Suppose that you wanted to design your own intelligence tests. You'd begin by writing a number of questions that you believed would be useful in measuring intelligence. Suppose further that you are a wealthy jet setter. You ask your friends and acquaintances from the country club, polo club, croquet club, and gourmet dining society to take your test. You find that, on the average, most of these people can answer questions about sonatas, stock investments, wine selection, and proper etiquette. Accordingly, you include these questions in your intelligence tests. If you administered this test to a group of migrant farm workers, how would they score? Consider the converse side of this example. Suppose a migrant farm worker were to write an intelligence test. How many questions could you answer about the most efficient way to pick strawberries, or harvest asparagus or the number of bushels of different crops you would need to pick to earn $10.00? (The issue of appropriate sampling which is being raised here is discussed more fully in the Thinking as Hypothesis Testing chapter.)

Some people feel that if a test is standardized on one group of people, it is not a valid test for people from a different group. Some intelligence tests were originally standardized on a white population, and later were given to black children and adults. Do the differences in the experiences of black and white people render tests standardized on one racial group unfair to the other racial group? This is part of a larger question of whether intelligence tests discriminate against minority groups. There are two possible answers to this question: No and Yes. Let's consider briefly how proponents of each of these positions present their side of the argument.

IS THERE BIAS IN INTELLIGENCE TESTING?

No

Jensen (1980, 1981) has called the argument that tests developed with one racial group are invalid for use with a different racial group the **Standardization Fallacy.** In support of his position, Jensen cites data in which a test that was standardized on one group of people was later given to a highly dissimilar group of people with the result that both groups obtained similar scores. For example, an intelligence test that was standardized in England and Scotland (Raven's Progressive Matrices) was given to Eskimos. The scores that the Eskimos received were similar to those obtained by the English and Scottish standardization group.

Jensen also argues that it is folly to believe that all groups of people are identical with regard to all traits and therefore should obtain the same test scores. He says that group differences in test scores should be expected. If one group scores higher than another on a test, it may not mean that the test is at fault. Jensen believes that since there are many well-documented differences among racial groups, why should intelligence be an exception?

Yes

There are many proponents of the idea that intelligence tests are biased against nonwhite populations and that the way the tests are standardized can account for much of this bias. One of the leading proponents of this position is Robert L. Williams (1972), who believes that there are many disparities in the cultural experiences of black and white Americans. As a result of these disparities, tests standardized on one racial group will always be unfair to the other. He devised a test that is based on expressions and terms that are indicative of Black American culture. His test, known as the **BITCH-100** (a catchy acronym for Black Intelligence Test of Cultural Homogenity) was developed from an earlier unpublished test of black intelligence known as the *Dove Counterbalance Intelligence Test,* which is attributed to Adrian Dove a black sociologist. Here are some test questions from the *Dove Counterbalance Intelligence Test.*

1. A "Gas Head" is a person who has a
   (a) Fast moving car
   (b) Stable of "lace"
   (c) "Process"
   (d) Habit of stealing cars
   (e) Long jail record for arson

2. If you throw the dice and "7" is showing on the top, what is facing down?
   (a) "Seven"
   (b) "Snake Eyes"
   (c) "Boxcars"
   (d) "Little Joes"
   (e) "Eleven"

3. Cheap chitlings (not the kind you purchase at a frozen-food counter) will taste rubbery unless they are cooked long enough. How soon can you quit cooking them to eat and enjoy them?
   (a) 45 minutes
   (b) 2 hours
   (c) 24 hours
   (d) 1 week (on a low flame)
   (e) 1 hour

4. If I was playing the dozens I'd be talking most about
   (a) Waterbread
   (b) Your Mamma
   (c) The digit man
   (d) Wrinkles
   (e) A together set

5. The first line of the original "Negro National Anthem" goes:
   (a) We shall overcome
   (b) Lift ev'ry voice and sing . . .

(c) We're a winner, and . . .
(d) Lord have mercy, Lord have mercy, L-O-R-D . . .
(e) Carry me back to old
(f) Keep on pushin'

6. Across the land the saying goes "Beep-beep, bang-bang . . . , BLACK POWER."
   (a) Can you dig it?
   (b) Umgawa
   (c) I can dig it
   (d) Delta Jabberwock
   (e) Say it loud!

7. A "handkerchief head" is
   (a) A cool cat
   (b) A porter
   (c) An Uncle Tom
   (d) A Murphey Man
   (e) A preacher

For those of you who are "culturally deprived" and consequently had difficulty answering these questions, the correct answers are: 1–c, 2–a, 3–c, 4–b, 5–b, 6–b, 7–c.

Many of the group differences in IQ scores seem to be related to differences in socioeconomic status (SES). One of the "truths" that psychologists have discovered is that SES is very often an important concept in understanding group differences. Middle class and wealthy people tend to perform better on standardized tests of intelligence than the poor. If you've read the chapter on Thinking as Hypothesis Testing, then you already know that we can't establish a causative relationship from a correlation between two variables. It is possible that the wealthy have greater opportunities to develop their intelligence, or that the intelligent migrate to the upper classes, or that the tests are biased toward the life experiences of the wealthy, or a host of other possible reasons.

The controversy over racial differences in intelligence and intelligence testing is unlikely to be easily resolved. We know that there are differences in living conditions among people of different SES and that these environmental differences could be responsible for IQ differences. Health care is not as available for the poor as it is for the middle and upper classes, and there is a disproportionate number of blacks in America and other countries living in poverty. The incidence of premature births is very high for black infants, probably due to poorer prenatal care. These are all factors that are clearly implicated in later intellectual functioning and could be responsible for racial differences in IQ scores.

Culture-Reduced Tests

You may be wondering if it is possible to measure intelligence in ways that are not influenced by cultural factors so that they would be fair to all racial groups. If we return to Sternberg's (1981) definition of intelligence as the ability to handle novel concepts and look at the items similar to the ones that appear in the WAIS, there is an obvious contradiction. In what way do questions like, "Who wrote *The Republic*?" measure the ability to function in nonentrenched tasks?

Several psychologists have attempted to devise intelligence tests (**Culture-Reduced Tests**) that minimize the influence of cultural background. It is not possible to write completely *Culture-Free Tests*. Culture-Reduced Tests employ questions about geometric shapes instead of questions from literature or music. Figure 9.1 shows sample items from the IPAT Culture-Fair Test developed by Cattel (1971). The term **Culture-Fair** suggests that it is a fair test for people from any culture. It has the same connotation as Culture-Reduced. As you work on the sample problems in Fig. 9.1, think about how each item is testing intelligence. Stop now and answer the items in Fig. 9.1. As you work on them, try to be aware of the thinking processes you're using to arrive at the correct answer. Don't go on until you've answered all the problems.

Answering the questions in Fig. 9.1 should have been an interesting exercise. The correct answer to 1 is E. Can you figure out why? The dot moved around the quadrants in a clockwise direction, while the X moved in a counter-clockwise direction. On the fourth move, the dot would be in the upper left hand quadrant and the X in the upper right hand quadrant.

Answering 2 involves examining several dimensions of the triangles to find one dimension that is different in only one triangle. Orientation cannot be the correct dimension since they all differ in orientation. The central area of the triangles can't be the critical dimension because they are all white. Only one figure has all three inner triangles the same—the answer must be D.

Problem 3 is also difficult. The dot in the example is in the intersecting area of two squares. The problem, however, is that alternatives B and D both have intersecting squares. Go back to the example and see how the dot relates to the circle. Only alternative D would allow you to place the dot inside both squares and the circle.

In the figural analogies problem, 4, a four-sided figure, the square, is compared to a three-sided figure, the triangle. The correct relationship involves the transformation of four vertical lines to three vertical lines. Thus, B is the correct answer to problem 4.

The matrices problem involves looking for parallel relationships. It is really a figural analogy of the form A is to B as C is to ? (A:B::C:?). Examine the circular figures in the top half of the matrix. The circle goes from unfilled to filled. The background stripes in the upper left hand quadrant are no longer found in the background, but instead are found in the figure in the upper right quadrant. The

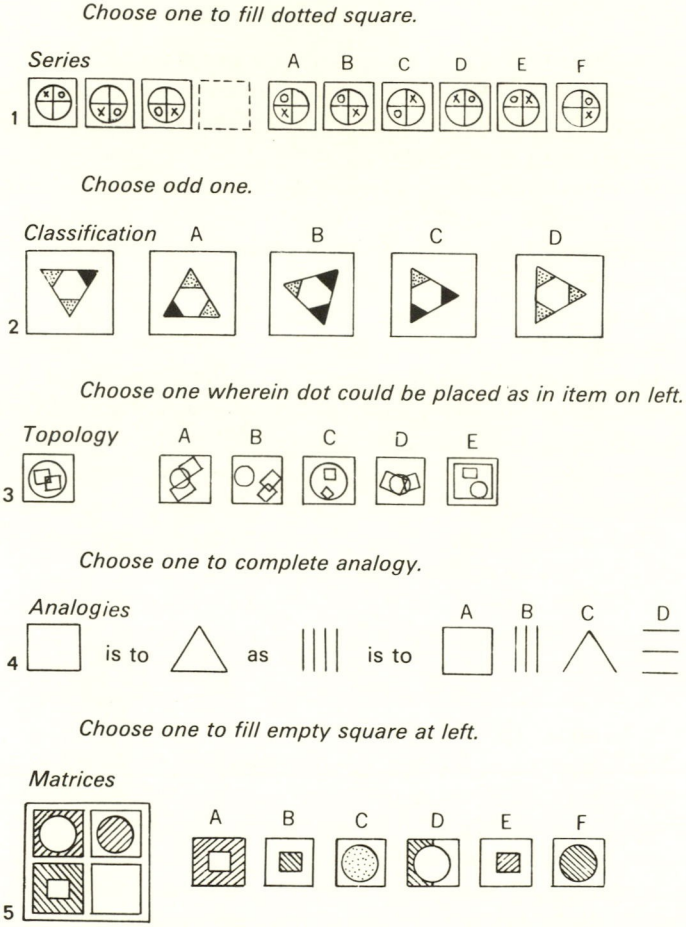

FIG. 9.1. From Form B, Scales II and III IPAT Culture-Fair Test. (Adapted from Cattell, 1971, *Abilities: Their structure, growth, and action*, Boston, Houghton Mifflin.)

alternative that maintains the same relationship to the square in the lower left hand quadrant is E.

While the notion of Culture-Reduced Intelligence Tests is appealing, there are some who believe it amounts to "throwing the baby out with the bath water." We need to function in a cultural context. It is our culture that provides us with the strategies or "intellectual tools" needed for competence. They would argue that reducing the cultural content of intelligence tests has drastically changed our notion of what intelligence is. There may be no right answer to the question of whether Culture-Reduced Intelligence Tests are beneficial. What do you think?

Stability

The **stability** of a test refers to the consistency of test scores. If you took an intelligence test when you were in sixth grade, are you likely to get the same score now? (This is sometimes referred to as *test-retest reliability*.) For most of the standardized intelligence tests, stability is high, but not perfect. If you scored an IQ = 113 in the sixth grade, a later testing will probably be somewhat higher or somewhat lower, but not drastically different from 113. Small fluctuations in test scores can be expected. IQ scores on the Stanford-Binet, for example, should be thought of as falling somewhere in a range from 5 points below the obtained score to 5 points above the obtained score. In practical terms, what does this mean? If you scored 113 and your poor friend only 110, does this mean that you are more intelligent than he is? No, because if you took the test again, he could just as easily score higher than you on the second test.

Since we earlier defined IQ = 100 as average, would a score of 102 signify smarter than average and 99 signify less than average intelligence? Again, the answer is no because the stability of any test is not perfect.

Validity

What good are intelligence tests? Are they true or **valid** measures of intelligence?

Intelligence tests have been used to predict success in school. In general, they have met with fairly good success, but it is important to remember that they are not perfect predictors of educational success.

Sometimes people who don't score well on intelligence tests do extremely well in school, while other times the reverse is true. Because of this, scores on standardized tests are considered along with other types of information like previous grades to determine who will be admitted to college or graduate school.

While intelligence tests are fairly good at predicting scholastic achievement, they are less good at predicting success after graduation. If you think about this, it should not be surprising. After all, it is difficult to measure life's success. Is the most successful person the one who makes the most money? I don't think so. If you were to decide to remain at home and raise children, you might be successful by your own definition. There is little in an intelligence test that could predict successful parenting, homemaking, or performance in skilled labor.

Sex Differences in Intelligence

Have you ever wondered if there are sex differences in intelligence? You have probably heard arguments advancing the notion that either the female or the male is the smarter sex. It may seem that it should be relatively easy to answer this question. All we have to do is find the IQ scores of a large sample of women and a large sample of men and determine which group has the higher average IQ. In fact, it is not possible to answer the question this way because intelligence tests are written so that both sexes will obtain the same average score.

It could be argued that if you look at the major accomplishments of women and men, you would have to conclude that men are the more intelligent sex. Think of the advances in chemistry, physics and medicine, the best known musical and artistic works, the major corporations—most of these are the products of men, although there are, of course notable exceptions. It would be unfair to judge women's and men's intelligence by looking at their achievements because women and men traditionally have performed different tasks in society. Medicine, science, government, and most other avenues to success had been virtually closed to women in the past. Thus, intelligence can't be assessed by examining women's achievements in these areas.

Two psychologists, Maccoby and Jacklin (1974), have conducted an extensive review of the literature on sex differences. On the basis of their review, they concluded that there is evidence for sex differences in four different areas. Three of the four areas of sex differences relate to intellectual functioning, the fourth is a personality variable:

1. *Verbal Ability.* Women and girls tend to score higher on tests of verbal ability then men and boys. It is important to keep in mind that we are dealing with group data, and that there are wide individual differences. Sex differences in verbal ability are most pronounced after puberty.

2. *Mathematical Ability.* The literature on sex differences in mathematical ability is a mirror image of the results obtained with respect to verbal ability. Men and boys tend to score higher on quantitative test items, with the largest sex differences found after puberty.

3. *Spatial Ability.* Sex differences are most consistently found in tests of spatial ability, with males outperforming females in this area. Spatial ability refers to the ability to visualize and work with various shapes. Examples of tasks used to assess spatial ability are imagining what a flat figure would look like if it were folded, visualizing what a scene would look like from another perspective, and finding a figure that is embedded in a larger and more complex figure. Sample items from tests of spatial ability are shown in Fig. 9.2.

4. *Aggression.* The fourth area in which Maccoby and Jacklin found sex differences is aggression. Typically, males have the dubious distinction of being more aggressive than females.

Although Maccoby and Jacklin found substantial evidence for these sex differences in the experimental investigations published in psychology journals, we

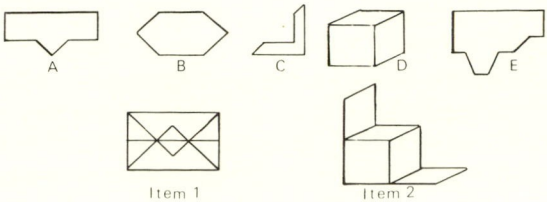

FIG. 9.2. Sample items from the Hidden Figures test. Which of the five simple figures at the top is concealed in each of the item figures? *Answers:* 1-A, 2-D. (This test is based upon figures originally designed by Gottschaldt, 1926.)

are still left with the problem of interpreting them. Are these differences inherent in the biology of women and men, or are they the products of contemporary socialization practices? It is possible that females outperform males in verbal skills because of our stereotypes about what women and men should do. Many males may avoid poetry and literature courses because they are not seen as "manly" topics to study. Conversely, women may often avoid math classes for fear of appearing unfeminine. A similar explanation for the male superiority on spatial tasks is also possible. It may be that males simply have more practice in performing spatial tasks, which are encouraged at an early age when they are given building blocks, tinker toys, and paper airplanes, while their sisters are given baby dolls and books. The fact that these differences emerge during adolescence provides further support for the idea that they are influenced by childhood experiences.

Sex differences in aggression could also be learned. Boys are often taught to fight and are given toy soldiers and "action figures" to play with. Many people feel that aggression is unseemly in women but is a prized trait in adult men that is needed for success in the business world and professional world.

It is not possible at this time to decide to what extent the sex differences Maccoby and Jacklin found are biologically determined and to what extent they are learned. This question can be answered only in a society that treats males and females as intellectual equals. Perhaps future generations will have the answer.

What do sex differences in intelligence imply about your own intelligence? Nothing. Even *if* there are real differences, and many other researchers have questioned their validity (e.g., Block, 1976), the magnitude of the effect is quite small. The results are based on averages taken from large groups of men and women. There are many men with outstanding verbal skills and many women with outstanding mathematical and spatial skills. Knowing that women may score slightly below men on math tests tells us nothing about your own ability. Information like this can never be used as a rationalization for your own failure or success.

LEARNING TO BE INTELLIGENT

Thus far, we have considered the concept of intelligence and its measurement. Since this text is concerned with thinking and getting you to learn how to improve your thinking, it seems reasonable to ask if you can learn to be more intelligent. If you learn all of the thinking skills presented in this text will you be smarter? The answer to this question depends on our elusive definition of intelligence.

Increasing IQ Scores

It is a relatively simple matter to increase IQ scores. Keep in mind that IQ is determined by a test score. If you simply want to improve your IQ, you could obtain a copy of the test that you will be administered, learn the answers to the questions that will be asked, and astound your friends with your high IQ. Obviously, this is not the same thing as becoming more intelligent. It would be unethical and begs the question of whether intelligence can be increased.

The real question is whether certain life experiences, like education, can make someone smarter. Many of you will recognize this as the **Nature–Nurture** (or **Heredity–Environment**) **Controversy.** Is intelligence determined by one's genetic make-up or his or her culture and environment? Without a doubt, both contribute to intelligence. A more controversial form of this question is which contributes more to intelligence—nurture or nature.

Psychologists who take a strong nature position (e.g., Jensen, 1970, 1980) argue that identical twins who are separated from birth and raised apart, thus having the same genetic make-up and different environments, tend to have highly similar IQ scores. Additional support for this position comes from adoption studies that show that unrelated siblings raised in the same home (thus having different heredities and the same environment) show only moderate similarity in IQ scores. The majority of psychologists and educators don't adhere to this view. Let's examine the other side of this issue, which states that intelligence is heavily dependent on life's experiences.

A Paradox

Gregory (1981) believes the current notions of intelligence are *paradoxical* or contradictory because they incorporate the following three propositions which are logically inconsistent (p. 296):

1. Intelligence is not supposed to be increased by education.
2. Abilities are supposed to be increased by education.
3. Intelligence is measured by abilities.

The paradox he is posing is, in simpler language: How can anyone claim that intelligence is unaffected by education and then measure intelligence by asking someone about things that are typically learned in school? If we think of intelligence as the knowledge you have stored somewhere in your head, then surely some experiences will allow you to acquire more knowledge than others. If we think of intelligence as the ability to solve novel problems, then experience in solving many types of problems should improve your proficiency at novel problem-solving tasks.

One way to resolve the intelligence paradox is by changing the first assumption and allowing the possibility that intelligence can be increased by education. An examination of some of the ways experimenters have attempted to "teach intelligence" will tell us if our resolution of the paradox is correct.

Each attempt to teach people to be more intelligent is based on a theory of what intelligence is. Different approaches, each based on a different theory of intelligence, are considered.

Development of Intelligence

L. L. Thurstone, an eminent psychologist and psychometrician (someone who measures mental abilities), devised a 7-factor theory of intelligence in 1938. He called the 7-factors **Primary Mental Abilities.** The 7 factors are:

1. Fluency with numbers
2. Fluency with words
3. Verbal comprehension
4. Memory
5. Reasoning (or Logic)
6. Visual and spatial ability
7. Perceptual speed

One attempt to train intelligence involved the development of a curriculum based on Thurstone's seven factors. The originators of this program were Sexton and Poling (1973). Sexton's interest in fully utilizing and increasing human intelligence began "while shining brass doorknobs on a US Navy cruiser in the South Pacific" (p. 2). Sexton and Poling developed methods of teaching Thurstone's Primary Mental Abilities for use in a program designed to raise intelligence. They added an eighth factor, creativity, to Thurstone's original list and included creativity training in their program.

The subjects were 13 students who took the course to increase their intelligence. The program entailed activities like vocabulary building, mathematics drills, and training in reading rapidly. The researchers report that their students' average IQ scores increased from 116 to 141. Sexton and Poling claimed they were unfamiliar with the intelligence test questions, so that objections that they *taught* the test questions could not be raised. Although they used a very small number of students, most of whom had high IQ scores before the course began, this study does suggest that specific short-term training courses can raise IQ scores. It is a more difficult matter to claim that the students actually became more intelligent. For example, we don't know if they reasoned more efficiently or used numbers with more proficiency outside of the classroom setting, nor do we know if they maintained their gain in IQ scores over the next several years. Sexton and Poling's subjects were also a highly select and well-motivated group of students. We don't know if they would have obtained the same results with randomly selected subjects.

There are several other claims that the IQ scores of adults can be improved with short-term thinking courses. A course designed by Samson (1975) provided specific instruction in word usage, "thing-making" (creating objects), qualification (similarities and differences), classification, structure analysis, operation analysis, and analogies. According to Samson, this course has increased the IQ scores of 256 college students an average of 10 points.

Other psychologists have provided similar evidence in support of the idea that intelligence is not a fixed characteristic and that it can be increased with appropriate training. Fox, Marsh, and Crandall (1983) have found that students enrolled in a course that he had designed to teach thinking skills show considerable gains on Piagetian tests of the ability to think abstractly. (See the next section for a description of this test.) Similarly, Rubinstein (1980) has reported that students at a midwestern university showed significant gains in IQ scores following a semester-long course on problem solving.

Although evidence has been accumulating to support the notion that IQ scores can be increased with training (see Whimby, 1976, for a review), and by implication, people learn to be more intelligent, it seems prudent to settle on the more modest conclusion that, "We don't know whether native intelligence may be increased, because we don't know what it is. But we can train people to solve problems they could not solve before" (Samson, 1975, p. ix).

A somewhat different approach to the question of whether people can learn to be more intelligent is to examine the kinds of problems that an individual can solve and use this knowledge to determine his or her intellectual level. Specific training on cognitive skills is then provided. The goal of these programs is to enhance the "level of thought" each individual is able to attain. This approach is based on a model of intelligence proposed by the Swiss psychologist, Jean Piaget.

PIAGETIAN MODEL OF INTELLIGENCE

Jean Piaget has probably done more to revolutionize the area of cognitive development than any other person in the world. He was primarily concerned with the way people acquire knowledge and the way cognitive processes change throughout childhood and early adulthood. According to Piaget, there are four broad developmental periods (each broken into stages). The first, the **Sensorimotor Thought Period** covers the period from birth to approximately 2 years of age. The central development at this stage is the differentiation of self from other people and objects. This stage culminates with the understanding that objects have a permanence to them and, thus, they don't cease to exist when they are out of the infant's view. It's during this period that infants learn about the touch, taste, and smell properties of objects in their environment. The second period is characterized by **Preoperational Thought.** This period spans early childhood from approximately two to seven years. During the Preoperational Stage, the child acquires the ability to classify objects and to perform seriation tasks (e.g., line up sticks in size order). At this stage, thought is characterized as egocentric. It is a major achievement when the child understands that the world does not appear to everyone exactly as she sees it. Preoperational children seem to be unable to integrate two dimensions and thus have difficulty with multiple classification (e.g., trucks that are large and red) and reasoning about moral issues. Piaget calls Preoperational thought pre-logical.

The third developmental period is **Concrete Operations** lasting from approximately seven to eleven years. During this period children learn to use symbolic representations and attain cognitive milestones like the understanding that the amount of liquid has not changed when it is poured from a flat dish into a tall, thin beaker. (This knowledge is called **conservation.**) At this stage, children understand the conditions under which quantities remain the same and change—the understanding of the nature of relevant and irrelevant transformations on quantities.

The final stage of development is **Formal Thought** or **Formal Operations,** which, according to Piaget, emerges at about 11 to 15 years of age and is characterized by logical thinking. It is a time when individuals can formulate hypotheses (What would happen if . . .) and manipulate abstract symbols such as the ones needed to understand algebra and geometry. Piaget later acknowledged that formal thought may not be as universal as he had formerly believed (Piaget, 1977). Rather, individuals may be able to reason abstractly about some topics, but not others.

There is considerable evidence that many people never progress beyond the mode of thought that is characteristic of Concrete Operations (Neimark, 1975). Consider the intellectual abilities associated with Formal Thought (Sime, 1973, p. 14): "Very simply, it is the period in which most of us become able to reason abstractly—to hypothesize and work from the abstract to the particular, instead of the other way round, or even to work from the abstract to the abstract. During this period we form and use concepts from abstractions, such as concepts of proportion (i.e., of a relation between relationships), of law, of justice, of infinity, and so forth." Most people would agree that these abilities are the hallmark of an intelligent individual. If the characteristics of Formal Thought could be taught, perhaps the level of intelligence could be raised with the appropriate instruction.

Researchers and educators who work in the Piagetian tradition, usually don't measure intelligence with IQ scores. More often, they look at performance on established tests that correspond to Piaget's levels of intellectual development. Here are some Piagetian tasks to work on. They were originally reported in Inhelder and Piaget's book *The Growth of Logical Thinking From Childhood to Adolescence* (1958). It's important that you actually work on these problems to understand how the skills required to solve them relate to intelligence.

Piagetian Tasks

Task 1 Mixing Colorless Chemicals. This task involves mixing chemicals until a yellow color is obtained. Suppose that you were given four bottles of odorless, colorless liquids. They appear to be identical except for being labeled 1, 2, 3, and 4. You are also given a fifth beaker labeled X, which is the "activating solution." The activating solution is always needed to obtain the yellow color, which results from a chemical reaction. How would you go about finding which of the chemicals in combination will yield the yellow color?

Some rules: The amount of each chemical is not important, nor is the order in which you combine them. It may help you in working on this problem to visualize the materials as presented in Fig. 9.3.

Stop now and think about how you would approach this problem. Do not go on until you have written down all of the tests you would perform.

Task 2 Bending Rods. This task is to determine which of several variables affects the flexibility of rods. Imagine that you are given a long vertical bar with

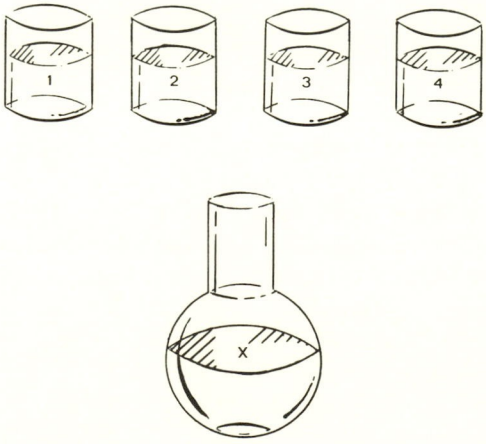

FIG. 9.3. Mixing colorless liquids. How would you determine which combinations of colorless liquids are needed to obtain a yellow color?

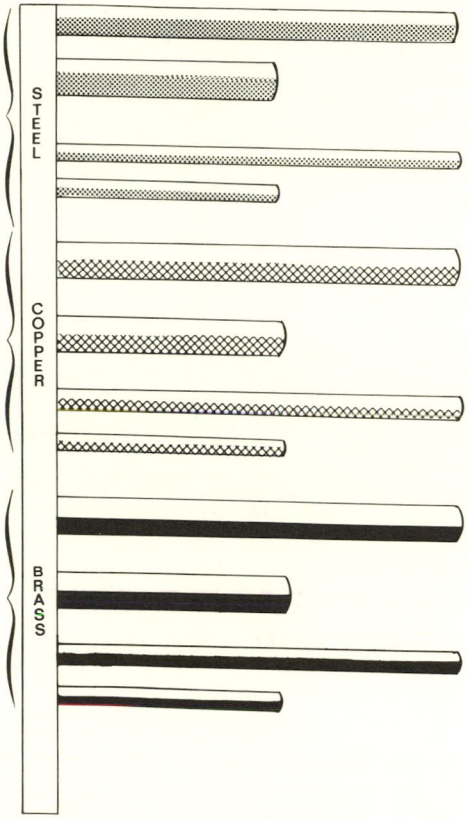

FIG. 9.4. Bending rods. How would you determine whether material, length, or thickness affects rod flexibility?

12 rods hanging from it. Each rod is made of either brass, copper, or steel. The rods come in two lengths and two thicknesses. Your task is to find which of the variables (material, length, or thickness) influence how much the rods will bend. You can test this by pressing down on each rod to see how much it bends. You may perform as many comparisons as you like until you can explain what factors are important in determining flexibility. It may help you to visualize the set-up as presented in Fig. 9.4.

What do you need to do to prove that length, or diameter, or the material rods are constructed from or some combination of these variables is important in determining flexibility? Stop now and write out your answer to this problem. Don't go on until you have finished this problem.

Task 3 Playing a Billboards-Type Game. In this task, you are presented with a table which has a ledge or "buffer" around its edges so that a ball cannot roll off. A cue stick and a ball are placed at one corner of the table. There is a small toy figure on the table. Your task is to shoot the ball from the corner of the

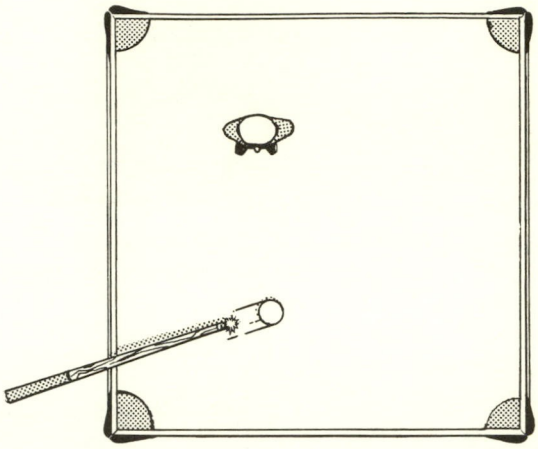

FIG. 9.5. Playing a billiards-type game. How would you position the cue stick so that the ball would bounce off the back wall and knock down the toy figure?

table so that it bounces off of the ledge and hits the toy figure. Consider the layout presented in Fig. 9.5.

How would you go about positioning the ball and the cue stick so that you can hit the toy figure?

Stop now and work out the strategy you would use for finding out how to bounce the ball off of the ledge so that it hits your target.

The three tasks presented here are only a few of the Piagetian tasks used to assess the level of intellectual achievement at which an individual is functioning. The kinds of answers you gave to these questions will indicate whether you are functioning at the level of Formal Thought.

Are You Functioning At The Level of Formal Thought?

To answer this question, let's review how you solved the sample Piagetian Tasks.

Task 1 Mixing Colorless Liquids. How did you approach this problem? Did you realize that you needed an organized plan or did you begin by randomly mixing the liquids? The best approach to this task is a very methodical one. It must include mixing each liquid separately with the activating solution (1+X, 2+X, 3+X, 4+X), then carefully mixing two liquids at a time with X (1+2+X, 1+3+X, 1+4+X, 2+3+X, 2+4+X, 3+4+X), then three at a time with X (1+2+3+X, 1+2+4+X, 1+3+4+X, 2+3+4+X), then all four at once (1+2+3+4+X), being careful to observe which combinations would yield the yellow color. If you carefully tested each combination, then you would score at the Formal Operations level on this task.

Task 2 Bending Rods. How did you go about exploring the effect of length, diameter, and material on rod flexibility? In order to solve this problem, you had to consider the possible factors that contribute to rod flexibility, and then systematically hold constant all of the variables except one. This is a basic concept in experimental methods. If you wanted to know if material was an important factor, which rods would you test? You would bend a brass rod, a copper rod, and a steel rod of the same length and diameter. This would hold constant the length and diameter variables while testing the material variable. Some possible tests of this would be to compare flexibility among the short and wide brass, copper and steel rods. Similarly, if you wanted to find out if length is important, you would bend a short and a long rod of the same diameter that was constructed with the same material. An example of this would be to compare the short and wide copper rod with the long and wide copper rod.

How would you decide if diameter influences rod flexibility? By now it should be clear that you would compare two rods of the same material and length and different diameters. You could test this by bending a short and wide steel rod with a short and thin steel rod.

Task 3 Playing a Billiards-Type Game. This is a difficult task to conceptualize without actually trying to perform it. I was hoping that you've had enough experience with similar games (e.g., billiards) to formulate the answer or, at least, the way you would go about finding the answer. If tasks like these were really being used to assess your level of intellectual functioning, you'd be able to actually manipulate the objects to derive an answer. A trial-and-error approach to this problem does not qualify as formal thinking. You must first realize that the ball travels in a straight line and hits the ledge at an angle which is determined by the position of the cue stick. You should also come to realize that the angle at which the ball strikes the ledge is equal to the angle at which it is reflected from the ledge. This is graphically demonstrated in Fig. 9.6

All of these tasks require the individual to develop an organized approach to the problem—to generate hypotheses and perform all of the appropriate tests. The combinatorial reasoning in the chemical task is similar to that required for geometrical proofs (Sime, 1973). The isolation and control of variables needed to solve the rods task is essential for research in any area, and the ability to discover the path a ball will take (called *reciprocal implication*) is a skill needed in all of the physical sciences.

You may be wondering if the skills needed to solve these tasks are peculiar to the sciences, or are they more general skills that are needed in other areas like the humanities and social sciences. A good criterion of intelligence must be applicable to a variety of endeavors, not just the sciences. For example, lawyers clearly

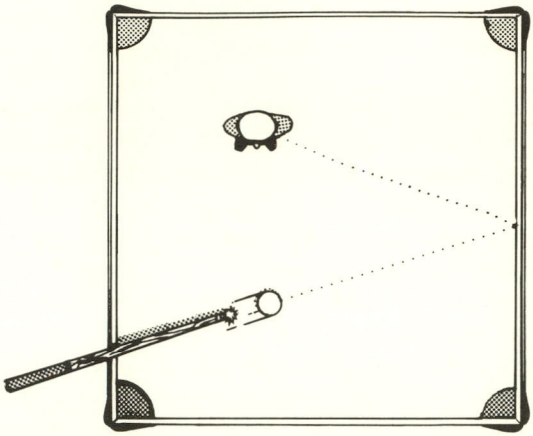

FIG. 9.6. Billiard game rebound diagram. The angle at which the ball strikes the ledge is equal to the angle at which it is reflected from the ledge.

must have the ability to reason abstractly and, therefore, would be expected to perform well on tasks that are indicative of Formal Thought. In a test of this hypothesis (Renner, 1976a), 81% of a sample of third year students at two law schools achieved at the Formal Thought level. It is likely that the same abstract thinking skills that are needed in the analysis of law, literature, and music are needed in mathematics and the sciences.

Can You Learn To Function at the Level of Formal Thought?

Using Piaget's conception of intelligence, can intelligence be taught? Joe E. McKinnon, one of the leading advocates of incorporating Piaget's theories into school curricula, answers this question with an enthusiastic, "Yes." McKinnon (1976) has been particularly concerned with the intellectual development of college students. McKinnon administered Piagetian tasks, like the ones presented earlier in this chapter, to college students at seven institutions. He found that approximately 50% of the students were not operating at the Formal Thought level. In response to the obvious need to teach thinking skills to college students, McKinnon developed an experimental curriculum that included "all the elements of inquiry—questioning, classifying, hypothesizing, verifying, restructuring, interpreting, and synthesizing" (p. 118). The success of this course was measured by comparing the number of students who had completed his experimental thinking course and had demonstrated that they were functioning at the Formal Thought level with the number of students who scored at this level without taking the course. Many more students from the experimental group (those who took the course) performed at the Formal thought level than from the control group (those who didn't take the course). It seems clear that certain educational experiences can help students to think at an abstract level.

Did the students learn to be smarter? If you go back to the first definition of intelligence presented in the beginning of this chapter, the "person on the street" definition, you would have to answer this question in the affirmative. If "reasons logically and well" is a major criterion of intelligence, then the gain in these skills as measured with Formal Thought Tasks, would attest to an increase in intelligence. If you use the second definition of intelligence, the ability to perform well on novel tasks, then the answer is probably. The Piagetian tasks they performed were novel to them; however, we don't know if they would show gains on other types of novel tasks. If you consider the third definition of intelligence, whatever intelligence tests test, the answer is "don't know" since we don't know if these students would show an increase in IQ scores obtained from standardized intelligence tests. This is the least relevant definition since programs designed in the Piagetian tradition are designed to advance the intellectual level at which an individual functions and not scores on intelligence tests. Renner (1976b) has concluded "The research . . . leaves no doubt that intellectual development can be an outcome of education" (p. 190).

CHAPTER SUMMARY

1. Most people believe that the concept of intelligence should include the ability to reason logically, read with comprehension, and function well in novel situations.

2. Intelligence is usually measured with an Intelligence Quotient (IQ). IQs for children are computed by multiplying the ratio of Mental Age (MA) to Chronological Age (CA) by 100. IQs for adults are computed by comparing their performance on an intelligence test to standardized norms for adults.

3. Intelligence tests are developed by administering them to a large group of people to determine which items are commonly missed and which items are commonly answered correctly. This process is called standardization. An important controversy concerns the question of whether it is legitimate to test the intelligence of one racial, socioeconomic, ethnic, or geographically distinct group of people with a test that was standardized on a different group of people.

4. Several psychologists have been developing culture-reduced tests that could be used to measure the intelligence of people from different cultures.

5. While sex differences in verbal, quantitative, and spatial abilities have been found, the magnitude of the group differences between women and men are small, while individual differences are large.

6. Psychologists are not in agreement on whether intelligence can be increased, even though several psychologists have provided small-scale studies showing gains in IQ points for students who have taken specific courses designed to improve thinking.

7. Piaget proposed that intelligence progresses in stages as individuals grow to adulthood. The final stage of adult thought is called formal thought or formal operations. Approximately 50% of college students are not operating at this level of thought.

Terms to Know:

You should be able to define or describe the following terms and concepts. If you find that you're having difficulty with any term, be sure to reread the section where it is discussed.

Intelligence
Nonentrenched Tasks
Intelligence Quotient (IQ)
Mental Age (MA)
Standardization
Standardization Fallacy
BITCH-100
Culture-Reduced Tests
Culture-Fair Tests
Stability
Validity
Nature–Nurture Controversy (also called Heredity–Environment Controversy)
Thurstone's Theory of Intelligence
Primary Mental Abilities
Piagetian Model of Intelligence
Sensorimotor Thought
Preoperational Thought
Concrete Operations
Conservation
Formal Thought

Be sure that you can answer the following questions:

1. Three different definitions of intelligence have been presented in this chapter. What are they? Why is intelligence so difficult to define?

2. What is the rationale for using nonentrenched tasks to measure intelligence?

3. What was the original purpose of intelligence tests? Why do the questions in intelligence tests vary by age?

4. Why is there so much concern about the way intelligence tests are standardized? Explain the argument that if a test is standardized on one group of people it is inherently unfair to another group. Why does Jensen call this the *Standardization Fallacy?* What do you think?

5. Why was the BITCH-100 developed? What are some possible reasons that explain why blacks, as a group, tend to score lower than whites on standardized intelligence tests?

6. What are the arguments for and against culture-reduced tests?

7. If a parent were told that his son's IQ is 103 and his daughter's IQ is 98, would he be justified in thinking of his son as "above average" in intelligence and daughter as "below average" in intelligence. Why not? (This should be a clue for the correct answer for the first part of this question.)

8. When Maccoby and Jacklin examined the question of sex differences, what did they conclude? What are some possible explanations for their findings?

9. In your own words, what is Gregory's paradox? How does it support the idea that intelligence can be learned?

10. Name and briefly describe the periods of intelligence development described by Piaget.

Exercises

Try out some problems that are similar to the ones used to assess intelligence and level of intellectual functioning.

1. *A Nonentrenched Task*

The following task was adapted from Sternberg (1981). It is a projection task similar to the one discussed in this chapter. Since you have already had some experience with projection tasks, it's not a truly novel task.

This task involves determining the color of a circle in the year 2000. A circle can be described as it physically appears: ○ or ●. It can also be described verbally with one of four color words: white, black, whack, and blite. A circle is defined as white if it appears white both in the present and in 2000. A circle is defined as black if it appears black both in the present and in 2000. A circle is defined as whack if it appears white in the present and black in 2000. A circle is defined as blite if it appears black in the present and white in 2000.

Your task is to use the information given to answer questions about what is true in the year 2000. Physical descriptions (● or ○) are always correct since they merely reflect how the circle appears when the observation is made. Verbal descriptions made in the present carry implications about the future which may or may not be correct. For example, if a circle appears black (●) in the present, it could either remain black and thus be labeled "Black" or it could change to white in which case it would be labeled "Blite." Thus, verbal descriptions made in the present require a guess about the future. Verbal descriptions made in the year 2000 are always correct since there is no longer any uncertainty about present or future events.

As in the example presented earlier in this chapter, sometimes inconsistent information will be given. In this case, select I (for inconsistent information) as the correct answer.

Question 1.1

A circle is Black at the present, and Black in 2000. Circle the correct answer.

○ ● I

(This is an easy problem which is presented as a warm-up. The answer must be ●.)

Question 1.2

A circle is Black at the present, and White in 2000. Circle the correct answer.

I ● ○

Question 1.3

A circle is Black at the present, and Blite in 2000. Circle the correct answer.

I ○ ●

Question 1.4

A circle is ● at the present, and White in 2000. Circle the correct answer.

○ ● I

Question 1.5

A circle is ○ in the present, and whack in 2000. Circle the correct answer.

○ ● I

Question 1.6

A circle is white in the present, and ● in 2000. Circle the correct answer.

Whack Black I

Question 1.7

A circle is blite in the present, and ● in 2000. What is the circle in 2000?

I Blite Black

Question 1.8

A circle is ● in the present, and ○ in 2000. Circle the correct answer.

Blite White Whack

2. Mental Age and Intelligence Quotients

Compute the Mental Age for a child who answers correctly all 6 questions at the 5-year level, all 6 questions at the 6-year level, 5 questions at the 7-year level, 2 questions at the 8-year level, 2 questions at the 9-year level, and no questions at the 10-year level. What is the child's IQ if she is 8 years and 4 months old? What is her IQ if she is 10 years, 6 months old?

Below are some additional problems to illustrate the Formal Thought level:

3. A scientist is interested in determining the number of birds on a large island. One day she captured 40 birds and placed a band around the leg of each. She returned one week later and captured 60 birds. Twelve of these birds had a band on their legs. Can she use this information to estimate the total number of birds on the island?

If you answered yes to this question, what is the best estimate of the total number of birds? Explain how you arrived at this answer.

4. You have taken a space trip to the mythical planet of Xob. On Earth you weigh 130 pounds. Your weight on Xob is 15 zerks. What is the weight in zerks of your 100-pound Earthling friend?

5. Several children want to play on a playground see-saw (also called a "teeter-totter") at the same time. They are all in kindergarten and are approximately the same weight. The see-saw is 6 feet long. Distances in one foot units have been marked off in the figures. Consider the situations in Fig. 9.7, both of which will keep the see-saw in balance.

Now consider the situation in Fig. 9.8.

Two children are sitting on the left hand side of the see-saw, at the positions indicated. If one child wanted to play with them, where should he sit to keep the board in balance? Explain your answer.

FIG. 9.7. These see-saws are in balance.

FIG. 9.8. Where should a third child sit to keep this see-saw in balance?

6. This problem was presented to children in fourth through ninth grade by Karplus, Karplus, and Wollman (1974). You should recognize this as an easier version of Exercise 4.

Here is a picture of Mr. Short.

There is a figure called Mr. Tall who is similar to Mr. Short, but larger. Mr. Short's height was measured with large buttons. He is four buttons tall. When Mr. Tall was measured with the same buttons, he was found to be six buttons tall. When Mr. Short's height is measured with small paper clips, he was found to be nine paper clips tall. What is Mr. Tall's height in paper clips?

7. Elliot is 5 feet tall. At 3 P.M. his shadow is 2 feet long. E.T. is 2½ feet tall. How long would his shadow be at 3 P.M.?

8. The Russians have a secret code. If you can break their code you will have access to their defense secrets. You know that they can only use the digits 4, 7, 8, and 9 and that the code can be one, two, three or four digits long. The same digit may *not* be used more than once in the code. How would you go about combining the digits 4, 7, 8, and 9 to break their code?

9. The American Heart Association wants to know how diet (high and low fat), exercise (frequent and never), and blood pressure (high and low) contribute to heart disease. How should they study the effect of diet on heart disease?

SUGGESTED READINGS

The psychological literature on intelligence is enormous. One of the major controversies is addressed in a book edited by Rubinstein and Slife (1982): *Taking Sides: Clashing Views on Controversial Psychological Issues.* "Is Intelligence Inherited?" is one of the issues they consider. An article written by Jensen answers this question with a "Yes," and an article written by Whimbey answers "No." Jensen expanded his position in his 1981 book, *Straight Talk About Mental Tests,* and in a more technical book written in 1980, *Bias in Mental Testing.* Lucid presentations of the "no" position can be found in

Kamin's (1974) *The Science and Politics of I.Q.* and Whimbey's (1976) *Intelligence Can Be Taught.* A collection of current papers on intelligence can be found in the book edited by Detterman and Sternberg (1982), *How and How Much Can Intelligence Be Increased.* An advanced treatment of intelligence appears in Gregory's (1981) *Mind in Science.*

General references on intelligence can be found in Cattell's (1971) classic text, *Abilities: Their Structure, Growth and Action,* Resnick's edited volume (1976) *The Nature of Intelligence,* and Sternberg and Detterman's edited book (1979) *Human Intelligence: Perspective on Its Theory and Measurement.*

An educational program that was designed to raise IQ scores has been written by Samson (1975). It can be found in his book *Thinking Skills: A Guide to Logic and Comprehension.* This is essentially a workbook with exercises graded in difficulty. A similar workbook that is also recommended is Whimbey and Lochhead's (1982) *Problem Solving and Comprehension* (3rd ed.).

There are several excellent accounts of the Piagetian approach to improving intelligence. An illustrated and easy-to-read book is Sime's (1973) *A Child's Eye View: Piaget for Young Parents and Teachers.* Several theoretical and empirical papers appear in *Research, Teaching, and Learning with the Piaget Model* (1976) by Renner, Stafford, Lawson, McKinnon, Friot, and Kellogg.

A philosophical overview on intelligence testing and its political ramifications can be found in a controversial book by Gould (1981), *The Mismeasure of Man.* A stern rejoinder to Gould and media treatment of the intelligence controversy entitled *I.Q. Testing and the Media* was written by Herrnstein. It appeared in *The Atlantic Monthly* in 1982.

10 Creative Thinking

Contents

Creativity 316
Lateral and Vertical Thinking 318
Sensitivity, Synergy and Serendipity 319
Measuring Creativity 322
Divergent Production Test 322
Remote Associations Test 324
Encouraging Creativity 325
Natural Abilities 325
Environmental Factors 326
Personality Factors 326
Strategies for Creative Thinking 327
Training Programs 327
Quantity Breeds Quality 329
Creative Ideas Checklist 331
Attribute Listing 332
Crovitz's Relational Algorithm 333
Browsing 334
Analogies and Metaphor 335
Visual Thinking 337
Putting It All Together 338

The history of civilization is essentially the record of man's creative ability.
—Osborn (1963, p. ix)

I recently spent a morning at a special summer program for "mentally gifted kids," the ones who score within the top one or two percent of all children in their age group on intelligence tests. Every morning, the second to tenth graders gather in a small auditorium to contemplate a "thought for the day," work on a puzzle, plan activities, and gripe about the usual things all kids gripe about. The puzzle for the day was "How can you take one away from 9 and get 10?" The kid sitting next to me whispered, "Do *you* know the answer?" After a few seconds thought, I gloated with a "Yes" response, pleased as punch that I could keep up with this elite group of short people.

Many hands went up in response to the puzzle. The first child to answer was a tiny, red-headed girl, reminiscent of Charlie Brown's heart throb. "It's easy," she said as she walked confidently to the chalkboard. "If you take away a *negative* one, the effect will be the same as addition." As she spoke, she wrote the following on the board:

$$9 - (-1) = 9 + 1 = 10$$

I was amazed. Why hadn't I thought of that? A second hand shot up and a young boy on the verge of adolescence explained another answer: "In Roman numerals, nine is written 'IX,' so if you take 'I' (one) away, you'll end up with 'X,' the Roman numeral for 10."

Another child responded with a sheepish grin, saying that, "This is a little silly, but, if you write 'q' and take the one, or vertical line, away and place it in front of the changed number, you'll have '10.'" I don't know why this was a silly answer—it was the one I had been thinking of.

Still more hands were up, anxious to demonstrate more ways to answer the puzzle. One child wrote out the word "NINE", then erased the second letter (the i that looked like a one), which left her with a "N NE." If you count the number of straight lines left in these letters, there are 10 (three in each "N" and four in the "E").

Actually there were even more answers, but I lost track as I sat with my mouth gaping open, trying to follow each explanation. The director of this summer program for gifted children is Dr. Barbara Clark from California State University, Los Angeles. Their usual summer curriculum includes activities designed to encourage creative thinking. Watching the children work on their daily puzzle made me keenly aware of the great creative potential in this small group of children.

CREATIVITY

A psychology of man is impossible without understanding man's ability to create.
—Arasteh & Arasteh (1976, p. 3)

Some people believe that creativity should not be a topic in its own right since it is sort of a "master thinking skill" that we employ to some extent every time we think. **Creativity** is a difficult word to define. Most people would agree that a creative act is an unusual one. If I take my garbage out to the curb every

Thursday morning, few people would be willing to claim that is a creative solution to my garbage problem. Yet, somewhere in the past, some unsung hero must have come up with the idea for curbside garbage pickup. This may have been a real breakthrough in how to handle the garbage problem. The idea originator was creative; the rest of us who trudge out weekly with our heavy tin cans are not. Thus, a definition of creativity must include a sense of originality, uniqueness, or unusualness.

Suppose that you are invited to supper at your friend Hazel's house. You know that she is an adventuresome cook and therefore you look forward to the meal with relish. The main dish is an original concoction of hot dogs and fruit salad in a cold mustard sauce. (This part is a true story. I was once served this at a friend's house.) The coup de grace is a dessert that she made on her new ice cream maker—liver flavored ice cream. While these are unusual dishes, few people would be willing to eat them. A definition of creativity must also include the notion that the idea or product be good or useful. Thus, creativity is a blend of unusual and good or useful ideas.

There is a problem with this definition of creativity because the terms "unusual" and "good" or "useful" are a matter of judgment, and people will often disagree on these topics. Pretend that you are given the task of discovering which students have musical creativity. One way to do this would be to amass musical experts and have them judge the student's performance. Suppose that you got together Itzhach Perlman, the great violinist, "Benny Goodman Big Band Sound" musicians, the popular rock star Alice Cooper, and the well known country music singer, Willie Nelson. Do you think that they would be able to agree on what constitutes musical creativity? Probably not!

It's easy to see why creativity has been an elusive topic to deal with. Someone or some group must judge an act or idea as unusual and good or useful before it can be labeled *creative*, and there will often be disagreement on the way these attributes are judged.

Prince (1970, p. i) offered a somewhat poetic definition of creativity, which, I believe, is itself creative. Consider his definition:

> CREATIVITY: an arbitrary harmony, an expected astonishment, a habitual revelation, a familiar surprise, a generous selfishness, an unexpected certainty, a formidable stubbornness, a vital triviality, a disciplined freedom, an intoxicating steadiness, a repeated initiation, a difficult delight, a predictable gamble, an ephemeral solidity, a unifying difference, a demanding satisfier, a miraculous expectation, an accustomed amazement.

However we choose to define creativity, we need it and we all possess it to some extent. Our everyday life is more pleasurable because of our creative actions; the arts depend on it for their existence; and the sciences and mathematics could not progress without it. Every time we express a complex thought or fill a blank piece of paper with our words, we are creating.

Lateral and Vertical Thinking

Vertical thinking is concerned with digging the same hole deeper. Lateral thinking is concerned with digging the hole somewhere else.

—DeBono (1977, p. 195)

The distinction between lateral and vertical thinking was first made by DeBono (1963, p. 11). It is best illustrated with a short story:

> Many years ago when a person who owed money could be thrown into jail, a merchant in London had the misfortune to owe a huge sum to a money-lender. The money-lender, who was old and ugly, fancied the merchant's beautiful teenage daughter. He proposed a bargain. He said he would cancel the merchant's debt if he could have the girl instead.
>
> Both the merchant and his daughter were horrified at the proposal. So the cunning money-lender proposed that they let Providence decide the matter. He told them that he would put a black pebble and a white pebble into an empty money-bag and then the girl would have to pick out one of the pebbles. If she chose the black pebble she would become his wife and her father's debt would be cancelled. If she chose the white pebble she would stay with her father and the debt would still be cancelled. But if she refused to pick out a pebble her father would be thrown into jail and she would starve.
>
> Reluctantly the merchant agreed. They were standing on a pebble-strewn path in the merchant's garden as they talked and the money-lender stopped down to pick up the two pebbles. As he picked up the pebbles the girl, sharp-eyed with fright, noticed that he picked up two black pebbles and put them into the money-bag. He then asked the girl to pick out the pebble that was to decide her fate and that of her father.

What would you do if you had been the girl? If you think about this problem in a careful, logical, straightforward way, you're using **vertical thinking,** a type of thinking that will not be much help in this situation. Typical "vertical thinking" answers are: let the girl sacrifice herself or expose him for the crook he is. Consider DeBono's suggested solution: The girl should fumble when she draws the pebble from the bag, dropping it onto the pebble-strewn path. She should then tell the villain that they can determine the color of the pebble she took by seeing the color of the one left in the bag. Since the remaining pebble must be black, the money-lender will be forced to admit that she had chosen the white pebble or expose himself as a crook.

Virtually everyone agrees that this is a good answer to the girl's dilemma. **Lateral thinking** is a way of thinking "around" a problem. "Lateral thinking generates the idea and vertical thinking develops them" (DeBono, 1968, p. 6).

Lateral thinking, then, is like creative thinking or idea discovery, while vertical thinking is the refinement and improvement of existing ideas.

The world's most famous fictional detective, Sherlock Holmes, often exhibited lateral thinking. One of my favorite examples was the use Holmes made in handling an idea by his faithful assistant, the good Dr. Watson. Watson pointed out that a certain dog would not be at all helpful in solving a mystery since the dog had done nothing the night of the murder. Sherlock cleverly noted that the dog was extremely important in solving the mystery precisely because he had done nothing on the night of the murder since dogs would be expected to bark or become excited at the sight of strangers or of violent struggles.

Sensitivity, Synergy and Serendipity

Creative thought is innovative, exploratory, venturesome.
—Kneller (1965, p. 6)

Creativity has been described as the three Ss: sensitivity, synergy, and serendipity (Parnes, Noller, & Biondi, 1977). **Sensitivity** is the use of our senses, our "windows to the world" that we use to touch, smell, taste, and see. Highly creative people may experience the physical world with greater intensity than the rest of us. One of the benchmarks of a creative person is the ability to find problems and not just solutions to them. Look at Fig. 10.1. This is called "Boring's Wife-and-Mother-In-Law." Can you guess why? Look closely. Can you see an old woman *and* a young woman in the picture. Look at Fig. 10.2. This is one of Escher's famous drawings. If you follow it carefully, the water seems to flow both uphill and downhill at the same time! Count the prongs on Fig. 10.3. Do they disappear as you count them? This is an impossible figure—impossible because it can't ever exist, except in an artist's mind. In creating each of these figures, the artists displayed a sensitivity to details that most of us lack.

Synergy is the bringing together of seemingly disparate parts into a useful and functioning whole. It is close to Koestler's notion of **bisociative thinking** in which two previously unconnected "frames of reference" are amalgamated. If you can take ideas from different domains and bring them together so that they work successfully in a new context, you have demonstrated synergy. Gordon (1961) has suggested that one way to promote creativity is to bring people from diverse fields together to find problems and to create solutions, the two mainstreams of the creative process.

Serendipity is a happy unexpected discovery that occurs when you least expect it. Biographies of great scientists often contain accounts of serendipitious events, some of them seemingly preposterous. I have often felt that focusing on serendipity did the scientist a great injustice. A new miracle drug may have been the result of an accidental spill, but it was the prepared scientist who could

FIG. 10.1. Boring's Wife and Mother-In-Law. Can you see both an old woman and a young woman in this picture?

appreciate the results of the accident that created the drug. While serendipity may have contributed to a creative act, the persistence, motivation, and hard work on the part of the creator allowed the serendipitious event to occur.

Consider how an artist friend of mine combined sensitivity, synergy, and serendipity to create a new form of art. Robert Perrine, a San Diego artist, decided to incorporate the glass that is used to cover pictures into the pictures themselves. He cut odd-shaped glass coverings and placed them over his water color paintings to see how the beveled edges in the glass would refract the paint beneath it and give it a glossy, shimmering appearance. It was a simple idea that brought together the framing process and the picture itself in a new art form. Creative ideas often seem simple and surprising.

Jokes, puns, and witticisms could also be considered as a form of creative expression. A joke brings together two ideas that are not usually combined.

Have you heard the one about the two former school mates who meet unexpectedly for the first time in 25 years? As they caught up on the details of their lives, one asked the other if he had any children. Sorrowfully he replied, "Yes, one living and one married." The listener was expecting the phrase "one living

FIG. 10.2. M. C. Eschler's Waterfall Lithograph. ©Beeldrecht, Amsterdam, VAGA, New York Collection Haags Gemeentemuseum—The Hague.

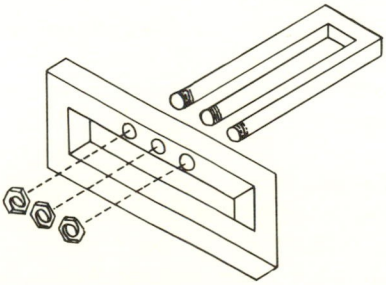

FIG. 10.3. An impossible figure. Try to count the prongs.

and one dead'' and the surprise juxtaposition of ''living and married'' is the humorous element in this joke. Laughter is often the response to original ideas also. The surprising combination of elements (synergy) makes for good jokes and creative ideas.

MEASURING CREATIVITY

The man with a new idea is a crank until the idea succeeds.
—Mark Twain

If you are very, very lucky, you could one day find yourself the recipient of the John D. and Catherine MacArthur Award. Grants of up to $300,000 are given to people to do exactly whatever they wish with the money. No strings attached. Of course, the coveted prize doesn't go to just anyone. It's given to people believed to possess special creative talents. The MacArthur Foundation believes that a wise way to help humanity is by allowing its most talented members to pursue their creative bent. The foundation selects their recipients based on an individual's past accomplishments and their own intuitive ''hunch'' as to who will continue to make creative contributions. While the MacArthur Foundation can afford to use the intuition of their advisers in these matters, psychologists have had to develop a more systematic and scientific approach to the question of creativity.

A problem for psychologists has been both to recognize and to quantify creativity. If we could devise reliable and valid tests of creativity, we could utilize this information in a variety of ways. **Psychometrics** is the branch of psychology that is concerned with the measurement of psychological traits such as creativity, intelligence, aggressiveness, androgeny, etc. Many tests have been devised to measure creative ability. Two of the most popular ones will be described here.

Divergent Production Test

When all think alike, no one is thinking.
—Walter Lippmann

Guilford (1967) made a distinction between *convergent* and *divergent* thinking. Consider the different types of thinking required by these questions:

What is the capital of Nebraska?
How many different uses can you think of for a carrot?

The first question has a single correct answer. Any answer other than ''Lincoln'' is incorrect. When you are required to come up with a single correct answer, you are engaging in **convergent thinking.** You are converging onto the correct answer. What is the correct answer to the second question? Obviously, there is no single correct answer. **Divergent thinking** is required when a person needs to generate many different responses to the same question. According to Guilford, divergent thinking is the essence of creativity. If you can produce several solutions to a given situation by thinking divergently and avoiding solutions you've relied upon in the past, you are a creative thinker. Guilford hypothesized that the human intellect comprises 120 different mental abilities. About one-fifth of these are creative or divergent thinking abilities. Guilford devised a test known as the *Divergent Production Test* to assess creative abilities. Three sample test items are presented in Fig. 10.4.

Example 1. Given a simple, familiar form, e.g., a circle, the examinee is to make as many objects as he can with a minimum of additional lines, as in the Sketches test.

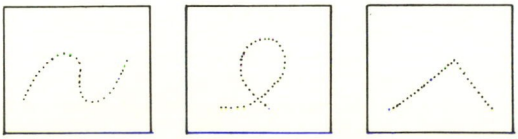

Example 2. In the Make a Mark test, the examinee is to make as many simple line figures as he can, keeping within a class specification. The examples given were in response to the instruction: make different simple, open figures in dotted lines.

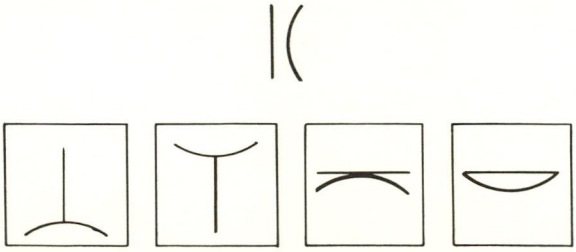

Example 3. In Make a Figure, given two line elements, the examinee is to combine them in a great variety of ways to make figures.

FIG. 10.4. Sample items from the Divergent Production Test (Guilford, 1967).

Another test of creativity that was devised by Guilford (1962, p. 159) is the Plot Titles Test. The test taker is to come up with as many different titles to a story that she can. One of the stories is about a missionary captured by cannibals who immediately placed him in a pot to boil. The cannibal princess intervenes and promises to save his life if he will marry her. He refuses and is boiled to death. Some examples of titles that were judged as not particularly creative are:

Defeat of a Princess
Eaten by Savages
The Princess
Boiled by Savages

Examples of creative titles are:

Pot's Plot
Potluck Dinner
Stewed Parson
Goil or Boil
A Mate Worse than Death
He Left a Dish for a Pot
Chaste in Haste
A Hot Price for Freedom

Remote Associations Test

The creative act owes little to logic and reason.
—Gardner (1978)

Creativity can be thought of as the ability to form new combinations of ideas to fulfill a need. Mednick and Mednick (1967) have created a test to tap this dimension of creativity. It is called the *Remote Associations Test* or RAT for short. Test takers are given three words and are asked to come up with a fourth word that relates to all three. As an example, what word relates to:

RIVER NOTE BLOOD

Can you come up with the relational word? (The answer is bank—river bank; bank note; blood bank.) Try some other remote associations similar to the ones on the RAT:

1.	BOARD	DUCK	DOLLAR
2.	FILE	HEAD	TOE
3.	BOILED	LID	FLOWER
4.	BALL	MALARIA	BUTTER
5.	CLASS	STAGE	SOCCER

(The answers are at the end of the chapter.)

Do creative people come up with remote associations when they think creatively? It seems that some do. An invention by Michael Reynolds of Taos, New Mexico seems to epitomize this type of thinking. He combined his knowledge of the high cost of housing with the problem of soda cans littering the countryside and the proverbial light bulb went on. He made these remote associations and constructed a house of aluminum soda cans. For his second house, he is filling the cans with water so that the solar heated cans of water can supplement his home energy needs.

Validity Issues

You are probably wondering if either of these tests can actually predict or assess creativity. There have been hundreds of studies using these and many other tests, showing mixed results. Some studies have found very little relationship between the scores that individuals get on these tests and their creative accomplishments in life, while others have found a low to moderate relationship. In addition, the scores that individuals get on both tests may not agree very well with each other.

The relative lack of success at predicting or measuring creativity seems to be inherent in the nature of creativity itself. First, remember that creativity is defined by its products. Creative thinkers are identified when the thinking is completed and their products are judged as worthy or not. People in art, science, or industry often cannot agree about which products are creative. Thus, any attempt to measure creativity is at least partially doomed because we have no clear-cut, universal standard for comparison.

A second problem concerns the kinds of activities we are willing to label creative. A successful homemaker with limited financial means may be quite creative in the ways she feeds her family or furnishes her home. Yet, the products of her creativity are likely to go unnoticed.

Third, creativity is a **multidimensional concept.** A multidimensional concept is one that varies in many qualitatively different ways. Creative thoughts can help us to understand past civilizations, solve pollution problems, or visualize futuristic societies. It is difficult to imagine a single test that could predict success in every possible area.

ENCOURAGING CREATIVITY

Natural Abilities

It is clear that creativity is not something that exists in an all-or-none fashion. People are more or less creative, just as they are more or less athletic or good-looking or prejudiced. The question of whether there is some inborn or inherited trait that is associated with high creativity has been difficult to answer. Most of the research has centered on the relationship between creativity and intelligence. Are intelligent people the most creative ones?

In general, people with above average scores on intelligence tests tend to be creative, while those with low IQ scores tend not to be; but the relationship is not a perfect one. It just isn't true that the very smartest people are always the most creative. It seems best to conclude that there is a certain minimum intelligence that is needed to be creative, but beyond the minimal level, IQ doesn't seem to matter much. Even if you're not a particularly intelligent person, you may have great creative potential.

Environmental Factors

Environmental factors are important. A quality education (both inside and outside of school) will give you the basis for the remote associations or divergent thoughts or novel ideas. You need a head filled with thoughts and facts in order to create with them.

Certain ethnic groups, notably the Jews and Asians are known for their outstanding creative abilities. Is this because of an inherited "creativity gene" or because of similarities in these diverse cultures that encourages creative thinking?

The Nobel Prize is usually considered the most prestigious prize in the world for creative achievement. A highly disproportionate number of these prizes have gone to Jews and Asians. Both cultures share a love of literacy, a reverance for education, a familiarity with abstract ideas (abstract God and religious laws), and a strong family life to pass these traditions onto their children. Cultures that encourage education produce creative thinkers. Of course, this doesn't address the possibility of an inherited tendency for creativity. Since both parents and children share their cultures and their gene pools, it is difficult to isolate the effects of each one.

However, the answer to the question of heritability is not useful, if you're interested in increasing your creative potential. There is little you can do about your heredity at this point and much you can do about your environment. Cultivate a love of learning; reward your own creative efforts; take the college courses that will fill your mind with new thoughts (and not just the easiest courses offered). Be your own Jewish or Asian mother, no matter what your background. Creative endeavors result from hard, intellectual work. Don't be afraid to engage in it.

Personality Factors

There are certain personality factors that are consonant with creativity. Since our definition of creativity requires an unusual or novel act, the creative individual must *not* be swayed by a need for conformity nor be resistant to change. Perhaps there is some validity to the notion of the "eccentric" artist or scholar.

The creative person must be self-motivated. Sometimes, school experiences tend to favor the noncreative students, as many traditional assignments don't call for creative responses. Creative people may have to create their own rewards for their actions as well as finding the creative process itself rewarding.

The ability to take risks is also needed for creative acts. When we try to do things differently, we sometimes fail. Most of the great discoveries in modern times were initially met with ridicule (a horseless carriage, a machine that could fly, etc.).

In a study of creative people (Barron, 1958), writers, artists, musicians, and mathematicians were given a battery of tests to determine if they had any personality traits in common. In general, these *highly* creative individuals were nonconforming, unconventional, and generally less concerned with "making a good impression." Of course, this does *not* mean that if you become nonconforming and unconventional, you'll then become highly creative.

STRATEGIES FOR CREATIVE THINKING

Training Programs

The nation that neglects creative thought today will assuredly have its nose ground into the dust of tomorrow.
—Fred Hoyle

Creativity has never been given the attention it deserved in standard educational settings. Lowenfeld (1962) has called creativity "education's stepchild." There seems to be no place in the traditional school curriculum for creativity training. There have been many programs developed with the specific goal of training people to be creative in order to fill this gap. Although there are considerable differences among these programs, they all share some basic common principles:

1. Teach the students to think of different ways to accomplish an objective and then how to select the best one.
2. Provide plenty of examples and exercises to model and practice creative skills.
3. Teach students how to ask relevant questions and *how* to discover when a problem exists.
4. Evaluate the quality of an idea by its consequences.
5. Reward original and relevant ideas. Let students know that their ideas are valuable.
6. Give students the confidence to speak freely.

The most famous creative training program was developed by Covington, Crutchfield & Davies in 1971 for 5th and 6th graders. The program consisted of a workbook in which the brother and sister team of Jim and Lila had to solve a series of detective stories. The reader, along with Jim and Lila had to formulate hypotheses, gather evidence, and ask questions in order to solve the crime. If you've already read the Thinking as Hypothesis Testing Chapter, you'll recognize this sequence as the steps used in experimental methods of discovery. All along Jim and Lila were guided by a wise "Uncle John" who would provide hints and explain their mistakes.

One of my favorite stories concerned a missing jewel. As guests arrived at a party, they brought wrapped gifts for the wealthy hostess. Suddenly, the lights went out, and when they went on again a valuable jewel was missing. Lila and Jim had to determine what had happened to the jewel. No one could have left the room or entered as the door had remained locked. The window was opened, but there were no footsteps in the fresh snow that covered the ground. Later we learn that there is a feather on the floor and that one of the boxes has a hole in the bottom. Have you solved the crime by now? A trained pigeon was taken from a wrapped box and used to transport the jewel to an accomplice.

It takes Lila and Jim a while to find and put together the clues in order to solve this crime. Crutchfield (1966) believes that with direct training with stories like this one, children can learn to think more creatively. The reader engages in the discovery process along with the protagonists, and may even solve the problem before Lila and Jim. Figure 10.5 demonstrates how the program attempts to encourage creative thinking.

There have been several evaluations of Covington, Crutchfield and Davies' program, most of them positive. However, it is important to keep in mind that the children are evaluated with material that is similar to the type used in training (detective stories). There is no good evidence that children trained with this

FIG. 10.5. An excerpt from Covington, Crutchfield and Davies' (1971) program of creativity training. (Reprinted by permission of Charles E. Merrill Publishing Co.).

method actually grow up to be more creative adults or that they ever apply these skills in real life settings. It was also found that the teacher was an important variable in the program's success. Children with rigid uninterested teachers did not improve as much as those with involved teachers.

Other creativity training programs have offered similar evidence of success. One of the more spectacular successes is attributed to a creativity training program at Sylvania Electric Company which resulted in "double profit; 2,100 new products; increased patent applications five-fold; saved $22 million" (Edwards, 1968). While these claims seem fantastic, we really have no idea what these figures should be compared to and therefore a more restrained enthusiasm is probably prudent.

While any single study or method may have its limitations and qualifications, numerous experimental programs indicate that creativity can be stimulated under proper conditions. It is not an inborn gift for a lucky few. We all can become more creative. Instead of attempting to review each of the training programs, let's examine some of the strategies and methods they've used so that you can apply them in your own life in an attempt to increase your creativity.

Quantity Breeds Quality

The notion that if you have lots of ideas, some of them will be good is the major thrust of **brainstorming.** Brainstorming was discussed in the chapter on the Development of Problem Solving Skills as a way to find solution paths that solve problems. It is a creative way to generate solution paths and is often used in creative problem solving. Brainstorming is a way of producing a list of ideas that can subsequently be evaluated. Although brainstorming can be done individually, it is more commonly considered a group activity. The only rule of brainstorming is that all judgment be deferred until some later time so that no one hesitates to offer unusual or off-beat ideas. Osborn (1963) offers many examples in his book, *Applied Imagination.* For example, Osborn reports that a 15-minute brainstorming session at American Cyanamid Corporation produced 92 ideas, or more than six ideas per minute. This was an average of eights ideas per participant.

The quantitative advantages of brainstorming are without question. But do more ideas necessarily imply better ones? Often, the best ideas result from the combination (synergy) and alteration of the ideas listed. The atmosphere of deferred judgment is clearly consistent with the discussion on environment presented earlier in the chapter. It encourages risk-taking and unconventionality, both of which are prerequisites to creative thinking. At the very least, brainstorming is fun. It is a recommended strategy for enhancing creative thought.

Osborn had a group of parents brainstorm on how to get their children to watch less television and read more books. Read carefully through the list of ideas the parents came up with. It seems to me that some combination of these ideas would surely be effective. (In fact, I intend to start using them at home with my own children.)

1. Pull plug in TV set.
2. Break up the set.
3. Set a definite time for looking at TV.
4. Arouse interest in books.
5. Acquire a bad horizontal tube.
6. Reorient antenna in order to get bad reception.
7. Select book that has been seen on TV.
8. Set example by reading yourself.
9. Buy portable radio for children.
10. Evaluate TV programs.
11. Encourage visits to library.
12. Have the children write book reports.
13. Give money for movies.
14. Donate a TV to library.
15. More outdoor companionship with parents.
16. As a result of seeing TV story (say Robinson Crusoe) children given same book to read and do research on.
17. Start reading aloud to them when young.
18. Read them good books.
19. Make reading as convenient as TV.
20. Give them their own bookcase in room.
21. Give records for Hi-Fi.
22. Give subscriptions to children's magazines.
23. Select books suitable to age.
24. Get them interested in daily newspapers, even if only the comics.
25. Help them with their homework.
26. Select type of news they read.
27. Discuss with them the books they have read.
28. Have them read to you.
29. At PTA meeting, have subject discussed with teachers; get teachers to recommend books.
30. Encourage group reading.
31. Buy them a good dictionary.
32. Always answer questions if you can.
33. Buy a good children's encyclopedia.
34. Institute games requiring the use of words and general knowledge.
35. Get local schools to have course in fast reading and good reading.
36. Have children checked physically—there may be some reason why they are unable to read.
37. In addition to their allowance, give them a fee for each good book that they read.

Creative Ideas Checklist

Another method for producing creative ideas is to present people with a checklist of diverse categories or adjectives or questions that could conceivably apply to the question or problem at hand. These lists are called **creative ideas checklists.**

In one study of the use of lists to stimulate creative ideas, Davis and Roweton (1968) gave students the following list which was labeled "Aids in Thinking of Physical Changes":

a. Add or Subtract Something
b. Change Color
c. Change the Materials
d. Change by Rearranging the Parts
e. Change Shape
f. Change Size
g. Change Design or Style

Students who were given this list were told to, "List as many physical changes as you can for a thumbtack." Davis and Roweton reported that the group that had received the checklist produced a greater number of ideas and more creative ideas than a control group that had not been given the checklist. Recently, a cookie manufacturer began making "reverse" chocolate chips cookies—chocolate cookies with white chocolate chips. They have become an overnight financial and taste success. You should recognize this simply as "d" in the above list—a change by rearranging the parts. This simple creative act has paid well for its innovator.

Perhaps the most famous checklist is a generalized one that can be applied in a variety of situations. Whiting (1958, p. 62) attributes this list to Osborn.

Put to Other Uses? New ways to use as is? Other uses if modified?

Adapt? What else is like this? What other idea does this suggest? Does past offer parallel? What could I copy? Whom could I emulate?

Modify? New twist? Change meaning, color, motion, odor, form, shape? Other changes?

Magnify? What to add? More time? Greater frequency? Stronger? Larger? Thicker? Extra value? Plus Ingredient? Duplicate? Multiply? Exaggerate?

Minify? What to substitute? Smaller? Condensed? Miniature? Lower? Shorter? Lighter? Omit? Streamline? Split Up? Understate?

Substitute? Who else instead? What else instead? Other ingredient? Other material? Other process? Other power? Other place? Other approach? Other tone of voice?

Rearrange? Interchange components? Other pattern? Other layout? Other sequence? Transpose cause and effect? Change pace? Change schedule?

Reverse? Transpose positive and negative? How about opponents? Turn it backward? Turn it upside down? Reverse roles? Change shoes? Turn tables? Turn other cheek?

Combine? How about a blend, an alloy, an assortment, an ensemble? Combine units? Combine purposes? Combine appeals? Combine ideas?

Although there are many such lists, a third one worth considering is from Parnes (1967, p. 231) who suggests that you ask yourself these idea-spurring questions when you're looking for new ideas:

1. Effects on objective?
2. Individuals and/or groups affected?
3. Costs involved?
4. Tangibles involved (material, equipment, etc.)?
5. Moral or legal implications?
6. Intangibles involved (opinions, attitudes, feelings, aesthetic values, etc.)?
7. New problems caused?
8. Difficulties or implementation and follow-up?
9. Repercussions of failure?
10. Timeliness?, etc.

While the purpose of creative ideas checklists is to create novel ideas, it is also possible that they could have an inhibiting effect. If you only considered the possibilities on a small checklist, you could miss other ideas by narrowing your search to ones that are suggested by the list.

We've all had the experience at one time or another or being "stuck," when ideas don't seem to flow. If you go through these checklists, pondering at each item, you're bound to get your thoughts flowing again.

Attribute Listing

In **attribute listing,** every characteristic or quality of the item or situations is listed and then examined for possible modification or recombination. Let's try an example.

Suppose you want to make something really different for dinner tonight. In fact, you want to make a food that no one else in the world has ever tasted before. How would you go about doing this? First, you could list many different foods:

eggs
hotdogs
Baked Alaska

stewed tomatoes
Steak Tartare
chocolate pudding
etc.

Alongside each food, you would list several of its attributes, such as shape, consistency, color, texture, odor, temperature, etc. You'd then randomly pair attributes to come up with a new food. You might think of the "soft and shimmery" attribute of jello and the cold, hard attribute of ice cream to combine the two so that you'd freeze the jello or whip the ice cream.

Attribute listing is a good procedure for fashion design. You could list every part of a dress, for example, and every attribute of that part. A partial example is:

Dress Part	*Attribute*
collars	pointed, rounded, none, Nehru
sleeves	raglan, short, rolled, long
waist	cinched, gathered, dropped, loose
skirt	full, straight, ruffled, pointed

A talented dress designer could combine possible dress attributes, coming up with thousands of unique designs (e.g., a dress with a Nehru collar, short sleeves, gathered waist and ruffled skirt).

Crovitz's Relational Algorithm

Those of you who have already read the chapter on the Development of Decision Making Skills know that an *algorithm* is a step-by-step guide that leads to a solution. Crovitz's (1970) **Relational Algorithm** is a solution guide that relies on changing the relations among items. Crovitz lists 42 "relational words" (p. 100). They are:

about	at	for	of	round	to
across	because	from	off	still	under
after	before	if	on	so	up
against	between	in	opposite	then	when
among	but	near	or	though	where
and	by	not	out	through	while
as	down	now	over	till	with

When you are in need of a creative solution, you have only to try different ways of "relating" the elements. Crovitz uses Duncker's classic X-ray problem as an example. Although this problem was described in the chapter on the Development of Problem Solving Skills, I'll present it again briefly. The problem is to get rid of an inoperable stomach tumor with X-rays without harming the healthy tissues. However, when the radiation is intense enough to destroy the tumor, it will also harm the healthy tissue surrounding it. The best solution involves using several weak rays through different parts of the body so that they will summate on the tumor. Crovitz demonstrates how the relational algorithm can be used to find a solution to this and other problems. The procedure is fairly simple. Form a sentence with each relational word using it as it might relate to the tumor. For example:

1. Take the rays *through* the esophagus.
2. Take the sensitivity *from* the tissues.
3. Take tissue *off* the tumor.
4. Take strong rays *after* weak rays.
5. Take a shield *on* stomach walls.
6. Take the tumor *across* the stomach.
7. Take a cannula *through* the stomach wall.
8. Take the power *from* the rays.
9. Take the tumor *to* the exterior.

(Crovitz, 1970, p. 102).

Crovitz claims that this method works well since it forces the individual to consider new relationships among the parts of the problem.

Browsing

In our society we have great institutions that function as repositories for ideas. They are called libraries. Wicker (1981) suggests that we "probe library sources" to generate new ideas. Pick up newspapers and magazines, case histories and biographies, scholarly journals, joke books, and even children's literature. Use a broad range of sources. You can't make "remote associations" or borrow ideas from other fields if your own knowledge is confined to a narrow discipline.

Use qualitative and quantitative information. Census reports can suggest new problems since they succinctly state what people are doing, where they are doing it, what the are eating, how they are living, and how they are dying. Learn something new every day. If you pick up a journal at random and read one new article a day, you'll be surprised at how the newly acquired information crops up in everyday contexts. Libraries are a great source for new ideas. You can also browse with quality television shows like Nova, Cosmos, and National Geographic. They contain a wealth of fascinating information on almost any topic of interest. Don't forget to go to museums, art galleries, theater, and the opera. If you feel that you can't afford these outings, many have a "free day" once a month and offer reduced rates for students, the elderly, and groups.

Analogies and Metaphor

Analogy is inevitable in human thought.
—Oppenheimer (1956, p. 129)

Analogies underlie much of our everyday thinking, our artistic expressions, and scientific achievements. Sternberg (1977, p. 353) has noted, "Reasoning by analogy is pervasive in everyday experience. We reason analogically whenever we make a decision about something new in our experience by drawing a parallel to something old. When we buy a new goldfish because we liked our old one, or when we listen to a friend's advice because it was correct once before, we are reasoning analogically." Thinking involves the ability to note resemblances or correspondence between two objects, while simultaneously discerning that there are also differences. When you use analogies you observe that two entities are similar with respect to some property, and dissimilar with respect to others.

We utilize analogies to make sense out of the world. They help us to understand new events by relating them to ones already known; they allow us to communicate our thoughts; they are the foundations of creative thinking. Analogies are one way of making the unfamiliar known.

Analogies are always imperfect since they imply a similarity between objects and events that are not identical. In evaluating and creating analogies, carefully consider the nature of the comparison. If I say that you are like your brother because you both have two eyes, you would certainly object since the number of eyes one has is not a relevant dimension for comparison. However, if I say that you are like your brother because you are both passive and stingy, you might still object, but the nature of the comparison is a relevant one.

A **metaphor** is an analogy that notes similarities between things that are basically dissimilar. (The English grammatical distinction between metaphor and simile is not being considered here since it is irrelevant to this discussion.) When Shakespeare wrote, "My love is like a red, red rose," he was speaking metaphorically since roses and humans are basically dissimilar. To use analogies and metaphors creatively, practice forming them, extending familiar ones, changing common ones, or reversing the process and seeking differences instead of similarities.

The most famous creative use of analogy is seen in the story of Archimedes. He was given the task of determining if the King's crown was pure gold—the only kind of crown worthy of a king. According to the legend, Archimedes did not know how to solve this problem because of the irregular shape of the crown. One day, while lowering himself into a bathtub full of water, the tub overflowed. The answer was immediately obvious. Like his body, a solid gold crown would display a volume of water identical to that displaced by a bar of gold that was equal in weight to that of the crown. The story goes on to say that in his excitement he ran naked through the streets yelling, "Eureka, I have found it!" He had a true creative insight mediated by the analogy of his body displacing his bathtub water and the knowledge that a gold crown would displace a predetermined volume of water. In case you're interested, the crown was pure gold and the king was very happy.

Analogies appear on most tests of intelligence since the ability to infer similarities is considered a high level cognitive skill. They usually involve four terms. The test taker has to infer the nature of the similarity between the first two terms and then verify if the same relationship exists between the last two. Some examples of analogies are:

thermometer:temperature	::	clock:time
dog:bark	::	cat:meow
tennis:racket	::	baseball:bat
kitchen:eat	::	bedroom:sleep
pharmacist:drugs	::	grocer:food

In each of these analogies, there is a relationship between the first two terms that also exists between the last two terms (instrument of measurement, type of sound, type of sporting good, function of the room, and items sold).

Making the Familiar Strange

While the usual function of analogies is to make the unfamiliar familiar, Gordon (1961; 1976), the founder of a creative technique known as *synectics* suggests that we reverse the process for creative results. Gordon suggests that we use analogies and metaphors by trying "strange new contexts in which to view a familiar problem" (1976, p. 251). Gordon suggests, as an example, that we consider a naive student examining a fish's heart for the first time. Since the student knows nothing about anatomy, the context is strange, yet the flow of blood through the heart may remind him of the filter system for a local swimming pool. The student's analogy is a creative contribution to his understanding of anatomy.

Gordon has suggested four specific types of analogies for use when attempting to solve a problem creatively. They are personal analogy, direct analogy, symbolic analogy, and fantasy analogy. Each is described in the chapter on the Development of Problem Solving Skills. Creative problem solving is one type of creativity. Analogies can also be used creatively to find problems. For example, executives at Bradford Associates (Westport, Connecticut) spent an afternoon sipping martinis and brainstorming about possible new products that would be marketable. Since they were enjoying their own liquid refreshments, they decided that the time had come "for a six-pack that a dog could ask for by name." They are now marketing a chicken-flavored soft-drink for dogs known as

"Arf'n'Arf." Here is a clear example of the use of analogies to find problems (the need for a doggie soft drink).

Bionics

Bionics is a special type of analogy. It relies on analogies from nature that can be adapted to human problems. For example, special properties of the eyes of beetles have suggested a new type of groundspeed indicator for airplanes, and the principles of adhesion used by cockleburs have served as the prototype for Velcro-type closures. Bionics is also concerned that the broad impact of solutions be considered because, borrowing another analogy from nature, small changes in our ecological system can result in disastrous consequences to other life forms in the food chain. Papanek (1977) calls this the "total-chain-of-design idea." It requires the creative consideration of entire systems and the interrelationships of parts.

Visual Thinking

When Mozart was asked where he got his ideas he said, "Whence *and* how *they come I know not; nor can I force them.*"
—(quoted in Vernon, 1970, p. 53)

Creative thinking often calls for images. The musician must first "hear" the sounds before she places the notes on paper; the poet must hear the rhyme before it is written; the painter must see the forms before his first brush stroke; and the chef must "taste" the combination of ingredients before the new recipe is created. It does seem that there are certain creative acts for which words are inadequate. Most people report that, at least some of the time, they think in images. An **image** is a picture-like representation in the mind. (See the chapter on the Development of Memory Skills for a discussion of imagery.)

The relationships among shapes can be used to characterize concepts. In fact, a suggested method for solving problems is to draw a diagram, thus transforming a verbal problem into a visual one. It has been said that President Kennedy would doodle in ways related to a problem when pondering difficult government and personal problems. Adams (1979) calls visual thinking an "alternative thinking language." It is an alternative to verbal-based thought. Adams suggests that we each take a drawing course to improve our ability to see and, in turn, to think creatively. He suggests that we can improve our visual thinking with practice.

Imagine the following (Adams, 1979, p. 91):

1. A pot of water coming to a boil and boiling over;
2. Your Boeing 747 being towed from the terminal, taxiing to the runway, waiting for a couple of other planes, and then taking off;

3. Your running cow changing slowly into a galloping racehorse;
4. An old person you know well changing back into a teenager;
5. A speeding car colliding with a giant feather pillow;
6. The image in (5) in reverse.

McKim's (1972) *Experiences in Visual Thinking* provides a series of guided exercises designed to enhance your ability to utilize visual modes of thought.

Putting It All Together

Several different strategies or methods to produce creative thoughts have been presented. It would be naive to believe that if you can recite each of these methods, you will automatically have creative thoughts. They are merely guidelines for hard work, and some of us will have to work harder than others.

It does seem clear that creative thinking is a skill that can be cultivated. The strategies are the plans for developing that skill. You may be wondering, where do I begin? You begin with a problem or a need. For some, creative ideas will immediately seem to flow; for others it will be more like pulling teeth. If you find yourself "out of fresh new ideas" try the techniques listed. Visualize the situation, use analogies and metaphors, consider relations, list attributes, mull checklists, and brainstorm. The creative process within you should ignite with some help from these strategies.

CHAPTER SUMMARY

1. Creativity involves the dual notion of unusual or unique and good or useful. It always involves judgment and people may not agree on which acts deserve to be labeled "creative."

2. DeBono has made a distinction between vertical thinking and lateral thinking. Vertical thinking is logical and straightforward, while lateral thinking is a creative way to think "around" a problem.

3. Creativity has been described as a blend of sensitivity, synergy, and serendipity. It is as if a fortuitous event brings together remote ideas in a person who is sensitive to their combination.

4. The Divergent Production Test and Remote Associations Test are the two most popular tests of creativity. Both have had low to moderate success in identifying creative individuals. Individuals who score high on one of these tests do not necessarily score high on the other.

5. While it is true that, in general, intelligent people are more creative than less intelligent people, it seems that a minimal level of intelligence is all that is needed for creative expression.

6. A proper environment is important in encouraging creativity. Ethnic groups that value education have a disproportionate number of highly creative individuals.

7. Several strategies to foster creative thinking were presented. Brainstorming is based on the supposition that if you have many ideas some of them will be good. Each item on a checklist of creative ideas can be applied to a problem to see if a creative spark is struck. Crovitz's relational algorithm relies on changing the relations among the parts of a problem to arrive at a solution. Ideas can also be "found" simply by browsing through library materials. Analogies and metaphors tune us in to similarities and differences that can be valuable in creating novel solutions. Visual thinking seems to be involved in many sorts of creative endeavors—especially the arts and sciences.

Terms to Know:

You should be able to define or describe the following terms and concepts. If you find that you're having difficulty with any term, be sure to reread the section where it is discussed.

Creativity
Lateral Thinking
Vertical Thinking
Sensitivity
Synergy
Bisociative Thinking
Serendipity
Psychometrics
Convergent Thinking
Divergent Thinking
Multidimensional Concept
Brainstorming
Creative Ideas Checklists
Attribute Listing
Relational Algorithm
Analogies
Metaphor
Bionics
Image

Be sure that you can answer the following questions:

1. Why is creativity difficult to define?
2. Contrast the terms "vertical" and "lateral" thinking. Give an example of each.
3. What does it mean to say that it takes a prepared mind to recognize a serendipitious event?
4. Why is it so difficult to design valid tests of creativity?
5. What is the relationship between intelligence and creativity?
6. What kind of environment will foster creativity?
7. Describe Crutchfield's program to foster creativity in children.
8. Why is it important to defer judgment during brainstorming?

9. How are creative ideas checklists used: Compare them with the strategy of attribute listing.

10. Why are analogies always imperfect? How are they used in creative thought? How does an analogy differ from a metaphor?

11. Why should we try to "make the familiar strange"?

Exercises

Using the strategies for creative thinking presented in this chapter, give creative solutions to the following problems. Notice which of the creativity strategies you try for each problem and which one seems to work.

1. The 1958 Rockefeller Report on "The Pursuit of Excellence: Education and the Future of America" raised a number of still timely problems in need of creative solutions. Select one of the problems listed below:

A. How can we improve conditions for 'giving free expression to creativity' within the realms of Science, Government, Business and Education?

B. In what ways can colleges and universities provide the Best Climate for the Creativity of the Individual without sacrificing the Benefits of Group Organization?

C. How can we more quickly and surely identify the creative person and enhance his individuality?

2. Morale is low on the automobile assembly line. There is a heat wave that is affecting everybody's work, causing them to slow down and destroying the pace on the assembly line. Generate possible solutions to this problem.

3. An architectural firm has been given a difficult contract. They must build an essentially rectangular building to keep construction costs down, yet they want it to be aesthetic and match its colonial sorroundings. What are some possible approaches?

4. If you've ever had the distasteful experience of trying to get a young child to take unpleasant tasting medicine, you'll know that this is a difficult task. How can you get a young child to take unpleasant tasting medication?

5. When college students move away from home and into the dorms, they often feel homesick. Since this seems like a childish problem, few will admit to it. What can be done to alleviate this problem?

6. Some young women literally starve themselves to death in order to gain the "super-thin" look that modern society endorses for women. What can we do about this problem?

7. You have been commissioned to create stained glass windows that depict the American Revolutionary War. What should you depict? How will you select your colors, etc.?

8. Your boss just called and is on his way over for dinner. Using only the ingredients you have in your house, what would you make for dinner?

9. How would you design a costume to represent what the well-dressed young man or woman will wear in the year 2000?

10. The headquarters of a large corporation is faced with rising costs and declining profits. In order to remedy this problem they could:

a. fire six employees
b. discontinue their new line of designer underwear
c. cheat on their taxes
d. require each employee to take a pay cut
e. ask each employee to work an extra hour each day
f. borrow money at high interest rates

Evaluate the impact of each of these solutions and recommend additional ones.

Evaluate the following analogies. How good is each comparison. Do the conclusions follow the analogical relationship?

11. The technicians who make false teeth are called "denturists." They have been seeking legislation that would allow them to also fit the teeth into people's mouths. They argue that they are the best professionals for fitting false teeth since they make them. Dentists, on the other hand, have been fighting this legislation. They argue that people who make heart valves are unable to perform cardiac surgery; similarly, the technicians who make false teeth are unable to fit them. Comment on this analogy.

12. At a recent meeting of the board of directors of an institution to serve the poor, someone suggested that the poor be represented at these meetings. The chair objected to this idea saying that it was like having the mentally incompetent administrating their own institution. Comment on this analogy.

13. Since some very well known politicians cheat on their income taxes, it must be all right.

14. Baboon mothers care for their young; therefore, it is only nature's way for women to assume the care of their infants.

Exercise your creative abilities in some of the following:

15. Write captions for cartoons.

16. Doodle.

17. Integrate principles learned in one class into another entirely different subject area.

18. Keep an idea file. Jot down ideas as they come to you. Review them periodically and use them.

19. Think of ways to improve on a favorite toy—like a teddy bear.

20. Enjoy your creative thoughts.

Answers to remote associations presented earlier in the chapter: 1. Bill 2. Nail 3. Pot 4. Fly 5. Coach

SUGGESTED READINGS

If you're seriously interested in increasing your creative potential, Parnes, Noller, and Biondi's (1977) *Guide to Creative Action: Revised Edition of Creative Behavior Guidebook* contains detailed instructions for 225 hours of creativity training, complete with practice exercises, an annotated bibliography, and articles on other creativity programs. An older edited volume filled with classic articles is Parnes and Harding (Eds.) (1962) *A Source Book for Creative Thinking*.

Osborn (1963) outlines the concept of brainstorming and other creativity strategies in his classic text *Applied Imagination: Principles and Procedures of Creative Problem Solving*. Another book that is filled with very good "self help" creativity ideas is Davis and Scott (Eds.) (1971) *Training Creative Thinking*.

The concepts of vertical and lateral thinking are developed in two books by DeBono (1967a) *The Use of Lateral Thinking* and (1968) *New Think*. Stein (1974; 1975) has a two-book series that comprises an excellent overall review of the topic. They are appropriately titled *Stimulating Creativity: Individual Procedures* (*Vol. I*) and *Stimulating Creativity: Group Procedures*, (*Vol. II*).

Adams' (1979) *Conceptual Blockbusting* is a very good little book on a big topic. Even if you find the area dull, you'll find this book entertaining. If you're interested in the life span development of creativity, Arasteh and Aresteh's (1976) *Creativity in Human Development* will fit your needs. It is divided into three sections that mirror human development—the young child, adolescence, and adult. The relevant literature for each portion of the life span is reviewed. Regretfully, old age is missing, possibly because we don't know much about creativity in old age.

Biographies of famous creative people always make fascinating reading. Ghiselin (1952) has compiled biographies from thirty-eight brilliant women and men entitled *The Creative Process*. You may find some of their stories inspirational. Arieti's (1978) book, *Creativity: The Magic Synthesis* is fairly heavy reading, although it's worth consulting because of the fascinating art it contains.

11 Applications of Critical Thinking Skills

Contents

Thinking is a Unitary Concept 343
Consumerism and Advertising Claims 344
  Why a Suntan? 344
  They're Not Sunglasses 344
  Mrs. B., There's Suds in Your Closet 345
Utilizing Research 345
  The Contraceptive Sponge 345
  Childhood Illnesses 346
  Reducing Serum Cholesterol 346
Legal Testimony 346
  Did You Steal The Money? 346
  Strike That From the Record 347
  A Probabilistic Determination of Guilt 347
Medical Decisions 347
  Fever 347
  Orthopedic Judgment 348
  Rare Diseases 349
Politics 349
  Victim's Bill of Rights? 349
  Public Opinion Polls 352
  Prison Sites 352
Games of Chance 352
Food Labels 353
Personal Decision Making and Life Planning 354

THINKING IS A UNITARY CONCEPT

There are very few activities that don't require at least some of the critical thinking skills presented in this book. Why then, a separate chapter on the application of thinking skills, especially since examples and exercises were presented in each chapter? Although each chapter discussed a separate thinking skill, it is important to remember that separating thinking into a number of different skills creates an artificial distinction since all of these skills are interdependent. We use probabilities when we reason; we make decisions when we test hypotheses; we utilize language and memory when we create, and so on. This final chapter is designed to "put thinking back together again." Several real-life examples are presented along with some hints as to how to go about thinking about them. Each example requires that you use several of the skills presented in this book, and thus serves the purpose of integrating the skills that were so neatly compartmentalized in each chapter.

CONSUMERISM AND ADVERTISING CLAIMS

Why a Suntan?

A brochure for a sun tan machine states the following:

> A deep, golden tan has become an accepted sign of beauty, vigor and also success. That healthy, successful look that comes with a good tan just naturally makes you feel better and in turn will make you more successful at anything you do.
>
> A deep golden tan also prevents sunburning to a certain degree. If you are an outdoor oriented person, a rich tan will allow you to stay in the sun longer than usual. Wear your tan like a beautiful coat and feel more secure.

What are the initial premises that are stated as true? Are they true? What conclusions do the sun tan machine manufacturers want you to infer? Do they logically follow from the premises? What methods of persuasion are being used to get you to purchase this product? Is the appeal essentially emotional or rational? What other important considerations have been omitted from this brochure?

They're Not Sunglasses

A recent ad in a magazine read:

> They're Not Sunglasses. They're Gargoyles.
>
> In fact, Gargoyles put sunglasses to shame . . . in looks comfort and performance. Fashionably designed for both women and men, Gargoyles are the beginning of a new era in classic eyewear.
>
> Impact Resistant
>
> Gargoyles' incredible strength was matched against the blast from a 12-gauge shotgun. The unique one-piece polycarbonate Lensframe survived with only a few small dents, proving that Gargoyles greatly exceed the performance standard of average safety glasses.

This ad uses research to support its claim. How good was the research? Does it "prove" the conclusion? What persuasive methods are being used? Was the proper test for safety made?

Mrs. B., There's Suds in Your Closet

A popular television ad runs something like this:

> The voice of an unseen male narrator beings: "Mrs. B., There's suds in your closet."
>
> Mrs. B. emphatically responds, "But that can't be because I just washed these clothes with my usual laundry product."
>
> Announcer: "If you don't believe me try dipping your clothes in a sink of water."
>
> Mrs. B. obediently obeys. When the inevitable suds appears, she exclaims, "Yucky suds! What can I do about them?"
>
> Announcer: "Switch to our low-suds brand for a cleaner, whiter wash."
>
> Mrs. B.: "I'll do that!"

What are the implicit assumptions in this commercial? Was Mrs. B.'s problem a realistic one? Besides switching laundry detergents, how else could she have solved her problem? What stereotypes are being perpetrated in this commercial? What methods are being used for persuasive appeal? Mrs. B. performed an experiment in this commercial. Comment on it.

UTILIZING RESEARCH

The Contraceptive Sponge

After 7 years of experimental and clinical trials with more than 2,000 women, the Food and Drug Administration has approved the use of a vaginal sponge contraceptive device. The sponge acts to prevent pregnancy both by its barrier action and with a spermicide that it contains.

A consumer group, the Empire State Consumer Association, has been working to keep the sponge off the market. The group cited two studies in which mice developed cancer after insertion of urethane sponges similar to the one being marketed. The president of the company about to market the sponge has countered these claims by noting that there are tens of thousands of chemically different urethanes and that the one used in the sponge is different from the one inserted in the mice. He went on to argue that this is like saying all car brakes are unsafe because the brakes on one kind of car are unsafe.

As a consumer of this research information, how would you respond to the dispute? Are the claims of the president of the contraceptive company relevant? Are they likely to be biased? Are they necessarily biased? The Food and Drug Administration has already granted its approval for the sponge to be marketed. How does this information affect the way you evaluate the information? Comment on his analogy between cancer in mice and car brakes. If you are female, would you be willing to use the contraceptive sponge; if you are male, would you endorse its use by a woman you care about? What additional information do you need to make a better informed decision?

Childhood Illnesses

A research team from the University of California at San Francisco has found that there are "twice as many children" limited in the activities that they can perform because of poor health than there were 25 years ago. There are many possible explanations for this distressing news, some of them artifacts of the way that the research has been reported. What are some possible explanations for this statistic?

Reducing Serum Cholesterol

A television commercial, featuring a well-respected senior actor, John Houseman, reports the results of some research that was designed to "reduce serum cholesterol." We are told that a group of adults exercised regularly, reduced dietary fats, and ate a particular brand of margarine. Clinical results showed that they substantially reduced their cholesterol levels following this regime. We are then told to make this brand of margarine part of our daily diets.

What are the implicit assumptions in this commercial? Comment on the way the research was conducted, given what you've been told about it. What does the research tell us about the use of margarine? Why was John Houseman selected to "play" this commercial? (His most famous television role was that of a tough knowledgeable professor.)

LEGAL TESTIMONY

Did You Steal The Money?

A person who takes the witness stand is liable for perjury (violating an oath to tell the truth) if she or he "asserts a falsehood," or, in more common language, tells a lie. However, witnesses are not liable if the words they speak merely *imply* something other than the truth.

Suppose that you are serving on a jury (most of you will at some time) and the prosecutor asks the witness, "did you steal the money?" The witness gives one of the following three answers (Harris & Monaco, 1978, p. 15).

1. I didn't steal the money.
2. I wasn't able to steal the money.
3. I wasn't forced into stealing the money.

Research with these alternatives has shown that in each instance, people remember that the witness claimed that he or she didn't steal the money. Look carefully at each of the three responses to the prosecutor's question. Are they equivalent? Can you infer that the witness is innocent from each of these statements? Using your knowledge of memory and language, discuss the differences among these three responses.

Strike That From The Record

Suppose, once again, that you are serving on a jury. The prosecutor asks the defendant: "Were you at all influenced in what you did on the night of March 5 by the fact that you (a) used to belong to the Ku Klux Klan, or (b) axed 15 people to death in Boston in 1955" (Harris & Monaco, 1978, p. 17).

As you can imagine, the defense attorney would object to this question. The judge would sustain the objection and then instruct the jury to disregard it. Jurors are to act as if they never heard it; they are directed to forget the question. Using what you've learned about memory and the decision-making process, discuss these directions from the judge. If a juror honestly tries to disregard the question, how might it still influence the decision process?

A Probabilistic Determination of Guilt

Suppose that you are an attorney representing a client who is charged with cold-blooded murder. These are the facts: Your client, Rob, is a member of the Young Punks Gang. Many members of the Young Punks were at a party when your client's arch enemy showed up with Rob's girlfriend. A fight ensued and the hated rival was shot dead. After studying all the available information, you conclude that there is only a 30% chance that Rob ever went to the party. However, if had been at the party, there is an 80% chance that he would have shot his arch enemy. How would you use these probability estimates to convince a jury that your client probably is innocent? What is the exact probability that Rob shot his rival? Criminal trials require that a defendent be convicted only if he has been found guilty "beyond a reasonable doubt." Use these probability figures to argue that there is substantial doubt over Rob's guilt.

MEDICAL DECISIONS

Fever

Medicine is a probabilistic science requiring sequential decisions and an acute awareness of trade-offs. A large portion of the pediatric physician's case load involves children with fevers. How should a physician go about diagnosing and treating a child with a fever? While I realize that you have not been to medical school, let's list some of the considerations that should contribute to this decision.

Studies that have examined what pediatricians do when faced with children who have fevers have shown that there are a large number of possible procedures. Physicians must consider the probability that a serious illness is underlying the fever. They must also consider the costs involved in testing for each possible cause. A urine test, for example, is noninvasive and inexpensive, while a lumbar puncture is painful and expensive. What sorts of other considerations should go into a physician's decision for treating a fever? Pantell, Naber, Lamar, and Dias (1980) suggested a heuristic for pediatricians: If infants are less than 3 months old and have a temperature above 38.3°C, then tests for serious underlying infection should be performed. What do you think about the use of heuristics in medicine? Can you think of any other possible medical heuristics? Why is it important for medical professionals to acknowledge trade-offs and assess risks?

Pantell et al. (1980) also reported that the risk of meningitis was more than three times greater for black infants than for white infants. How should physicians use this statistical information?

Orthopedic Judgment

In a study on the development of judgment skills in orthopedic surgery residents, Knafl and Burkett (1975) concluded that the ability to make correct orthopedic decisions is at least as important as the highly developed technical skills the residents learn. While surgical and treatment decisions are often made in groups, evaluations of the outcome are usually not given the same scrutiny as the decision. Here is a brief excerpt from Knafl and Burkett's (1975, p. 401) paper:

> I followed Mitchell on rounds. He begins to unwrap the man's foot and says to me, "Look at that, he's really doing well, see how well it's healing. Only one spot that's a little bit moist. We were able to save almost the entire ball of the foot. That will make it easier for walking." I ask, "Did you do this case?" Mitchell replies, "Yes, I did."

In this example, why should the evaluation have been done by someone other than Mitchell, the surgeon who performed the operation? How could his own expectations have influenced the outcome, either positively or negatively? Resident surgeons receive extensive training in the technical skills that they will need in their profession and almost no explicit training in how to solve problems, make decisions, find creative solutions, or use probabilities. Comment on these missing aspects of medical education.

Rare Diseases

Suppose that you return from a trip to a primitive tropical country with severe cramping, nausea, and vomiting. You are afraid that you may have contracted a rare tropical disease. Your physician tells you that it is probably the flu, since only 3% of the visitors to this mythical country ever contract the rare tropical disease. Suppose further that there is a blood test designed to test for the disease. However, the test is not perfectly accurate. The test will indicate if you have the disease with 85% accuracy. The test also gives false positive results for 20% of the people who do not have the disease. Reluctantly, you agree to the test. The results are positive, indicating that you have the disease. What is the actual probability that the test is correct and you have the disease?

POLITICS

Victim's Bill of Rights?

Politics has been described as "deciding who gets what" and "the process of deciding who decides." Political problems and their resolution often have worldwide impact. The business of running a country is big business. Have you ever wondered how our political decisions are made?

Many of the important decisions are hammered out in committees and then approved or rejected by the president. Different presidents are known to have different "styles" of decision making. No matter what the style, the tasks remain the same. A single individual will need to make many decisions about many different topics. According to Hill et al. (1979), Roosevelt set up all sorts of committees and councils, Eisenhower delegated authority to "save him from immersion in trivia," and Carter used decision balance sheets like the one described in the text. Here is an excerpt from New York Times Magazine (June 8, 1978, p. 30) that was reprinted by Hill et al. (1979, p. 99):

> Last June (1977) Carter was approaching a decision on the B-1 bomber, [and] he was caught in a political cross fire. He met with both sides and called for memos from the Pentagon, the State Department, the National Security Council staff and other agencies. Then he retired to his study to pore over the memos. . . . As if he were back at Annapolis doing a staff study, he wrote out the pros and cons on a yellow legal pad—47 arguments in all. Neatly, in the margin, he assigned numerical weights to each. . . . The arithmetic went against the B-1. So did President Carter. . . . Above all, Jimmy Carter is a problem solving President and that essential cast of mind explains many of his strengths and weaknesses as a leader.

As a voter you are a decision maker. How do you go about making your own political decisions?

One of the best ways that people can gather information on the myriad of political issues that face them on ballots at least twice a year is to read the ballot pamphlets that some states publish and mail to each voter's home address. The pamphlets contain short summaries of each issue and pro and con arguments. One issue that has been hotly debated is the so-called "Victim's Bill of Rights."

Presented here is a portion of the "Analysis by the Legislative Analyst," which is supposedly an unbiased informational summary of the proposition (California Ballot Primary, Primary Election, June 8, 1982, compiled by March Fong Eu, p. 32):

Proposal

This initiative proposes many changes in the State Constitution and statutory law that would alter criminal justice procedures and punishments and constitutional rights. The major changes are summarized below.

Restitution. Under existing law, victims of crime are not automatically entitled to receive "restitution" from the person convicted of the crime. (Restitution would involve, for example, replacement of stolen or damaged property, or reimbursement for costs that the victim incurred as a result of the crime.) In some cases, however, the courts release a convicted person on probation, on the condition that restitution be provided to the victim or victims.

Safe Schools. The Constitution currently provides that all people have the inalienable right of "pursuing and obtaining safety, happiness, and privacy." In addition, statutory law prohibits various acts upon school grounds which disturb the peace of students or staff, or which disrupt the peaceful conduct of school activities. This measure would add a section to the State Constitution declaring that students and staff of public elementary and secondary schools have the "inalienable right to attend campuses which are safe, secure and peaceful."

Here is one of the "Arguments in Favor" of this proposition (p. 34):

It is time for the people to take decisive action against violent crime. For too long our courts and the professional politicians in Sacramento have demonstrated more concern with the rights of criminals than with the rights of innocent victims. This trend must be reversed. By voting "yes" on the Victims' Bill of Rights you will restore balance to the rules governing the use of evidence against criminals, you will limit the ability of violent criminals to hide behind the insanity defense, and you will give us a tool to stop extremely dangerous offenders from being released on bail to commit more violent crimes. Your action is as vital and necessary today as it was in 1978 when I urged Californians to take property taxes into their own hands and pass Proposition 13. If you believe as I do that the first responsibility of our criminal justice system is to protect the innocent, then I urge you to vote "yes" on Proposition 8.

Mike Curb
Lieutenant Governor

Contrast Curb's argument with a selected portion of the "Argument Against" this proposition (p. 35):

> You're afraid of crime—and you have the right to be. If Proposition 8 would end crime, we would be the first to urge you to vote for it.
>
> But Proposition 8 is a hoax . . . there is no other way to describe it.
>
> Some ambitious politicians may think this ill-conceived measure helps them. It will certainly help keep an army of appellate lawyers fully employed . . .
>
> But it will not reduce crime, help victims, or get dangerous criminals off the streets.
>
> As professionals, charged with the responsibility of controlling crime and prosecuting criminals . . . we ask YOU to PLEASE VOTE NO on PROPOSITION 8.
>
> Proposition 8 is so badly written it mangles nearly every aspect of the criminal justice system it touches.
>
> READ the PROBLEMS it will cause:
>
> UNCONSTITUTIONAL INITIATIVE TAKES CONVICTED KILLERS OFF DEATH ROW
>
> Even some of Proposition 8's supporters agree it may be unconstitutional. But unconstitutional laws cause sentences to be overturned. Thirty convicted killers were recently taken off death row because of one unconstitutional line in the 1978 Death Penalty Initiative.
>
> COURTS IN CHARGE OF PUBLIC SCHOOLS
>
> Nobody knows what the so-called "safe schools" section means. The likely result of this provision is constant court battles over compliance. This will no doubt lead to judges running some of our schools. It also could give children the constitutional right to refuse to attend school.
>
> VICTIM RESTITUTION—A MEANINGLESS PROMISE
>
> What good is a right to restitution when so many victims are harmed by criminals who can't pay? (Ever been hit by an uninsured motorist?) Besides, victims already have the right to collect from criminals who can pay.
>
> It may be good politics, but it is bad law.
>
> PLEASE, VOTE NO ON PROPOSITION 8.
>
> RICHARD L. GILBERT
> District Attorney, Yoho County
>
> STANLEY M. RODEN
> District Attorney, Santa Barbara County
>
> TERRY GOGGIN
> Member of the Assembly, 66th District
> Chairman, Committee on Criminal Justice

Given this information, how would you vote on the "Victim's Bill of Rights"? Comment on the label for this bill. What would you call it if you wanted people to vote against it? What are some of the premises and conclusions used by proponents of each side of the issue?

Public Opinion Polls

If you were a senator (or worked for a senator) from a large state who wanted to know which issues your constituency found most important, how would you gather this information? How would you phrase the questions? How would you ask them?

When an elected official claims that "the voters in my district are for issue X," what questions should you ask of him or her about this statement?

Critically review the results of a recent public opinion pool. Can you think of some ways it may have been biased, either deliberately or inadvertantly, or could have been improved?

Prison Sites

There are a number of "hot issues" or "headaches" that continue to be of major political concern. One such issue involves prison facilities. Even when voters have approved funds for new prison facilities, the problem of finding an appropriate site can delay construction for years. It seems that no one wants a prison in her or his community. How would you go about finding an acceptable prison site? Use your problem-solving and decision-making skills. If you come up with a creative solution, why not send it off to the appropriate prison officials.

Alternatively, select a different political problem. There are so many to choose from, you should have no difficulty finding a good one (e.g., where to dump toxic waste, how to raise money for education, what to do about vagrants, when to renovate abandoned houses, etc.).

GAMES OF CHANCE

Keno

Keno is a game of chance with a long history. According to legend, it was used by the Chinese to raise the revenues needed to build the Great Wall of China (Spencer, 1977). Keno is a popular casino game that is played with eighty numbered balls. Before the game starts, players mark which of the numbers from one to eighty they wish to bet on. A total of twenty numbered balls is drawn from a cage by the Keno dealer. If several of the numbers selected by the player are drawn, then the player wins an amount of money determined by a payoff table.

For example, if you select nine numbers and pay $7.00 to play, then you would win $23.00 if five of your numbers are selected, $300.00 if six of your numbers are selected, $2,000.00 for seven of them, $25,000.00 for eight or nine of them.

Let's change the rules slightly for the purposes of illustration. Pretend that after the Keno dealer draws a ball from the cage, she or he returns it before drawing the next ball.

What is the probability that one of the numbers you select will be drawn on the first draw if you decide to select seven numbers?

I strongly advise you to avoid playing Keno because it has a low expected value. Explain what this means.

Russian Roulette

Russian Roulette is another game that I strongly advise you to avoid. As you probably know, it is played with a revolver that has been loaded with one bullet. The other five bullet chambers are empty. Let's not get too realistic and just pretend the following:

A fiendish enemy talks you into playing Russian Roulette. If you pull the trigger three times without firing the bullet, you'll win $3,000.00. However, if you fire the bullet, the entire proceeds of your life insurance policy will go to your fiendish enemy. You'll lose $20,000.00, not to mention your life. What is the expected value of this game in dollars?

Horse Racing

There are eight horses racing in the first race in today's daily double and six horses racing in the second race. What is the probability of winning both races by picking a horse at random from each race?

FOOD LABELS

If it's true that we are what we eat, then we're in trouble. Very often, the words we use to label our foods have little in common with their ingredients. Food manufacturers are required by law to list all ingredients, in order of quantity so that the first item listed contributes the greatest weight to the item, with the other ingredients listed in descending order.

Listed below are the ingredients for five common foods. What are they?

Food 1: Water, hydrogenated coconut and palm kernel oils, sugar, corn syrup, sodium caseinate, dextrose, natural and artificial flavors polysorbate 60, sorbitan monostearate, xanthan gum, guar gum and artificial color.

Food 2: Farina, brown sugar, sugar, dehydrated apples, guar gum, wheat germ, salt, calcium carbonate, cinnamon, natural flavor, malic acid, caramel color, reduced iron, partially hydrogenated soybean oil, niacin, BHA (preservative),

Vitamin A acetate, pyridoxine hydrochloride (Vitamin B_6), mono and diglycerides, thiamin mononitrade (Vitamin B_1) riboflavin (Vitamin B_2), folic acid (a B-Vitamin).

Food 3: Sugar, gelatin, adipic acid (for tartness), disodium phosphate (controls acidity), fumaric acid (for tartness), artificial color, artificial flavor.

Food 4: Salt, hydrolyzed vegetable protein, sugar, chicken fat, (BHA and citric acid), chicken meat, onion powder, natural and artificial flavor, parsley flakes, celery see, tumeric extractives, garlic power, spice, disodium guanylate and disodium inosinate.

Food 5: Sugar, wheat starch, shortening (BHA and BHT), dried corn syrup, salt, nonfat dry milk, artificial flavor, mono and diglycerides, soy lecithin, polysorbate 60, artificial color.

Have you lost your appetite? These are all common foods, gleaned from my refigerator and cabinet. *Food 1:* Cool Whip; *Food 2:* Apple 'n Cinnamon Cream of Wheat; *Food 3:* Strawberry Jello; *Food 4:* Steero Instant Chicken Flavor Bouillon; *Food 5:* Betty Crocker Creamy White Frosting Mix.

A consumer group tried to pass a law requiring that foods be named by their ingredients. For example, if a chicken soup is primarily salt, it would have to be labeled: "Salt Chicken Soup." Similarly, a tomato sauce that is mostly water would have to be labeled "Watered Tomato Sauce." The consumer group believed that this would be a more honest approach to labeling, and one that would make consumers aware of the foods that they're eating. The law obviously never passed.

Look around your own cabinets at home. You'll be surprised at how many foods contain salt, BHA, polysorbate 60, guar gum and mono and diglycerides. Do you know what most of these ingredients are? Of course, preservatives must be added to many of our foods, but as consumers we should utilize the readily available information about ingredients to plan wise diets.

Consider the ingredient and nutritional information found on food packages. How could you change this information so that it would be more meaningful to consumers?

PERSONAL DECISION MAKING AND LIFE PLANNING

The problems we solve and decisions we make have the greatest impact when the topic concerns our own life situations and plans. Here are a few examples.

Health Insurance

Consumers are faced with a vast array of health insurance options—many of them available for the first time. Consider the choice between traditional health plans with a deductible (fixed amount that you must pay before the insurance takes over) that allow you to choose your own physician and health maintenance organizations that cover all expenses, but restrict you to physicians at their own hospitals. How do you choose? You need to weigh the alternatives on a number of considerations. If you are on a very tight budget, the cost advantage of a health maintenance organization will be weighted heavily. On the other hand, if you have a private physician whom you trust and respect, this consideration will weigh heavily for the traditional deductible plan. Decide between these two alternatives.

Financial Investments

Money seems to be a problem for almost everyone. Consider a realistic budget that includes savings. How can you get the most yield from your savings? There are passbook accounts that offer safe, easy access to your money, term accounts that offer higher interest rates and safety, but don't allow you to use your money for a specified term. There are stock market investments and other more creative ways to increase savings. Explore the possibilities and establish a personal financial plan.

Career Decisions

Probably the biggest problem for college students is planning for the next step in their life—what to do after graduation. Assess your strengths and weaknesses, collect information about the job market, graduate and professional schools. Decide which things are important to you and which are not. Consider subjective and objective probabilities of success. Consult academic and career counselors. Use all of your critical thinking abilities to plan well for your life.

Glossary

Acquisition. Used to describe learning in the Human Information Processing model. Also known as encoding, or putting information into memory

Algorithm. A problem-solving procedure that will always yield the solution to a particular problem if it is followed exactly. Compare with heuristic

Ambiguous. An utterance is ambiguous when it can have more than one meaning or underlying representation

Analogies. (in problem solving) Problem-solving strategies in which similarities are noted between two or more situations, while simultaneously discerning that there are also differences; for example, by noting similarities between two different problems, the problem solver may discover that similar solutions are applicable

Anatomy of a Problem. Newell and Simon (1972) have conceptualized all problems as consisting of parts or components—an initial state, a goal state, and solution paths that link the initial state to the goal state.

Antecedent. In "if, then" statements, it is the information given in the "if" clause

Appeals to Pity. A propaganda technique that asks for your compassion instead of appealing to your reason

Appeals to Pride or Snobbery. The use of praise or flattery to get its recipient to agree with a position

Arguments Against the Person. A form of propaganda that attacks the people who support a cause, and not the cause itself

Artificial Intelligence (AI). The attempt to develop intelligent systems with use of computer programs, without attempting to simulate human thought processes

Atmosphere Effect. When reasoning with syllogisms, the quantifiers create a set which causes people to accept certain conclusions as valid. Whenever one or more of the premises is negative, people tend to accept a negative conclusion; whenever one or more of the premises contains the word "some," people tend to accept conclusions that contain the word "some"; whenever both premises contain the word "all," people tend to accept premises that contain the word "all."

Attribute Listing. A method of generating creative solutions in which every characteristic or quality of the item or situation is listed and then examined for possible modification or recombination

Availability Heuristic. A decision making "rule of thumb" that is used when estimates of frequency or probability are made based on the ease with which instances come to mind; for example, many college students believe that there are more professors in America than farmers because they can think of more professors whom they know than farmers.

Band Wagon. A propaganda technique that is persuasive because it relies on the need for conformity. It suggests that since "everyone does it," it must be right.

Base-Rate Biases. A decision-making predilection in which people fail to consider the frequency with which an event occurs in the population (the base rate) when making decisions about its probability. When we are given probabilistic information about unusual events (e.g., a 70% chance of a rare disease), we tend to overestimate the likelihood of the event.

Bayes Theorem. A mathematical formula for determining posteriori probabilities, or the probability that an event has occurred given that we already know something about the occurrence of a related event

Belief Bias. The interference of one's personal beliefs with the ability to reason logically

Belief in the Fairness of Chance. Belief that random processes are self-correcting so that if a random event has not occurred recently, it is believed to be more likely to occur

Biased Discounting. Predilection to discount or reduce the magnitude or probability of risk

Biased Sample. A sample that is not representative of the population from which it was drawn

Bionics. The use of analogies from nature that can be adapted to human problems

Bisociative Thinking. Bringing together two previously unassociated ideas or "frames of reference"

BITCH-100. An acronym for Black Intelligence Test of Cultural Homogeneity. It is an intelligence test written by R. L. Williams with items reflecting Black American culture.

Black-or-White Fallacy. A persuasive technique that offers its recipients the choice between two extreme positions, without considering intermediate or alternative positions

Brainstorming. A group or individual method for generating solution paths for problems. Problem solvers are encouraged to think up wild, imaginative solutions and to defer judgment on these solutions until a later time when they may be modified or combined. The goal is to produce a large number of possible solutions.

Brain Waves. The electrical activity of the brain recorded by electrodes that are attached to a person's skull

Breaking Set. Overcoming predispositions to respond in fixed ways

Bureaucratese. The use of formal, stilted language that is often unfamiliar to people who lack special training

Card Stacking. A propaganda technique that omits important information that might support an unfavored view

Categorical Reasoning. Also known as syllogistic reasoning. Use of the quantifiers "some," "all," "no," and "none" to indicate category membership

Chunking. A memory process in which a number of related items are stored and retrieved as a unit in order to facilitate memory

Cocktail Party Effect. Information that is being attended to will be remembered, while information that is not being attended to will be forgotten or never learned. Phenomenon is named for the way people switch their attention among different simultaneous conversations at large parties.

Cognitive Dissonance. A theory based on the notion that people want their beliefs, attitudes, and actions to be consistent. When they are not consistent an unpleasant internal state arises—dissonance—which needs to be reduced. We reduce dissonance by changing our beliefs and attitudes so that they are in accord with our actions.

Comprehension. The arrival at the speaker's (or writer's) intended meaning by a listener (or reader)

Computer Programs. Explicit, logical, and sequential instructions that tell the computer what to do

Computer Simulation. Computer programs that are written to simulate or imitate human thought, and thus may use processes and strategies that are similar to the ones people use in solving problems

Conclusion. An inferential belief that is derived from premises

Concrete Operations. The third stage in Piaget's theory of intellectual development. Children from approximately 7 to 11 years learn to use symbolic representations of concrete objects. Children at this stage acquire the concepts of conservation, classification, and serial order.

Conditional Logic. Also known as propositional logic. Logical statements that are expressed in an "if, then" format.

Confirmation Bias. The predilection to seek and utilize information that supports or confirms one's hypothesis or premises while ignoring disconfirming information

Confounding. When experimental groups differ in more than one way, it's not possible to separate the effects due to each variable. For example, if you found that teenage girls scored higher on a test of verbal ability than preteen boys, you wouldn't know if the results were due to sex differences or age differences between the two groups.

Consequent. In "if, then" statements, it is the information given in the "then" clause

Conservation. According to Piaget it is a developmental intellectual milestone that is obtained by children from approximately 7 to 11 years old. It is the knowledge that quantities and volumes do not change when the arrangement of their parts or the size or shape of their containers change.

Content Effect. When we reason we do not automatically accept the given premises as true. We use our knowledge about the topic (content) to judge the veracity of the premises and to supply additional information that influences which conclusion we will accept as valid.

Contingency Relationships. Relationships that are expressed with "if, then" statements. The consequent is contingent or dependent upon the antecedent.

Contradiction. A problem-solving strategy with which the problem solver shows that a goal cannot be obtained from the givens because of inconsistencies

Convenience Samples. The use of a group of people who are readily available as participants in an experiment. Such samples may be biased in that they may not be representative of the population from which they were drawn.

Convergent Thinking. The kind of thinking you engage in when you are required to come up with a single correct answer to a question or a problem. Compare with divergent thinking

Convergent Validity. The use of several different measures or techniques that all suggest the same conclusion

Correlated Variables. Two or more variables that are related. See negative correlation and positive correlation

Creative Ideas Checklists. Lists that suggest ways to generate creative ideas by varying a problem's components and relationships among the components

Creativity. The act of producing something that is original and useful

Critical Thinking. Thinking that is purposeful and goal directed. Also known as directed thinking. Compare with nondirected thinking.

Culture Fair Tests. An intelligence test that fairly assesses the intelligence of people from any culture

Culture-Free Tests. An intelligence test in which the test items do not reflect any particular culture. It is not possible to write a test that is totally free of all cultural influences.

Culture-Reduced Tests. Intelligence tests that minimize the influence of cultural background so that they can measure fairly the intelligence of people from any culture

Decision Trees. Branching diagrams that are used to assess mathematically the probability or likelihood of uncertain outcomes

Deductive Method. A method of testing hypotheses in which you formulate a hypothesis that you believe to be true and then deduce consequences from it. Systematic observations are then made to verify if your hypothesis is correct.

Deductive Reasoning. Use of stated premises to formulate conclusions that can logically be inferred from them

Degree of Belief. The use of probability values to indicate our beliefs about the likelihood of an event

Dependent Variable. The variable that is measured in an experiment to determine if its value depends on the independent variable. Compare with independent variable.

Detour Problems. Problems in which the path to the goal is not a direct linear one. Intermediate steps are required that seem directly opposite to the goal.

Dichotic Listening. A laboratory procedure that is used to study attention. Individuals wear headphones with different messages coming into each ear. They are asked to attend to only one message and are tested for their memory of the unattended message.

Dimensional Comparison. A method for calculating a decision from a worksheet. The choice that has "won" the greatest number of considerations would be selected. Compare with overall assessment and ⅔ ideal rule.

Direct Analogy. A problem-solving strategy suggested by Gordon (1961) in which you note similarities between your problem and related problems in other domains

Directed Thinking. Thinking that is purposeful and goal directed. Also known as critical thinking. Compare with nondirected thinking.

Divergent Thinking. The kind of thinking required when a person needs to generate many different responses to the same question or problem. Compare with convergent thinking.

Dove Counterbalance Intelligence Test. An intelligence test with items reflecting Black American culture. It was later developed by R. Williams and renamed the BITCH-100 (Black Intelligence Test of Cultural Homogeneity).

Ecological Validity. Concerns the real world validity or applications of a concept outside of the laboratory

Electroencephalograph. A recording of the electrical activity of the brain that is produced when electrodes are attached to a person's skull

Elimination by Aspects. A decision-making strategy in which choices are sequentially eliminated if they fail to meet one or more considerations

Entrapment. A situation in which an individual has already invested much money, time, or effort and therefore decides to continue in this situation because of the initial investment

Euphemism. The substitution of a desirable term for a less desirable or offensive one

Expected Value. The amount of money you would expect to win in the long run in a betting situation. The mathematical formula for determining expected values is the probability of winning times the value of winning plus the probability of losing times the value of losing.

Extraneous Variables. Variables that you're not interested in that can influence hypothesis testing results

Extrapolation. The estimation of a value from a trend suggested by known values

Extrasensory Perception. Knowledge or perception of events through an "extra" sense and not through the usual ones that operate via our eyes, nose, mouth, ears, and skin

Facts. Information that has a varifiable truth value. Compare with opinion

Failure to Accept the Logical Task. In everyday reasoning we alter the statements we're given according to our personal beliefs and then decide if a conclusion follows from the altered statements. We reject the logical task of deciding if a conclusion follows from the statements as they are given.

Fallacy. An error or mistake in the thinking process

Fantasy Analogy. A problem-solving strategy suggested by Gordon (1961) in which problem solvers utilize their imagination to conceptualize ideal solutions

First Letter Mnemonics. A mnemonic device or memory aid in which the first letters of each word to be learned are combined into a single word

Flowchart. A diagram of the sequence of operations that a computer is instructed to perform

Formal Thought. (Also known as formal operations) The fourth stage in Piaget's theory of intellectual development. It emerges between 11 to 15 years of age when people develop the ability to formulate hypotheses, reason logically, and deal with abstractions.

Forward-Looking Strategy. A problem-solving strategy in which all of the planning is done by considering operations that move the problem solver closer to subgoals and the goal. This method is usually contrasted with working backwards from the goal.

Four-Card Selection Task. A task that is often used to demonstrate confirmation biases. Subjects are required to indicate which of four cards they need to turn over in order to verify a rule about the contents of each side of the card. Overwhelmingly, subjects only select cards that will confirm the hypothesis that they are considering instead of seeking information that would disconfirm their hypothesis.

Functional Fixedness. A type of mental set in which individuals only consider the usual use (function) of objects

Gambler's Fallacy. The mistaken belief that chance events are self-correcting. Many people believe that if a random event has not recently occurred, it becomes more likely.

Generalization. (1) Using the results obtained in a sample to infer that similar results would have been obtained from the population if everyone in the population had been measured. (2) A problem-solving strategy in which the problem is considered as an example of a larger class of problems.

General Problem Solver. A generally applicable computer program developed by Newell and Simon that can solve a wide variety of problems. It utilizes means-ends analysis as its problem-solving strategy.

Gist. The interpretation or meaning of a message

Given/New Distinction. The ratio of known (given) information to new information in a communication. It is the primary determinant of the difficulty of a communication.

Givens. (1) In communication, it is the information already known by both the listener and speaker. (2) In problem solving, it is the information or rules that place constraints upon a problem. The givens are used to find a solution.

Goal State. The desired end state in a problem. When a problem solver finds "paths" to the goal, the problem is solved.

Guilt by Association. The propaganda technique of associating a position or a person with an undesirable position or person in order to create a negative impression. Compare with virtue by association.

Hemisphere. The human brain is divided into two halves, called the right or left hemisphere

Heuristic. A general "rule of thumb" or strategy that we use to solve problems and make decisions. While it doesn't always produce a correct answer, it is usually a helpful aid. Compare with algorithm.

Hierarchical Trees. Branching diagrams that serve as a representational aid in solving problems. Instances of categories provide the "nodes" of the trees.

Hindsight. Reevaluation of a decision after it has been made and its consequences have occurred with the belief that the consequences should have been known before the decision was made.

Hints. Additional information that is given after an individual has begun to work on a problem

Human Information Processing (HIP). A model of human thinking that uses the flow of information through a computer as an analogy of human thought. Like a computer, we take in information from the environment (input), process the information, and then output information.

Hypothesis. A set of beliefs about the nature of the world, usually concerning the relationship between two or more variables

Hypothesis Testing. The scientific method of collecting observations to confirm or disconfirm beliefs about the relationships among variables

Hypothetical Constructs. Terms like learning, memory, and perception that are used as labels for the theoretical processes that underlie human thought and behavior

If, Then Statements. Statements of a contingency relationship such that *if* the antecedent is true, *then* the consequent must be true

Ill-Defined Problems. Problems with many possible correct answers. The difficulty with these problems lies in evaluating possible solutions to decide which is best. Often the goal in these problems is vague or incomplete.

Illicit Conversions. Transformations of the premises in a syllogism into nonequivalent forms (e.g., converting "All A are B" into "All B are A")

Illogical. Reaching conclusions that are not in accord with the rules of logic

Illusory Correlation. The belief that two variables are correlated, when in fact they are uncorrelated

Illusory Validity. The belief that a measure is valid (measures what you want it to) when, in fact, it is not. This belief causes people to be overconfident in their judgments.

Image. A picture-like representation in the mind

Imagery. The use of an internal picture-like representation while thinking

Incubation. A period in problem solving when the problem solver is not actively working on the problem. Sometimes people report that a solution comes to them during this "time out" period.

Independent. In probability calculations, two events are independent when the occurrence of one of them does not influence the occurrence of the other.

Independent Variable. The variable that is selected (or manipulated) by the experimenter who is testing a hypothesis to see if changes in the independent variable will result in changes the dependent variable. For example, if you want to know if people are more readily persuaded by threats or rational appeals, you could present either a threatening message or a rational appeal to two groups of people (message type is the independent variable), and then determine how much their attitudes toward the topic have changed (the dependent variable).

Inductive Method. A method of formulating hypotheses in which you observe events and then devise a hypothesis about the events you observed

Inductive Reasoning. Observations are collected that suggest or lead to the formulation of a conclusion or hypothesis

Initial State. The starting or beginning place in a problem. A problem is solved when the problem solver can find "paths" from the initial state to the goal.

Input. According to the Human Information Processing model of the human mind, input is the initial information that is acquired.

Insight. Sudden knowledge of a solution to a problem. Also known as the *Aha! experience*

Intelligence. A general cognitive aptitude. Most people believe that it is manifested in the ability to reason logically and well and the ability to read with high comprehension.

Intelligence Quotient (IQ). A measure of intelligence. For children, it is calculated by taking the ratio of the child's mental age (MA) to her or his chronological age, then multiplying by 100. For adults, an intelligence quotient of 100 indicates average adult performance, with values greater than 100 indicating above average performance and values less than 100 indicating below average performance.

Interference Theory of Forgetting. A theory of how we forget that attributes forgetting to "interference" or displacement of the to-be-remembered items by other material that has been previously or subsequently learned

Intuitive Scientist. Term coined by Nisbett and Ross (1980) to describe their observation that people commonly use procedures that are similar to scientific methods to verify their personal theories about the causes of social and physical events

Judgment or Evaluation Stage. The third stage in problem solving during which time the problem solver evaluates the solution paths in order to select the best one

Keywords. A mnemonic device or memory aid in which a previously learned list of words or rhymes serve as associates or "hooks" for the to-be-remembered items

Lateral Thinking. Thinking "around" a problem. Used to generate new ideas. Compare with vertical thinking.

Law of Small Numbers. The willingness to believe that results obtained from a few subjects can be generalized to the entire population

Linear Ordering. (Also known as linear syllogism) Reasoning that involves the inference of orderly relationships (e.g., size, position) among terms

Linear Syllogism. See linear ordering

Logic. A branch of philosophy that explicitly states the rules for deriving valid (correct) conclusions

Long-Term Memory. The memory system that retains information over long retention intervals—perhaps as long as a lifetime. Compare with sensory memory and short-term memory.

Marked Adjectives. Adjectives that connote a bias when they appear in a question (e.g., poor, dumb, or small). When asked "How poor is he," it is presumed that the response will be towards the poor extreme and not towards the rich extreme.

Matrix. A rectangular array of numbers that is used as a means of representing problems that contain categories of information

Mean. A measure of central tendency that is calculated by taking the sum of all of the values divided by the total number of values

Means-End Analysis. A general problem-solving strategy in which operations are used to reduce the distance between the problem solver's current state and the nearest possible subgoal or goal

Measures of Central Tendency. Numbers calculated on samples or populations that give a single number summary of all of the values. Three measures of central tendency are the mean, median, and mode.

Mechanization. A routinized approach to solving commonly encountered problems.

Median. A measure of central tendency that is calculated by finding the middle value in a set of scores

Mental Age (MA). A measure of intelligence that signifies that an individual is functioning like the average person of that age. Thus, a mental age of ten years means that the individual is intellectually similar to an average 10 year old.

Mere Exposure Effect. Very often, repeated exposure to a stimulus will enhance your liking for it

Metacognition. Our knowledge about our memory and thought process. Colloquially, what we know about what we know.

Metamemory. A person's knowledge about his or her own memory system; for example, knowing that you have to repeat a series of digits in order to maintain them in memory.

Metaphor. Formed when we note similarities between things that are basically dissimilar. Often used in creative thinking.

Method of Places. (Also known as method of loci) A mnemonic device or memory aid in which a familiar route is selected and the to-be-remembered items are imaged at intervals along the route. At recall, the individual "mentally traverses" the route to retrieve the items.

Mnemonics. Memory aids or techniques that are utilized to improve memory

Mode. A measure of central tendency that is calculated by finding the most frequent value in a set of scores

Model. An "as if" statement. Models of human thought processes are used to help psychologists understand how the mind works.

Mood. Used to classify the premises and conclusions of a syllogism. There are four moods that are dependent upon the quantifiers used in the statements. The four moods are: universal affirmative (all A are B); particular affirmative (some A are B); universal negative (no A are B); and particular negative (some A are not B).

Multidimensional Comparison. When the choices in a decision-making task vary in many different ways, people compare them on all of their differences and combine all of the information to make their decisions. For example, if three homes differed in price, size, and location, the information about these three considerations would be combined when making a choice.

Multidimensional Concept. A concept that varies in many qualitatively different ways

Narrative Stories. A mnemonic device or memory aid in which the words to be remembered are incorporated in a meaningful story

Nature-Nurture Controversy. (also known as Heredity-Environment Controversy) The controversy over whether each individual's intellect and personality depends primarily on his or her genetic make-up (nature) or his or her culture and life experiences (nurture)

Negative Correlation. Two or more variables that are related such that increases in one variable are associated with decreases in the other variable

Neuron. The smallest unit in the nervous system

Nondirectional Thinking. Daydreams, night dreams, and other sorts of thinking that are not engaged in for a specific purpose. Compare with directed (or critical) thinking.

Nonentrenched Tasks. R. Sternberg's term for novel tasks that can be used to assess intelligence by noting how people go about solving them

Objective Probability. Mathematically determined statements about the likelihood of events with known frequencies

Odds. A mathematical method for indicating probability that is commonly used in sporting events

Operational Definition. An explicit set of procedures that tell the reader how to recognize and measure the concept that you're interested in

Operations. The transformations of the "givens" in a problem into solution paths that will solve a problem

Opinion. Information that reflects how an individual or group has assessed a position or product. Compare with fact.

Optimization. In decision making, it refers to making the best possible decision in any situation

Overall Assessment. A method of calculating a decision from a worksheet. The choice with the highest worksheet total would be selected. Compare with dimensional comparison and ⅔ ideal rule.

Paired-Associates Learning. A learning paradigm in which a subject learns to respond to words in a list with other words that have previously been paired with each list word

Paralogic. While people do not behave according to the laws of formal logic, they do utilize logic-like standards when interpreting premises. These logic-like standards are called paralogic.

Particular Affirmative. The mood of statements in a syllogism with the format, "Some A are B"

Particular Negative. The mood of statements in a syllogism with the format, "Some A are not B"

Perceptual Reorganization. Seeing or restructuring a problem in a new way so that attempts to find a solution will be facilitated. Perceptual reorganization is one way to break mental sets or predispositions to respond in fixed ways.

Periodic Review. Memories for highly emotional events are often retrieved and retold many times. The frequent retrieval of these memories can alter how they are remembered.

Perseverence Phenomenon. The tendency to persist in optimistic predictions that favorable events are more likely to occur than unfavorable ones

Phonetic System. A mnemonic device in which a consonant sound is associated with a digit. When a string of numbers is to be remembered, it is converted into a meaningful word using the associated consonants and supplying vowels as needed.

Population. For statistical and hypothesis testing purposes, a population is the entire group of people (or animals or entities) in which one is interested and to which one wishes to generalize

Positive Correlation. Two or more variables that are related so that increases (or decreases) in one variable occur concomitantly with increases (or decreases) in the other variable

Posteriori Probabilities. Probability values that take into account the fact that some events have already occurred. They are used when we know that an event has already occurred and we need to determine its most likely cause.

Personal Analogy. A problem-solving strategy suggested by Gordon (1961) in which you think of yourself as a participant in the phenomenon that you want to understand

Premises. Statements that allow the inference of logical conclusions

Preoperational Thought. The second stage in Piaget's theory of intellectual development. Children from approximately 2 to 7 years develop common concepts like dogs, trucks, and toys.

Preparation of Familiarization Stage. The first stage in problem solving, which includes the time spent in understanding the nature of the problem, the desired goal, and the givens

Primary Mental Abilities. Thurstone's theory that intelligence is comprised of the following seven factors: fluency with numbers, fluency with words, verbal comprehension, memory, reasoning (or logic), visual and spatial ability, and perceptual speed.

Probability. The number of ways a particular event can occur divided by the number of possible outcomes. It is a measure of how often we expect an event to occur in the long run.

Probabilogical. Term coined to label the joint influences of probability and logic on the way we think

Problem Space. All possible paths from the initial state to the goal state in a problem

Production Stage. The second stage in problem solving. During this state, the problem solver produces the solution paths that define the problem space.

Programmed Learning. An approach to learning in which students proceed through a set of materials in "small steps," often with repetition deliberately built into the learning materials

Programmer. A person who writes the instructions that tell computers what to do

Projection Task. A nonentrenched or novel task used to assess intelligence. For example, using a set of rules and symbols, people are required to decide which alternative in a set will be true in the year 2000.

Propaganda. A communication presented by people who want others to believe that what they are saying is true. The purpose of propaganda is to persuade people.

Propositional Logic. See conditional logic

Prospective Research. A method of conducting research in which possible causative factors of an event are identified before the event occurs. Experimenters then wait to see if the hypothesized event occurs. Compare with retrospective research.

Protocol Analysis. A think-aloud protocol is broken into sections so that each can be separately analyzed in order to provide a model of how people think

Prototype. The most common or representative form of an object or method

Psychoanalysis. Refers to Sigmund Freud's theory of psychology and the form of psychotherapy he developed

Psycholinguistics. The branch of psychology that is concerned with the production, comprehension, and usage of language

Psychometrics. The branch of psychology that is concerned with the measurement of psychological traits such as creativity, intelligence, etc.

Quantifiers. Terms like "all," "some," "none," and "no" that are used in syllogisms to indicate category membership

Random Sample. A sample in which everyone in a population has an equal chance of being selected

Random Search. A problem-solving strategy in which all possible solution paths from the initial state to the goal are considered in an unsystematic (random) manner. This method is usually contrasted with *trial-and-error* search.

Reasoning. Has two forms: deductive and inductive. When reasoning deductively, we use our knowledge of two or more premises to infer if a conclusion is valid. When reasoning inductively, we collect observations and formulate hypotheses based upon them.

Regression Toward the Mean. In general, when someone scores extremely high or low on some measure, she or he will tend to score closer toward the mean (average) on a second measurement

Relational Algorithm. A method for generating creative ideas which relies on changing the relations among items using relational words such as on, between, under, and through

Relative Frequency. How often an event occurs relative to the size of the population of events at the time of its occurrence

Reliability. The consistency of a measure (e.g., a test) on repeated occasions

Representativeness Heuristic. A decision making "rule of thumb" in which the determination of a sample's likelihood is made by noting its similarity to a random process. If it "looks like" a random process, it is judged to be more probable than if it appears orderly or patterned.

Repression. According to Freudian theory, the inability to recall traumatic events is mediated by an unconscious process that won't allow the memory to become conscious because it would overwhelm the individual

Restating the Problem. A problem-solving strategy that is best suited for ill-defined problems. It is sometimes easier to find a solution to a problem when it is expressed in different words.

Retention Interval. The time interval between the acquisition of new information (learning) and its retrieval

Retrieval. The act of recalling or remembering information that had been previously acquired (learned)

Retrospective Experiments. After an event has occurred, the experimenter looks backward in time to determine its cause. Compare with prospective research.

Rules. The principles that underlie some problems. For example, solutions to problems that require a prediction of the next element in a series depend on the discovery of their rules.

Sample. A subset of a population that is studied in order to make inferences about the population

Sample Size. The number of people selected for a study

Sapir–Whorf Hypothesis of Linguistic Relativity. The hypothesis that language, at least in part, determines or influences thought

Satisficing. Terminating the decision-making process when an alternative that is "good enough" to satisfy most of the important considerations is found

Self-Fulfilling Prophecy. We tend to act in ways that influence experimental results so that we obtain results that are consistent with our expectations

Sensitive Measures. Measures that are able to detect small changes in the dependent variable

Sensitivity. Responsiveness to the information we perceive through our senses

Sensorimotor Thought. The first stage in Piaget's theory of intellectual development. Infants from birth to 2 years learn about their environment through the sensations that they derive from interacting with objects in the world.

Sensory Memory. Refers to "memories" that last only 1 or 2 seconds. These very brief memories are closely tied to the ways our sensory systems function. Compare with short-term and long-term memory.

Serendipity. A happy, unexpected discovery that occurs when you don't expect it

Set. A predisposition to respond in a particular way. A "rut" in the thinking process that is often difficult to overcome. See "breaking set."

Short-Term Memory. Refers to the limited capacity memory system that "stores" memories that last up to approximately one minute. Also called working memory. Compare with sensory and long-term memory.

Significant Difference. A difference between two groups or observations that is so large that it probably didn't occur by chance

Simplification. (1) A problem-solving strategy in which as much of the complexity as possible is removed from the problem in order to facilitate a solution. (2) A propaganda technique in which complex issues are made to appear simple so as to suggest an intended solution.

Solution Paths. Methods or means for solving problems. Routes that lead from the initial state to the goal state in a problem

Specialization. A problem-solving strategy in which the problem is considered as a special case drawn from a larger set of problems

Split-Half Method. A problem-solving strategy that is useful when there is no a priori reason for selecting among a sequentially organized set of possible solution paths. The method consists of continually selecting a point that is halfway between the present state and the goal as a systematic means for "guessing" at the solution.

Stability. The consistency of test scores when individuals repeatedly take the same test at different times. Sometimes called "test-retest reliability"

Standardization. The computation of norms (or standards) for intelligence tests. Intelligence tests are developed by including those questions that are answered correctly by some proportion of the people in the standardization group.

Standardization Fallacy. This term was coined by Jensen as a label for the notion that tests developed with one racial or ethnic group are invalid for use with a different racial or ethnic group. Many people disagree with this concept. They believe that standardization is a valid concern that creates racial and ethnic biases on intelligence tests.

Standardization Group. The sample used to develop norms (or standards) for intelligence tests

State-Dependent Memory. The ability to recall certain events is facilitated when individuals are in a mood or drug state at recall that is similar to the one they were in at acquisition

Statistic. A number that has been calculated on a sample. (In its plural form it is the branch of mathematics that is concerned with probabilities and mathematical characteristics of distributions of numbers.)

Subgoal. When difficulty is encountered in solving a problem, it can be broken down into several smaller problems called "subproblems." Each subproblem has its own goal, called a "subgoal."

Subproblems. When difficulty is encountered in solving a problem, it can be broken down into several smaller problems or "subproblems"

Subject. A person, animal, or entity who serves as a participant in an experiment

Subjective Probability. Personal estimates of the probability or likelihood of events

Surface Structure. The sounds of an utterance or the outward appearance of a language expression. Compare with underlying representation.

Syllogism. Two or more premises that are used to derive valid conclusions

Syllogistic Reasoning. A form of reasoning that involves quantifiers. Also known as categorical reasoning because the quantifiers indicate category membership.

Symbolic Activity. The deliberate use of visual imagery or other symbolic representation as a problem-solving aid

Synergy. The bringing together of seemingly disparate parts into a useful and functioning whole. Creative thinking often seems to involve such combinations.

Temporal. Used to refer to the passage of time or processes that occur over time

Testimonials. The endorsement of a position or product by respected individuals

Think Aloud Protocols. Verbatim records of what a subject says she or he is doing while solving a problem. They are used to formulate models of how people think.

Thinking. An often unconscious, dynamic, private "activity" that involves combinations of information stored in memory so that we end up with something more than and different from what we started with

Transitivity. The property of numbers such that if $A > B$ and $B > C$, then $A > C$

Tree Diagrams. Branching diagrams that are used to compute probabilities by considering all possible outcomes in a sequence of events

Trial-and-Error. A problem-solving strategy in which all solution paths from the initial state to the goal are searched systematically. This method is usually contrasted with random search.

Turing's Test. A test to determine if computers can think. According to A. M. Turing, if people can't determine if responses to their questions have come from a human or a computer, then it has been demonstrated that computers can think.

⅔ Ideal Rule. A method for calculating a decision from a worksheet. Only choices whose worksheet totals are at least ⅔ as large as the ideal choice would be chosen. Compare with dimensional comparison and overall assessment.

Underlying Representation. The meaning component of language. It's the thought that you want to convey with an utterance. Compare with surface structure.

Unidimensional Comparison. When the choices in a decision-making task vary in only one way, the decision is straightforward and relies only on the differences on this dimension. For example, if three hats were identical, varying only in price, then price alone would dictate the choice.

Universal Affirmative. The mood of statements in a syllogism, with the format, "All A are B"

Universal Negative. The mood of statements in a syllogism with the format, "No A are B"

Unmarked Adjectives. Adjectives that are neutral in that they don't connote a particular direction when they appear in a question (e.g., big, smart, tall). When asked, "How big is he," the response could be a larger or a small number. Compare with marked adjective.

Vagueness. A lack of precision in a communication. A communication is vague if it does not specify enough details for its intended purpose.

Validity. The extent to which a measure (e.g., a test) is measuring what you want it to

(A) Variable. A quantifiable characteristic that can take on more than one value (e.g., height, gender, age, race)

Variability. Term used to denote the fact that people (and animals) differ in the way they respond to experimental stimuli

Vertical Thinking. Thinking that is logical and straight-forward. Used in the refinement and development of ideas. Compare with lateral thinking, which is sometimes considered to be more creative.

Virtue by Association. The propaganda technique of associating a position or a person with a desirable position or person in order to create a favorable impression. Compare with guilt by association.

Wechsler Adult Intelligence Scale (WAIS). An intelligence test for adults designed by David Wechsler. It yields three measures of intelligence: verbal, performance, and full-scale.

Well-Defined Problems. Problems with a single correct answer

Wishful Thinking. People tend to overestimate their chances of success or the likelihood of a desirable outcome

Working Backwards. A problem-solving strategy in which operations are planned that move from the goal to the present or initial state. This method is usually contrasted with the forward-looking strategy.

World View Constraints. Limitations on the way we approach problems placed upon us by our social class, nationality, or political views

References

Adams, J. L. (1979). *Conceptual blockbusting: A guide to better ideas* (2nd Ed.). New York: Norton.

Adler, R. B., Rosenfeld, L. B., & Towne, N. (1980). *Interplay: The process of interpersonal communication*. New York: Holt, Rinehart & Winston.

Alcock, J. E. (1981). *Parapsychology: Science or magic?* Oxford: Pergamon Press.

Allport, G. W. (1954). *The nature of prejudice*. Cambridge, MA: Addison-Wesley.

Anderson, B. F. (1980). *The complete thinker: A handbook of techniques for creative and critical problem solving*. Englewood Cliffs, NJ: Prentice-Hall.

Anderson, J. R. (1980). *Cognitive psychology and its implications*. San Francisco: W. H. Freeman.

Arasteh, A. R., & Arasteh, J. D. (1976). *Creativity in human development*. New York: Schenkman Publishing Co.

Arieti, S. (1978). *Creativity: The magic synthesis*. New York: Basic Books.

Arnheim, R. (1971). *Visual thinking*. Berkeley: University of California Press.

Atkinson, R. C. (1975). Mnemotechnics in second-language learning. *American Psychologist, 30*, 821–828.

Ayer, A. J. (1965). Chance. *Scientific American, 213*, 45–54.

Baddeley, A. D. (1972). Selective attention and performance in dangerous environments. *British Journal of Psychology, 63*, 537–546.

Baddeley, A. D. (1976). *The psychology of memory*. New York: Basic Books.

Barron, F. (1958).The psychology of imagination. *Scientific American, 199*, 151–166.

Barry, V. (1983). *Good reason for writing*. Belmont, CA.: Wadsworth Publishing Co.

Bartlett, F. C. (1932). *Remembering: A study in experimental and social psychology*. England: Cambridge University Press.

Bartlett, F. C. (1958). *Thinking: An experimental and social study*. London: Allen & Unwin, Ltd.

Beardsley, M. C. (1950). *Practical logic*. Englewood Cliffs, N.J.: Prentice Hall, Inc.

Begg, I., & Denny, J. P. (1969). Empirical reconciliation of atmosphere and conversion interpretations of syllogistic reasoning errors. *Journal of Experimental Psychology, 81*, 351–354.

Bell, R., & Caplans, J. (1976). *Decisions decisions: Game theory and you*. New York: W. W. Norton.

Berlin, B., & Kay, P. (1969). *Basic color terms: Their universality and evolution*. Berkeley: University of California Press.

Berliner, H. J. (1977). Some necessary conditions for a master chess program. In P. N. Johnson-Laird, & P. C. Wason (Eds.), *Thinking: Readings in cognitive science*. England: Cambridge University Press.

Block, J. (1976). Issues, problems, and pitfalls in assessing sex differences: A critical review of The psychology of sex differences. *Merrill-Palmer Quarterly, 24*, 283–308.

Bloom, B. S., & Broder, L. J. (1950). *Problem-solving processes of college students*. IL: The University of Chicago Press.

Boillot, M. H., Gleason, G. M., & Horn, L. W. (1979). *Essentials of flowcharting* (2nd Ed.). Dubuque, IA: Wm. C. Brown.

Boring, E. G. (1923). Intelligence as the tests test it. *New Republic, 35,* 35–37.

Bourne, L. E., Ekstrand, B. R., & Dominowski, R. L. (1971). *The psychology of thinking.* Englewood Cliffs, NJ: Prentice Hall.

Bousfield, W. A. (1953). The occurrence of clustering in the recall of randomly arranged associates. *Journal of General Psychology, 49,* 229–240.

Bower, G. H. (1970). Analysis of a mnemonic device. *American Scientist, 58,* 496–510.

Bower, G. H. (1972). Mental imagery and associative learning. In L. Gregg (Ed.), *Cognition in learning and memory.* New York: Wiley.

Bower, G. H. (1981). Mood and memory. *American Psychologist, 36,* 129–148.

Bower, G. H., & Clark, M. C. (1969). Narrative stories as mediators for serial learning. *Psychonomic Science, 14,* 181–182.

Braine, M. D. S. (1978). On the relation between the natural logic of reasoning and standard logic. *Psychological Review. 85,* 1–21.

Bransford, D. (1979). *Human cognition: Learning, understanding and remembering.* Belmont, CA: Wadsworth Publishing Company.

Bransford, J. D., & Johnson, M. K. (1972). Contextual prerequisites for understanding: Some investigations of comprehension and recall. *Journal of Verbal Learning and Verbal Behavior, 11,* 717–726.

Bransford, J. D., & Johnson, M. K. (1973). Considerations of some problems of comprehension. In W. G. Chase (Ed.), *Visual information processing.* New York: Academic Press.

Brehm, J. W. (1956). Postdecision changes in the desirability of alternatives. *Journal of Abnormal and Social Psychology, 52,* 384–389.

Brim, O. G., Jr. (1966). High and low self-estimates of intelligence. In O. G. Brim, Jr., R. S. Crutchfield, & W. H. Holtzman (Eds.), *Intelligence: Perspectives 1965.* New York: Harcourt, Brace & World.

Bross, I. D. J. (1973). Languages in cancer research. In G. P. Murphy, D. Pressman, & E. A. Mirand (Eds.), *Perspectives in cancer research and treatment* (pp. 213–221). New York: Alan R. Liss.

Brown, R. (1958). *Words and things.* New York: The Free Press.

Bruce, D. J., Evans, C. R., Fenwick, P. B. C., & Spencer, V. (1970). Effect of presenting novel verbal material during slow-wave sleep. *Nature, 225,* 873–874.

Bruner, J. S. (1957). On going beyond the information given. In *Contemporary approaches to cognition* (pp. 41–69). Cambridge, MA: Harvard University Press.

Bruner, J. S., Goodnow, J. J. & Austin, G. A. (1956). *A study of thinking.* New York: Wiley.

California Ballot Primary *Primary Election* (June 8, 1982). Compiled by March Fong Eu.

Camer, R. (1983). Dubious fact. *Psychology Today, 17,* 73.

Campbell, S. K. (1974). *Flaws and fallacies in statistical thinking.* Englewood Cliffs, NJ: Prentice-Hall.

Carey, J., Foltz, K., & Allan, R. A. (February 7, 1983). The mind of the machine. *Newsweek.*

Carkhuff, R. R. (1973). *The art of problem-solving.* Amherst, Mass.: Human Resource Development Press.

Carpenter, E. J. (1981). Piagetian interviews of college students. In R. G. Fuller et al. (Eds.), *Piagetian programs in higher education* (pp. 15–22.) Lincoln: University of Nebraska.

Cattell, R. B. (1971). *Abilities: Their structure, growth and action.* Boston: Houghton-Mifflin.

Ceraso, J. & Protivera, A. (1971). Sources of error in syllogistic reasoning. *Cognitive Psychology, 2,* 400–410.

Chapman, L. J., & Chapman, J. P. (1959). Atmosphere effect reexamined. *Journal of Experimental Psychology, 58,* 220–226.

Chapman, L. J., & Chapman, J. P. (1967). The genesis of popular but erroneous psychodiagnostic observations. *Journal of Abnormal Psychology, 72,* 193–204.

Chapman, L. J., & Chapman, J. P. (1969). Illusory correlation as an obstacle to the use of valid psychodiagnostic signs. *Journal of Abnormal Psychology, 74,* 271–280.

Cherry, E. C. (1953). Some experiments on the recognition of speech with one and two ears. *Journal of the Acoustical Society of America, 25,* 975–979.

Clark, H. H., & Clark, E. V. (1977). *Psychology and language: An introduction to psycholinguistics.* New York: Harcourt Brace Jovanovich.

Clark, H. H., & Haviland, S. E. (1977). Comprehension and the given-new contract. In R. O. Freedle (Ed.), *Discourse production and comprehension.* Norwood, NJ: Ablex Publishing.

Cohen, J. (1973). *Psychological probability or the art of doubt.* Cambridge, MA: Schenkman Publishing Co.

Copi, I. M. (1978). *Introduction to logic* (5th ed.). New York: Macmillan.

Cordes, C. (April, 1983). Search goes on for "best" ways to learn science. *American Psychological Association Monitor,* pp. 7–8.

Covington, M. V., Crutchfield, R. S., & Davies, L. B. (1971). *The productive thinking program.* Columbus, OH: Charles E. Merrill Publishing Co.

Crovitz, H. F. (1970). *Galton's walk: Methods for the analysis of thinking, intelligence and creativity.* New York: Harper & Row.

Crutchfield, R. S. (1966). Creative thinking in children: Its teaching and testing. In O. G. Brim, Jr., R. S. Crutchfield, & W. H. Holtzman, *Intelligence: Perspectives 1965, The Terman–Otis Memorial Lectures.* New York: Harcourt, Brace & World.

Cyert, R. M. (1980). Problem solving and educational policy. In D. T. Tuma, & F. Reif (Eds.), *Problem solving and education: Issues in teaching and research,* Hillsdale, NJ: Lawrence Erlbaum Associates.

Darley, C. F., Tinklenberg, J. R., Roth, W. T., Hollister, L. E., & Atkinson, R. C. (1973). The influence of marijuana on storage and retrieval process in memory. *Memory & Cognition, 1,* 196–200.

Davis, G. A., & Roweton, W. (1968). Using idea checklists with college students: Overcoming resistance. *Journal of Psychology, 70,* 221–226.

Davis, G. A., & Scott, J. A. (Eds.). (1971). *Training creative thinking.* New York: Holt, Rinehart and Winston.

DeBono, E. (1967a). *The use of lateral thinking.* Great Britain: Ebenezer Bayles and Son, Limited.

DeBono, E. (1967b). *The five day course in thinking.* New York: Basic Books.

DeBono, E. (1968). *New think: The use of lateral thinking in the generation of new ideas.* New York: Basic Books.

DeBono, E. (1977). Information processing and new ideas—lateral and vertical thinking. In S. J. Parnes, R. B. Noller, & A. M. Biondi (Eds.), *Guide to creative action: Revised edition of creative behavior guidebook.* New York: Charles Scribner's Sons.

deGroot, A. D. (1966). Perception and memory versus thought: Some old ideas and recent findings. In B. Kleinmuntz (Ed.), *Problem solving: Research, method and theory.* New York: Wiley.

DeSoto, C. G., London, M., & Handel, S. (1965). Social reasoning and spatial paralogic. *Journal of Personality and Social Psychology, 2,* 513–521.

Detterman, D. K., & Sternberg, R. J. (1982). *How and how much can intelligence be increased.* Norwood, NJ: Ablex Publishing.

Doherty, M. E., Mynatt, C. R., Tweney, R. D., & Schiavo, M. D. (1981). Pseudodiagnosticity. In R. D. Tweney, M. E. Doherty, & C. R. Mynatt, *On scientific thinking.* New York: Columbia University Press.

Drew, C. J. (1976). *Introduction to designing research and evaluation.* Saint Louis: C. V. Mosby Co.

Duncan, C. P. (1961). Attempts to influence performance on an insight problem. *Psychological Reports, 9,* 35–42.

Duncker, K. (1945). On problem solving. *Psychological Monographs,* (Whole No. 270) 1–113.

Edwards, M. W. (1968). A survey of problem-solving courses. *Journal of Creative Behavior, 2,* 33–51.

Einhorn, H. J., & Hogarth, R. M. (1978). Confidence in judgment: Persistence of the illusion of validity. *Psychological Review, 85,* 395–416.

Erickson, J. R., & Jones, M. R. (1978). Thinking. *Annual Review of Psychology, 29,* 61–91.

Estes, W. K. (1976). The cognitive side of probability learning. *Psychological Review, 83,* 37–64.

Evans, J., St. B. T. (1972). Reasoning with negatives. *British Journal of Psychology, 63,* 213–219.

Evans, J., St. B. T. (1982). *The psychology of deductive reasoning.* London: Routledge & Kegan Paul.

Ferguson, G. (1981). Architecture. In N. L. Smith (Ed.), *Metaphors for evaluation: Sources of new methods.* Beverly Hills, CA: Sage Publications.

Festinger, L. (1957). *A theory of cognitive dissonance.* CA: Stanford University Press.

Festinger, L. (Ed.). (1964). *Conflict, decision and dissonance.* CA: Stanford University Press.

Festinger, L., Riecken, H. W., & Schacter, S. (1956). *When prophecy fails.* Minneapolis: University of Minnesota Press.

Feyerabend, P. (1975). *Against method.* London: Verso.

Fischer, D. H. (1970). *Historians' fallacies.* London: Routledge Kegan Paul.

Fischoff, B. (1975). Hindsight ≠ foresight: The effect of outcome knowledge on judgment under uncertainty. *Journal of Experimental Psychology: Human Perception and Performance, 1,* 288–299.

Fischoff, B., Lichtenstein, S., Slovic, P., Derby, S. L., & Keeney, R. L. (1981). *Acceptable risk.* England: Cambridge University Press.

Fixx, J. F. (1978). *Solve it.* New York: Doubleday.

Flesch, R. (1951). *The art of clear thinking.* New York: Harper & Row.

Fox, L. S., Marsh, G., & Crandall, Jr., J. C. (April 30, 1983). *The Effect of College Classroom Experiences on Formal Operational Thinking.* Paper presented at the 1983 Annual Convention of the Western Psychological Association, San Francisco, CA.

Gardner, M. (1978). *Aha! Insight.* New York: W. H. Freeman.

Ghiselin, B. (Ed.). (1952). *The creative process.* Berkeley, University of California Press. (Reprinted in 1955, New York: Mentor Books).

Gick, M. L., & Holyoak, K. J. (1980). Analogical problem solving. *Cognitive Psychology, 12,* 306–355.

Glucksberg, S., & Weisberg, R. W. (1966). Verbal behavior and problem solving: Some effects of labeling in a functional fixedness problem. *Journal of Experimental Psychology, 71,* 659–664.

Gordon, W. J. J. (1961). *Synectics.* New York: Harper & Row.

Gordon, W. J. J. (1976). Metaphor and invention. In A. Rothenberg, & C. R. Hausman (Eds.), *The creativity question.* Durham, NC: Duke University Press.

Gould, S. (1981). *The mismeasure of man.* New York: W. W. Norton.

Greeno, J. G. (1973). The structure of memory and the process of solving problems. In R. L. Solso (Ed.), *Contemporary issues in cognitive psychology.* Washington D.C.: Winston.

Greeno, J. G. (1977). Process of understanding in problem solving. In N. J. Castellan, Jr., D. B. Pisoni, & G. R. Potts (Eds.), *Cognitive theory* (Vol. 2). Hillsdale, NJ: Lawrence Erlbaum Associates.

Gregory, R. L. (1981). *Mind in science.* England: Cambridge University Press.

Griffiths, D. H. (1976). Physics teaching: Does it hinder intellectual development? *American Journal of Physics, 44,* 81–85.

Gruneberg, M. M., & Morris, P. E. (Eds.). (1979). *Applied problems in memory.* New York: Academic Press.

Guilford, J. P. (1962). Creativity: Its measurement and development. In S. J. Parnes & H. F. Harding (Eds.), *A source book for creative thinking.* New York: Charles Scribner's Sons.

Guilford, J. P. (1967). *The nature of human intelligence.* New York: McGraw-Hill.

Gunther, M. (1977). *The luck factor.* New York: MacMillan.

Hadamard, J. (1945). *The psychology of invention in the mathematical field.* NJ: Princeton University Press.

Halpern, D. F. (in press). The influence of sex role stereotypes on prose recall. *Sex roles.*

Halpern, D. F., & Blackman, S. (in press). Magazines vs. physicians: Information source influences attitudes toward oral contraceptives. *Women and Health.*

Halpern, D. F., & Irwin, F. W. (1973). Selection of hypotheses as affected by their preference values. *Journal of Experimental Psychology, 101,* 105–108.

Halpern, H. (1983). *Development and construct validation of a multidimensional scale of attitudes toward homosexuality.* Unpublished doctoral dissertation. University of Cincinnati.

Hammond, K. R., McClelland, G. H. & Mumpower, J. (1980). *Human judgment and decision making.* New York: Praeger Publishers.

Hanson, N. R. (1958). *Patterns of discovery.* England: Cambridge University Press.

Harris, R. J. (1977). Comprehension and pragmatic implications in advertising. *Journal of Applied Psychology, 62,* 603–608.

Harris, R. J., & Monaco, G. E. (1978). Psychology of pragmatic implication: Information processing between the lines. *Journal of Experimental Psychology: General, 107,* 1–22.

Hayes, J. R. (1978). *Cognitive psychology.* Homewood, IL: Dorsey Press.

Hayes, J. R. (1981). *The complete problem solver.* Philadelphia: The Franklin Institute Press.

Hayes, J. R. (1982). Issues in protocol analysis In G. R. Ungson, & D. N. Braunstein (Eds.), Decision making: An interdisciplinary approach. Boston: Kent Publishing Co.

Henle, M. (1962). On the relation between logic and thinking. *Psychological Review, 69,* 366–378.

Herrnstein, R. J. (August, 1982). I.Q. testing and the media, *The Atlantic, 250,* 68.

Hill, P., Bedau, H., Checile, R., Crochetiere, W., Kellerman, B., Dunjian, D., Pauker, S., & Rubin, J. (1979). *Making decisions: A multidisciplinary introduction.* Reading, MA: Addison-Wesley.

Hitchcock, D. (1983). *Critical thinking: A guide to evaluating information.* Toronto, Canada: Methuen Publications.

Hogarth, R. M. (1980). *Judgement and choice: The psychology of decision.* Chichester: Wiley.

Holt, J. (1964). *How children fail.* New York: Dell.

Huff, D. (1954). *How to lie with statistics.* New York: W. W. Norton & Company.

Hunt, M. (1982). *The universe within: A new science explores the human mind.* New York: Simon & Schuster.

Inhelder, B., & Piaget, J. (1958). *The growth of logical thinking from childhood to adolsecence.* New York: Basic Books.

Janis, I. L., & Mann, L. (1977). *Decision making: A psychological analysis of conflict, choice and commitment.* New York: The Free Press.

Jenkins, J. G., & Dallenbach, K. M., (1924). Oblivescence during sleep and waking. *American Journal of Psychology, 35,* 605–612.

Jensen, A. R. (1970). IQ's of identical twins reared apart. *Behavior Genetics, 1,* 133–148.

Jensen, A. R. (1980). *Bias in mental testing.* New York: The Free Press.

Jensen, A. R. (1981). *Straight talk about mental tests.* New York: The Free Press.

Johnson, D. M. (1972). *A systematic introduction to the psychology of thinking.* New York: Harper and Row.

Johnson-Laird, P. N., Legrenzi, P., & Legrenzi, M. (1972). Reasoning and a sense of reality. *British Journal of Psychology, 63,* 395–400.

Johnson-Laird, P. N., & Steedman, M. (1978). The psychology of syllogisms. *Cognitive Psychology, 10,* 64–99.

Johnson-Laird, P. N., & Wason, P. C. (1970). A theoretical analysis of insight into a reasoning task. *Cognitive Psychology, 1,* 134–148.

Johnson-Laird, P. N., & Wason, P. C. (Eds.). (1977). *Thinking: Readings in cognitive science.* England: Cambridge University Press.

Kahane, H. (1980). *Logic and contemporary rhetoric: The use of reason in everyday life.* (3rd Ed.). Belmont, CA: Wadsworth Publishing Co.

Kahneman, D., & Tversky, A. (1972). Subjective probability: A judgment of representativeness. *Cognitive Psychology, 3,* 430–454.

Kahneman, D., & Tversky, A. (1973). On the psychology of prediction. *Psychological Review, 80,* 237–251.

Kamin, L. J. (1974). *The science and politics of I.Q.* New York: Wiley

Kaplin, M. F., & Schwartz, S. (Eds.). (1975). *Human judgment and decision processes.* New York: Academic Press.

Karplus, R., Karplus, E., & Wollman, W. (1974). Intellectual development beyond elementary school IV: Ratio, the influence of cognitive style. *School Science and Mathematics, 74,* 476–482.

Kerlinger, F. N. (1979). *Behavioral research: A conceptual approach.* New York: Holt, Rinehart and Winston.

Klatzky, R. L. (1980). *Human memory: Structures and processes* (2nd Ed.). San Francisco: Freeman.

Klein, G. A., & Weizenfeld, J. (1978). Improvement of skills for solving ill-defined problems. *Educational Psychologist, 13,* 31–41.

Knafl, K., & Burkett, G. (1975). Professional socialization in a surgical speciality: Acquiring medical judgment. *Social Science and Medicine, 9,* 397–404.

Kneller, G. F. (1965). The art and science of creativity. New York: Holt, Rinehart and Winston.

Koestler, A. (1964). *The act of creation.* London: Hutchinson.

Köhler, W. (1925). *The mentality of apes.* New York: Harcourt Brace and World.

Köhler, W. (1969). *The task of Gestalt psychology.* NJ: Princeton University Press.

Kyburg, H. E., & Smoker, H. E. (Eds.). (1980). *Studies in subjective probability* (2nd Ed.). Melbourne, Florida: Krieger.

Lee, A. M. (1953). *How to understand propaganda.* New York: Rinehart and Company.

Leedy, P. D. (1981). *How to read research and understand it.* New York: MacMillan.

Lewin, M. (1979). *Understanding psychological research.* New York: Wiley.

Lichtenstein, S., Slovic, P., Fischoff, B., Layman, M., & Combs, B. (1978). Judged frequency of lethal events. *Journal of Experimental Psychology: Human Learning and Memory, 4,* 551–578.

Lindsay, P. H., & Norman, D. A. (1977). *Human information processing: An introduction to psychology* (2nd Ed.). New York: Academic Press.

Lipson, S. (1982). *It's basic: The ABC's of computer programming.* New York: Holt, Rinehart and Winston.

Lochhead, J. & Clement, J. (Eds.). (1979). *Cognitive process instruction: Research on teaching thinking skills.* Philadelphia, PA: Franklin Institute Press.

Loftus, E. F. (1975). Leading questions and the eyewitness report. *Cognitive Psychology, 7,* 560–672.

Loftus, E. F. (1979). *Eyewitness testimony.* Cambridge, MA: Harvard University Press.

Loftus, E. F. (1980). *Memory: Surprising new insights into how we remember and why we forget.* Reading, MA: Addison-Wesley.

Loftus, G. F., & Loftus, E. F. (1976). *Human memory: The processing of information.* Hillsdale, NJ: Lawrence Erlbaum Associates.

Loftus, G. F., & Loftus, E. F. (1982). *Essence of statistics.* Monterey, CA: Brooks/Cole Publishing Co.

Loisette, A. (1896). *Assimilative memory or how to attend and never forget.* New York: Funk & Wagnalls.

Lorayne, H. (1975). *Remembering people.* New York: Stein & Day.

Lorayne, H., & Lucas, J. (1974). *The memory book.* New York: Stein and Day (Also published in paperback by Ballantine Books, 1975).

Lowenfeld, V. (1962). Creativity: Education's stepchild. In S. J. Parnes & H. F. Harding (Eds.), *A source book for creative thinking*. New York: Charles Scribner's Sons.

Luchins, A. S. (1942). Mechanization in problem solving: The effect of Einstellung. *Psychological Monographs*, 54:6, (Whole No. 248).

Luria, A. R. (1968). *The mind of a mnemonist*. New York: Basic Books.

Maccoby, E. E., & Jacklin, C. N. (1974). *The psychology of sex differences* (Vol. I). CA: Stanford University Press.

Maier, N. R. F. (1931). Reasoning in humans II: The solution of a problem and its appearance in consciousness. *Journal of Comparative Psychology, 12*, 181–194.

Mandler, G. (1975). *Mind and emotion*. New York: Wiley.

Manis, M., Dovalina, I., Avis, N. E., & Cardoze, S. (1980). Base rates can affect individual predictions. *Journal of Personality and Social Psychology, 38*, 231–248.

Mann, L. (1972). Use of a "balance sheet" procedure to improve the quality of personal decision making: A field experiment with college applicants. *Journal of Vocational Behavior, 2*, 291–300.

Markle, S. M. (1977). Teaching conceptual networks. *Journal of Instructional Development, 1*, 13–17.

Marsh, J. G., & Shapira, Z. (1982). Behavioral decision theory and organizational decision theory. In G. R. Ungson, & D. N. Braunstein (Eds.), *Decision making: An interdisciplinary inquiry*. Boston MA: Kent Publishing Co.

McCauley, C., & Jacques, S. (1979). The popularity of conspiracy theories of presidential assassination: A Bayesian analysis. *Journal of Personality and Social Psychology, 37*, 637–644.

McCracken, D. D. (1965). *A guide to Fortran IV programming*. New York: Wiley.

McGuire, W. J. (1981). The probabilogical model of cognitive structure and attitude change. In R. E. Petty, T. M. Ostrom, & T. C. Brock (Eds.), *Cognitive responses in persuasion*. Hillsdale, NJ: Lawrence Erlbaum Associates.

McKim, R. (1972). *Experiences in visual thinking*. Monterey, CA: Brooks/Cole.

McKim, R. H. (1980). *Thinking visually: A strategy manual for problem solving*. Belmont, CA: Wadsworth.

McKinnon, J. W. (1976). The college student and formal operations. In J. W. Renner, D. G. Stafford, A. E. Lawson, J. W. McKinnon, F. E. Friot, & D. H. Kellog (Eds.), *Research, training and learning with the Piaget model* (pp. 110–129). Norman: University of Oklahoma Press.

McKinnon, J. W., & Renner, J. W. (1971). Are colleges concerned with intellectual development? *American Journal of Psychology, 39*, 1047–1052.

Mednick, S. A., & Mednick, M. T. (1967). *Remote associates test: Examiners manual*. Boston MA: Houghton Mifflin.

Miller, G. A. (1956). The magical number seven plus or minus two: Some limits on our capacity for processing information. *Psychological Review. 63*, 81–97.

Miller, J. E., Jr. (1972). *Word, self, reality: The rhetoric of imagination*. New York: Dodd, Mead.

Mitroff, I. I. (1974). Norms and counter-norms in a select group of the Apollo moon scientists: A case study of the ambivalence of scientists. *American Sociological Review,39*, 579–595.

Moray, N. (1959). Attention in dichotic listening: Affective cues and the influence of instructions. *Quarterly Journal of Experimental Psychology, 11*, 56–60.

Morgan, J. J. B., & Morton, J. T. (1944). The distortion of syllogistic reasoning produced by personal convictions. *Journal of Social Psychology, 20*, 39–59.

Morlock, H. (1967). The effect of outcome desirability on information required for decision. *Behavioral Science, 12*, 269–300.

Morris, W. (Ed.). (1969). *The American heritage dictionary of the English language*. Boston: Houghton Mifflin Co.

Moss, J. (1950). *How to win at poker*. Garden City, NY: Garden City Books.

Mowrey, J. D., Doherty, M. E., & Keeley, S. M. (1979). The influence of negation and task complexity on illusory correlation. *Journal of Abnormal Psychology, 88,* 334–337.

Munson, R. (1976). *The way of words.* Boston, MA: Houghton Mifflin.

Mynatt, C. R., Doherty, M. E., & Tweney, R. D. (1978). Consequences of confirmation and disconfirmation in a simulated research environment. *Quarterly Journal of Experimental Psychology, 30,* 395–406.

Neimark, E. D. (1975). Intellectual development during adolescence. In F. D. Horowitz (Ed.), *Review of Child Development Research* (Vol. 4). Chicago: University of Chicago Press.

Neisser, U. (1982). *Memory observed: Remembering in natural contexts.* San Francisco: W. H. Freeman and Company.

Newell, A., & Simon, H. A. (1972). *Human problem solving.* Englewood Cliffs, NJ: Prentice-Hall.

Nickerson, R. S., & Adams, M. J. (1979). Long-term memory for a common object. *Cognitive Psychology, 11,* 287–307.

Nisbett, R., & Ross, L. (1980). *Human inference: Strategies and shortcomings of social judgment.* Englewood Cliffs, NJ: Prentice-Hall.

Nisbett, R. E., & Wilson, T. D. (1977). Telling more than we can know: Verbal reports on mental processes. *Psychological Review, 7,* 231–259.

Nixon, R. M. (1962). *Six crises.* Garden City, NY: Doubleday.

Norman, D. A. (1976). *Memory and attention: An introduction to human information processing.* New York: Wiley.

Oppenheimer, J. R. (1956). Analogy in science. *American Psychologist. 11,* 127–135.

Orthopharmaceutical Corp. (1979). *The Pill—After Your Doctor Prescribes. . . .* Raritan, NJ.

Orwell, G. (1949). *1984.* New York: Harcourt, Brace.

Osborn, A. (1963). *Applied imagination: Principles and procedures of creative problem solving* (3rd Revised Edition). New York: Charles Scribner's Sons.

Osgood, C. E. (1953). *Method and theory in experimental psychology.* New York: Oxford University Press.

Oskamp, S. (1965). Overconfidence in case-study judgments. *Journal of Consulting Psychology. 29,* 261–265.

Pantell, R. H., Naber, M., Lamar, R., & Dias, J. K. (1980). Fever in the first six months of life. *Clinical Pediatrics, 19,* 77–82.

Papanek, V. J. (1977). Tree of life: Bionics. In S. J. Parnes, R. B. Noller, & A. M. Biondi (Eds.), *Guide to creative action: Revised edition of creative behavior guidebook.* New York: Charles Scribner's Sons.

Parducci, A. (1968). The relativism of absolute judgments. *Scientific American, 219,* 84–90.

Parnes, S. J. (1967). *Creative behavior workbook.* New York: Scribner.

Parnes, S. J., & Harding, H. F. (Eds.). (1962). *A source book for creative thinking.* New York: Scribner.

Parnes, S. J., Noller, R. B., & Biondi, A. M. (1977). *Guide to creative action: Revised edition of creative behavior guidebook.* New York: Charles Scribner's Sons.

Perfetto, G. A., Bransford, J. D., & Franks, J. J. (1983). Constraints on access in a problem solving context. *Memory & Cognition, 11,* 24–31.

Perkins, D. N. (1981). *The mind's best work: A new psychology of creative thinking.* Cambridge, MA: Harvard University Press.

Phillips, H. (1961). *My best puzzles in logic and reasoning.* New York: Dover Publications.

Piaget, J. (1962). Play, dreams, and imitation in childhood. New York: W. W. Norton.

Piaget, J. (1977). Intellectual evolution from adolescence to adulthood. In P. N. Johnson-Laird, & P. C. Wason (Eds.), *Thinking: Readings in cognitive science.* England: Cambridge University Press.

Pickren, J. W., & Gamarra, M. C. (1975). Effects of smoking. In G. P. Murphy, D. Pressman, & E. A. Mirand (Eds.), *Perspectives in cancer research and treatment.* NY: Alan R. Liss, Inc.

Pitt, J., & Leavenworth, R. (1968). *Logic for argument*. New York: Random House.

Poincare, H. (1929). *The foundations of science*. New York: Science House.

Pollio, H. F., Barlow, J. M., Fine, H. J., & Pollio, M. R. (1977). *Psychology and the poetics of growth*. Hillsdale, NJ: Lawrence Erlbaum Associates.

Polya, G. (1957). *How to solve it: A new aspect of mathematical method* (2nd Ed.). New York: Doubleday.

Polya, G. (1962). *Mathematical discovery* (Volume 1). New York: Wiley.

Posner, M. I. (1973). *Cognition: An introduction*. Glenview, IL: Scott, Foresman.

Potts, G. R. (1972). Information processing strategies used in the encoding of linear orderings. *Journal of Verbal Learning and Verbal Behavior, 11*, 727–740.

Prince, G. M. (1970). *The practice of creativity*. New York: Harper.

Quattrone, G. A., & Jones, E. E. (1980). The perception of variability within in-groups and out-groups: Implications for the law of small numbers. *Journal of Personality and Social Psychology, 38*, 141–152.

Reed, S. K. (1982). *Cognition: Theory and applications*. Monterey, CA: Brooks/Cole Publishing Co.

Renner, J. S. (1976a). Formal operational thought and its identification. In J. W. Renner, D. G. Stafford, A. E. Lawson, J. W. McKinnon, F. E. Friot, & D. H. Kellogg (Eds.), *Research, teaching, and learning with the Piaget model* (pp. 64–78). Norman: Oklahoma University Press.

Renner, J. S. (1976b). What this research says to schools. In J. W. Renner, D. G. Stafford, A. E. Lawson, J. W. McKinnon, F. E. Friot, & D. H. Kellogg (Eds.), *Research, teaching and learning with the Piaget model (pp. 174–191). Norman: Okalahoma University Press.*

Renner, J. W., Stafford, D. G., Lawson, A. E., McKinnon, J. W., Friot, F. E., & Kellogg, D. H. (Eds.). (1976). *Research, teaching, and learning with the Piaget model*. Norman: Oklahoma University Press.

Resnick, L. B. (Ed.). (1976). *The nature of intelligence*. Hillsdale, NJ: Lawrence Erlbaum Associates.

Revlin, R., & Mayer, R. E. (1978). *Human reasoning* Washington, D.C.: Winston.

Rosch, E. (1977). Human categorization. In N. Warren (Ed.), *Studies in cross-cultural psychology* (Vol. 1). New York: Academic Press.

Rosenthal, R., & Fode, K. L. (1963). The effect of experimental bias on the performance of the albino rat. *Behavioral Science, 8*, 183–187.

Rosenthal, R., & Jacobson, L. (1968). *Pygmalion in the classroom. Teacher expectations and pupils' intellectual development*. New York: Holt.

Ross, J., & Laurence, K. A. (1968). Some observations on memory artifice. *Psychonomic Science, 13*, 107–108.

Rubinstein, J., & Slife, B. D. (1982). *Taking sides: Clashing views on controversial psychological issues*. Guilford, CT: Dushkin Publishing Group.

Rubinstein, M. F. (1975). *Patterns of problem solving*. Englewood Cliffs, NJ: Prentice-Hall.

Rubinstein, M. F. (1980). A decade of experience in teaching an interdisciplinary problem-solving course. In D. J. Tuma, & F. Reif (Eds.), *Problem solving and education: Issues in teaching and research*. Hillsdale, NJ: Lawrence Erlbaum Associates.

Rubinstein, M. F., & Pfeiffer, K. R. (1980). *Concepts in problem solving*. Englewood Cliffs, NJ: Prentice-Hall.

Salmon, W. (1973). *Logic* (2nd Ed.). Englewood Cliffs, NJ: Prentice-Hall.

Samson, R. W. (1975). *Thinking skills: A guide to logic and comprehension*. CT: Innovative Science, Inc.

Sapir, E. (1960). *Culture, language and personality*. Berkeley: University of California Press.

Savage, D. (April 14, 1983). Math scores of students up in national test. *Los Angeles Times*, pp. 1, 19.

Scheerer, M. (1963). Problem solving. *Scientific American, 208*, 118–128.

Schoenfeld, A. H. (1979). Can heuristics be taught? In J. Lochhead, & J. Clement (Eds.), *Cognitive process instruction: Research on teaching thinking skills*. Philadelphia: Franklin Institute.

Schoenfeld, A. H., & Herrmann, D. J. (1982). Problem perception and knowledge structure in expert and novice mathematical problem solvers. *Journal of Experimental Psychology: Learning, Memory, and Cognition, 8*, 484–494.

Schwartz, B. (1982). Reinforcement-Induced behavioral stereotypy: How not to teach people to discover rules. *Journal of Experimental Psychology: General, 3*, 23–59.

Scriven, M. (1976). *Reasoning*. New York: McGraw-Hill.

Seamon, J. G. (Ed.). (1980). *Human memory: Contemporary readings*. New York: Oxford University Press.

Sexton, T. G., & Poling, D. R. (1973). *Can intelligence be taught?*. Bloomington, IN: Phi Delta Kappa Educational Foundation.

Shubik, M. (1971). The dollar auction game: A paradox in noncooperative behavior and escalation. *Journal of Conflict Resolution, 15*, 109–111.

Siegler, R. S. (1978). The origins of scientific reasoning. In R. S. Siegler (Ed.), *Children's thinking: What develops?* (pp. 109–149). Hillsdale, NJ: Lawrence Erlbaum Associates.

Siegler, R. S. (Ed.). (1978). *Children's thinking: What develops?*. Hillsdale, NJ: Lawrence Erlbaum Associates.

Sime, M. (1973). *A child's eye view: Piaget for young parents and teachers*. New York: Harper & Row.

Simon, H. A. (1977). The psychology of scientific problem solving. In H. A. Simon (Ed.), *Models of discovery*. Dordrecht, Holland: D. Reidel.

Simpson, M. E., & Johnson, D. M. (1966). Atmosphere and conversion errors in syllogistic reasoning. *Journal of Experimental Psychology, 72*, 197–200.

Skinner, B. J. (1968). *The technology of teaching*. New York: Appleton-Century-Crofts.

Slobin, D. I. (1974). *Psycholinguistics*. London: Scott, Foresman and Co.

Slovic, P., & Lichtenstein, S. (1968). Relative importance of probabilities and payoffs in risk taking. *Journal of Experimental Psychology Monograph, 78*, (3, Pt. 2).

Smedslund, J. (1963). The concept of correlation in adults. *Scandinavian Journal of Psychology, 44*, 165–173.

Snyder, M., & Uranowitz, S. W. (1978). Reconstructing the past: Some cognitive consequences of person perception. *Journal of Personality and Social Psychology, 36*, 941–950.

Sorensen, T. C. (1965). *Kennedy*. New York: Harper & Row.

Sparke, W., Taines, B., & Sidell, S. (1975). *Doublespeak: Language for sale*. New York: Harper's College Press.

Spencer, D. (1977). *Game playing with basic*. Rochelle Park, NJ: Hayden Book Co.

Stein, M. I. (1974). *Stimulating creativity: Individual procedures* (Vol. I.). New York: Academic Press.

Stein, M. (1975). *Stimulating creativity: Group procedures* (Vol. II). New York: Academic Press.

Sternberg, R. J. (1977). Component processes in analogical reasoning. *Psychological Review, 84*, 353–373.

Sternberg, R. J. (1981). Intelligence and nonentrenchment. *Journal of Educational Psychology. 73*, 1–16.

Sternberg, R. J. (1982). Who's intelligent? *Psychology Today, 16*, pp. 30–33, 35–36, 37–39.

Sternberg, R. J., & Detterman, D. K. (Eds.). (1979). *Human intelligence: Perspective on its theory and measurement*. Norwood, NJ: Ablex.

Summers, G. J. (1968). *New puzzles in logical deduction*. New York: Dover Publications.

Summers, G. J. (1972). *Test your logic: 50 puzzles in deductive reasoning*. New York: Dover Publications, Inc.

Taplin, J. E., & Staudenmayer, H. (1973). Interpretation of abstract conditional sentences in deductive reasoning. *Journal of Verbal Learning and Verbal Behavior, 12*, 530–542.

Teger, A. I. (1979). *Too much invested to quit: The psychology of escalation of conflict.* New York: Pergamon Press.

Thomas, S. (1977). *Practical reasoning in natural language.* Englewood Cliffs, NJ: Prentice-Hall.

Thouless, R. H. (1932). *Straight and crooked thinking.* New York: Simon & Schuster.

Thouless, R. H. (1939). *Tests of logical reasoning: How to think straight.* New York: Simon and Schuster.

Thurstone, L. L. (1938). *Primary mental abilities.* Psychometric Monographs, No. 1. IL: University of Chicago Press.

Treisman, A. M. (1964). Verbal cues, language, and meaning in selective attention. *American Journal of Psychology, 77,* 206–219.

Tuma, D. J., & Reif, F. (Eds.). (1980). *Problem solving and education: Issues in teaching and research.* Hillsdale, NJ: Lawrence Erlbaum Associates.

Turing, A. (1950). Computing machinery and intelligence. *Mind, 59,* 433–460.

Tversky, A. (1969). Intransitivity of preferences. *Psychological Review, 76,* 31–48.

Tversky, A. (1972). Elimination by aspects. A theory of choice. *Psychological Review, 79,* 281–299.

Tversky, A., & Kahneman, D. (1971). Belief in the law of small numbers. *Psychological Bulletin, 76,* 104–110.

Tversky, A., & Kahneman, D. (1974). Judgment under uncertainty: Heuristics and biases. *Science, 185,* 1124–1131.

Tversky, A., & Kahneman, D. (1981). The framing of decisions and the psychology of choice. *Science, 211,* 453–458.

Ungson, G. R., & Braunstein, D. N. (Eds.). (1982). *Decision making: An interdisciplinary inquiry.* Boston: Kent Publishing Co.

Vernon, P. (1970). *Creativity.* Harmondsworth, England: Penguin Books.

Wallas, G. (1926). *The art of thought.* New York: Harcourt, Brace & World.

Wallsten, T. S. (1980). *Cognitive processes in choice and decision behavior.* Hillsdale, NJ: Lawrence Erlbaum Associates.

Wanous, J. P. (1973). Effects of a realistic job preview on job acceptance, job attitudes, and job survival. *Journal of Applied Psychology, 58,* 327–332.

Wason, P. C. (1960). On the failure to eliminate hypotheses in a conceptual task. *Quarterly Journal of Experimental Psychology, 12,* 129–140.

Wason, P. C. (1968). On the failure to eliminate hypotheses: A second look. In P. C. Wason, & P. N. Johnson-Laird (Eds.), *Thinking and reasoning.* Baltimore: Penguin.

Wason, P. C. (1969). Structure simplicity and psychological complexity. *Bulletin of the British Psychological Society, 22,* 281–284.

Wason, P. C., & Johnson-Laird, P. N. (Eds.). (1968). *Thinking and reasoning.* Harmondsworth, England: Penguin Books.

Wason, P. C., & Johnson-Laird, P. N. (1972). *Psychology of Reasoning.* Cambridge MA: Harvard University Press.

Weisberg, R., DiCamillo, M., & Phillips, D. (1978). Transferring old associations to new situations: A nonautomatic process. *Journal of Verbal Learning and Verbal Behavior, 17,* 219–228.

Weizenbaum, J. (1966). ELIZA—A computer program for the study of natural language communication between man and machine. *Communications of the Association for Computing Machinery, 9,* 36–43.

Wertheimer, M. (1959). *Productive thinking* (2nd Ed.). New York: Harper.

Wheeler, D. D., & Janis, I. L. (1980). *A practical guide for making decisions.* New York: The Free Press.

Whimbey, A. (1976). *Intelligence can be taught.* New York: Bantam.

Whimbey, A., & Lochhead, J. (1982). *Problem solving and comprehension* (3rd Ed.). Philadelphia: Franklin Institute Press.

White, D. (1975). *Decision methodology*. New York: Wiley.

Whiting, C. S. (1958). *Creative thinking*. New York: Reinhold.

Whorf, B. (1956). *Language, thought, and reality*. Cambridge, MA: M.I.T. Press.

Wickelgren, W. (1974). *How to solve problems*. San Francisco: W. H. Freeman and Co.

Wicker, A. W. (1981). *Getting out of our conceptual ruts: Strategies for generating new perspectives on familiar research problems*. Paper presented at the 1981 Annual Convention of the Western Psychological Association, Los Angeles.

Williams, R. L. (1972). *The BITCH Test (Black Intelligence Test of Cultural Homogeneity)*. St. Louis, MO: Black Studies Programs, Washington University.

Wilson, T. D., & Nisbett, R. E. (1978). The accuracy of verbal reports about the effects of stimuli on evaluations and behavior. *Social Psychology, 41*, 118–131.

Woodworth, R. S., & Sells, S. B. (1935). An atmosphere effect in formal syllogistic reasoning. *Journal of Experimental Psychology, 18*, 451–460.

Wright, L. (1982). *Better reasoning: Techniques for handling argument, evidence and abstraction*. New York: Holt, Rinehart and Winston.

Yates, F. A. (1966). *The art of memory*. London: Routledge & Kegan Paul.

Zechmeister, E. B., & Nyberg, S. E. (1982). *Human Memory: An introduction to research and theory*. Monterey, CA: Brooks, Cole Publishing Co.

Author Index

Numbers in *italics* indicate pages with complete bibliographic information.

A

Adams, J. L., 200, 201, 208, 337, 342, *373*
Adams, M. J., 249, *380*
Adler, R. B., 48, *373*
Alcock, J. E., 153, 158, *373*
Allan, R. A., 15, *374*
Allport, G. W., 100, *373*
Anderson, B. F., 71, 277, *373*
Anderson, J. R., 69, *373*
Arasteh, A. R., 316, 342, *373*
Arasteh, J. D., 316, 342, *373*
Arieti, S., 342, *373*
Arnheim, R., 23, *373*
Atkinson, R. C., 262, 271, 277, *373, 375*
Austin, G. A., 91, *374*
Avis, N. E., 146, *379*
Ayer, A. J., 158, *373*

B

Baddeley, A. D., 264, 278, 327, *373*
Barlow, J. M., 48, *381*
Barron, F., 327, *373*
Barry, V., 48, *373*
Bartlett, F. C., 24, 253, 279, *373*
Beardsley, M. C., 19, *373*
Bedau, H., 241, 349, *377*
Begg, I., 66, *373*
Bell, R., 241, *373*
Berlin, B., 28, *373*
Berliner, H. J., 13, *373*
Biondi, A. M., 20, 319, 341, *380*
Blackman, S., 124, *377*
Block, J., 297, *373*
Bloom, B. S., 19, *373*
Boillot, M. H., 91, *373*
Boring, E. G., 285, *374*
Bourne, L. E., 4, 24, *374*
Bousfield, W. A., 261, *374*
Bower, G. H., 261, 266, 270, 274, *374*
Braine, M. D. S., 70, 71, *77*
Bransford, J. D., 193, 254, 256, 267, 279, *374, 380*
Braunstein, D. N., 241, *383*
Brehm, J. W., 236, *374*
Brim, O. G., Jr., 282, *374*
Broder, L. J., 19, *373*
Bross, I. D. J., 11, *374*
Brown, R., 48, *374*
Bruce, D. J., 258, *374*
Bruner, J. S., 4, 91, 258, *374*
Burkett, G., 348, *378*

C

Camer, R., 137, *374*
Campbell, S. K., 158, *374*
Caplans, J., 241, *373*
Cardoze, S., 146, *379*
Carey, J., 15, *374*
Carkhuff, R. R., 15, 234, 241, *374*
Carpenter, E. J., 19, *374*
Cattell, R. B., 239, 294, 312, *374*
Ceraso, J., 64, 66, *374*
Chapman, J. P., 65, 106, 108, *374*
Chapman, L. J., 65, 106, 108, *374*
Checile, R., 241, 349, *377*
Cherry, E. C., 249, *375*
Clark, E. V., 48, 279, *375*
Clark, H. H., 31, 48, 279, *375*
Clark, M. C., 261, 274, *374*
Clement, J., 6, 24, *378*
Cohen, J., 136, *375*
Combs, B., 139, 140, *378*
Copi, I. M., 158, *375*
Cordes, C., 13, *375*
Covington, M. V., 327, *375*
Crandall, Jr., J. C., 6, 300, *376*
Crochetiere, W., 241, 349, *377*
Crovitz, H. F., 279, 333, *375*
Crutchfield, R. S., 327, 328, *375*
Cyert, R. M., 6, *375*

D

Dallenbach, K. M., 258, *377*
Darley, C. F., 262, *375*
Davis, G. A., 331, 342, *375*
Davis, L. B., 327, *375*
DeBono, E., 24, 197, 318, 338, 342, *375*
deGroot, A. D., 256, *375*
Denny, J. P., 66, *373*
Derby, S. L., 158, *376*
DeSoto, C. G., 72, *375*
Detterman, D. K., 312, *375, 382*
Dias, J. K., 348, *380*
DiCamillo, M., 192, *383*
Doherty, M. E., 107, 143, 216, *375, 379, 380*
Dominowski, R. L., 4, 24, *374*
Dovalina, I., 146, *379*
Drew, C. J., 116, *375*
Duncan, C. P., 174, 175, 191, *375*
Duncker, K., 9, 192, 196, 197, *375*
Dunjian, D., 241, 349, *377*

E

Edwards, M. W., 329, *375*
Einhorn, H. J., 115, *376*
Ekstrand, B. R., 4, 24, *374*
Erickson, J. R., 24, *376*
Estes, W. K., 158, *376*
Evans, C. R., 258, *374*
Evans, J. St., B. T., 79, 92, *376*

F

Fenwick, P. B. C., 258, *374*
Ferguson, G., 30, *376*
Festinger, L., 236, 241, *376*
Feyerabend, P., 116, *376*
Fine, H. J., 48, *381*
Fischer, D. H., 152, *376*
Fischoff, B., 139, 140, 158, 237, *376, 378*
Fixx, J. F., 185, 201, 208, *376*
Flesch, R., 23, 48, *376*
Fode, K. L., 111, *381*
Foltz, K., 15, *374*
Fox, L. S., 6, 300, *376*
Franks, J. J., 193, *380*
Friot, F. E., 313, *381*

G

Gamarra, M. C., 116, *380*
Gardner, M., 207, *376*
Ghiselin, B., 342, *376*
Gick, M. L., 195, *376*
Gleason, G. M., 91, *373*
Glucksberg, S., 9, *376*
Goodnow, J. J., 91, *374*
Gordon, W. J. J., 196, 319, 336, 361, 362, 367, *376*
Gould, S., 313, *376*
Greeno, J. G., 167, *376*
Gregory, R. L., 298, 312, *376*
Griffiths, D. H., 17, *376*
Gruneberg, M. M., 279, *376*
Guilford, J. P., 322, 323, *376*
Gunther, M., 153, 158, *376*

H

Hadamard, J., 195, *377*
Halpern, D. F., 124, 148, 221, 252, *377*
Halpern, H., 94, *377*

Hammond, K. R., 241, *377*
Handel, S., 72, *375*
Hanson, N. R., 255, *377*
Harding, H. F., 342, *380*
Harris, R. J., 34, 346, 347, *377*
Haviland, S. E., 31, *375*
Hayes, J. R., 12, 161, 208, *377*
Henle, M., 53, *377*
Hernstein, R. J., 313, *377*
Herrmann, D. J., 208, *382*
Hill, P., 241, 349, *377*
Hitchcock, D., 49, 81, *377*
Hogarth, R. M., 115, 158, 222, 241, *376, 377*
Hollister, L. E., 262, *375*
Holt, J., 250, *377*
Holyoak, K. J., 195, *376*
Horn, L. W., 91, *373*
Huff, D., 149, 158, *377*
Hunt, M., 53, 70, *377*

I

Inhelder, B., 302, *377*
Irwin, F. W., 148, 221, *377*

J

Jacklin, C. N., 296, *379*
Jacobson, L., 116, *381*
Jacques, S., 146, *379*
Janis, I. L., 224, 230, 236, 241, *377, 383*
Jenkins, J. G., 258, *377*
Jensen, A. R., 288, 290, 298, 312, *377*
Johnson, D. M., 24, 69, *377, 382*
Johnson, M. K., 254, 256, *374*
Johnson-Laird, P. N., 62, 80, 81, 91, 241, *377, 383*
Jones, E. E., 102, *381*
Jones, M. R., 24, *376*

K

Kahane, H., 49, 53, 158, *378*
Kahneman, D., 29, 102, 135, 147, 158, 217, 218, 220, 221, 225, 235, *378, 378*
Kamin, L. J., 312, *378*
Kaplin, M. F., 241, *378*
Karplus, E., 311, *378*
Karplus, R., 311, *378*
Kay, P., 28, *373*
Keeley, S. M., 107, *379*
Keeney, R. L., 158, *376*
Kellerman, B., 241, 349, *377*
Kellogg, D. H., 313, *381*
Kerlinger, F. N., 116, *378*
Klatzky, R. L., 278, *378*
Klein, G. A., 167, 208, *378*
Knafl, K., 348, *378*
Kneller, G. F., 319, *378*
Koestler, A., 9, 24, *378*
Köhler, W., 164, 170, *378*
Kyburg, H. E., 158, *378*

L

Lamar, R., 348, *380*
Laurence, K. A., 273, *381*
Lawson, A. E., 313, *381*
Layman, M., 139, 140, *378*
Leavenworth, R., 26, *380*
Lee, A. M., 49, *378*
Leedy, P. D., 94, 116, *378*
Legrenzi, M., 81, *377*
Legrenzi, P., 81, *377*
Lewin, M., 116, *378*
Lichtenstein, S., 139, 140, 158, *376, 378, 382*
Lindsay, P. H., 279, *378*
Lipson, S., 91, *378*
Loftus, E. F., 30, 135, 252, 268, 278, *378*
Loftus, G. F., 135, 268, *378*
Loisette, A., 270, *378*
London, M., 72, *375*
Lorayne, H., 268, 271, 279, *378*
Lowenfeld, V., 327, *378*
Lucas, J., 268, *378*
Luchins, A. S., 202, *379*
Luria, A. R., 279, *379*

M

Maccoby, E. E., 296, *379*
Maier, N. R. F., 191, *379*
Mandler, G., 4, *379*
Manis, M., 146, *379*
Mann, L., 224, 230, 235, 236, 241, *377, 379*
Markle, S. M., 21, *379*
Marsh, G., 6, 300, *376*
Marsh, J. G., 235, *379*
Mayer, R. E., 91, *381*
McCauley, C., 146, *379*
McClelland, G. H., 241, *377*
McCracken, D. D., 83, 146, *379*

McGuire, W. J., 79, *379*
McKim, R. H., 23, 338, *379*
McKinnon, J. W., 3, 306, 313, *379, 381*
Mednick, M. T., 324, *379*
Mednick, S. A., 324, *379*
Miller, G. A., 228, *379*
Miller, J. E., Jr., 26, 27, 48, *379*
Mitroff, I. I., 148, *379*
Monaco, G. E., 346, 347, *377*
Moray, N., 249, *379*
Morgan, J. J. B., 69, 70, *379*
Morlock, H., 148, *379*
Morris, P. E., 279, *376*
Morris, W., 36, *379*
Morton, J. T., 69, 70, *379*
Moss, J., 257, *379*
Mowrey, J. D., 107, *379*
Mumpower, J., 241, *377*
Munson, R., 4, 106, *379*
Mynatt, C. R., 143, 216, *375, 380*

N

Naber, M., 348, *380*
Neimark, E. D., 301, *380*
Neisser, U., 243, 279, *380*
Newell, A., 161, 162, 184, 206, 357, *380*
Nickerson, R. S., 249, *380*
Nisbett, R., 16, 94, 117, 158, 364, *380, 384*
Nixon, R. M., 210, *380*
Noller, R. B., 20, 319, 341, *380*
Norman, D. A., 268, 269, 279, *378, 380*
Nyberg, S. E., 278, *384*

O

Oppenheimer, J. R., 335, *380*
Orwell, G., 4, 27, *380*
Osborn, A., 193, 315, 329, 342, *380*
Osgood, C. E., 255, *380*
Oskamp, S., 110, *380*

P

Pantell, R. H., 348, *380*
Papanek, V. J., 337, *380*
Parducci, A., 332, *380*
Parnes, S. J., 20, 319, 332, 341, 342, *380*
Pauker, S., 241, 349, *377*
Perfetto, G. A., 193, *380*
Perkins, D. N., 24, *380*
Pfeiffer, K. R., 157, 158, 208, *381*
Phillips, D., 192, *383*
Phillips, H., 177, 208, *380*
Piaget, J., 263, 264, 301, 302, *377, 380*
Pickren, J. W., 116, *380*
Pitt, J., 26, *380*
Poincare, H., 163, *380*
Poling, D. R., 299, *382*
Pollio, H. F., 48, *381*
Pollio, M. R., 48, *381*
Polya, G., 78, 161, 166, 167, 208, *381*
Posner, M. I., 182, *381*
Potts, G. R., 73, *381*
Prince, G. M., 317, *381*
Protivera, A., 64, 66, *374*

Q

Quattrone, G. A., 102, *381*

R

Reed, S. K., 206, *381*
Reif, F., 24, *383*
Renner, J. W., 3, 306, 307, 313, *379, 381*
Resnick, L. B., 312, *381*
Revlin, R., 91, *381*
Riecken, H. W., 241, *376*
Rosch, E., 28, *381*
Rosenfeld, L. B., 48, *373*
Rosenthal, R., 111, 116, *381*
Ross, J., 273, *381*
Ross, L., 94, 117, 158, 364, *380*
Roth, W. T., 262, *375*
Roweton, W., 331, *375*
Rubin, J., 241, 349, *377*
Rubinstein, J., 6, 157, 158, 208, 300, 312, *381*

S

Salmon, W., 91, *381*
Samson, R. W., 300, 313, *381*
Sapir, E., 27, *381*
Savage, D., 18, *381*
Schachter, S., 241, *376*
Scheerer, M., 205, 206, *381*
Schiavo, M. D., 143, *375*
Schoenfeld, A. H., 166, 208, *381, 382*
Schwartz, B., 18, *382*

Schwartz, S., 241, *378*
Scott, J. A., 342, *375*
Scriven, M., 82, *382*
Seamon, J. G., 279, *382*
Sells, S. B., 66, *384*
Sexton, T. G., 299, *382*
Shapira, Z., 235, *379*
Shubik, M., 222, *382*
Sidell, S., 48, *382*
Siegler, R. S., 116, *382*
Sime, M., 301, 305, 313, *382*
Simon, H. A., 161, 162, 162, 184, 206, 357, *380, 382*
Simpson, M. E., 69, *382*
Skinner, B. J., 18, *382*
Slife, B. D., 312, *381*
Slobin, D. I., 48, *382*
Slovic, P., 139, 140, 158, *378, 378, 382*
Smedslund, J., 213, *382*
Smoker, H. E., 158, *378*
Snyder, M., 251, *382*
Sorensen, T. C., 210, *282*
Sparke, W., 48, *382*
Spencer, D., 352, *382*
Spencer, V., 258, *374*
Stafford, D. G., 313, *381*
Staudenmayer, H., 77, *382*
Steedman, M., 62, *377*
Stein, M. I., 342, *382*
Sternberg, R. J., 282, 283, 293, 309, 312, 335, *375, 382*
Summers, G. J., 91, *382*

T

Taines, B., 48, *382*
Taplin, J. E., 77, *382*
Teger, A. I., 198, *382*
Thomas, S., 241, *383*
Thouless, R. H., 48, 91, *383*
Thurstone, L. L., 299, *383*
Tinklenberg, J. R., 262, *375*
Towne, N., 48, *373*
Treisman, A. M., 249, *383*
Tuma, D. J., 24, *383*
Turing, A., 14, *383*
Tversky, A., 29, 102, 135, 147, 158, 217, 218, 220, 221, 225, 235, *378, 383*
Tweney, R. D., 143, 216, *375, 380*

U

Ungson, G. R., 241, *383*
Uranowitz, S. W., 251, *382*

V

Vernon, P., 337, *383*

W

Wallas, G., 163, *383*
Wallsten, T. S., 241, *383*
Wanous, J. P., 235, *383*
Wason, P. C., 79, 80, 81, 214, 241, *283, 377*
Weisberg, R. W., 9, 192, *376, 383*
Weizenbaum, J., 13, *383*
Weizenfeld, J., 167, 208, *378*
Wertheimer, M., 165, *383*
Wheeler, D. D., 241, *383*
White, D., 241, *383*
Whiting, C. S., 331, *383*
Whimbey, A., 176, 208, 267, 300, 312, *383*
Whorf, B., 27, *384*
Wickelgren, W., 16, 167, 194, 206, 208, *384*
Wicker, A. W., 334, *384*
Williams, R. L., 291, *384*
Wilson, T. D., 16, *380, 384*
Woodworth, R. S., 66, *384*
Wollman, W., 311, *378*
Wright, L., 91, *384*

Y

Yates, F. A., 272, *384*

Z

Zechmeister, E. B., 278, *384*

Subject Index

A

Adjectives
  marked, 74
  unmarked, 74
Advertising
  appeals to pity in, 39
  appeals to pride or snobbery in, 41–42
  card stacking in, 42
  critical thinking skills and, 5, 344–345
  defending against persuasive techniques in, 42–43
  distinguishing fact from opinion in, 44–45
  euphemisms in, 35
  evaluating source in, 43
  if, then statements in, 75–76
  implication and inference in, 33–34
  reasoning examples in, 83
  repetition in, 37
  testimonials in, 40
  validity of measurement in, 109
  word choice and consumer judgment in, 29
Affirming the antecedent, 75, 76
Affirming the consequent, 75
Aggression, and intelligence tests, 296, 297
Algorithms, 216
Analogies
  creative thinking and, 335–336
  problem solving and, 195–197
  types of, 196–197
Antecedent in if, then statements, 75
  affirming, 75, 76
  denying, 75
  negation in, 79–80
Anxiety, and memory, 264–265
Appeals to pity, 39
Appeals to snobbery or pride, 41–42
Artificial intelligence, 13–14
Asians, and creativity, 326
Aspects, elimination by, 225
Assassinations, conspiracy theories of, 146–147
Association effect in language, 38
Atmosphere effects in syllogistic reasoning, 66–69
Attention
  cocktail party effect and, 248
  experimental studies of, 248–249
  memory and, 247–250
  properties of, 248
Attribute listing in creative thinking, 332–333
Availability heuristic, 216–219
Averages
  kinds of, 149
  statistics and, 149–150

B

Backward-looking strategy in problem solving, 184–185

Bar graphs, 173
Base-rate biases in probability, 140–143
Bayes Theorem, 144–147
Belief, and probability, 122
Belief biases, and syllogistic reasoning, 69–70
Bets, and expected values (EV) in probability, 132–135
Bias
  base-rate, in probability, 140–143
  confirmation, and decision making, 215–216
  confirmation, in if, then statements, 80–81
  intelligence tests and, 290–297
  syllogistic reasoning and, 69–70
Biased discounting, 225
Bionics, 337
BITCH-100 (intelligence test), 291
Black or white fallacy, 40–41
Brainstorming
  creative thinking and, 329–330
  problem solving and, 193–194
Brain waves, 6–7
Browsing, and creative thinking, 334
Bumper stickers, 82, 83
Bureaucratese, 35

C

Cards
  extrasensory perception (ESP) testing with, 153–154
  probability and, 125–126
Card stacking in propaganda, 42
Career decisions, 355
Categorical reasoning, 56; *see also* Syllogistic reasoning
Cat-in-tree problem, 185–188
Cause
  convergent validity in, 109
  correlation and, 104–108
  determining, 102–111
  hypothesis testing and, 94
  illusory validity and, 110–111
  isolation and control of variables in, 102–104
  measurement in, 108–109
  posteriori probability and, 143
  prospective and retrospective research in, 104
  reliability and, 111
  self-fulfilling prophecies and, 111–112
Census Bureau, 152
Chance, games of
  critical thinking skills in, 352–354
  probability and, 125–127
Chance, laws of, and decision making, 220
Chunking, and memory, 257
Class, and problem solving, 201–202
Cocktail party effect, 248
Cognitive dissonance, 236–237
Cognitive process instruction, 3
Cognitive psychology, 3
Coin toss, and probability, 127–130
Communication
  barriers to, 34–36
  comprehension and, 30–36
  context and, 32–33
  given/new distinction in, 31–32
  implication and inference in, 33–34
  rules for clear, 31–33
  surface structure of language and, 26–27
  thinking as silent speech and, 9–11
  vagueness and, 36
Comparisons
  decision making and, 225–227
  linear ordering and, 72, 73, 74
Comprehension
  barriers to, 34–36
  bureaucratese and euphemism and, 35
  implication and inference and, 33–34
  meaningfulness and, 254
  rules for clear communication and, 31–33
  vagueness and, 36
Computers and computer programs
  artificial intelligence and, 13–14
  capacity for thinking of, 14–15
  flowcharts in, 83–86
  logic in, 83–86
  as model of human thought, 246–247
  problem solving with, 183–184
  Rogerian therapy with, 13–14
  structural programming with, 6
  think aloud protocols in, 12–13
  thinking skills and, 6, 18
  Turing's test in, 14
Conclusion
  inductive and deductive reasoning and, 54–55
  syllogism and, 53, 57
Concrete operations thought period, 301
Conditional logic, 74; *see also* If, then statements

Confirmation bias
decision making and, 215–216
if, then statements and, 80–81
Confounding in samples, 100
Consequent in if, then statements, 75
Conservation in concrete operations period, 301
Conspiracy theories of presidential assassinations, 146–147
Consumers and consumerism
critical thinking skills and, 344–345
decision making variables for, 16
Content effects
if, then statements with, 77
syllogistic reasoning with, 70–71
Context, and communication, 32–33
Contingency relationships, 74
Contradiction in problem solving, 194
Control in hypothesis testing, 94–95
Convenience samples, 100
Convergent thinking, 322–323
Convergent validity, and cause, 109
Correlation
cause and, 104–105
illusory, 106–108
negative, 105
positive, 105
Creative thinking, 315–339
analogies and metaphors in, 335–336
attribute listing in, 332–333
bionics in, 337
brainstorming and, 329–330
browsing and, 334
creative ideas checklist in, 331–332
medical decisions and, 347–349
relational algorithm in, 333–334
strategies for, 327–338
synectics in, 336
training programs for, 327–329
visual thinking in, 337–338
Creativity, 316–322
convergent and divergent thinking in, 322–323
decision making and problem solving and, 162
definition of, 317
divergent production test in, 322–324
encouraging, 325–327
environmental factors in, 326
lateral and vertical thinking in, 318–319
measuring, 322–325
as multidimensional concept, 325
natural abilities and, 325–326
personality factors and, 326–327
remote association test and, 324–325
sensitivity, synergy and serendipity in, 319–322
Critical thinking skills
applications of, 343–355
consumerism and advertising claims and, 344–345
directed and nondirected thought in, 3
examples of need for, 5–6
games of chance and, 352–354
improving skills in, 4, 6
need for, 2–6
personal decision making and life planning and, 354–355
politics and, 349–352
utilizing research and, 345–346
Cues in memory retrieval, 258–260
Cultural factors, and ways of thinking, 27
Culture-free intelligence tests, 293
Culture-reduced intelligence tests, 293–294

D

Decision making, 209–239
alternatives of action in, 210–211
alternative ways of formulating problem, problem in, 212
assessing risks in, 223–225
availability heuristic in, 216–219
belief in fairness of laws of chance in, 220
biased discounting in, 225
cognitive dissonance and, 236–237
commitment and evaluation after, 236–238
confirmation bias and, 215–216
creativity and problem solving and, 162
critical thinking skills in, 354–355
definition of problem in, 211–212
dilemmas in, 235–236
educational programs for, 2–3
elimination by aspects in, 225
entrapment and, 222–223
failure to seek disconfirming evidence in, 214–216
fallacy in, 213
gambler's fallacy in, 220
hindsight and forethought in, 237–238
law of small numbers and, 220–221

Decision making (*continued*)
medical examples in, 209–210, 213, 215–216, 218
multidimensional comparisons in, 225–227
pitfalls and pratfalls in, 213–223
process in, 210–212
representativeness heuristic in, 219–220
sample size and, 220–221
trained professionals and, 212–213
transitivity in, 226–227
2/3 ideal rule in, 234–235
uncertainty and risks in, 223–225
variables influencing, 16
wishful thinking in, 221–222
worksheet preparation in, 228–236
Deductive reasoning
hypothesis testing with, 95–96
reasoning skills with, 54–56
Denying the antecedent, 75
Denying the consequent, 75
Dependent variables in hypothesis testing, 98–99
Detour problems, 181
Developmental periods, Piagetian, 301–302
Diagrams, and problem solving, 167–174, 181
Dice throw, and probability, 132–135
Dichotic listening, 248
Differences in thinking, 19–20
Dimensional comparison in decision making, 233–234
Direct analogy, 197
Directed thinking, 3; *see also* Critical thinking skills
Distortion, and memory, 253
Divergent thinking, 322–323
Dominance in brain, 7
Dove Counterbalance Intelligence Test, 291

E

Ecological validity, and syllogisms, 63–64
Education
Piagetian tasks in, 19
problem solving skills and, 167
programmed learning and, 17–19
tests for learning assessment in, 18
thinking skills and, 2–3, 6, 16–17
Elections, and mere exposure effect, 27
Electroencephalograph, 6–7
Elimination by aspects, 225
Emotions
memory and, 263–267
reasoning and, 70
Entrapment, and decision making, 222–223
Environmental factors
creativity and, 326
intelligence and, 292, 298
Euler Diagrams, 59
Euphemism, 35
Evaluation
decision making and, 236–238
problem solving and, 163
Evidence
decision making and, 214–216
illusory validity and, 110
Examinations, in learning assessment, 18
Expected value (EV), and probability, 132–135
Experts, and problem solving, 198
Explanation, and hypothesis testing, 94–95
Extraneous variables in hypothesis testing, 99
Extrapolation in statistics, 152
Extrasensory perception (ESP), 153–154
Eyewitness testimony, and memory, 253–254

F

Fact, distinguishing opinion from, 43–45
Failure to accept logical task, 54
Fallacy in decision making, 213
False dichotomy in propaganda, 40–41
Familiarization stage in problem solving, 163
Family tree, 176
Fantasy analogy, 197
Film, and propaganda, 36
First letter mnemonics, 273–274
Flowcharts, 83–86
examples of, 84, 85
symbols in, 83–84, 85
Forethought, and decision making, 237–238
Forgetting, 257–258
Formal thought development period, 301, 304–307
Forward-looking strategy in problem solving, 184
Four-card selection task, 80–81
Frequency
determining, 139–140
probability and, 137–139
relative frequency distinguished from, 137–138

Functional fixedness, and problem solving, 199–201

G

Gambler's fallacy
  decision making and, 220
  probability and, 136–137
Gambling, and probability, 125–126
Games of chance
  critical thinking skills and, 352–354
  probability and, 125–127
Generalization
  hypothesis testing with, 99
  problem solving with, 188–189
General Problem Solver (computer program), 183–184
Gist, and memory, 256
Given/new distinction, 31–32
Goal, and problem solving, 166
Graphs in problem solving, 167–173
Guilt by association, 38

H

Handedness, 7
Hemispheres in brain, 7
Heredity
  creativity and, 326
  intelligence and, 298
Heuristics in decision making
  availability, 216–219
  representativeness, 219–220
Hierarchical trees in problem solving, 174–176
Hindsight, 237–238
Hints in problem solving, 190–192
Horse racing, 353
Human information processing (HIP), and memory, 245–261
Hypnosis, 266–267
Hypothesis, definition of, 94
Hypothesis testing, 93–113
  convergent validity in, 109
  definition of, 94
  determining cause in, 102–111
  explanation, prediction and control in, 94–95
  generalization in, 99
  illusory validity in, 110–111
  independent and dependent variables in, 98–99
  inductive and deductive reasoning in, 54–55, 95–96
  measurement and, 108–109
  operational definitions in, 97
  populations and samples in, 99–102
  reliability and, 111
  self-fulfilling prophecies and, 111–112
  thinking as intuitive science and, 112
  understanding, 94–102

I

If, then statements, 63, 74–81
  computer flowcharts with, 86
  confirmation bias in, 80–81
  contingency relationships and, 74
  content effects in, 77
  in everyday contexts, 82–83
  examples of, 74–75
  kinds of reasoning in, 75, 76
  negation and, 79–80
  probabilistic reasoning in, 77–79
Ill-defined problems, 165–166
Illicit conversions in syllogistic reasoning, 65–66
Illusory correlation, 106–108
Illusory validity, 110–111
Images and imagery
  mnemonics with, 270–271
  syllogisms and, 63
  thinking as, 7–11
Implication, and communication, 33–34
Incubation stage in problem solving, 163–164
Independent variables in hypothesis testing, 98–99
Individual differences in thinking, 19–20
Inductive reasoning, and hypothesis testing, 54–56, 95–96
Inference
  communication and, 33–34
  learning and memory and, 244, 253
Information processing
  memory and, 245–261
  thinking as, 11–15
Insight in problem solving, 164–165
Intellectual skills, and brain research, 7
Intelligence, 281–308
  artificial, 13–14
  definitions of, 282–283, 285, 307
  development of, 299–300
  example of nature of, 283–285

Intelligence (*continued*)
learning for increase in, 298–300
measurement of, 285
nature-nurture controversy in, 298
nature of, 282–285
paradox in notions of, 298–299
Piagetian model of, 300–301
primary mental abilities in, 299
sex differences in, 295–297
Thurstone theory of, 299–300
Intelligence quotient (IQ), 285–290
determining, 285–287
mental age (MA) and, 286–287
Intelligence tests, 285–290
bias in, 290–297
creativity and, 325–326
culture-free, 293
culture-reduced, 293–294
environmental factors in, 202
increasing scores on, 298
problems on, 190, 288–289
racial factors in, 290–292
sex differences in intelligence and, 295–297
socioeconomic status (SES) and, 292
stability of, 295
standardization of, 289–290
test-retest reliability of, 295
validity of, 295
Interference theory of forgetting, 257–258
IQ, *see* Intelligence quotient (IQ)

J

Jargon
bureaucratese in, 35
communication and, 10–11
thinking by students and, 16–17, 19
Jews, and creativity, 326
Judgment
context in communication and, 33
problem solving and, 163
word choice and, 29–30

K

Keno, 352–353
Keywords in mnemonics, 269–272
Knowledge acquisition, and memory, 243–244

L

Language
association effect in, 38
bureaucratese and euphemism in, 35
comprehension and, 30–36
distinguishing fact from opinion in, 43–45
linear ordering and, 73
negation in if, then statements and, 79–80
Orwellian example of thought and, 27–28
persuasion and propaganda and, 36–43
psycholinguistics in, 26
Sapir-Whorf hypothesis of linguistic relativity in, 27–29
surface structure of, 26–27
thinking as silent speech and, 9–11
thought and, 25–30
underlying representation of, 26–27
see also Jargon
Lateral thinking, 318–319
Law and legal profession
appeals to pity in, 39
bureaucratese in, 35
critical thinking skills in, 346–347
logical thinking in, 56, 70
problem solving by, 305–306
syllogistic reasoning in, 63
Law of small samples, 102
Laws of chance, and decision making, 220
Learning
examinations assessing, 18
memory and, 244–245
metamemory and, 267
mnemonic devices and, 268–275
programmed, 17–19
sleep and, 258, 267
time line for retention interval in, 245
Left handedness, 7
Legal profession, *see* Law and legal profession
Life planning, and critical thinking skills, 354–355
Linear ordering, 63, 71–74
in everyday contexts, 82, 83, 85
examples of, 71–73
paralogic and, 72
psychological principles of, 73–74
Listening, and attention, 248
Logic
computer, 83–86
conclusions in, 53

definition of, 53
failure to accept task in, 54
flowcharts with, 83–86
paralogic and, 72
probabilogical thinking with, 79
reasoning skills and, 53–56
Long-term memory, 250–251

M

Marijuana, and memory, 261–263
Marked adjectives, 74
Mathematical ability in intelligence tests, 296, 297
Mathematics
problem solving in, 166–167, 170
thinking skills in, 6, 16–17
Matrix in problem solving, 176–179, 181
Mazes, 185
Mean
regression toward, and probability, 147–148
statistics and, 149–150
Meaning
implication and inference and, 33–34
surface structure of language and, 26–27
Meaningfulness, and memory, 254–257
Means-ends analysis, 182–186
Measurement
cause and, 108–109
convergent validity in, 109
reliability of, 111
sensitivity of, 108–109
validity of, 109
Mechanization in problem solving, 202
Medicine
base rates in probability in, 143
critical thinking skills needed in, 345–349
decision making in, 209–210, 213, 215–216, 218, 347–349
euphemism in, 35
probability and, 124
Memory, 243–276
acquisition of information in, 247
anxiety and stress and, 264–265
attention in, 247–250
chunking in, 257
computer as model of human thought in, 246–247
constructive nature of, 251–257
emotions and, 263–267
eyewitness testimony and, 253–254
forgetting and, 257–258
gist and, 256
human information processing (HIP) in, 245–261
hypnosis and, 266–267
illusory validity and selective nature of, 110
inference and distortion and, 253
knowledge acquisition and, 243–244
learning and, 244–245
long-term, 250–251
marijuana and, 261–263
meaningfulness and, 254–257
metamemory and, 267–268
mnemonics and, 268–275
organization and, 260–261
periodic review and, 263–264
prior knowledge and, 251–252
repression and, 265–267
retention and, 245, 247, 250–251
retrieval in, 257–261
sensory, 250
short-term, 250
sleeping and, 258
state-dependent, 266
stereotype and prejudice and, 251–252
time line for retention interval in, 245
types of, 250–251
Men, and intelligence tests, 296–297
Mental age (MA), and intelligence tests, 286–287
Mental set, and problem solving, 199–201
Mere exposure effect, 37
Metacognition, 15–20
Metamemory, 267–268
Metaphor
creative thinking and, 335–336
problem solving and, 195–197
Method of place in mnemonics, 272–273
Mnemonics, 268–275
applications for, 275
first letter, 273–274
images in, 270–271
keywords in, 269–272
method of place in, 272–273
narrative stories in, 274
principles of, 274–275
rhymes in, 271–272
Mode in statistics, 150
Models in problem solving, 179–181

Mood in syllogism, 57
Multidimensional comparisons in decision making, 225–227

N

Name calling, 38–39
Narrative stories in mnemonics, 274
Nationality, and problem solving, 201–202
Negation, in if, then statements, 79–80
Negative correlation, 105, 106
Nervous system, and thinking, 6–7
News media
  distinguishing fact from opinion in, 44
  reasoning examples in, 83
  statistical abuse in, 151
Nondirected thinking, 3
Nonentrenched tasks, 283

O

Odds
  cards and, 125–126
  probability and, 122–123
Operational definitions in hypothesis testing, 97, 98–99
Operations in problem solving, 167
Opinion, distinguishing fact from, 43–45
Optimism, and decision making, 221–222
Organization, and memory, 260–261

P

Paralogic, 72
Perceptual reorganization, 165
Perseverence phenomenon in probability, 148
Personal analogy, 196
Personality factors, and creativity, 326–327
Persuasion
  card stacking in, 42
  defending against, 42–43
  propaganda and, 26–43
Physics, 16
Piagetian model of intelligence, 300–307
  development periods in, 301–302
  tasks in, 19, 302–304
Pity, appeals to, 39
Place in mnemonics, 272–273
Plot Title Test, 324
Politics
  appeals to pride or snobbery in, 41–42
  critical thinking skills in, 4–5, 350–352
  problem solving and, 201–202
  reasoning in, 55–56, 83
  syllogistic reasoning in, 63, 70
Pollyanna principle, 221–222
Popularity technique in propaganda, 39–40
Populations
  hypothesis testing with, 99–102
  statistics with, 149
Positive correlation, 105, 106
Posteriori probability, 143–147
Precision with statistics, 150–151
Prediction in hypothesis testing, 94–95
Preference, and word choice, 29–30
Prejudice
  decision making and, 218
  memory and, 251–252
Premises, and reasoning, 55, 57
Preoperational thought development period, 301
Preparation stage in problem solving, 165
Presidential assassinations, conspiracy theories of, 146–147
Pride, appeals to, 41–42
Probabilistic reasoning, and if, then statements, 77–79
Probabilities, 119–155
  application of models in, 153–154
  averages in, 149–150
  base-rate biases in, 140–143
  Bayes Theorem in, 144–147
  cards and, 125–126
  computing in multiple outcome situations and, 127–131
  definition of, 120
  degree of belief in, 122
  desirability of outcome in, 148
  example of, 120–122
  expected values (EV) in, 132–135
  experimental example of, 135–136
  extrasensory perception (ESP) and, 153–154
  frequency and relative frequency in, 137–143
  frequency judgments in, 139–140
  games of chance and, 125–127
  implicit use of, 124–125
  likelihood and uncertainty in, 120–122
  mean in, 149–150

mode in, 150
nonregressive judgments in, 147–148
objective, 135
odds in, 122–123
perseverance phenomenon in, 148
posteriori, 143–147
precision in, 150–151
regression toward mean in, 147–148
roulette and, 126–127
subjective, 136–148
tree diagrams in, 127–131
using, 123–130
Probabilogical thinking, 79
Problem solving skills, 159–203
analogies and metaphors in, 195–197
anatomy of problem in, 160–161
bar graphs in, 173
brainstorming in, 193–194
cat-in-tree problem in, 185–188
consulting expert in, 189
contradiction in, 194
decision making and creativity and, 162
detour problem in, 181
drawing graph or diagram in, 167–174
educational programs for, 6
factors causing problems in, 199–202
forward-looking strategy in, 184
functional fixedness and mental set in, 199–201
generalization and specialization in, 188–189
goal state of problems in, 160
hierarchical trees in, 174–176
hints in, 190–192
incubation stage in, 163–165
initial state of problem in, 160
insight in, 164–165
instruction in, 167
judgment or evaluation stage in, 163
matrix in, 176–179
means-ends analysis in, 182–184
mechanization in, 202
misleading and irrelevant information in, 201
models in, 179–181
operations in, 167
perceptual reorganization in, 165
Piagetian tasks and, 302–306
preparation or familiarization stage in, 163
problem space in, 160
production stage in, 163
random search and trial-and-error in, 189
representing problems in, 167–182
restating problem in, 194–195
rules in, 189–190
selecting best representation of problem in, 181–182
selecting best strategy in, 185–189
solution paths in, 160
split-half method in, 192–193
stages in, 163–164
strategies in, 166–199
syllogistic reasoning and, 63
table formats in, 173
Tower of Hanoi problem in, 182–183
two-string problem in, 191
well-defined and ill-defined problems in, 165–166
working backwards in, 184–185
world view constraints in, 201–202
writing problem down in, 167
Production stage in problem solving, 163
Professionals, and technical jargon, 10–11
Programmed learning, 17–19
Programs, computer, *see* Computers and computer programs
Projection task, 283
Propaganda, 36–43
appeals to pity in, 39
appeals to pride and snobbery in, 41–42
arguments against person in, 38–39
association effect in, 38
card stacking in, 42
defending against persuasive techniques in, 42–43
definition of, 36
evaluating source in, 43
false dichotomy in, 40–41
language and, 36–43
mere exposure effect in, 37
popularity and testimonials in, 39–40
purpose of, 36
Prophecies, self-fulfilling, 111–112
Propositional logic, 74; *see also* If, then statements
Prospective research, and cause, 104
Protocol analysis, 11–13
Pseudodiagnosticity, 144
Psychoanalysis, 265–266
Psycholinguistics, 26

Psychology
reasoning skills and, 53–56
study of thinking in, 3
Psychometrics, 322
Psychotherapy, 266
computers and, 13–14

Q

Quantifiers in syllogistic reasoning, 56

R

Racial factors
eyewitness testimony and, 253–254
intelligence tests and, 290–292
Racing, 353
Random samples, 101
Random search in problem solving, 189
Raven's Progressive Matrices, 290
Reasoning skills
definition of, 53
development of, 51–86
in everyday contexts, 82–86
failure to accept logical task in, 54
if, then statements in, 74–81
individual differences in, 19–20
inductive and deductive, 54–56
linear ordering and, 71–74
logical and psychological approaches to, 53–56
syllogistic reasoning in, 56–71
Regression toward mean, 147–148
Relational algorithm in creative thinking, 333–334
Relative frequency, and probability, 137–138
Reliability, and cause, 111
Remote Association Test (RAT), 324–325
Repetition in advertising, 37
Repression of memory, 265–267
Research, and critical thinking skills, 345–346
Retention, and memory, 245, 247, 250–251
Retrieval
cues in, 258–260
memory and, 245, 257–261
Retrospective research, and cause, 104
Review, and memory, 263–264
Rhymes in mnemonics, 271–272
Right handedness, 7
Risks
assessing, 223–225
creativity and, 327
decision making and, 223–225
Rogerian therapy, 13–14
Rorschach inkblots, 107–108
Roulette, 126–127
Rubik's cube, 162
Rules in problem solving, 189–190
Rules of thumb in decision making, 216–217
Russian roulette, 353

S

Samples
biased and unbiased, 99–100
confounding, 100
convenience, 100
decision making and size of, 220–221
generalization in, 99
hypothesis testing with, 99–102
law of small numbers in, 102
random, 101
significant differences and size of, 150
statistics and, 149
subject in, 100
variability in, 101
Sapir-Whorf hypothesis of linguistic relativity, 27–29
Science and scientists
decision making by, 216
everyday thought similarities to, 94–95
Piagetian tasks in, 19
problem solving in, 166–167, 170, 305
thinking skills in, 16–17
Self-fulfilling prophecies, 111–112
Sensitivity
creativity and, 319–322
measurement and, 108–109
Sensorimotor thought development period, 301
Sensory memory, 250
Serendipidity, and creativity, 319–322
Sex differences in intelligence, 295–297
Short-term memory, 250
intelligence tests and, 300
problem solving and, 164
Simplification
problem solving and, 185–188
propaganda and, 40–41

Size of sample
decision making and, 220–221
statistics and, 150
Sleeping
learning and, 258, 267
memory and, 258
Slogans, 40
Snobbery, appeals to, 41–42
Socioeconomic status (SES), and intelligence tests, 292
Solution paths, in problem solving, 160
Spatial ability on intelligence tests, 296, 297
Spatial problems, 170
Specialization in problem solving, 188–189
Speech, thinking as silent, 7–11
Split-half method in problem solving, 192–193
Stability of intelligence tests, 295
Stanford-Binet intelligence test, 288, 295
State-dependent memory, 266
Statistical significance, 103
Statistics, 148–152
abuse of, 148–152
averages in, 149–150
definition of, 149
extrapolation in, 152
mean in, 149–150
measure of central tendency in, 150
median in, 150
mode in, 150
population in, 149
precision in, 150–151
sample in, 149
significant differences in, 151–152
Stereotypes
decision making and, 218
illusory correlations and, 108
memory and, 251–252
Stress, and memory, 264–265
Structured programming, 6
Style, and communication, 32
Subgoals, 182
Subject in samples, 100
Subjective probability, 135–148
base-rate biases in, 140–143
Bayes Theorem and, 144–147
desirability of outcome in, 148
experimental example of, 135–136
frequency and relative frequency in, 137–143
frequency judgments in, 139–140
gambler's fallacy in, 136–137
nonregressive judgments in, 147–148
perseverance phenomenon in, 148
posteriori probability in, 143–147
regression toward mean in, 147–148
Subproblems, 182
Supreme Court, 56, 70
Syllogistic reasoning, 56–71
atmosphere effects in, 66–69
belief biases in, 69–70
common errors in, 64–71
content effects in, 70–71
definition of, 56
ecological validity in, 63–64
Euler Diagrams in, 57
everyday examples of, 57–58, 63–64, 82
illicit conversions in, 65–66
linear, *see* Linear ordering
mood in, 57
premises and conclusion in, 57
quantifiers in, 56
understanding how people solve, 62–63
Venn Diagrams in, 58–63, 64
Symbolic analogy, 196
Synectics, 196, 336
Synergy, and creativity, 319–322

T

Table formats, 173
Technical jargon
communication and, 10–11
thinking by students and, 16–17, 19
Testimonials in advertising, 40
Testimony
critical thinking skills in, 346–347
memory and, 253–254
Tests
intelligence, *see* Intelligence tests
learning assessment and, 18
Tetrahydrocannabinol (THC), 262
Think aloud protocols in computer simulation, 11–13
Thinking
artificial intelligence and, 13–14
awareness of process of, 16–19
as biological process, 6–7
brain wave recordings during, 6–7
computer as model of, 246–247

Thinking (*continued*)
computer capacity for, 14–15
conceptualizations about, 6–15
definitions of, 4, 14
directed and nondirected thought in, 3
distinguishing fact from opinion in, 43–45
educational programs for, 2–3, 6, 16–17
examples of situations needing, 5–6
as human information processing, 11–15
hypothesis testing and, 112
as imagery, 7–11
improving skills in, 4, 6, 20
individual differences in, 19–20
as intuitive scientist, 112
language and, 25–30
learning, 3–4
metacognition and, 15–20
need for skills in, 2–6
persuasion and propaganda and, 36–43
programmed learning and, 17–19
as silent speech, 8, 9–11
variables influencing, 16
Tower of Hanoi problem, 182–183
Training programs, and creative thinking, 327–329
Transitivity in decision making, 226–227
Tree diagrams
base rates in probability with, 140–143
computing probability with, 127–131
dice throwing outcomes with, 133
problem solving with, 174–176, 188–189
Trial-and-error in problem solving, 189
Truth, and communication, 32
Turing's Test, 14
Two-string problem, 191
2/3 ideal rule, 234–235

U V

Uncertainty in decision making, 223–225
Unidimensional comparison, 226
Unmarked adjectives, 74
Vagueness, and communication, 36
Validity
convergent, 109
illusory, 110–111
of intelligence tests, 295
syllogism and, 63–64
Variability of samples, 101
Variables
definition of, 98
dependent, 98–99
extraneous, 99
hypothesis testing with, 98–99
isolation and control of, 102–104
statistical significance and, 103
Venn Diagrams, 58–63, 64
atmosphere effects on, 67–68
examples of, 59–62
illicit conversions with, 65, 66
Verbal ability in intelligence tests, 288, 296, 297
Vertical thinking, 318–319
Victim's bill of rights, 349–352
Viewpoint, and problem solving, 201–202
Virtue by association, 38
Visual imagery, thinking as, 7–11
Visual thinking, 337–338

W

Wechsler Adult Intelligence Scale (WAIS), 288
Wechsler Intelligence Scale for Children (WISC), 288
Well-defined problems, 165–166
Wheel of fortune, 136–137
Wishful thinking, and decision making, 221–222
Women, and intelligence tests, 295–297
Word choice
association effect and, 38
bureaucratese and euphemism and, 35
human judgment and preference and, 29–30
linear ordering and, 73
meaning of language and, 26–27
negation in if, then statements and, 79–80
Sapir-Whorf hypothesis of linguistic relativity and, 27
thinking as silent speech and, 9–11
see also Technical jargon
Worksheet procedure in decision making, 228–236
calculating decision in, 232–235
defining problem in, 228
dimensional comparison in, 233–236
generating alternatives in, 229
listing considerations in, 229–230
overall assessment in, 233
2/3 ideal rule in, 234–235
validity of, 235–236
weighting alternatives in, 231–232
weighting considerations in, 230

Zener cards, 153–154